Managing Software
Requirements

MANAGING SOFTWARE REQUIREMENTS

A Unified Approach

Dean Leffingwell
Don Widrig

Addison-Wesley

An imprint of Addison Wesley Longman, Inc.

Reading, Massachusetts • Harlow, England • Menlo Park, California
Berkeley, California • Don Mills, Ontario • Sydney
Bonn • Amsterdam • Tokyo • Mexico City

The publisher offers discounts on this book when ordered in quantity for special sales.

For more information, please contact:

Pearson Education Corporate Sales Division
One Lake Street
Upper Saddle River, NJ 07458
(800) 382-3419

Visit AWL on the Web: www.awl.com/cseng/

Library of Congress Cataloging-in-Publication Data
Leffingwell, Dean
   Managing software requirements: a unified approach/Dean
Leffingwell, Don Widrig.
      p. cm. -- (The Addison-Wesley object technology series)
   Includes bibliographical references and index.
   ISBN 0-201-61593-2
   1. Computer software--Development--Management. I. Widrig,
Don. II. Title. III.
   Series.
   QA76.76.D47 L44 1999
   005.1'068--dc21   99-046571

Executive Editor: J. Carter Shanklin
Project Editor: Krysia Bebick
Editorial Assistant: Kristin Erickson
Production Manager: John Fuller
Cover Design: Simone R. Payment
Design and composition: Kim Arney

ISBN 0-201-61593-2
Text printed on recycled paper.
2 3 4 5 6 7 8 9 10—MA—03020100
Second printing, February 2000

This book is dedicated to Becky, my wife and my best friend.

—Dean

This book is dedicated to my book partner, Dean, who made this effort worthwhile, and to my life partner, Barbara, who makes life worthwhile.

—Don

Contents

FOREWORD

The Rock Problem

One of my students summarized the issues discussed in this book as the "rock" problem. She works as a software engineer in a research laboratory, and her customers often give her project assignments that she describes as "Bring me a rock." But when you deliver the rock, the customer looks at it for a moment and says, "Yes, *but*, actually, what I really wanted was a *small blue* rock." The delivery of a small blue rock elicits the further request for a *spherical* small blue rock.

Ultimately, it may turn out that the customer was thinking all along of a small blue marble—or maybe he wasn't sure what he wanted, but a small blue marble—well, perhaps even a cat's eye small blue marble—would have sufficed. And he probably changed his mind about his requirements between the delivery of the first (large) rock and the third (small blue) rock.

At each subsequent meeting with the customer, it's common for the developer to exclaim, "You want it to do *what?*" The developer is frustrated because she had something entirely different in mind when she worked long and hard to produce a rock with the prescribed characteristics; the customer is equally frustrated because, even though he might find it difficult to articulate what he wants, he's convinced that he's expressed it clearly. These developers just don't get it!

To complicate matters, in most real projects, more than two individuals are involved. In addition to the customer and the developer—who may, of course, have very different names and titles—there are likely to be marketing people, testing and quality assurance people, product managers, general managers, and a variety of "stakeholders" whose day-to-day operations will be affected by the development of the new system.

All of these people can become frustrated by the problems of specifying an acceptable "rock," particularly because there often isn't enough time in today's competitive, fast-moving business world to scrap an expensive, 2-year "rock project" and do it all over again. We've got to get it right the first time yet also provide for the iterative process in which the customer ultimately discovers what kind of rock he wants.

It's difficult enough to do this when we're dealing with tangible, physical artifacts like a rock. Most business organizations and government agencies today are "information-intensive," so even if they're nominally in the business of building and selling rocks, there's a good chance that the rock contains an embedded computer system. Even if it doesn't, there's a good chance that the business needs elaborate systems to keep track of its e-commerce rock sales, its rock customers, its rock competitors and suppliers, and all of the other information that it needs to remain competitive in the rock business.

Software systems, by their nature, are intangible, abstract, complex and—in theory, at least—infinitely changeable. So, if the customer begins articulating vague requirements for a "rock system," he often does so on the assumption that he can clarify, change, and fill in the details as time goes on. It would be wonderful if the developers—and everyone else involved in the creation, testing, deployment, and maintenance of the rock system—could accomplish this in zero time, and at zero cost, but it doesn't work that way.

In fact, it often doesn't work at all: More than half of the software systems projects taking place today are substantially over budget and behind schedule, and as much as 25%–33% of the projects are canceled before completion, often at a staggering cost.

Preventing these failures and providing a rational approach for building the system the customer does want is the objective of this book. It's important to realize, though, that this is *not* a book about programming, and it's not written just for the software developer. This is a book about managing requirements for complex software applications. *As such, this book is written for every member of the software team—analysts, developers, tester and QA personnel, project management, documentation folks, and the like—as well as those members of the external "customer" team—users and other stakeholders, marketing, and management—*everyone, really, who has the need and requirement to contribute to the requirements solution.

You'll discover that it is crucial that the members of both teams, including the nontechnical members of the external team, master the skills required to successfully define and manage the requirements process for your new system—for the simple reason that *they* are the ones who create the requirements in the first place and who ultimately determine the success or failure of the system. The stand-alone, hero programmer is an anachronism of the past: May he rest in peace.

A simple metaphor: If you were a building contractor, you wouldn't need to be convinced that a series of carefully orchestrated conversations with the homeowner are necessary; otherwise, you might end up building a two-bedroom house when your customer wanted a three-bedroom house. But it's equally important that these "requirements" be discussed and negotiated with the government authorities concerned with building codes and zoning regulations, and you may need to check with the next-door neighbors before you decide to cut down any trees on the property where the house will be built.

The building inspector and the next-door neighbors are among the stakeholders who, along with the person who intends to pay for and inhabit the house, will determine whether the finished house meets the full set of requirements. It's also clear that many important stakeholders of your system, such as neighbors and zoning officials, are not users (homeowners), and it seems equally obvious that their perspectives on what makes a quality home system may vary widely.

Again, we're discussing software applications in this book, not houses or rocks. The requirements of a house might be described, at least in part, with a set of blueprints and engineering drawings; similarly, a software system can be described with models and diagrams. But just as the blueprints for a house are intended as a communication and negotiation mechanism between laypeople and engineers—and lawyers and inspectors and nosy neighbors—so the technical diagrams associated with a software system can also be created in such a way that "ordinary" people can understand them.

Many of the crucially important requirements don't need any diagrams at all; the prospective house buyer, for example, can write a requirement in ordinary English that says, "My house must have three bedrooms, and it must have a garage large enough to hold two cars and six bicycles." As you'll see in this book, the majority of the crucial requirements for a software system can be written in plain English.

Many of the *team skills* you will need to master in order to address this challenge can also be described in terms of practical, common-sense advice. "Make sure you talk to the building inspector," we might advise our novice house builder, "*before* you dig the foundation for the house, not after you've poured the cement and begun building the walls and the roof." In a software project, we will be offering similar advice: "Make sure you ask the right questions, make sure that you prioritize the requirements, and *don't* let the customer tell you that 100 percent of the requirements are critical, because you're not likely to have time to finish them all before the deadline."

About This Book

In this book, Leffingwell and Widrig have taken a pragmatic approach to describing the solution to the rock problem. They have organized the book into seven parts. The introduction provides some of the context, definitions, and background that you'll need to understand what follows. Chapter 1 reviews the systems development "challenge." The data shows that some software project failures are indeed caused by sloppy programming, but a number of recent studies demonstrate rather convincingly that poor requirements management may be the single largest cause of project failure. And though I've described the basic concept of requirements management in a loose, informal fashion in this foreword, the authors will define it more carefully in Chapter 2, in order to lay the groundwork for the chapters that follow. Chapter 3 provides a brief introduction to some of the characteristics of modern software teams, so that they can relate the team skills that will be developed to the team context, wherein the skills must be applied.

The book is structured on the six requisite team skills for effective requirements management.

Each of the next six major parts is intended to help you and your team understand and master one of the *six requisite team skills for effective requirements management*.

- To begin, of course, you will need a proper understanding of the problem that's intended to be solved with a new software system. That is addressed in Team Skill 1, Analyzing the Problem.
- Team Skill 2, Understanding User and Stakeholder Needs, is also crucial. Those skills form the basis for Team Skill 2.
- Team Skill 3, Defining the System, describes the initial process of defining a system to address those needs.
- Team Skill 4, Managing Scope, covers that absolutely crucial, and often ignored, process of managing the scope of the project.
- Team Skill 5, Refining the System Definition, illustrates key techniques that you will use in order to elaborate on the system to a level of detail sufficient to drive design and implementation, so the entire extended team knows exactly what kind of system you are building.
- Team Skill 6, Building the Right System, discusses the processes associated with building a system that does fulfill the requirements. Team Skill 6 also discusses techniques you can use to validate that the

system meets the requirements and, further, to help ensure that the system doesn't do anything malevolent to its users or otherwise exhibit unpleasant behaviors that are *not* defined by the requirements. And, since requirements for any nontrivial application cannot be frozen in time, the authors describe ways in which the team can actively manage change without destroying the system that is being designed and built.

Finally, after a brief summary, the authors provide a prescription that you and your team can use to manage requirements in your next project. They conclude with this in a Chapter 35, Getting Started.

We hope that armed with these newly acquired team skills, you, too, will be able to build the perfect marble. But it will never be easy; even with the best techniques and processes, and even with automated tool support for all of this, you'll still find that it's hard work. And it's still risky; even with these team skills, some projects will fail because we're "pushing the envelope" in many organizations, attempting to build ever more complex systems in ever less time. But the skills defined in this book will go a long way toward reducing the risk and thereby helping you achieve the success you deserve.

—Ed Yourdon

PREFACE

By Dean Leffingwell

Context and Acknowledgments

The knowledge delivered in this book represents the cumulative experience of a number of individuals who have spent their careers defining, developing, and delivering world-class software systems. This book is *not* an academic treatment of requirements management. During the 1980s, Don Widrig and I were executives in a small company producing software solutions for customers. When we developed many of the requirements management practices described in this book, our perspective was of those accountable for both the outcomes of the software systems we developed and the results that had to be delivered to shareholders. As the performance of the delivered software was critical to the success of the business venture itself, we tended to discourage petty biases, personal preferences, and experimentation with unproven techniques.

Over the past decade, the techniques have evolved and have been enhanced by new experiences, extended with the help of additional expertise, in different companies and in different circumstances. But all of the techniques presented are "real-world" proven and have withstood the test of time. Perhaps even more important, they have withstood the technological change that has occurred in the industry during this period. Indeed, most of the principles in this book are independent of changing trends in software technology. We can therefore at least hope that the knowledge expressed herein can deliver some lasting value.

Requirements Lessons from Building Software for Others

At first, I just hated computers. ("What? I stayed here all night and I have to submit this batch job again because I left out a 'space'? Are you crazy? Let me in that room. . . .") My first "real computer" was a minicomputer, which, although incredibly limited in performance by today's standards, was unique in that I could touch it, program it, and make it do what I wanted. It was *mine*.

My early research applied the computer to analyze physiological signals from the human body, primarily EKGs, and the dedicated computer was a wonderful tool for this job. Out of this experience, I began to apply my programming skills and experience with real time software systems to the needs of the industry.

 Eventually, I incorporated RELA, Inc., and began a long, and perhaps unusually difficult, career as CEO of a contract software development business. My coauthor, Don Widrig, joined me at RELA in the early years as Vice President of Research and Development. He had the primary accountability for the success of the many systems that we developed.

Over the years, the company grew rapidly. Today, the company employs many hundreds of people and has diversified beyond providing just software to providing complete medical devices and systems that encompass software, as well as mechanical, electronic, optical, and fluidics-handling subsystems. However, at the heart of each and every machine, including the latest DNA fingerprinting in-vitro diagnostic clinical laboratory, lies one or more computers, reliably and routinely delivering their steady heartbeats through the rhythm of a real-time multitasking system.

Initially, we would program anything for anybody, from antenna-positioning software to such games as laser tag, automated guided vehicles for amusement parks, educational products, welding robots, and automated machine controls. We even developed a large distributed computer system that automatically detected and counted the presence of commercials on television. (Our motto then was "We make computers to watch commercials so you don't have to!") *Perhaps the only thing the software we developed had in common was that we developed it for others—we were not domain experts in the field, and we couldn't cover our own paychecks if we had to. We were completely dependent on the customer's satisfaction as the final determination of outcome. In many ways,* such an environment was very conducive to effective requirements management. Here's why:

- We knew little about the domain, so we were dependent on customers for the requirements. There was little temptation to simply make them up; we had to ask, and we had to learn how to ask the right questions the right way, at the right time.
- Our customers often knew little about computers, so they were dependent on us to translate their needs and wishes into technical requirements.
- The fact that money changed hands created a rigorous interface between the developer and the customer.
- Quality was easy to measure: We either got paid or we didn't.

Big Question 1:
"Exactly what is this software supposed to do?"

It was in this environment that we discovered the first of two fundamental questions that face software developers on each and every project. This question dominated our behavior for many years and remains today as perhaps *the* toughest question to answer in any software project. And the Big Question is:

> *"So, exactly what is this software supposed to do?"*

The principles and techniques presented in Team Skill 1, Analyzing the Problem; Team Skill 2, Understanding User Needs, and Team Skill 3, Defining the System, were developed over more than a decade as a means to discover the answer to this question. Each of these techniques has proved its worth and has demonstrated its effectiveness in many real-world projects. It was also during this period that I first became aware of the work of Donald Gause and Jerry Weinberg, especially their book *Exploring Requirements: Quality Before Design"* (1989). Because their book heavily influenced our work, we have borrowed a few key concepts from it for this book, both because the concepts work and because we thought it only fair that you share the Gause and Weinberg experience.

Lessons from Building High-Assurance Systems

Over time, RELA began to specialize in the development of various types of computer-based medical devices and systems: portable ventilators (breathing machines), infusion pumps, pacemaker programmers, clinical diagnostic systems, blood pumps, patient-monitoring equipment, and a plethora of other diagnostic and therapeutic devices.

It was early during the ventilator development project that the ultimate accountability for what we were doing really hit us: *Whoa, if we screw this up, somebody could die*! Our primary concern was for the patient and for the family of the patient who was tethered to the device, a device on which we were executing some of the earliest, most time-critical, resource-limited software the world had yet seen. (Imagine the challenge of alpha and beta testing. You go first!)

Clearly, this high-stakes endeavor caused us to take software very seriously at a fairly early time in the evolution of the embedded-systems industry. It became clear very quickly that sustainable success would require a combination of

- A pragmatic process for defining and managing the requirements for the software
- A solid methodology for the design and development of software
- The application of various proven, innovative, techniques for verifying and validating that the software was safe and effective
- Extraordinary skills and commitment on the part of both the software development and software quality assurance teams

I strongly believed at that time, and I am even more convinced today, that *all of those elements are required to deliver any reasonably reliable software system of any significant scope*. At RELA, Inc., this was to be the only way we could possibly ensure each patient's safety, the very survival of our company, and the economic futures of the employees and their families who depended on the company.

Big Question 2: "How, exactly, will we know when the software does exactly that and nothing else?"

Given our earlier success in the development and application of the various techniques we used to answer Big Question 1, we now moved on to the second fundamental question facing software development teams worldwide. Big Question 2 is

"How, exactly, will we know when the software does exactly that and nothing else?"

The techniques we used to answer this question form the basis of Team Skill 5, Refining the System Definition, and Team Skill 6, Building the Right System.

So, you can be confident that the techniques presented in this book are road hardened and well proven. Also, even if you are not in the business of developing safety-critical systems, you can rest assured that what follows is useful, practical, and cost-effective advice that you can use to develop software systems of the highest quality.

Although the techniques that we borrowed, modified, developed, and applied at RELA, Inc., to address the two big questions were highly effective, I must also admit to one nagging uncertainty that kept me awake during the most serious crunch times on these projects:

> *"Given the highly manual nature of the requirements process, how long would it be before we made a single, but potentially dangerous, mistake?"*

And there was also the matter of cost, as manual verification and validation were expensive and error prone. During this period, the discipline of mechanical engineering had advanced from a mechanical drawing arm to 3-D computer-aided design systems. In the same period, our software advances were limited, for all practical purposes, to having increased the level of abstraction in our programming languages: a good thing, for certain, but defect rates, lines-of-code productivity factors, and quality measures were relatively constant. Our experiments with the CASE tools of that period were met with mixed results. Frankly, as a software engineer and entrepreneur, I found the state of the art in "software engineering" to be embarrassing.

Although it was obvious that automation would never eliminate the critical-thinking skills required in software development, I did become convinced that automating some of the manual, record-keeping, and change management aspects of the process would free scarce resources to focus on higher value-added activities. And, of course, we anticipated that development costs would be lower while reliability would be increased!

Lessons from the Requirements Management Business

So, in 1993, REQUISITE, Inc., was born, and a number of us committed to a course of action to develop and to market an innovative requirements management tool: RequisitePro. As we were continuously helping customers address their requirements management challenges during this time, much additional material for this book was born. We owe much of this work to those customers, and the customers at RELA, who essentially taught us everything we know on the subject.

This portion of my career was heavily influenced by Dr. Alan Davis, who was Editor in Chief of *IEEE Software* magazine and held the El Pomar Endowed Chair of Software Engineering at the University of Colorado in Colorado Springs. Al joined the company as a director and advisor early on and was instrumental in influencing our technology and the business direction. He is well known for his leadership in the field of requirements engineering. Al was also active in consulting activities and had developed a number of techniques for helping companies improve their requirements process. These techniques were merged with some of the RELA-derived techniques and became the basis of a professional training offering called Requirements College, the basis for parts of this book.

In addition, operating under the insufficiently popular business theory of *"you can never have too much professional help,"* we recruited renowned software author and expert Ed Yourdon to join the board of the company. Ed was also highly influential in guiding the course of the technology and business direction. Both Ed and Al were earlier contributors to this work, and many of the words that appear in this book are theirs. Indeed, we had intended to release the book jointly a few years ago. But times change, and Ed and Al have graciously donated all of their earlier work to us. However, you will often hear them speaking through these words.

Experiences at Rational Software

Rational Software Corporation purchased Requisite, Inc., in 1997. At Rational, we have gained significant additional experience in requirements management as it applies to developing and releasing a full family of application development tools, as well as continuing to help customers address their requirements problems. Don continues to work with us and help refine the techniques. In addition, at Rational, I have had the pleasure of working with software experts and authors Grady Booch, Ivar Jacobson, James Rumbaugh, Walker Royce, and Philippe Kruchten. Each of them contributed to my view of the requirements management challenge, and Walker and Philippe were early reviewers of this work.

We also became exposed to the use case technique for requirements capture, and to the notion of using use cases within the design model to provide a common thread to drive architecture, implementation, and testing.

I am also a fan of Rational's promulgation of the *iterative approach* for software development, of which I like to think that we were early practitioners at RELA, as well as the Rational Unified Process, a full lifecycle software development process.

Rational helped me complete this work, and for that I am grateful. Also, Rational graciously provided permission to use certain ideas, text, and diagrams.

Finally, we would also like to thank the reviewers and many others who contributed to this work, including Al Davis, Ed Yourdon, Grady Booch, Philippe Kruchten, Leslee Probasco, Ian Spence, Jean Bell, Walker Royce, Joe Marasco, Elemer Magaziner, and the following A-W reviewers: Ag Marsonia, Granville Miller, Frank Armour, Dr. Ralph R. Young (Director of Software Engineering, Litton PRC Systems and Process Engineering), Professor David Rine (George Mason University), and Dan Rawsthorn (ACCESS).

Summary

In a sense, few, if any, ideas in this book are original. Instead, it represents harvesting the shared software development experiences of two decades, with a focused, consistent, and measured emphasis on the requirements challenge. In so doing, the work, we hope, assimilates the experiences and opinions of some of the best minds in the industry on this unique and difficult software challenge. We firmly believe that the result—these *six requisite team skills for effective requirements management*—will help you deliver quality software systems on time and on budget.

INTRODUCTION

It Doesn't Seem Like It Should Be This Hard

Sit down with the customer. Figure out what the customer wants the system to do. Use cool new software languages and tools that didn't even exist two years ago. Craft the application, using the latest languages and tools. Simulate and debug with efficiency and aplomb. Download the new client application remotely. Sit back and wait for awards to come in. Take the entire holiday off. Watch for that bonus check!

Reality Seems Entirely Different

However, for most of us, much of the time, reality seems entirely different. Our lives are dominated by late nights, changing requirements, fickle customers, serious software quality issues, technology that obsolesces before we deploy it for the first time, significant project delays, and missed commitments. In the best cases, our customers are thrilled and we are well rewarded. But even then, it comes at a personal cost and we *know* we could have done better. In the worst cases, we encounter canceled projects and complete frustration. Bring on the next project! Goodness gracious, we *love* this business!

Background

Chapter 1 introduces the concept of requirements management and also summarizes some of the ongoing challenges and problems associated with software development and the causes of project successes and failures. The chapter also provides a rationale for investing time and resources in doing a better job of managing application requirements. If you're a veteran software developer, a veteran project manager, or any other kind of software veteran with lots of scars from complex projects gone awry, you may be tempted to skip this discussion and turn directly to Chapter 2.

But if you are new to the industry or spend most of your time outside the software development department of your company—if you're in the marketing department, perhaps, and you're charged with defining a new software product or if you're the quality assurance department chartered to acquire an ISO 9000 accreditation for the entire company, or if you're in a "user department" that needs to have information systems developed to support its activities—you should read Chapter 1, as well as the rest of the book!

You are most likely aware that systems development projects tend to be difficult, expensive, risky, and prone to failure, but you may not know *why* this is a common situation in most organizations. Indeed, if you think that no other organization on Earth could be as screwed up as yours, you'll be relieved to discover, from the statistics in Chapter 1, that almost every organization suffers from the same kinds of problems. Knowing *why* these problems exist and where they tend to be the most severe and expensive is a crucial first step for improvement.

In Chapter 2, we introduce the concepts of requirements management that we'll be discussing throughout the remainder of the book. Even if you think you know what "requirement" means—and after all, who *doesn't?*—we urge you to read this material, for it provides some definitions and foundation-level assumptions that we depend on in subsequent chapters.

Finally, in Chapter 3, we introduce the software team.

Effective require-
ments management
can be accom-
plished only via an
effective software
team.

This not a book about teams, however, and the important topics of building high-performance teams, motivating them, and even managing them within the context of software development are outside the scope of this book. But this *is* a book on managing software requirements, and to accomplish this challenge, we will need the support of the entire software team. The reason is that, perhaps more than with any other specific software development activity, requirements management is a process that touches every team member, both inside the core team and in the extended team of the customer and stakeholders. Indeed, it is a premise of this book that in all but the most trivial projects, *effective requirements management can be applied only via an effective software team.* Further, to achieve success, every member of the team must participate in the process, albeit in different ways, and each team member will need to be knowledgeable about his or her role in requirements management.

Chapter 1

THE REQUIREMENTS PROBLEM

Key Points

- The goal of software development is to develop quality software—on time and on budget—that meets customers' real needs.
- Project success depends on good requirements management.
- Requirements errors are the most common type of systems development error and the most costly to fix.
- A few key skills can significantly reduce requirements errors and thus improve software quality.

The Goal

Thousands of software development teams worldwide are engaged right now in developing widely different software applications in widely different industries. But although we work in different industries and speak and write in different languages, we all work with the same technologies worldwide, we read the same magazines, we went to the same schools, and fortunately, have the same clear goal: *to develop quality software—on time and on budget—that meets customers' real needs.*

Though our customers are quite different . . .

- For some of us, the customer is an external entity, purchase order in hand, whom we must convince to disregard our competitor's claims and to buy *our* shrink-wrapped software product because it's easier to use, has more functionality, and, in the final analysis, is just better.
- For others of us, the customer is a company that has hired us to develop its software, based on expectations that the software developed will be of the highest quality achievable at today's state of the

art and will transform the company into a more competitive, more profitable organization in their marketplace.

- For perhaps most of us, the customer is sitting down the hall or downstairs or across the country, waiting anxiously for that new application to enter sales orders more efficiently or to use e-commerce for selling the company's goods and services so that the company *we* work for will ultimately be more profitable and our jobs more rewarding and just more fun.

So, although our customers are varied, we can take some comfort in the fact that the goal is the same.

A Look at the Data

In a nutshell: We software developers must admit to having a spotty track record when it comes to building nontrivial software systems. Of course, some systems work quite well, and amateurs and veterans alike are often dazzled by what we've been able to accomplish: the Internet, simpler user interfaces, hand-held computing devices, smart appliances, real-time process control, online interactive brokerage accounts, and the like. It's also true that there's a wide spectrum of possibilities between perfection and failure. For example, the word processor and the PC operating system we used to write this book collectively caused about two system crashes a day while we were writing this chapter, as well as exhibiting a number of other annoying quirks, idiosyncrasies, and "gotchas." But overall, the word processor and the operating system were "good enough" to support the task of writing this chapter, but they certainly weren't examples of perfect software.

But in many cases, the results are far more serious. A study by the Standish Group (1994) reported:

> In the United States, we spend more than $250 billion each year on IT application development of approximately 175,000 projects. The average cost of a development project for a large company is $2,322,000; for a medium company, it is $1,331,000, and for a small company, it is $434,000. . . .
>
> The Standish Group research shows a staggering 31% of projects will be canceled before they ever get completed. Further results indicate 52.7% of projects will cost 189% of their original estimates. . . .
>
> Based on this research, the Standish Group estimates that . . . American companies and government agencies will spend $81 billion for canceled software projects. These same organizations will pay an additional $59 bil-

lion for software projects that will be completed but will exceed their original time estimates.[1]

It is generally wise to take any such data "with a grain of salt," but it's fairly easy for any of us in the industry to relate to such data. We all have a pet project that never went to market or an information system "tar pit" that we built and are still suffering from. So, when there's reasonable empirical evidence that we have a problem and that evidence correlates with our own experience, it's best to admit that we have a problem and to move on to problem solving. After all, that's what we do best. Right? Right?????

Root Causes of Project Success and Failure

The first step in resolving any problem is to *understand the root causes*. Fortunately, the Standish Group survey went beyond the assessment phase and asked survey respondents to identify the most significant factors that contributed to projects that were rated "success," "challenged" (late and did not meet expectations), and "impaired" (canceled), respectively.

It's here that we discover that the emphasis in this book on requirements management is not frivolous or arbitrary; it's a response to accumulating evidence that many of the most common, most serious problems associated with software development are related to requirements. The Standish Group (1994) study noted the three most commonly cited factors that caused projects to be "challenged":

- Lack of user input: 13 percent of all projects
- Incomplete requirements and specifications: 12 percent of projects
- Changing requirements and specifications: 12 percent of all projects

Thereafter, the data diverges rapidly. Of course, your project could fail because of an unrealistic schedule or time frame (4 percent of the projects cited this), inadequate staffing and resources (6 percent), or inadequate technology skills (7 percent), various other reasons. But to the extent that the Standish figures are representative of the overall industry, it appears that at least a third of development projects run into trouble for reasons that are directly related to requirements gathering, requirements documenting, and requirements management.

---

1. Used with permission.

Although the majority of projects do seem to experience schedule/budget overruns, if not outright cancellation, the Standish Group found that some 9 percent of the projects in large companies were delivered on time and on budget; 16 percent of the projects in small companies enjoyed a similar success. And that leads to an obvious question: What were the primary "success factors" for those projects? According to the Standish study, the three most important factors were

- User involvement: 16 percent of all successful projects
- Executive management support: 14 percent of all successful projects
- Clear statement of requirements: 12 percent of all successful projects

Other surveys have even more striking results. For example, the European Software Process Improvement Training Initiative (ESPITI) conducted a survey (1995) to identify the relative importance of various types of software problems in industry. The results of this large-scale survey, based on 3,800 responses, are indicated in Figure 1–1.

The two largest problems, appearing in about half the responses, were

1. Requirements specifications
2. Managing customer requirements

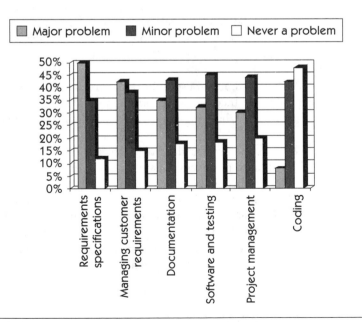

Figure 1–1   Largest software development problems by category

Again, corroborating the Standish survey, coding issues were a "nonproblem," relatively speaking.

It seems clear that requirements deserve their place as a leading root cause of software problems. Let's take a look at the economic factors associated with this particular root cause.

The Frequency of Requirements Errors

Both the Standish and the ESPITI studies provide qualitative data indicating that respondents feel that requirements problems *appear* to transcend other issues in terms of the risks and problems they pose to application development. But do requirements problems affect the delivered code?

Table 1–1 summarizes a 1994 study by Capers Jones that provided data regarding the likely number of "potential" defects in a development project and the typical "efficiency" with which a development organization removes those defects through various combinations of testing, inspections, and other strategies.

The Defect Potentials column normalizes the defects such that each category contributes to the total potential of 5.00, an arbitrary normalization that does not imply anything about the absolute number of defects. The Delivered Defects column, referring to what the user sees, is normalized in the same way.

Requirements errors top the delivered defects and contribute approximately one third of the total delivered defects to the defect pile. Thus, this study provides yet another confirmation that requirements errors are the most common category of systems development errors.

Table 1–1   Defect summary

Defect Origins	Defect Potentials	Removal Efficiency	Delivered Defects
Requirements	1.00	77%	0.23
Design	1.25	85%	0.19
Coding	1.75	95%	0.09
Documentation	0.60	80%	0.12
Bad fixes	0.40	70%	0.12
Total	5.00	85%	0.75

The High Cost of Requirements Errors

If requirements errors can be fixed quickly, easily, and economically, we still may not have a huge problem. But this last statistic delivers the final blow. Just the opposite tends to be true. Studies performed at companies including GTE, TRW, IBM, and HP have measured and assigned costs to errors occurring at various phases of the project lifecycle. Davis (1993) summarized a number of these studies, as Figure 1–2 illustrates. Although these studies were run independently, they all reached roughly the same conclusion: If a unit cost of *one* is assigned to the effort required to detect and repair an error during the coding stage, then the cost to detect and repair an error during the requirements stage is between *five* to *ten* times less. Furthermore, the cost to detect and repair an error during the maintenance stage is *twenty* times more.

Altogether, the figure illustrates that as much as a 200:1 cost savings results from finding errors in the requirements stage versus finding errors in the maintenance stage of the software lifecycle.

While this may be the exaggerated case, it's easy to see that there is a multiplicative factor at work. The reason is that many of these errors are not detected until well after they have been made.

If you've read this section carefully, you may have noticed that we muddled two issues together in Figure 1–2: the relative costs of various categories of

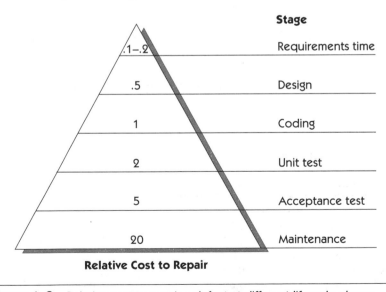

Figure 1–2   Relative cost to repair a defect at different lifecycle phases

errors *and* the cost of fixing them at different stages in the software lifecycle. For example, the item "requirements time" literally means *all* errors that were detected and fixed during the period officially designated as "requirements definition." But since it's unlikely that any technical design or programming activities will have been carried out at this early stage—ignoring, for the moment, the possibility of prototyping activities that might be taking place—the mistakes that we detect and fix at this stage *are* requirements errors.

But the errors that are discovered during the design phase of a development project could be one of two categories: (1) errors that occurred when the development staff created a technical design from a correct set of requirements *or* (2) errors that should have been detected as requirements errors somewhat earlier in the process but that somehow "leaked" into the design phase of the project. It's the latter category of errors that turn out to be particularly expensive, for two reasons.

1. By the time the requirements-oriented error is discovered, the development group will have invested time and effort in building a design from those erroneous requirements. As a result, the design will probably have to be thrown away or reworked.

2. The true nature of the error may be disguised; everyone assumes that they're looking for design errors during the testing or inspection activities that take place during this phase, and considerable time and effort may be wasted until someone says, "Wait a minute! This isn't a design mistake after all; we've got the wrong requirements."

Confirming the details of the requirements error means tracking down the user who provided the requirements details in the first place. But that person may not be readily available, may have forgotten the requirements instruction to the development team or the rationale for identifying the original requirements in the first place, or just had a change of mind. Similarly, the development team member who was involved in that stage of the project—often, a person with the title of "business analyst" or "systems analyst"—may have moved on to a different project or may suffer a similar form of short-term amnesia. All of this involves a certain amount of "spinning of wheels" and lost time.

These problems associated with "leakage" of defects from one lifecycle phase to the next are fairly obvious when you think about them, but most organizations haven't investigated them very carefully. One organization that *has* done so is Hughes Aircraft; a study by Snyder (1992) follows the leakage phenomenon for a large collection of projects Hughes has conducted over the past 15 years. The study indicates that 74 percent of the requirements-oriented defects were discovered during the requirements-analysis phase of the project—that is, the formal phase during which customers and systems analysts are discussing, brainstorming, negotiating, and documenting the project requirements. That's the ideal time and place to discover such errors, and it's likely to be the most inexpensive time and place. However, the study also shows that 4 percent of the requirements defects "leak" into the preliminary, or high-level, design phase of the project and that 7 percent leak further into detailed design. The leakage continues throughout the lifecycle, and a total of 4 percent of the requirements errors aren't found until the maintenance phase—that is, when the system has been released to the customers and is presumably in full-scale operation.

Thus, depending on when and where a defect is discovered in a software application development project, we're likely to experience the effect of 50–100 times cost. The reason is that in order to repair the defect, we are likely to experience costs in some or all of the following areas:

- Respecification.
- Redesign.
- Recoding.
- Retesting.
- Change orders—telling users and operators to replace a defective version of the system with the corrected version.
- Corrective action—undoing whatever damage may have been done by erroneous operation of the improperly specified system, which could involve sending refund checks to angry customers, rerunning computer jobs, and so on.
- Scrap—including code and design and test cases that were carried out with the best of intentions but then had to be thrown away when it was discovered that they were based on incorrect requirements.
- Recall of defective versions of shrink-wrapped software and associated manuals from users. But since software is now embedded in products ranging from digital wristwatches to microwave ovens to automobiles, the recall could include both tangible products and the software embedded within them.
- Warranty costs.
- Product liability—if the customer sues for damages caused by the defective software.
- Service costs for a company representative to visit a customer's field location to reinstall the new software.
- Documentation.

Conclusion

In summary, this data demonstrates two things.

1. Requirements errors are likely to be the most common class of error.
2. Requirements errors are likely to be the most expensive errors to fix.

Requirements errors are likely to consume 25%–40% of the total project budget.

Given the frequency of requirements errors and the multiplicative effect of the "cost to fix" factor, it's easy to predict that requirements errors will contribute the majority—often 70 percent or more—of the rework costs. And since rework typically consumes 30%–50% of a typical project budget (Boehm and Papaccio 1988b), it follows that requirements errors can easily consume *25%–40%* of the total project budget!

Our own experiences support this data, and that is the primary reason we wrote this book. If, with a small investment in a few key skills, we can do a better job in this area, we can save significant amounts of money, increase productivity, save precious time on the project calendar, and ultimately deliver higher-quality results to the customer, not to mention saving some of the wear and tear on the software *team*.

Chapter 2

INTRODUCTION TO REQUIREMENTS MANAGEMENT

Key Points

- A requirement is a capability that the system must deliver.
- Requirements management is a process of systematically eliciting, organizing, and documenting requirements for a complex system.
- *Our* problem is to understand *users'* problems in *their* culture and *their* language and to build systems that meet *their* needs.
- A feature is a service that the system provides to fulfill one or more stakeholder needs.
- A use case describes a sequence of actions, performed by a system, that yields a result of value to a user.

Based on the data presented in the Chapter 1, you can see why we're interested in focusing on requirements management. But before we can begin explaining the various techniques and strategies, we need to provide some definitions and examples. We'll need to start by defining what we mean by a requirement.

Definitions

What Is a Requirement?

Although many definitions of software requirements have been used throughout the years, the one provided by requirements engineering authors Dorfman and Thayer (1990) is quite workable:

- A software capability needed by the user to solve a problem to achieve an objective
- A software capability that must be met or possessed by a system or system component to satisfy a contract, standard, specification, or other formally imposed documentation

This definition may appear to be a little vague, but we'll develop these concepts further, so this definition will do quite well for now.

What Is Requirements Management?

Requirements define capabilities that the systems must deliver, and conformance or lack of conformance to a set of requirements often determines the success or failure of projects. It makes sense, therefore, to find out what the requirements are, write them down, organize them, and track them in the event that they change. Stated another way, we'll define requirements management as

> *a systematic approach to eliciting, organizing, and documenting the requirements of the system, and a process that establishes and maintains agreement between the customer and the project team on the changing requirements of the system.*

- Anyone who has ever been involved with complex software systems—whether from the perspective of a customer or a developer—knows that a crucial skill is the ability to *elicit* the requirements from users and stakeholders.
- Since hundreds, if not thousands, of requirements are likely to be associated with a system, it's important to *organize* them.
- Since most of us can't keep more than a few dozen pieces of information in our heads, *documenting* the requirements is necessary to support effective communication among the various stakeholders. The requirements have to be recorded in an accessible medium: a document, model, database, or a list on the whiteboard.

But what do these elements have to do with *managing* requirements? Project size and complexity are major factors here: nobody would bother talking about "managing" requirements in a two-person project that had only 10 requirements to fulfill. But to verify 1,000 requirements—a small purchased software product—or 300,000 requirements—a Boeing 777—it's obvious that we will be faced with problems of organizing, prioritizing, controlling access to, and providing resources for the various requirements.

- Which project team members are responsible for the wind speed requirement (#278), and which ones are allowed to modify it or delete it?
- If requirement #278 is modified, what other requirements will be affected?
- How can we be sure that someone has written the code in a software system to fulfill requirement #278, and which test cases in the overall test suite are intended to verify that the requirements have indeed been fulfilled?

That, along with some other, similar activities, is what requirements management is all about.

This is not something new that we've invented on our own; it's one of those "common sense" activities that most development organizations claim to do in some fashion or other. But it's typically informal and carried out inconsistently from one project to another, and some of the key activities are likely to be overlooked or short-changed because of the pressures and politics associated with many development projects. So, requirements management could be regarded as a set of organized, standardized, and systematic processes and techniques for dealing with the requirements of a significant, complex project.

We're certainly not the first to suggest the idea of organized, formalized processes; two well-known efforts of this kind are the Software Engineering Institute's Capability Maturity Model (SEI-CMM) and the ISO 9000 quality management standards. We'll discuss the SEI-CMM and ISO 9000 views on requirements management in Appendix D.

Application of Requirements Management Techniques

Types of Software Applications

Earlier, we suggested that software applications can be categorized as follows:

- Information systems and other applications developed for use within a company. (Such as the payroll system that is being used to calculate the take-home pay for our next paycheck.) This category is the basis for the information system/information technology industry, or IS/IT.
- Software we develop and sell as commercial products (such as the word processor we are using to write this chapter). Companies developing this type of software are often referred to as independent software vendors, or ISVs.
- Software that runs on computers embedded in other devices, machines, or complex systems (Such as those contained in the airplane we are writing this in; the cell phones we just used to call our spouses; the automobile we'll use to get to our eventual destination). We'll call this type of software embedded-systems applications, or embedded applications.

The nature of the applications we develop for these three different types of systems is extremely diverse. They could consist of 5,000,000 lines of

COBOL on a mainframe host environment developed over a period of ten or more years by 50–100 individuals. They could consist of 10,000 lines of Java on a Web client application written in one year by a one- or two-person team. Or, they could be 1,000,000 lines of extremely time-critical C code on a complex real-time telephony system.

We'll maintain that the requirements management techniques presented throughout this book can be applied to any of these types of systems. Many of the techniques are independent of application type; others may need to be tuned for the application-specific context before being applied. To enhance your understanding, we'll provide a mix of examples to illustrate the application of the various techniques.

Systems Applications

Requirements management also can be applied to systems development. Most of the techniques in this book will deliver value in managing requirements of arbitrarily complex systems consisting of mechanical subsystems, computer subsystems, and chemical subsystems and their interrelated pieces and parts. Clearly, this is a broad discipline, and we will have to show some discretion to be able to deliver value to the average software team member. So, we'll focus on a requirements management process and specific techniques that can be applied most directly to *significant software applications of the IS/IT, ISV, or embedded-systems* types.

The Road Map

Since we are embarking on a journey to *develop quality software—on time and on budget—that meets customers' real needs*, it may well be helpful to have a map of the territory. But this is a difficult challenge in that the variety of people you encounter on this particular journey, and the languages they speak, are quite diverse. Many questions will arise.

- Is this a need or a requirement?
- Is this a nice-to-have or a must-have?
- Is this a statement of the problem or a statement of the solution?
- Is this a goal of the system or a contractual requirement?
- Do we have to program in Java? Says who?
- Who is it that doesn't like the new system, and where was that person when we visited here before?

In order to successfully navigate through the territory, we'll need to understand where we are at any point in time, who these people are that we meet, what language they are speaking, and what information we need from them to successfully complete our journey. Let's start in the "land of the problem."

The Problem Domain

Most successful requirements journeys begin with a trip to the land of the problem. This *problem domain* is the home of real users and other stake-holders, people whose needs must be addressed in order for us to build the perfect system. This is the home of the people who need the rock or a new sales order entry system or a configuration management system good enough to blow the competition away. In all probability, these people are not like us. Their technical and economic backgrounds are different from ours, they speak in funny acronyms, they go to different parties and drink different beers, they don't wear T-shirts to work, and they have motiva-tions that seem strange and unfathomable. (What, you don't like *Star Trek?*)

On rare occasions, they are just like us. They are programmers looking for a new tool or system developers who have asked you to develop a portion of the system. In these rare cases, this portion of the journey *might* be easier, but it might also be more difficult.

But typically, this is not the case, and we are in the land of the alien user. These users have *business* or *technical problems* that they need our help to solve. So, it becomes *our* problem to understand *their* problems, in *their* cul-ture and *their* language and to build systems that meet *their* needs. Since this territory can seem a little foggy, we'll represent it as a cloud. This will be a constant reminder to us to make sure that we are seeing all the issues in the problem space clearly.

Problem domain

Within the problem domain, we use a set of *team skills* as our map and com-pass to *understand the problem to be solved*. While we are here, we need to gain an understanding of the problem and the needs that must be filled to address this problem.

Stakeholder Needs

It is also our responsibility to understand the needs of users and other stake-holders whose lives will be affected by our solution. As we elicit those needs, we'll stack them in a little pile called stakeholder needs, which we represent as a pyramid.

Moving Toward the Solution Domain

Fortunately, the journey through the problem domain is not necessarily difficult, and the artifacts collected there are not many. However, with even this little bit of data, we will be well provisioned for the part of the journey that we have perhaps been better prepared for: providing a solution to the problem at hand. In this solution space, we focus on defining a solution to the user's problem; this is the realm of computers, programming, operating systems, networks, and processing nodes. Here, we can apply the skills we have learned much more directly.

Features of the System

First, however, it will be helpful to state what we learned in the problem domain and how we intend to deliver that via the solution. This is not a very long list and consists of such items as

- "The car will have power windows."
- "Defect-trending charts will provide a visual means of assessing progress."
- "Web-enabled entry of sales orders."
- "Automatic step-and-repeat weld cycle."

These are simple descriptions, in the user's language, that we will use as labels to communicate with the user how our system addresses the problem. These labels will become part of our everyday language, and much energy will be spent in defining them, debating them, and prioritizing them. We'll call these descriptions "*features*" of the system to be built and will define a feature as

a service that the system provides to fulfill one or more stakeholder needs.

Graphically, we'll represent features as a base for the previous needs pyramid.

Software Requirements

Once we have established the feature set and have gained agreement with the customer, we can move on to defining the more specific requirements that we will need to impose on the solution. If we build a system that conforms to those requirements, we can be certain that the system we develop will deliver the features we promised. In turn, since the features address one or more stakeholder needs, we will have addressed those needs directly in the solution.

These more specific requirements are the *software requirements*. We'll represent them as a block within our pyramid in a similar manner to the features. We also note that these appear pretty far down on the pyramid, and this implies, correctly, that we have much work to do before we get to that level of specificity later in the book.

An Introduction to Use Cases

One final key construct will help us on our journey. This key construct is the *use case*, which we'll use in a variety of ways throughout the rest of the book. Most simply, a use case describes a *sequence of actions, performed by a system, that yields a result of value to a user.* In other words, a use case describes a series of user/system interactions that helps the user accomplish something. We'll represent the use case with a simple oval icon containing the name of the use case. For example, if we were to describe a use case whereby a user uses a computer to simply turn a light on or off, we might call it simply "control light," and we'd put that term in the oval.

Summary

Now let's take a look at the map we've built. In Figure 2–1, you can see that we have made a subtle yet important transition in our thinking in this process. We

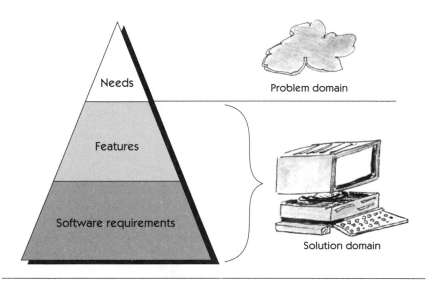

Figure 2–1   Overview of problem/solution domains

have moved from the problem domain, represented by the cloud and the user needs we discovered, to a definition of a system that will constitute the solution domain, represented by the features of the system and the software requirements that will drive its design and implementation. Moreover, we have done so in a logical, stepwise fashion, making sure to understand the problem and the user's needs before we envision or define the solution. This road map, along with its important distinctions, will continue to be important throughout this book.

Chapter 3
THE SOFTWARE TEAM

"Computer programming is a human activity." (Weinberg 1971)

Key Points

- Requirements management touches every team member, albeit in different ways.
- Effective requirements management can only be accomplished by an effective software team.
- Six team skills are needed for requirements management.

Individuals choose software development as their career domain for a variety of reasons. Some read *Popular Science* and *Popular Mechanics* at home, gravitated to the one programming course available in high school, majored in engineering or computer science in college, and thereby directed their lives down this specific technical path. For others, it was serendipity; being at a place in space and time when the need for software was apparent, we could participate in meeting that need, and it gradually evolved into a full-time commitment in the field.

In any case, it was the allure of *technology* that kept the flame burning: We love the bits and bytes, the operating systems, the databases, the development tools, the keyboard shortcuts, the languages. Who else but software developers could have developed the UNIX operating system? We are focused on technology, and that is our driving motivation. Perhaps because of an innate genetic tendency or perhaps because we skipped all the "softer" classes in college—psychology, drama, or, even worse, English!—we are generally focused less on the people side of our business and more on the bits and bytes. We tend not to party well,[1] and some of us have trouble relating to people outside

---

1. During a 1979 RELA open house, for example, one programmer remained at his desk throughout the party, programming happily, even though his desk was in the *middle* of the party room. After finishing his work, he simply got up, arranged his desk, and left the building without a word to anyone. What is unusual about this behavior? In our industry? Nothing!

of work, when there is no common technology substrate on which to base a discussion.

One result of this, which was further compounded by the simple single-user nature of the tools we used and the more limited size of the applications we developed, was the tendency toward software development as an individual activity. The programmer defined, designed, wrote, and, typically, tested his or her own work. Perhaps testers were around to help with the heavy lifting at the end, but the focus clearly was on individual activity. The programmer as hero was the common paradigm.

Software Development as a Team Activity

"Software Development has become a team sport." (Booch 1998)

At some point, the game changed. Why? Watts Humphrey (1989) observed that

"The history of software development is one of increasing scale."

> *"the history of software development is one of increasing scale. Initially, a few individuals could hand craft small programs; the work soon grew beyond them. Teams of one or two dozen individuals were then used, but success was mixed. While many organizations have solved these small-system problems, the scale of our work continues to grow. Today, large projects typically require the coordinated work of many teams."*

Humphrey goes on to observe that complexity continues to outpace one's ability to solve these problems intuitively as they appear. For example, we are involved in a requirements project that simultaneously affects approximately 30 products in a broad product family. The requirements that are being generated influence, in real time, the software being written by more than 400 programmers at distributed locations. Making this project a success requires intense coordination of a "team of teams" all working in a common methodology to address the requirements challenge.

The requirements management process touches every team member, albeit in different ways.

Effective requirements management can be accomplished only via an effective software team.

What's to be done? Clearly, we have to make the "team thing" work and work well. As Boehm (1981) points out in the COCOMO cost estimation model, the capability of the team has the greatest impact on software production. Davis (1995b) supports this conclusion in his discussion of team productivity: "optimizing the productivity of all individuals does not necessarily result in optimizing the productivity of the team" (p. 170). So, it seems logical that we invest some of our resources in making software *teams* more productive.

Requisite Team Skills for Effective Requirements Management

This book is organized around the six team skills that are necessary for a modern software team to address the requirements challenge.

- In Team Skill 1, Analyzing the Problem, we develop a set of techniques the team can use to gain a proper understanding of the *problem* that a new software system is intended to solve.
- In Team Skill 2, Understanding User Needs, we introduce a variety of techniques the team can use to *elicit requirements* from the system users and stakeholders. No one set of techniques will work in all situations; nor will it be necessary for the team to master all of the techniques. But with a little practice and some judicious picking and choosing, the team will gain a much better ability to understand the real needs that the system must address.
- In Team Skill 3, Defining the System, we describe the initial process by which the team converts an understanding of the problem and the user's needs to the initial definition of a system that will address those needs.
- In Team Skill 4, Managing Scope, we arm the team with the ability to do a better job of managing the scope of the project. After all, no matter how well understood the needs are, the team cannot do the impossible, and it will often be necessary to negotiate an acceptable deliverable before success can be achieved.
- In Team Skill 5, Refining the System Definition, we help the team *organize* the requirements information. Further, we introduce a set of techniques the team can use to *elaborate* on the system definition, or refine it to a level suitable to drive design and implementation, so that the entire extended team knows exactly what kind of system it is building.
- Finally, in Team Skill 6, Building the Right System, we cover some of the more technical aspects of *design assurance, verification, validation testing,* and *change management,* and we show how *traceability* can be used to help ensure a quality outcome.

Team Members Have Different Skills

One of the most interesting things about teams is that individual team members have different skills. After all, that's what makes a team a team. Walker Royce (1998) points out that

balance and coverage are two of the most important aspects of an excellent team. . . . A football team has a need for diverse skills, very much like a

> *software development team. . . . There has rarely been a great football team that didn't have great coverage, offense, defense, and special teams, coaching and personnel, first string and reserve players, passing and running. Great teams need coverage across key positions with strong individual players. But a team loaded with superstars, all striving to set individual records and competing to be the team leader, can be embarrassed by a balanced team of solid players with a few leaders focused on the team result of winning the game.*

In the software team, we hope that some players have proven their ability to work with the *customers* effectively, that others have software *programming* abilities, and that others have *testing* abilities. Still other team players will need *design and architecture* abilities. Many more skills are required as well. We also expect that the requisite team skills for requirements management will affect various members of the teams in various ways. So, in a sense, we'll hope to develop every team member's ability to help manage requirements effectively. And we'll try to indicate, where we can, which team members may be best suited to a particular and necessary skill.

The Organization of Software Teams

Software development is exceedingly complex, and the domains in which we apply our skills vary tremendously. It therefore seems unlikely that one specific way to organize a software team will work in all cases or is inherently more efficient than other approaches. Nonetheless, certain common elements occur in many successful teams. Therefore, we think it's important to establish a hypothetical team construct. But rather than invent an ideal team, which would be too easy and too academic, we decided to pattern our hypothetical team on a real software development team.

The team we'll model is based on a real-world software team that has proved effective in two major areas: (1) effective requirements management and (2) delivering on time and on budget. (Of course, we believe that this is an obvious cause-and-effect relationship!) Yet we also admit that many other skills must be present in a team that truly delivers the goods year in and year out. In our case study, the team works for a company called Lumenations, Ltd., that is developing a next-generation "home lighting automation system" for high-end residential use.

The Case Study

We can meet another objective in this book if we can develop a case study we can track from requirements start to requirements finish. In this way, we will be able to not only apply the techniques that we are about to discuss to our example but also provide example work products, or artifacts, to further illustrate key points and to serve as examples for your own projects. Appendix A of this book provides a sample set of artifacts from the case study.

Background for the Case Study

Lumenations, Ltd., has been a worldwide supplier of commercial lighting systems for use in professional theater and amateur stage productions for more than 40 years. In 1999, its annual revenues peaked at approximately $120 million, and sales are flattening. Lumenations is a public company and the lack of growth in sales—no, worse, the lack of any reasonable prospect for improving growth in sales—is taking its toll on the company and its shareholders. The last annual meeting was quite uncomfortable, as there was little new to report about the company's prospects for growth. The stock climbed briefly to $25 last spring on a spate of new orders but has since crept back down to around $15.

The theater equipment industry as a whole is flat with little new development. The industry is mature and already well consolidated. Since Lumenations' stock is in the tank and its capitalization is only modest, acquisition is not an option for the company.

What's needed is a *new* marketplace, not too remote from what the company does best, but one in which there is substantial opportunity for growth in revenue and profits. After a thorough market research project and spending many dollars on marketing consultants, the company has decided to enter a new market: *lighting automation for high-end residential systems.* This market is apparently growing at 25%–35% a year. Even better, the market is immature, and none of the established players has a dominant market position. Lumenations' strong worldwide distribution channel will be a real asset in the marketplace, and the distributors are hungry for new products. Looks like a great opportunity!

The HOLIS Software Development Team

The project we choose will be the development of HOLIS, our code name for an innovative new HOme Lighting automation System to be marketed by Lumenations. The HOLIS team is typical in its size and scope. For the purposes of our case study, we've made it a fairly small team, composed of only 15 team members, but it's large enough to have all the necessary skills fairly well represented by individuals with some degree of specialization in their roles. Also, it's the structure of the team that's most important, and by adding more developers and testers, the structure of the HOLIS team

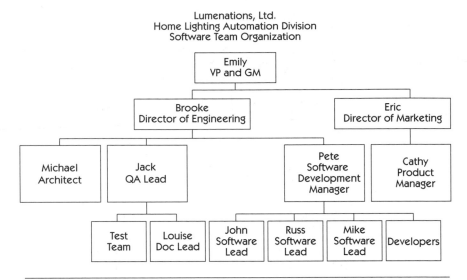

Figure 3–1   The HOLIS software development team

proved to scale well to a size of 30–50 people and commensurately larger software applications than HOLIS will require.

To address the new marketplace, Lumenations has set up a new division, the Home Lighting Automation Division. Since the division and technology are mostly new to Lumenations, the HOLIS team has been assembled mostly from new hires, although a few team members have been transferred from the commercial lighting division.

Figure 3–1 is an organization chart of the development team and the relationships among the team members. We'll revisit this team periodically throughout the book and see how it applies its new skills to the requirements challenge for HOLIS.

Summary

It's difficult for anyone to argue rationally *against* the idea of managing and documenting the requirements of a system in order to ensure that we deliver what the customer really wanted. However, as we have seen, the data demonstrate that, as an industry, we often do a poor job of doing so. *Lack of user input, incomplete requirements and specifications, and changing requirements and specifications* are commonly cited problem causes in projects that failed to meet their objectives. And we do know that a significant number of software projects do fail to meet their objectives.

A common attitude among developers and customers alike is that "even if we're not really sure of the details of what we want, it's better to get started with implementation now, because we're behind schedule and in a hurry. We can pin down the requirements later." But all too often, this well-intentioned approach degenerates into a chaotic development effort, with no one quite sure what the user really wanted or what the current system really does. With today's powerful and easy-to-use prototyping tools, there's a perception that if the developers can build a rough approximation of the user's needs in a prototype, the user can point out the features that need to be added, deleted, or modified. This *can* work, and it is an important aspect of iterative development. But due in part to the extremely high cost of fixing requirement errors, this process must be within the context of an overall *requirements management strategy*, or chaos results.

How do we know what the system is supposed to do? How do we keep track of the current status of requirements? How do we determine the impact of a change? It's because of issues like these that requirements management has begun to emerge as both a necessary and a practical software engineering discipline. We have introduced an encompassing philosophy of requirements management and have provided a set of definitions that support these activities.

Since the history of software development—and the future for at least as far as we can currently envision it—is one of increasing complexity, we also understand that the software development problem is one that must be addressed by well-structured and well-trained software *teams*. In the requirements management discipline in particular, every team member will eventually be involved in helping manage the requirements for the project. These teams must develop the requisite skills to understand the user needs, to manage the scope of the application, and to build systems that meet these user needs. The team must work, *as a team*, to address the requirements management challenge.

In order to do so, the first step in the requirements management process is to ensure that the developers understand the "problem" the user is trying to solve. We'll cover that topic in the next three chapters as Team Skill 1, Analyzing the Problem.

Analyzing the Problem

The last few years have seen an unprecedented increase in the power of the tools and technologies that software developers use to build today's enterprise applications. New languages have increased the level of abstraction and improved the productivity with which we can address and solve user problems. The application of object-oriented methods has produced designs that are more robust and extensible. Tools for version management, requirements management, design and analysis, defect tracking, and automated testing have helped software developers to manage the complexity of thousands of requirements and hundreds of thousands of lines of code.

As the productivity of the software development environment has increased, it should now be easier than ever before to develop systems that satisfy real business needs. However, as we have seen, the data demonstrate that we remain challenged in our ability to truly understand and to satisfy these needs. Perhaps there is a simpler explanation for this difficulty that may represent the *"problem behind the problem." Development teams spend too little time understanding the real business problems, the needs of the users and other stakeholders, and the nature of the environment in which their applications must thrive.* Instead, we developers tend to forge ahead, providing technological solutions based on an inadequate understanding of the problem to be solved.

> Development teams tend to forge ahead, providing solutions based on an inadequate understanding of the problem to be solved.

The resulting systems do not fit the needs of the users and stakeholders as well as could have been reasonably expected. The consequences of this mismatch are inadequate economic rewards for the customers and developers of the system, dissatisfied users, and career challenges. It seems obvious, therefore, that an incremental investment in an analysis of the problem will produce handsome rewards downstream. The goals of this team skill are to provide guidelines for problem analysis and to define specific goals for this skill in application development.

In the following chapters, we will explore ways and means of defining just exactly what the problem is. After all, if your team can't define the problem, it's going to be difficult to figure out a proper solution.

Chapter 4
THE FIVE STEPS
IN PROBLEM ANALYSIS

Key Points

- Problem analysis is the process of understanding real-world problems and user's needs and proposing solutions to meet those needs.
- The goal of problem analysis is to gain a better understanding, before development begins, of the problem being solved.
- To identify the root cause, or the problem behind the problem, ask the people directly involved.
- Identifying the actors on the system is a key step in problem analysis.

This chapter focuses on ways in which the development team can understand the real-world needs of the stakeholders and users of a new system or application. As most systems are built to solve a particular problem, we'll use *problem analysis* techniques to make sure we understand what the problem is.

But we should also recognize that not every application is developed to solve a problem; some are built to take advantage of *opportunities* that the market presents, even when the existence of a problem is not clear. For example, unique software applications, such as SimCity and Myst, have proved their worth to those who like computer games and mental challenges or who just enjoy modeling and simulating or playing games on their computers. So, although it's difficult to say what problem SimCity or Myst solved—well, perhaps the problem of "not having enough fun things to do with your computer" or the problem of "too much spare time on one's hands"—it seems clear that the products provide real value to a large number of users.

In a sense, problems and opportunities are just flip sides of the same coin; your problem is my opportunity. It's a matter of perspective. But since most systems do address some identifiable problem, we can simplify the discussion and avoid the problem/opportunity schizophrenia by focusing on the problem side of the coin only. After all, we like to think of ourselves as problem solvers.

We'll define problem analysis as

the process of understanding real-world problems and user needs and proposing solutions to meet those needs.

In so doing, the problem domain must be analyzed and understood, and a variety of solution domains must be explored. Usually, a variety of solutions are possible, and our job is to find the solution that is the optimum fit for the problem being solved.

In order to be able to *do* problem analysis, it would be helpful to define what a problem is. According to Gause and Weinberg (1989),

"a problem can be defined as the difference between things as perceived and things as derived."

This seems like a sensible definition, one that at least should eliminate the common problem of developers often thinking that the real problem is that the user doesn't understand what the real problem is! According to the definition, if the user perceives something as a problem, it's a real problem, and it's worthy of addressing.

Sometimes, the simplest solution is a workaround, or revised business process, rather than a new system.

Still, based on this definition, our colleague Elemer Magaziner notes that there are a number of ways to address a problem. For example, changing the user's *desire* or *perception* may be the most cost-effective approach. Doing so may be a matter of setting and managing expectations, providing workarounds or incremental improvements to existing systems, providing alternative solutions that do not require new system development, or providing additional training. Practical experience shows many examples where changing the perception of the difference has led to the highest-quality, fastest, and cheapest solutions available! As problem solvers, it is incumbent on us to explore these alternative solutions before leaping into a new system solution.

However, when these alternative activities fail to sufficiently reduce the gap in perception and desire, we are left with the largest and most expensive challenge: to actively change the distance between perception and reality. This we must accomplish by defining and implementing *new systems* that narrow the difference between *as desired* and *as perceived*.

As with any complex problem-solving exercise, we must start with the goal in mind. The goal of problem analysis is to gain a better understanding,

The goal of problem analysis is to gain a better understanding of the problem being solved *before* development begins.

before development begins, of the problem being solved. The specific steps that must be taken in order to achieve the goal are

1. Gain agreement on the problem definition.
2. Understand the root causes—the problem behind the problem.
3. Identify the stakeholders and the users.
4. Define the solution system boundary.
5. Identify the constraints to be imposed on the solution.

Let's work through each of these steps and see if we can develop the team skills that we need to move on to solution providing!

Step 1: Gain Agreement on the Problem Definition

The first step is to gain agreement on the definition of the problem to be solved. One of the simplest ways to gain this agreement is to *simply write the problem down and see whether everyone agrees.*

As part of this process, it is often beneficial to understand some of the benefits of a proposed solution, being careful to make certain that the benefits are described in the terms provided by the customers/users. Having the user describe the benefits provides additional contextual background on the real problem. In seeing the benefits from the customer's point of view, we also gain a better understanding of the stakeholder's view of the problem itself.

The Problem Statement

You may find it helpful to write your problem down in a standardized format (Table 4–1). Filling the table in for your application is a simple yet powerful technique to ensure that all stakeholders on your project are working toward the same goal.

Spending the time it takes to gain agreement on the problem being solved may seem like a small and insignificant step, and in most circumstances, it is. But sometimes, it is not. For example, one of our clients, an equipment manufacturer, was engaged in a major upgrade to its IS/IT system, which provided invoicing and financial reporting between the company and its dealers. The theme for the new program was to "improve dealer communications." As such, the team had embarked on a significant new system development effort.

Table 4–1   Problem statement format

Element	Description
The problem of	Describe the problem.
affects	Identify stakeholders affected by the problem.
the result of which	Describe the impact of this problem on stakeholders and business activity.
Benefits of	Indicate the proposed solution and list a few key benefits.

An exercise in gaining agreement on the problem being solved was enlightening. The development team–defined solution envisioned a powerful new system that provided better financial reporting, improved invoice and statement formats, online parts ordering, and electronic mail. And oh, by the way, the team eventually *hoped* to provide the capability for electronic funds transfer between the company and the dealer.

During the problem statement exercise, company management had the opportunity to provide input. Management's vision was substantially different: The primary goal of the new system was to *provide electronic funds transfer that would improve the cash flow of the company.* After a raucous discussion, it became clear that the first-order problem to be addressed by the new system was electronic funds transfer; e-mail and other dealer communication features were considered simply "nice to have." Needless to say, there was a substantial reorientation of the objectives of the new system, including a new problem definition that identified electronic funds transfer as the problem being solved. This reorientation also triggered the development of a different system architecture than had been envisioned, complete with the security capability consistent with the risks inherent in electronic banking.

Step 2: Understand the Root Causes— The Problem Behind the Problem

Your team can use a variety of techniques to gain an understanding of the real problem and its real causes. One such technique is "root cause" analysis, which is a systematic way of uncovering the root, or underlying, cause of an identified problem or a symptom of a problem.

For example, consider a real-world example: a mail-order catalog company, called GoodsAreUs, that manufactures and sells a variety of inexpensive, miscellaneous items for home and personal use. As the company addresses the problem of insufficient profitability, it uses total quality management (TQM) techniques for problem solving learned in their quality program. Based on this experience, the company quickly focused on its *cost of nonconformance*, which is the cost of all of the things that go wrong and produce waste, scrap, and other excess costs. This cost includes rework, scrap, customer dissatisfaction, employee turnover, and other factors that are negative-value activities. As the company quantified its cost of nonquality, it suspected that production waste, or "scrap," was one of the largest contributors.

The next step in getting to the *root cause*, or *the problem behind the problem in scrap*, is to determine what factors contribute to the scrap problem. TQM teaches us the use of the *fishbone diagram* (see Figure 4–1) to identify the problems behind the problem. In our specific analysis, the company identified many sources that contributed to scrap. Each source was listed as one of the "bones" on the diagram.

OK, so how do you determine the root causes? Well, it just depends. In many cases, it's a simple matter of asking the people directly involved what they think the root cause is. It's amazing how much people *do* know about the problem behind the problem; it's just that no one—by which we usually mean management—had taken the time to *ask* them before. So, *ask* them and then *ask* them *again*.

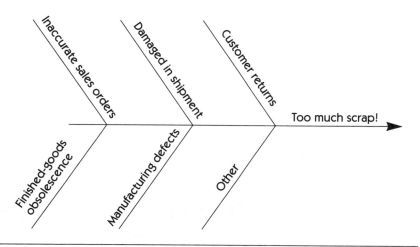

Figure 4–1   Fishbone diagram of root causes

If the problem is more serious and simply asking those affected doesn't create a sense of comfort, it may be necessary to perform a detailed investigation of each contributing problem and to quantify its individual impact. This could vary from perhaps simple brainstorming by participants who have knowledge of the space to a small data collection project or, potentially, to a more rigorous and scientific investigation. In any case, the goal is to quantify the likely contribution of each root cause.

Addressing the Root Cause

Quality data demonstrates that many root causes are simply not worth fixing.

Of course, the engineer in all of us would like to fix *all* of the root causes on the "bones" of the diagram. This seems like the right thing to do. But is it? Often, *it is not; quality data routinely shows that a number of root causes are simply not worth fixing*, as the cost of the fix exceeds the cost of the problem. How do you know which ones to fix? *Answer*: You must determine the materiality, or contribution, of each root cause. The results of this investigation can be plotted as a *Pareto chart*, or simple histogram that visually exposes the real culprits.

Back to our example: Let's suppose that the results of data gathering produced the results shown in Figure 4–2. As you can see, the team discovered that a *single* root cause—"inaccurate sales orders"—produced half of all scrap. If, in turn, the existing sales order system was found to be a poor example of legacy code, complete with a user-vicious interface and nonexistent online error handling, there may indeed be opportunity to cut scrap through development of new software.

At this point, *and only at this point*, is the team justified in proposing a replacement for the existing sales order entry system. Further, the cost justification

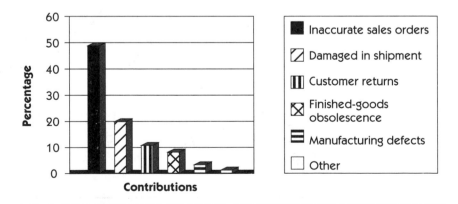

Figure 4–2 Pareto chart of root causes

Table 4–2 Sales order problem statement

Elements	Description
The problem of	inaccuracies in sales orders
affects	sales order personnel, customers, manufacturing, shipping, and customer service,
the result of which	is increased scrap, excessive handling costs, customer dissatisfaction, and decreased profitability.
Benefits of	a new system to address the problem include
	■ Increased accuracy of sales orders at point of entry
	■ Improved reporting of sales data to management
	■ And, ultimately, higher profitability

for such a system can be quantified by determining the estimated cost of development and the return on this investment through a reduction in scrap.

A further fishbone analysis could then be used to determine what specific types of errors contribute to the inaccurate sales order problem. This new, more detailed, data can then be used to define the features of the software system to address those errors. For our purposes, however, we can conclude our analysis by agreeing that a replacement of the sales order system can be at least a partial solution to the problem of too much scrap.

Once we have identified inaccurate sales orders as a root cause of a problem worth solving, we can create a problem statement for the sales order entry problem, as seen in Table 4–2.

Once written, the problem statement can be circulated to the stakeholders for comment and feedback. When finalized, the problem statement communicates the mission to all members of the project team so that everyone is working toward the same objective.

Step 3: Identify the Stakeholders and the Users

Effectively solving any complex problem typically involves satisfying the needs of a diverse group of stakeholders. Stakeholders will typically have

Understanding the
needs of the users
and other stake-
holders is a key fac-
tor in developing an
effective solution.

varying perspectives on the problem and various needs that must be addressed by the solution. We'll define a stakeholder as

> *anyone who could be materially affected by the implementation of a new system or application.*

Many stakeholders are users of the system, and their needs are easy to focus on because they will be directly involved with system definition and use. However, some stakeholders are only *indirect* users of the system or are affected only by the business outcomes that the system influences. These stakeholders tend to be found elsewhere within the business, or in "the surrounds" of the particular application environment. In yet other cases, these stakeholders are even further removed from the application environment. For example, they include the people and organizations involved in the development of the system, subcontractors, the customer's customer, outside agencies, such as the U.S. Federal Aviation Administration (FAA) or the Food and Drug Administration (FDA), or other agencies that interact with the system or the development process. Each of these classes of stakeholders may influence the requirements for the system or will in some way be involved with the system outcome.

Non-user stake-
holder needs must
also be identified
and addressed.

An understanding of who these stakeholders are and their particular needs is an important factor in developing an effective solution. Depending on the domain expertise of the development team, identifying the stakeholders may be a trivial or nontrivial step in problem analysis. Often, this simply involves interviewing decision makers, potential users, and other interested parties. The following questions can be helpful in this process:

- Who are the users of the system?
- Who is the customer (economic buyer) for the system?
- Who else will be affected by the outputs that the system produces?
- Who will evaluate and bless the system when it is delivered and deployed?
- Are there any other internal or external users of the system whose needs must be addressed?
- Who will maintain the new system?
- Is there anyone else?

In our example of a replacement sales order system, the primary and most obvious users were the sales order entry clerks. These users are obviously stakeholders in that their productivity, convenience, comfort, job performance, and job satisfaction are affected by the system. What other stakeholders can we identify?

Table 4–3   Users and Stakeholders of New System

Users	Other Stakeholders
Sales order entry clerks	MIS director and development team
Sales order supervisor	Chief financial officer
Production control	Production manager
Billing clerk	

Other stakeholders, such as the sales order entry supervisor, are directly affected by the system but access the system through different user interfaces and reports. Still other folks, such as the chief financial officer of the company, are clearly stakeholders in that the system can be expected to have an effect on the productivity, quality, and profitability of the company. Lest we forget, the MIS director and members of the application development team are also stakeholders in that they will be responsible for developing and maintaining the system. They will have to live with the result, as will the users. Table 4–3 summarizes the results of the stakeholder analysis and identifies the users and stakeholders of the new sales order system.

Step 4: Define the Solution System Boundary

Once the problem statement is agreed to and the users and stakeholders are identified, we can turn our attention to *defining a system* that can be deployed to address the problem. In so doing, we enter an important transition state wherein we have to keep two things in mind: an understanding of the problem and the considerations of a potential solution.

The next important step is to determine the boundaries of the solution system. The system boundary defines the border between the solution and the real world that surrounds the solution (Figure 4–3). In other words, the system

Figure 4–3   The input/system/output relationship

boundary describes an envelope in which the solution system is contained. Information, in the form of inputs and outputs, is passed back and forth from the system to the users living outside the system. All interactions with the system occur via interfaces between the system and the external world.

In other words, if we are going to have to build it or modify it, it's part of our solution and within the boundary; if not, it's external to our system. Thus, we divide the world into two interesting classes of things:

We divide the world in two:
1. Our system
2. Things that interact with our system

  1. Our system
  2. Things that interact with our system

Let's identify the "things that interact with our system" generically as "actors on our system." After all, they do have a *role to play* in making our system do its thing. We'll represent an actor with a simple stick figure icon. We'll define an actor as

Actor

  someone or something, outside the system, that interacts with the system.

Once we have the notion of an actor in hand, we can illustrate a system boundary as shown in Figure 4–4.

In many cases, the boundaries of the system are obvious. For example, a single-user, shrink-wrap personal contact manager that runs on a stand-alone Windows 2000 platform has relatively well-defined boundaries. There is only one user and one platform. The interfaces between the user and the application consist of the interface dialogs the user uses to access information in the system and any output reports and communication paths that the system uses to document or transmit that information.

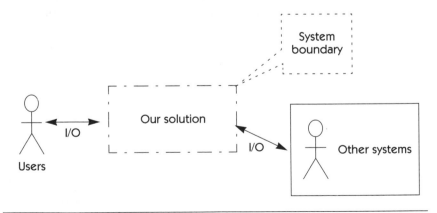

Figure 4–4   System boundary

In our order entry system example, which is to be integrated into an existing legacy system, the boundaries are not so clear. The analyst must determine whether data is shared with other applications, whether the new application is to be distributed across various hosts or clients, and who the users are. For example, are the production people to have online access to sales orders? Is there a quality control or audit function to be provided? Will the system run on the mainframe or on a new client/server front end? Are specialized management reports to be provided?

Although it seems fairly obvious, identifying the actors is a key analytical step in problem analysis. How do we find these actors? Here are some helpful questions to ask:

- Who will supply, use, or remove information from the system?
- Who will operate the system?
- Who will perform any system maintenance?
- Where will the system be used?
- Where does the system get its information?
- What other external systems will interact with the system?

With the answers to these questions in hand, the analyst can now create a "system perspective," a block diagram that describes the boundaries of the system, the users, and other interfaces. Figure 4–5 provides a simplified system perspective for the new sales order system.

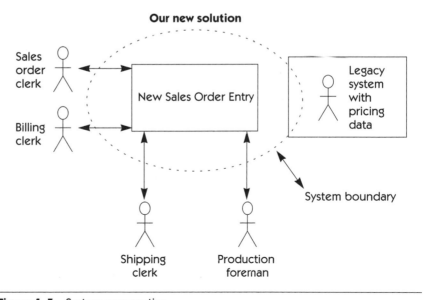

Figure 4–5 System perspective

The dotted line illustrates the system boundary for the proposed solution. The diagram shows that the bulk of the new application will be deployed on the new sales order entry system but a portion of the solution code must be developed and deployed on the existing legacy system.

Step 5: Identify the Constraints to Be Imposed on the Solution

Constraints are restrictions on the degrees of freedom we have in providing a solution.

Before launching a well-intended trillion-dollar effort to revolutionize the state of the art in sales order entry, we must stop and consider the constraints that will be imposed on the solution. We'll define a constraint as

a restriction on the degree of freedom we have in providing a solution.

Each constraint has the potential to severely restrict our ability to deliver a solution as we envision it. Therefore, each constraint must be carefully considered as part of the planning process, and many may even cause us to reconsider the technological approach we have initially envisioned.

A variety of sources of constraints must be considered. These include schedule, return on investment, budget for labor and equipment, environmental issues, operating systems, databases, hosts and client systems, technical issues, political issues within the organization, purchased software, company policies and procedures, choices of tools and languages, personnel or other resource constraints, and a host of other considerations. These constraints may be given to us before we even begin ("No new hardware"), or we may have to actively elicit them.

As an aid to elicitation, it would be helpful to know what kinds of things we should be looking for. Table 4–4 lists potential sources of system constraints. Asking the questions listed in the table should elicit the majority of the constraints that will affect your solution. It will probably also be helpful to identify the rationale for the constraint, both to make sure that you understand the perspective of the constraint and so that you can recognize when and if the constraint might no longer apply to your solution. The less constrained, the better.

Once identified, some of these constraints will become requirements for the new system ("use the MRP system provided via our current accounting system

Table 4–4 Potential system constraints

Source	Sample Considerations
Economic	▪ What financial or budgetary constraints are applicable? ▪ Are there costs of goods sold or any product pricing considerations? ▪ Are there any licensing issues?
Political	▪ Are there internal or external political issues that affect potential solutions? ▪ Interdepartmental problems or issues?
Technical	▪ Are we restricted in our choice of technologies? ▪ Are we constrained to work within existing platforms or technologies? ▪ Are we prohibited from any new technologies? ▪ Are we to use any purchased software packages?
System	▪ Is the solution to be built on our existing systems? ▪ Must we maintain compatibility with existing solutions? ▪ What operating systems and environments must be supported?
Environmental	▪ Are there environmental or regulatory constraints? ▪ Legal? ▪ Security requirements? ▪ What other standards might we be restricted by?
Schedule and resources	▪ Is the schedule defined? ▪ Are we restricted to existing resources? ▪ Can we use outside labor? ▪ Can we expand resources? Temporary? Permanent?

vendor"). Other constraints will affect resources, implementation plans, and project plans. It is the problem solver's responsibility to understand the potential sources of constraints for each specific application environment and to determine the impact of each constraint on the potential solution spaces.

Returning to our example, what constraints might be imposed on the new sales order system? Table 4–5 summarizes the sources and constraints that were imposed on the new system.

Table 4–5   Constraints, sources, and rationale for sales order entry system

Source	Constraint	Rationale
Operational	An exact copy of sales order data must remain on the legacy database for up to one year.	The risk of data loss is too great; we will need to run in parallel for up to one year.
Systems and OS	The applications footprint on the server must be less than 20 megabytes.	We have limited server memory available.
Equipment budget	The system must be developed on existing server and host; new client hardware for users may be provided.	Cost control and maintenance of existing systems.
Personnel budget	Fixed staffing resource; no outsourcing.	Fixed operating costs as per the current budget.
Technology mandate	New OO methodology to be used.	We believe that this technology will increase productivity and increase reliability of the software.

Summary

With this step complete, we can be reasonably confident that we have

- A good understanding of the problem to be solved and the root causes for the problem
- Identified the stakeholders whose collective judgment will ultimately determine the success or failure of our system
- A notion of where the boundaries of the solution are likely to be found
- An understanding of the constraints and the degrees of freedom we have to solve the problem.

Looking Ahead

With this background, we can now turn our attention to two more specific problem-solving techniques that can be applied in certain application domains. In Chapter 5, we'll look at *business modeling* a technique we can apply in our IS/IT type of applications. In Chapter 6, we'll look at *systems engineering* for software-intensive systems, which can be applied to applications in the embedded-system domain.

As for the third domain, that of the ISVs (independent software vendors), problem analysis techniques are typically focused on such activities as

- Identifying market opportunities and market segments
- Identifying classes of potential users and their particular needs
- Studying the demographics of the potential user base
- Understanding potential demand, pricing, and pricing elasticity
- Understanding sales strategies and distribution channels

Clearly, these are interesting topics, but to help us manage the scope of this book, we will not explore these specific issues further. However, you can rest assured that the team skills we explore in later chapters apply equally well to this class of application, as we will illustrate.

Note: One of the most difficult things about writing this book was attempting to present a variety of techniques to build the team skills sets. No one technique works In all situations; no two situations are the same.

In the prior chapters, we focused on a general philosophical approach to problem analysis that appears to work in most systems contexts. However, this problem of "selection of technique to apply" becomes even more acute in the following chapters of the book, wherein we define the technique for business modeling, a technique for system engineering, and then go on to define a variety of techniques in Team Skill 2, Understanding User Needs, where we will present a wide variety of techniques that can be used to understand the needs of stakeholders and users with respect to *"a system that you are about to build."*

However, we think it's important to point out that the techniques described in this book—from problem analysis to brainstorming—can be used in many different parts of the software process, not just in the part of the process where we have chosen to describe them. For example, the team could use problem analysis to define a sales order entry system problem or to resolve a technical problem within its implementation. Similarly, the team could use brainstorming to determine the potential root causes in a problem analysis exercise or to determine potential new features for a system as it's used in Chapter 5. We will make no attempt to describe every circumstance under which a particular technique will apply but will focus instead on having the team develop the skills so that it can add these techniques to its bag of tricks—to be pulled out and used at the appropriate point in the project.

Chapter 5

BUSINESS MODELING

Key Points

- Business modeling is a problem analysis technique especially suitable for the IS/IT environment.
- The business model is used to help define systems and their applications.
- A business use case model, consisting of actors and use cases, is a model of the intended functions of the business.
- A business object model describes the entities that deliver the functionality to realize the business use cases, and how these entities interact.

In the context of the information system/information technology (IS/IT) environment, the first problem to be solved has an even broader context than we described in Chapter 4. In this environment, business complexity abounds, and one typically needs to understand some of this complexity before even attempting to define a specific problem worth solving. This environment consists not simply of a user or two and their interface to a computer but rather of organizations, business units, departments, functions, wide area networks, the corporate intranet and extranet, customers, users, human resources, material requirement planning (MRP) systems, inventory, management systems, and more.

In addition, even when we are focused on a specific application to be implemented, we must continually remind ourselves of the broader context in which the application operates. Perhaps this can be accomplished successfully by asking the right questions, but as with any technique, there's more that can be done in a specific context than in the more generic case.

In the IS/IT context, it would be helpful to have a technique by which we could determine the answers to the following questions:

- Why build a system at all?
- Where should it be located?
- How can we determine what functionality is optimum to locate on a particular system?
- When should we use manual-processing steps or workarounds?
- When should we consider restructuring the organization itself in order to solve the problem?

Fortunately, there is a technique that's ideally suited to addressing this particular problem, and that technique is *business modeling*.

Purpose of Business Modeling

Within the context of this book, we can think of the terms "business" and "business modeling" in the broadest possible context. For example, your business may be the business of software development or manufacturing welding robots, or you may wish to model a not-for-profit business or service organization or an intradepartmental process or internal work flow.

In any case, the purpose of business modeling is twofold:

- To understand the structure and dynamics of the organization
- To ensure that customers, end users, and developers have a common understanding of the organization

This approach gives the team a logical approach to defining where software applications can improve the productivity of the business and to assist in determining requirements for those applications.

Using Software Engineering Techniques for Business Modeling

Of course, a variety of techniques can be applied to business modeling. However, it's rather convenient that, as software developers, we have at our disposal a rich set of tools and techniques that we already use to model our software. Indeed, we already know how to model entities (objects and

With the right choice of business modeling technique, some of the work products, such as use cases and object models, will be useful in the solution activity.

classes), relationships (dependencies, associations, and so on), complex processes (sequences of activities, state transitions, events, conditionality, and so on), and other constructs that occur naturally in the context of designing our software applications.

If we could apply these same techniques to business modeling, we would be speaking the same language in both contexts. For example, a "thing," such as a payroll withholding stub, described in the business domain might relate to a "thing" that appears again in the software domain—payroll withholding record, for example. If we can be fortunate enough to use the same techniques or very similar techniques for both problem analysis and solution design, the two activities can share these same work products.

Choosing the Right Technique

Historically, we have seen that modeling techniques that were developed and matured in the software domain inspire new ways of visualizing an organization. Since object-oriented visual modeling techniques have become common for new software projects, using similar techniques in the business domain comes naturally. This methodology has been well developed by Jacobson, Ericsson, and Jacobson (1994) and others.

The 1980s and 1990s saw a rapid proliferation of both business modeling techniques and software development methodologies. However, they were all different! At the center of this activity were the various object-oriented (OO) methods and notations developed by various software engineering experts and methodologists.[1] Fortunately, these methodology "wars" are over, and the industry has settled on an industry standard—the Unified Modeling Language, or UML—for modeling software-intensive systems.

The Unified Modeling Language (UML)

In late 1997, a graphical language "for visualizing, specifying constructing, and documenting the artifacts of a software intensive system" was adopted as an industry standard (Booch, Jacobson, and Rumbaugh). The Unified

---

1. Various OO methods included the Booch method, by Grady Booch from Rational Software; the Object Modeling Technique by James Rumbaugh, then at GE; Responsibility-Driven Design, by Rebecca Wirfs-Brock at Tektronix; Object Oriented Software Engineering, by Ivar Jacobson, then at Objectory in Sweden; the Coad-Yourdon method, by Peter Coad and Ed Yourdon; and a half dozen more.

Modeling Language[2] provides a set of modeling elements, notations, relationships, and rules for use that could be applied to a software development activity. However, the UML can also be used to model other applications, such as system modeling and business modeling. A tutorial on UML is outside the scope of this book. (For this, refer to the three companion books on the UML: Booch, Rumbaugh, and Jackson (1999), *The United Modeling Language User Guide*; Jacobson, Booch, and Rumbaugh (1999), *The Unified Software Development Process*; and Rumbaugh, Booch, and Jacobson (1998), *The Unified Modeling Language Reference Manual*.) However, we will use some key concepts from the UML in this section and will build on this foundation in succeeding sections of this book.

Business Modeling Using UML Concepts

One of the goals of business models is to develop a model of the business that can be used to drive application development. Two key modeling constructs that can be used for this purpose are a *business use-case model* and *a business object model*.

A *business use-case model* is a model of the intended functions of the business and is used as an essential input to identify roles and deliverables in the organization. As such, the business use-case model consists of the actors—users and systems that interact with the business—and the use cases—sequences of events by which the actors interact with the business elements to get their job done. Together, the actors and the use cases describe who is involved in the business activities and how these activities take place. Figure 5–1 shows

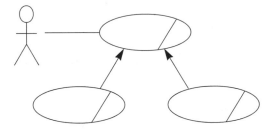

Figure 5–1   Business use-case model

2. UML v1.1 was adopted by the international Object Management Group (OMG) in 1997 after the original creators at Rational Software (Booch, Jacobson, and Rumbaugh) built a broad-based industry consortium and included concepts from other methods, as well as a public feedback and revision process.

the business use-case model. Note that the oval icon used to represent the business use-case has a slash, indicating a business-level use case rather than a system-level use case.[3]

A business use-case model, then, consists of business actors and business use cases, with the actors representing roles external to the business (for example, employees and customers) and the business use cases representing processes. Examples of a business use-case model might be

- "Deliver electronic pay stub to employee."
- "Meet with customer to negotiate contract terms."

Examples of business actors might include

1. "Customer"
2. "Employee"
3. "Software developer"

The *business object model* describes the entities—departments, paychecks, systems—and how they interact to deliver the functionality necessary to realize the business use cases. Figure 5–2 represents the business object model. The actor-circle icon represents a worker who appears within the business process, such as a payroll clerk or a system administrator. The slashed circle represents a business entity or something that business workers produce, such as a paycheck or a ball bearing or a source file.[4]

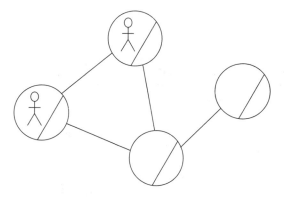

Figure 5–2　Business object model

---

3. The icon is one of many standard UML stereotypes. For further discussion of the modeling icons, see Rational Software Corporation (1999).
4. Ibid.

A business object model also includes business use-case realizations that show how the business use cases are "performed" in terms of interacting business workers and business entities. To reflect groups or departments in an organization, business workers and business entities may be grouped into organizational units.

Taken together, the two models provide a comprehensive overview of how the business works and allow the development team to focus on the areas in which systems can be provided that will improve the overall efficiency of the business. The models also help the team to understand what changes will have to take place within the business processes themselves in order for the new system to be effectively implemented.

From the Business Models to the Systems Model

One advantage of this approach to business modeling is the clear and concise way of showing dependencies between models of the business and models of the system. This clarity improves the productivity of the software development process and also helps ensure that the system being developed solves the real business need. See Figure 5–3.

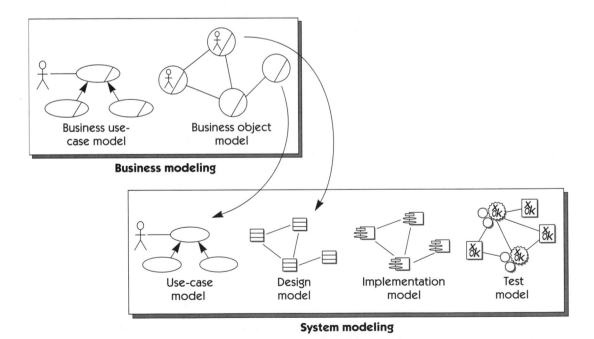

Figure 5–3   Business/system models

The translation between the two can briefly be summarized as follows.

- Business workers will become actors to the system we are developing.
- Behaviors described for business workers are things that can be automated, so they help us find system use cases and define needed functionality.
- Business entities are things we may want the system to help us maintain, so they help us find entity classes in the analysis model of the system.

In performing the translation, business modeling facilitates the process of moving from an understanding of the business and problems within the business to the potential applications that may be implemented to deliver solutions to the problems identified.

When to Use Business Modeling

Business modeling is not something that we recommend for every software engineering effort. Business models add most value when the application environment is complex and multidimensional, and when many people are directly involved in using the system. For example, if you were building an additional feature to an existing telecommunication switch, you would not consider business modeling. On the other hand, if you were building the order entry system for GoodsAreUs, we could have used business modeling to good advantage to support problem analysis.

Summary

In this chapter, we discussed a specific problem analysis technique, business modeling. In so doing, we defined

- Why you might need to model the business
- How, using the UML, we transpose techniques developed for software engineering and use them for business modeling
- The primary artifacts of business modeling, the business use-case model, and the business object model
- How you can define software applications and derive software requirement from models of the business.

Looking Ahead

In the next chapter, we'll look at systems engineering of software systems, another problem analysis technique, that will help give a shape to applications of the embedded-systems type.

Chapter 6

SYSTEMS ENGINEERING
OF SOFTWARE-INTENSIVE SYSTEMS

Key Points

- Systems engineering is a problem analysis technique especially suitable for embedded systems development.
- System engineering helps us understand the requirements imposed on software applications that run within the solution system.
- Requirements flowdown is primarily a matter of ensuring that all system requirements are filled by a subsystem or a set of sub-systems collaborating.
- Today, the system must often be optimized for software costs rather than for hardware costs.

In Chapter 5, we looked at business modeling, a problem analysis technique for IS/IT applications. Business modeling helps us to determine what application we should build and where we should run that application, within the context of the computing environment of the company and the departments, buildings, and political and physical constructs of the company itself. In other words, this analysis can help us to determine *why* and *where* an application should come into existence. In so doing, of course, we make a subtle shift from the *problem space* to an initial look at the *solution space*, wherein the functionality that resolves the problem will exist on one or more applications that meet the user's ultimate need.

In the embedded-systems business, however, the problem domain and the solution domain look entirely different. Instead of departments, people, and processes, the domains consist of connectors and power supplies, racks of equipment, electronic and electrical components, hydraulic and fluidic handling devices, other software systems, mechanical and optics subsystems, and the like. Here, business modeling cannot provide much value. Instead, we must look to a different strategy to help us determine the *why* and *where* questions. Here, we find ourselves in the realm of the *systems engineer*.

What Is Systems Engineering?

According to the International Council on Engineering Systems (INCOSE 1999):

> *Systems engineering is an interdisciplinary approach and means to enable the realization of successful systems. It focuses on defining customer needs and required functionality early in the development cycle, documenting requirements, then proceeding with design synthesis and system validation while considering the complete problem:*
>
> - *Operations*
> - *Performance*
> - *Test*
> - *Manufacturing*
> - *Cost and Schedule*
> - *Training and Support*
> - *Disposal*
>
> *Systems engineering integrates all the disciplines and specialty groups into a team effort forming a structured development process that proceeds from concept to production to operation. Systems Engineering considers both the business and the technical needs of all customers with the goal of providing a quality product that meets the needs of the user.*

Phew. That's a long one. From this definition, however, it does appear that systems engineering can be considered a problem analysis technique, albeit one that we can't hope to fully cover a book on software requirements management! (For more on systems engineering, see Rechtin (1997).)

Within the scope of this book, however, systems engineering can help us understand the needs of the problem space and the requirements that are to be imposed on the solution. In this context, *systems engineering helps us understand the requirements that are going to be imposed on any software applications that run within the solution system*. In other words, we'll apply systems engineering as a problem analysis technique to help us understand the requirements for our software applications, whether they run on an embedded microprocessor or a UNIX system within the context of a worldwide tele-communications system.

Pragmatic Principles of Systems Engineering

If we choose to view systems engineering as a problem analysis technique, the specific steps, or at least the basic principles of the discipline, should provide us with the steps we need to apply to use systems engineering to analyze the problem in our requirements context. The INCOSE Systems Engineering Practices working group (INCOSE 1993) defined a basic set of eight systems engineering principles.

Systems engineering provides eight pragmatic principles.

- Know the problem, know the customer, and know the consumer.
- Use effectiveness criteria based on needs to make the system decisions.
- Establish and manage requirements.
- Identify and assess alternatives so as to converge on a solution.
- Verify and validate requirements and solution performance.
- Maintain the integrity of the system.
- Use an articulated and documented process.
- Manage against a plan.

This list identifies some pragmatic systems engineering principles. In point of fact, however, a subset of the systems engineering discipline is based on another process, the successive decomposition of complex systems into simpler ones.

The Composition and Decomposition of Complex Systems

With this process, a complex problem, the system (Figure 6–1), is decomposed into smaller problems—subsystems (Figure 6–2). Each subsystem can

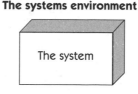

The systems environment

The system

Figure 6–1 A system in its environment

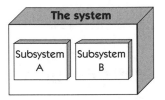

Figure 6–2   A system composed of two subsystems

be reasoned about, successfully designed and manufactured, and then integrated to produce the solution system. The engineering disciplines that support the approach to system decomposition are implied in the attributes of the preceding definition, such as understanding the operational characteristics, manufacturability, testability, and so on.

This decomposition, or successive refinement, process proceeds until the systems engineer achieves the *right* results, as provided by quantitative measures that are specific to the specific systems engineering domain. In most cases, the subsystems defined in the initial composition are themselves further decomposed into subsubsystems, with the result appearing as in Figure 6–3.

In the most complex systems, this process continues until a large number of subsystems are developed. (The F22 fighter aircraft, for example, is said to be composed of 152 such subsystems.)

The systems engineer knows that the job is done and is "right" when

- Distribution and partitioning of functionality are optimized to achieve the overall functionality of the system with minimal costs and maximum flexibility.

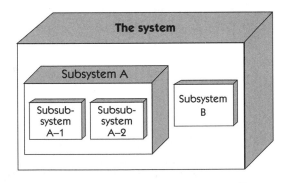

Figure 6–3   A subsystem composed of two subsystems

- Each subsystem can be defined, designed, and built by a small, or at least modest-sized, team.
- Each subsystem can be manufactured within the physical constraints and technologies of the available manufacturing processes.
- Each subsystem can be reliably tested as a subsystem, subject to the availability of suitable fixtures and harnesses that simulate the interfaces to the other system.
- Appropriate deference is given to the physical domain—the size, weight, location, and distribution of the subsystems—that has been optimized in the overall system context.

Requirements Allocation in Systems Engineering

Requirements flow-down allocates system functionality to subsystems.

Assuming that the systems engineering has resulted in a good job of defining the requirements for the system, the requirements management problem is still not complete. For what of these subsystems? What requirements are to be imposed on them? In some cases, the process is one of assigning a system-level requirement to a subsystem ("subsystem B will execute the windspeed algorithm and drive the heads-up display directly"). This *requirements flow-down* process is primarily a matter of making sure that all system requirements are fulfilled by a subsystem somewhere or by a set of subsystems collaborating together.

On Derived Requirements

Sometimes, we discover that we have created a whole new requirements class—*derived requirements*—that must be imposed on the subsystem(s). Typically, there are two subclasses of derived requirements.

1. *Subsystem requirements* are those that must be imposed on the subsystems themselves but that do not necessarily provide a direct benefit to the end user ("Subsystem A must execute the algorithm that computes the wind speed of the aircraft").
2. *Interface requirements* may arise when the subsystems need to communicate with one another to accomplish an overall result. They will need to share data or power or a useful computing algorithm. In these cases, the creation of subsystems also further engenders the creation of *interfaces* between subsystems (see Figure 6–4).

But are these derived requirements "true" requirements? Do we treat them the same as other requirements? They don't seem to meet the definitions in

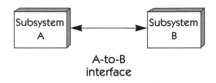

Figure 6–4   Interface between two subsystems

Chapter 2 (although they may well meet the definitions of design constraints that we'll provide later in this book).

The important thing to recognize is that these requirements, although crucial to the project success, are *derived* from the systems decomposition process. As such, alternative decompositions would have created alternative derived requirements, so these requirements are not first-class citizens in the sense that they do not reflect requirements that came from our customer. However, from the viewpoint of a subsystem supplier, they *are* first-class citizens because they reflect requirements imposed by the customer (the system developer).

No magic answer exists. How we treat these requirements is based on the development team's role in the project, the systems decomposition, and other technological factors as well. So, the important thing to know is "how we got here" and to treat the requirements appropriately to the case. The important thing to recognize is that the specification of derived requirements will ultimately affect the ability of the system to do its job, as well as the maintainability and robustness of the system.

A Quiet Revolution

In industry after industry, the intelligence of the device has moved from the hardware components to the software components.

System engineering has traditionally been a discipline applied primarily to physical systems, such as aircraft and airframes, brakes and brake pads, power supplies and power consuming devices, and so on. However, during the last 20 or so years, a quiet revolution has occurred in the systems engineering of complex systems. Gradually, in transportation, telecommunication, industrial equipment, medical equipment, scientific instruments, and many others industries, the systems and devices have become smarter and smarter and smarter. To meet this increasing demand for complexity and sophistication, more and more of the delivered functionality has become allocated to software subsystems rather than to hardware components. Software is *softer* after all, and many algorithms for measuring, metering, assaying, and detecting are much easier, or at least much cheaper in terms of parts cost, to implement in software than they are in hardware. More important, they are much easier to change.

So, in industry after industry, the innate intelligence of the device has moved from the hardware components, where they were previously implemented in a combination of electrical and electronic systems, mechanical systems, and even physical chemistry systems, to the software components, where they are implemented in software or firmware on microprocessors or complete minicomputer subsystems.

When Generations Collide: Graybeard Meets Young Whippersnapper

For decades, systems engineers were some of the most senior project engineers in the industry. Battle scarred and field tested, many of these *senior systems engineers* were specialists in specific disciplines, such as mechanical and electronic engineering, and many were some of the best generalists on the team. They had witnessed the largest disasters and had experienced many triumphs. Older and wiser now, they knew the specific application domain—radios, airplanes, HVAC, robotics, materials-handling equipment—incredibly well and were also aware of the differing technical, economic, and political facets of technology implementation.

But suddenly, a new breed of individual invaded their turf. These newcomers—the *programmers*, or on a good day, software engineers—were relatively inexperienced in complex systems and didn't know weight and balance or global systems optimization from their navel, but they could make a microprocessor sing in assembly language. In addition, they seem to have been formed from a different gene pool, or at least a different generation, which added the complexities of culture and generation clash to the systems engineering process. Many interesting situations developed.

For a while, the turf battle was even, and the systems engineers made the ultimate calls for system partitioning and allocation of functionality. But in many industries, software technology gradually took over, and systems engineering became dominated, at least in part, by the need to engineer for flexible *software* functionality within the system. There were a number of solid technical reasons for this transition. Over time, a number of facts became obvious.

- Software, not hardware, will determine the ultimate functionality of the system and the success of the system in the end user's hands and in the marketplace.
- Software, not hardware, will consume the majority of the costs of research and system development.

- Software, not hardware, will be on the critical path and will, therefore, ultimately determine when the system goes to the marketplace.
- Software, not hardware, will absorb most of the changes that occur during system development and will be evolved over the next few years to meet the changing needs of the system.

And perhaps most surprisingly,

- The cost of software development and maintenance, taken in the aggregate and amortized over the full life of the product, became material to, or in some cases equal to or greater than, the contribution of hardware costs of goods sold to that holy grail of systems manufacturers: *total manufacturing costs*.

Many systems must now be optimized for software, not hardware, capability.

This last one was a killer, because it meant that you must consider optimizing the system not for hardware or manufacturing costs but for *development, maintenance, evolution, and enhancement of the software contained in the system*. This changed the game significantly. For now, the systems engineering must be performed with one eye on the computers to be used. Often, this meant

- Maximizing the system's ability to execute software by providing more than adequate computing resources, even at the expense of cost of goods sold, adding more microprocessors, RAM, ROM, mass storage, bandwidth, or whatever resources the system requires to execute its software.
- Providing adequate communication interfaces between subsystems and ensuring that the communications mechanism chosen (Ethernet, Firewire, serial port, or single data line) is extensible, via the addition of software, not hardware.

In turn, this change affected the requirements management challenge in two ways.

- Each of these dimensions will create new *requirements* that the hardware system must fulfill in order for a successful solution to be built.
- The bulk of the requirements problem moved to the software application.

Fortunately, at least for the latter, that is the subject of this book, and we hope to prepare you well for this particular problem.

Avoiding the Stovepipe System Problem

This is all, or at least mostly, well and good. Dealing with systems of complexity requires nontrivial approaches, and a system of subsystems is a means to this end. Surely, the alternatives are worse, as we would end up with incredibly complex systems that no one could possibly understand, with indeterminate behavior, and design based on shared functionality, poor partitioning, and threaded code in such a way as could never be unraveled. Systems engineering seems like a good thing.

How does this affect requirements management? When the final tally is made, we will discover that subsystem requirements are far more numerous than external requirements, or those that affect the behavior of the system in the user's environment. In the end, we will invest far more in prioritizing, managing, and identifying the subsystem requirements than those that affect the end user. This doesn't seem like a completely positive thing.

 And what happens if we don't do a good job of systems engineering? The system will become brittle and will resist change because the weight of the requirements assets will "bind" us to the implementation. Our subsystem requirements have taken control of our design flexibility, and a change in one will have a ripple effect in other subsystems. These are the "stovepipe" systems of legend, and such systems *resist* change. In their interfaces, the problems may be worse. If the interfaces are not properly specified, the system will be fragile and will not be able to evolve to meet changing needs without the wholesale replacement of interfaces and entire subsystems that were based on them.

When Subsystems Are Subcontracts

A further complication often arises. Since subsystems are typically developed by different teams—after all, that's one of the reasons we create subsystems—the subsystem requirements and interfaces tend, in effect, to become *contracts* between the teams. ("My subsystem delivers the results of the wind speed computation in exactly this format. . . .") Indeed, in some cases, the subsystem may be developed by a subcontractor whose paystub has a different logo from yours. In this case, our requirements challenge has left the system and technical context and has instead become a political "football." ("Darn. The requirements cannot be changed unless the contract is renegotiated.") Soon, the project can be all "bound up in its shorts." A severe word of warning: *Many large-scale system efforts have met their death at the hands of this problem.*

Making It Work Out Right

What should we do? Well, doing a good job of systems engineering is a primary goal. As you participate in this activity for software-intensive systems, you may want to consider the following recommendations

- Develop, understand, and maintain the high-level requirements and use cases that *span* the subsystems and that describe the overall system functionality. These use cases will provide context for how the system is supposed to work and will make sure that you "don't miss the forest for the trees." They will also help ensure that the systems architecture is designed to support the most likely usage scenarios.
- Do the best possible job of partitioning and isolating functionality within subsystems. Use object technology principles: encapsulation and information hiding, interface by contract, messaging rather than data sharing—in your systems engineering work.
- If possible, develop software as a whole, not as several individual pieces, one for each physical subsystem. One of the characteristics of stovepipe systems is that on both sides of the interface (well or badly defined), the software needs to reconstruct the state of key elements (objects) that are needed for making decisions on both sides; unlike hardware, the allocation of requirements to both sides does not represent a clear partition.
- When coding the interfaces, use common code on both sides of the interface. Otherwise, there will likely be subtle variations, often blamed on "optimizations," that will make this synchronization of states very difficult. Then, if the boundary between the two physical subsystems later disappears—that is, systems engineering finds out that processors are good enough to support both subsystems A and B—software engineers will have a hard time "merging" the two bodies of software.
- Define interface specifications that can do more than would be necessary to simply meet the known conditions. Invest in a little extra bandwidth, an extra I/O port, or some IC real estate to provide room for expansion.

Finally, see whether you can find one of those graybeards to help you with your systems engineering. They've been down this path before, and their experience will serve you wisely. Besides, you might help close the generation gap in the process!

A Story: On Partitioning Large-Scale Software Systems into Subsystems for Distributed Development Teams

In class one day, Rusty, an experienced software manager, approached us and stated the following problem. We had the following dialogue.

Rusty: We are building a large-scale application that runs on a single host system. Our development resources consist of two separate teams of 30 people each; one team lives on the east side of the river in New York City, and the other lives on the west side. The two teams have different managers and different competencies. How can we divide the work and create a system that will run when we are done?

Us: *Well, Rusty, one way to think of this problem is as a systems engineering problem. That is, figure out how you would partition the system into two sensible subsystems. Call them East and West, and allocate requirements to the subsystems as if they were in separate physical systems. Define an interface, complete with the definition of common classes and common services to be used, that allows the two subsystems (applications) to cooperate to accomplish the overall system functionality.*

Rusty: But won't I have then created an arbitrary system that is not driven by true architectural concerns?

Us: *True enough, in the technical sense. But separating concerns along project team logistical lines and specific competencies may be just as important.*

Rusty: But won't I also create artificial interfaces and a potential stovepipe system?

Us: *Yes, in a sense, but we'd recommend that you have the interface code for both sides developed by only one team. Otherwise, there will be a lot of redundant work done between the two teams. In so doing, you will indeed create new requirements for the system, including interfaces that would otherwise not have been necessary, or at least not as formalized as you will now make them. And yes, it's important to be aware of the stovepipe problem and to do everything you can to minimize coupling between systems and to minimize the political issues that are likely to result.*

The Case Study

So much for a brief introduction to systems engineering. Now let's try to apply what we have learned to HOLIS, our home lighting automation system. At this point, we haven't spent much time trying to understand the requirements for HOLIS. We'll do that in later chapters of the book. So in a sense, systems engineering is premature. On the other hand, we probably understand enough to make some first-level system design decisions, based on our experience, and our understanding of likely requirements. In any case, we haven't committed anything to hardware or software yet, and we can revisit these decisions later on. In the iterative process described later, we'll visit systems architecture and system requirements interactively, so this is not a bad time to begin.

Preliminary User Needs

Let's assume that a few reasonably well-understood user needs have already been defined for HOLIS.

- HOLIS will need to support "soft" key switches—individually programmable key switches used to activate the lighting features in various rooms.
- Homeowners have requested that there be a means to program HOLIS from a remote center so they can simply call in their needs and not be bothered with "programming" HOLIS at all.
- Other prospective buyers have requested that HOLIS be programmable from their home PCs and that they be provided with the ability to do all of the installation, programming, and maintenance themselves.
- Still others have requested that the system provide a simple, push-button control panel–type interface they can use to change HOLIS programming, vacation settings, and so on, without having to use a PC.
- HOLIS needs to provide an emergency-contact system of some kind.

Problem Analysis

In analyzing the problem, the team first decided to develop three problem statements, one of which seemed to state the obvious problem from the company's perspective.

Problem Statement—For Lumenations	
The problem of	slowing growth in the company's core professional theater marketplaces
affects	the company, its employees, and its shareholders,
the result of which	is unacceptable business performance and lack of substantive opportunities for growth in revenue and profitability.
Benefits of	of new products and a potential new marketplace for the company's products and services include
	■ Revitalizing the company and its employees
	■ Increased loyalty and retention of the company's distributors
	■ Higher revenue growth and profitability
	■ Upturn in the company's stock price

The team also decided to see whether it could understand the "problem" from the perspectives of a future customer (end user) and potential distributors/builders (Lumenations' customers). Here's what the team came up with

Problem Statement for the Homeowner	
The problem of	the lack of product choices, limited functionality, and high cost of existing home lighting automation systems
affects	the homeowners of high-end residential systems,
the result of which	is unacceptable performance of the purchased systems or, more often than not, a decision "not to automate."

Problem Statement for the Homeowner	
Benefits of	the "right" lighting automation solution could include
	▪ Higher homeowner satisfaction and pride of ownership
	▪ Increased flexibility and usability of the residence
	▪ Improved safety, comfort, and convenience

Problem Statement for the Distributor	
The problem of	the lack of product choices, limited functionality, and high cost of existing home lighting automation systems
affects	the distributors and builders of high-end residential systems,
the result of which	is few opportunities for marketplace differentiation and no new opportunities for higher-margin products.
Benefits of	the "right" lighting automation solution could include
	▪ Differentiation
	▪ Higher revenues and higher profitability
	▪ Increased market share

HOLIS: The System, Actors, and Stakeholders

Let's get back to our systems engineering project. From a systems perspective, our first impression of the HOLIS system is simply that of a system inside the homeowner's house. Figure 6–5 is a simple systems diagram showing HOLIS in the context of the homeowner's home.

Step 3 of problem analysis requires that *we identify the stakeholder and users of the system*. Step 4 of problem analysis is to *define the system boundary of the solution*

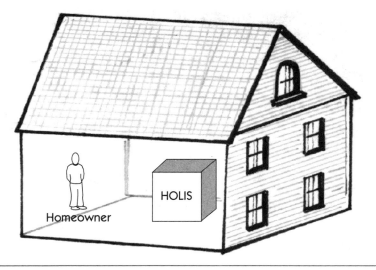

Figure 6–5   System context: HOLIS in its environment

system. Given the additional user need data we have just been given, we can now improve our understanding of HOLIS's system context by identifying the actors that will interact with HOLIS. Figure 6–6, shows the four actors:

1. The homeowner who uses HOLIS to control the lighting
2. The various lights that HOLIS, in turn, controls

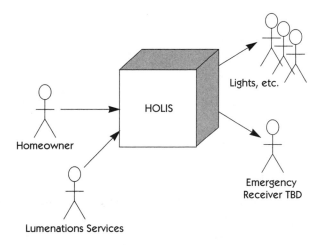

Figure 6–6   HOLIS with actors

3. Lumenations Services, the manufacturer that has the ability to remotely dial HOLIS and perform the remote programming
4. Emergency Receiver, an undefined actor who will likely receive emergency messages

Of course, the team also discovers that a number of *"nonactor" stakeholders*, both internal and external to the company, care about the requirements for HOLIS, as Table 6–1 shows.

HOLIS Systems Engineering

Now that we understand the external actors for HOLIS, let's do some systems-level thinking to consider how we might partition HOLIS into subsystems. This process could well be driven by the following kinds of systems engineering thinking

- It would be good if we could have common software within both the controller device and the homeowner's PC; we'll pick a PC-based implementation for both elements of the system.
- We're not yet certain what flexibility we are going to need in the remote softkey switches, but it's clear that there will be many of them, that some of them will be a fair distance from the main control unit, and that we'll probably need some intelligent communication between those and the control unit.

Table 6–1   Nonactor stakeholders for HOLIS

Item Name	Comments
External	
Distributors	Lumenations' direct customer
Builders	Lumenations' customer's customer: the general contractor responsible to the homeowner for the end result
Electrical contractors	Responsible for installation and support
Internal	
Development team	Lumenations' team
Marketing/product management	Will be presented by Cathy, product manager
Lumenations general management	Funding and outcome accountability

With this minimalist thinking, we can come up with a new system perspective, one in which HOLIS, the system, is composed of three subsystems: *Control Switch*, the programmable remote switching device; *Central Control Unit*, the central computer control system; and *PC Programmer*, the optional PC system that some homeowners have requested. Now the block diagram appears as in Figure 6–7.

Note that we seem to have identified a *fifth* actor—the homeowner again—but who this time is using the PC to program HOLIS rather than to turn lights on and off. This *homeowner/programmer* actor has different needs for the system in that role and therefore is a separate actor to the system. We'll look again later to see the various behaviors that this actor will expect of HOLIS.

The Subsystems of HOLIS

From a systems engineering and requirements perspective, the problem become little more complex. In addition to needing to understand the requirements for HOLIS, the system, we'll now also need to understand the unique requirements for each of HOLIS's three subsystems. We can use our

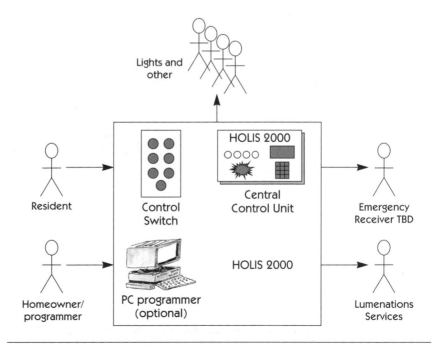

Figure 6–7 HOLIS with subsystems and actors

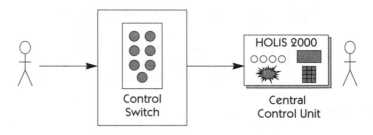

Figure 6–8 Control switch subsystem with actors

actor paradigm again, at the next level of system decomposition. In so doing, we come up with three new block diagrams: Figures 6–8, 6–9, and 6–10.

In Figure 6-8, when we look at the system perspective from the Control Switch standpoint, we find yet another actor: Central Control Unit (CCU), another subsystem. In other words, from a subsystem perspective, *CCU is an actor on Control Switch*, and we'll need later to understand what kinds of requirements and use cases CCU will impose on Control Switch. This set of requirements is derived from our system decomposition.

In Figure 6-9, the systems perspective from the viewpoint of the homeowner's PC, we don't seem to learn anything new, at least in terms of actors and subsystems, as they've all been identified before. Figure 6-10, however, presents a slightly richer view, and we see that CCU has more actors than anyone else. This seems to make intuitive sense, as we have started thinking about CCU as the brains of HOLIS, so it makes sense to think that it has the most stuff to do and the most actors to do it for.

To complete the problem analysis, look at Table 6-2, which itemizes the constraints that the team identified, discussed, and agreed to between the HOLIS development team and Lumenations management.

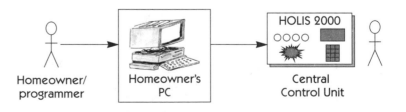

Figure 6–9 PC Programmer subsystem with actors

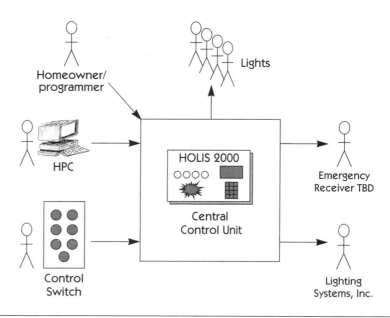

Figure 6–10   Central Control Unit subsystem with actors

Table 6–2   Constraints for HOLIS project

ID #	Description	Rationale
1	Version 1.0 would be released to manufacturing by January 5, 2000.	The only product launch opportunity this year.
2	The team would adopt UML modeling, OO-based methodologies, and the Unified Software Development Process.	We believe these technologies will provide increased productivity and more robust systems.
3	The software for the Central Control Unit and PC Programmer would be written in C++. Assembly language would be used for the Control Switch.	For consistency and maintainability; also, the team knows these languages.
4	A prototype system *must* be displayed at the December Home Automation trade show.	To take distributors' orders for Q1 FY 2000.

Table continued on next page.

Table 6–2 Constraints for HOLIS project (*continued*)

ID #	Description	Rationale
5	The microprocessor subsystem for the Central Control Unit would be copied from the professional division's advanced lighting system project (ALSP).	An existing design and an inventoried part.
6	The only Homeowner PC Programmer configuration supported would be compatible with Windows 98.	Scope management for release 1.0.
7	The team would be allowed to hire two new full-time employees after a successful inception phase, with whatever skill set was determined to be necessary.	Maximum allowable budget expansion.
8	The KCH5444 single-chip microprocessor would be used in the control switch.	Already in use in the company.
9	Purchased software components were permissible, so long as there was no continuing royalty obligation to the company.	No long-term cost of goods sold impact for software.

That's enough problem analysis and systems engineering on HOLIS for now. We'll revisit the case study in subsequent chapters.

Team Skill 1 Summary

Team Skill 1, Analyzing the Problem, introduced a set of skills that your team can apply to *understand the problem to be solved before application development begins.* We introduced a simple, five-step problem analysis technique that can help your team gain a better understanding of the problem to be solved.

1. Gain agreement on the problem definition.
2. Understand the root causes of the problem.
3. Identify the stakeholders and users whose collective judgment will ultimately determine the success or failure of your system.
4. Determine where the boundaries of the solution are likely to be found.
5. Understand the constraints that will be imposed on your team and on the solution.

Analyzing the problem in this systematic fashion will improve your team's ability to address the challenge ahead— *providing a solution to the problem to be solved.*

We also noted the variety of techniques that can be used in problem analysis. Specifically, we looked at business modeling, which works quite well in complex information systems that support key business infrastructures. The team can use business modeling both to understand the way in which the business evolves and to define where within the system we can deploy applications most productively. We also recognized that the business model we defined will have parallel constructs in the software application, and we use this commonality to seed the software design phases. We will also use the business use cases we discovered again later to help define requirements for the application itself.

For the class of software applications that we classify as embedded systems, we used the systems engineering process as a problem analysis technique to help us decompose a complex system into subsystems. This process helps us to understand where software applications should lie and what overall purpose they serve. In so doing, we also learned that we complicate requirements matters somewhat by defining new subsystems, for which we must in turn come to understand the requirements to be imposed.

Team Skill 2

UNDERSTANDING USER NEEDS

The most commonly cited factor on challenged projects was "lack of user input." (Standish Group, 1994)

The Standish Group survey cited "lack of user input" as the most common factor in challenged projects. Although 13 percent of respondents picked that cause as the primary root cause, an additional 12 percent of respondents picked "incomplete requirements and specifications." From this data, it's apparent that, for over one quarter of all challenged projects, a lack of understanding of the users' (and most likely other stakeholders') real requirements was a serious problem that interfered with the success of the project.

Unless we imagine that users worldwide are going to suddenly wake up one day and start doing a better job of both understanding and communicating their requirements, it's obvious that our development teams are going to have to take the initiative. In other words, our teams need to develop the necessary skills to elicit these requirements.

In Team Skill 1, we developed the skills that will help you understand the problem being solved. In Team Skill 2, we describe a number of techniques the development team can use to gather and to understand the real needs of prospective users and other stakeholders. In so doing, we'll also start to gain an understanding of the potential requirements for a system that we will develop to address these needs. While we do this, we will be focusing primarily on stakeholder needs, which live at the top of the requirements pyramid.

The techniques we look at range from simple, inexpensive, and straightforward techniques, such as interviewing, to modestly expensive and quite technical techniques, such as prototyping. Although no one technique is perfect in every case, exposure to a variety of techniques will provide the team with a rich set of skills to choose from. For each specific project, the team can then pick from the available techniques and apply the experience and knowledge gained from the elicitation effort on prior projects. In this way, the team will develop a set of skills that are unique and well suited to their environment and that can actively contribute to improved outcomes.

Chapter 7

THE CHALLENGE OF
REQUIREMENTS ELICITATION

Key Points

- Requirement elicitation is complicated by three endemic syndromes.
- The "Yes, But" syndrome stems from human nature and the users' inability to experience the software as they might a physical device.
- Searching for requirements is like searching for "Undiscovered Ruins"; the more you find, the more you know remain.
- The "User and the Developer" syndrome reflects the profound differences between the two, making communication difficult.

In the next few chapters, we will look at a variety of techniques for eliciting requirements from the users and other stakeholders of the system.[1] This process seems so straightforward. Sit down with the future users of the system and other stakeholders and ask them what they need the system to do.

Why is this so difficult? Why do we need so many techniques? Indeed, why do we need this team skill at all? In order to gain a fuller appreciation of this particular problem, let's first take a look at three syndromes that seem to complicate these matters immensely.

---

1. We use the term "user" generically in this context. The techniques apply to eliciting requirements from all stakeholders, both users and non-users.

Barriers to Elicitation

The "Yes, But" Syndrome

One of the most frustrating, pervasive, and seemingly downright sinister problems in all of application development is what we have come to call the "Yes, But" syndrome, being our observation of the users' reaction to every piece of software we have ever developed. *For whatever reason, we always observe two immediate, distinct, and separate reactions when the users see the system implementation for the first time*:

- "Wow, this is so cool; we can really use this, what a neat job, atta boy," and so on.
- "Yes, but, hmmmmm, now that I see it, what about this . . . ? Wouldn't it be nice if . . . ? Whatever happened to . . . ?"

The roots of the "Yes, But" syndrome appear to lie deep in the nature of software as an intangible intellectual process. To make matters worse, our development teams typically *compound* the problem by rarely providing anything earlier than production code for the users to interact with and to evaluate.

The users' reaction is simply human nature and it occurs in various other day-to-day circumstances. The users haven't seen your new system or anything like it before; they didn't understand what you meant when you described it earlier, and now that it's in front of them—now, for the first time after months or years of waiting—they have the opportunity to interact with the system. And guess what: It's not exactly what they expected!

By analogy, let's compare this software process to the development of mechanical devices whose technology and development process predate software by a mere few hundred years or so. Mechanical systems have a reasonably well-defined discipline of proof-of-principle models, mockups, models, incremental prototyping, pilot production devices, and so on, all of which have tangible aspects and most of which look, feel, and act somewhat like the device under development.

The users can see the early devices, touch them, reason about it, and even interact with them *well* before detailed implementation is complete. Indeed, specific technologies, such as stereo lithography, wherein a rapid prototype is constructed overnight out of a vat of goo, have been developed exclusively for the purpose of providing early and immediate feedback on the conceptual definition of the product. Yet in software, with its enormous complexity, we are expected to get it right the first time!

As frustrating as it is, accepting the "Yes, But" syndrome as reality may lead to real insights that will help team members mitigate this syndrome in future projects

- The *"Yes, But"* syndrome is human nature and is an integral part of application development.
- We can drastically reduce this syndrome by applying techniques that get the "buts" out early. In so doing, we elicit the "Yes, But" response early, and we then can begin to invest the majority of our development efforts in software that has already passed the "Yes, But" test.

The "Undiscovered Ruins" Syndrome

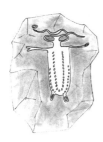

One of our friends was once a tour bus guide in the Four Corners area, an area defined by the common borders of Colorado, New Mexico, Utah, and Arizona. The tour bus route included the majestic peaks of the La Plata mountain range and the sprawling ancient Anasazi ruins of Mesa Verde and the surrounding area. Tourists' questions are a constant source of amusement among the tour guide crew and create a certain folk lore of the tour business. In one summer season, our friend's favorite silliest-question-ever-posed-by-a-stupid-tourist was, "So, ummm, how many undiscovered ruins are there?"

In many ways, the search for requirements is like a search for undiscovered ruins: *The more that are found, the more you know remain.* You never really feel as though you have found them all, and perhaps you never will. Indeed, software development teams everywhere continually struggle to determine when they are done with requirements elicitation, that is, when have they found all of the requirements that are material or have found at least enough.

In order to help the team address this problem, we'll provide a variety of techniques, both in the Team Skill 2 chapters and later ones. Of course, as we described in Chapter 1, taking the time in problem analysis to identify all of the stakeholders of the system is of tremendous value, because many of these nonuser stakeholders are often holders of otherwise undiscovered requirements. However, as with finding all of the undiscovered ruins, we must acknowledge that we are on a mission that can never be completed. But we also understand that at some point, we will be able to say with confidence, "We have discovered enough."

The "User and the Developer" Syndrome

Techniques for requirements elicitation are not new. Application developers have strived for more than 40 years to do a better job. What could possibly

Table 7–1 The user and the developer syndrome

Problem	Solution
Users do not know what they want, or they know what they want but cannot articulate it.	Recognize and appreciate the user as domain expert; try alternative communication and elicitation techniques.
Users think they know what they want until developers give them what they said they wanted.	Provide alternative elicitation techniques earlier: storyboarding, role playing, throwaway prototypes, and so on.
Analysts think they understand user problems better than users do.	Put the analyst in the user's place. Try role playing for an hour or a day.
Everybody believes everybody else is politically motivated.	Yes, its part of human nature, so let's get on with the program.

account for the fact that understanding user needs remains one of our largest problems? Well, considering the fact that few application developers have any training in *any* elicitation techniques, it's perhaps not all that surprising.

The third syndrome arises from the *communication gap* between the user and the developer. We call this syndrome the "User and the Developer" syndrome. Users and developers are typically from different worlds, speaking different languages and having different backgrounds, motivations, and objectives.

Somehow, we must learn to communicate more effectively with these "users from the other tribe." In an article on this subject, Laura Scharer (1981) describes this syndrome and provides some guidelines to help mitigate the problem. Combining her words with our own experiences, Table 7–1 both summarizes the reasons for this problem and suggests some solutions.

The hope is that with a better understanding of both the nature of these problems and some approaches to mitigate them, developers will be better prepared for the interesting work ahead.

Techniques for Requirements Elicitation

Gaining a better understanding of user needs moves us from the domain of bits and bytes, where many developers are more comfortable, into the domain of real people and real-world problems. Just as a variety of techniques can be used for analyzing and designing software solutions, a variety of techniques can be used to understand user and stakeholder requirements. Some techniques are suited to particular project teams and circumstances.

In Chapters 4, 5, and 6, we started down that path with problem analysis, a set of questions we can ask about the constraints to be imposed on the system, the business modeling technique we can use for many applications, and the systems engineering technique that we can apply to complex systems. In the following chapters, we'll describe techniques that have proved effective in addressing the three syndromes just discussed. Among the techniques we will discuss are

- Interviewing and questionnaires
- Requirements workshops
- Brainstorming and idea reduction
- Storyboards
- Use cases
- Role playing
- Prototyping

The choice of a specific technique will vary, based on the type of application, the skill and sophistication of the development team, the skill and sophistication of the customer, the scale of the problem, the criticality of the application, the technology used, and the uniqueness of the application.

Chapter 8

THE FEATURES OF
A PRODUCT OR SYSTEM

Key Points

- The development team needs to play a more active role in eliciting the requirements for the system.
- Product or system features are high-level expressions of desired system behavior.
- System features should be limited to 25–99, with fewer than 50 preferred.
- Attributes provide additional information about a feature.

G iven some of the problems we've described in the earlier chapters, it seems clear that the development team is rarely, if ever, handed a perfect, or perhaps even reasonable, specification to use as the basis for system development. In Chapter 7, we learned about the reasons for this. One conclusion we can draw is that if we are not going to be given better definitions, we are going to have to go out and *get* them. In other words, in order to achieve success, the development team is going to have to play a much more active role in eliciting the requirements. As we'll discover, although we can delegate the majority of this responsibility to a senior lead, analyst, or product manager, in the end, the entire team will be involved at one or more points in the process.

Stakeholder and User Needs

It seems obvious that the development team will build a better system only if it understands the true needs of the stakeholder. That information will give the team the information it needs to make better decisions in the definition and implementation of the system. This set of inputs, which we call *stakeholder* or *user needs*, or just user needs, provides a crucial piece of the puzzle.

Often, these user needs will be vague and ambiguous. "I need easier ways to understand the status of my inventory" or "I'd like to see a big increase in the productivity of sales order entry," your stakeholder might say. Yet, these statements set a most important context for all of the activities that follow. Since they are so important, we'll spend some significant time and energy time trying to understand them. We'll define a stakeholder need as

a reflection of the business, personal, or operational problem (or opportunity) that must be addressed in order to justify consideration, purchase, or use of a new system.

Features

Interestingly, when interviewed about their needs or requirements for a new system, stakeholders typically describe neither of these things, at least not in terms of the definitions we've provided thus far. That is, stakeholders often tell you neither their real need—"If I don't increase productivity in this department, I won't get my bonus this year" or "I want to be able to slow this vehicle down as quickly as possible without skidding"—nor the actual requirement for the system—"I must reduce sales order entry transaction processing time by 50 percent" or "The vehicle shall have a computer control system for each wheel." Instead, they describe what seems to be an abstraction somewhere between "I need a new GUI-based order entry screen" and "I want a vehicle with ABS."

We call these high-level expressions of desired system behavior the *features* of a product or system. These features are often not well defined and may even be in conflict with one another. "I want increased order processing rates" and "I want to provide a far more user-friendly interface to help our new employees learn the system"—but they are a representation of real needs nevertheless.

What is happening in this discussion? The stakeholder has already translated the real need (productivity or safety) into a system behavior that they have reason to believe will solve the real need (see Figure 8–1). In so doing, the *what* ("I need") has subtly shifted the to the *how* ("what I think the system should do to address this need"). This is not a bad thing, as the user oftentimes has real expertise in the domain and real insight into the value of the feature. Also, because it is easy to discuss these features in natural language and to document them and to communicate them to others, they add tremendous richness to the requirements schema.

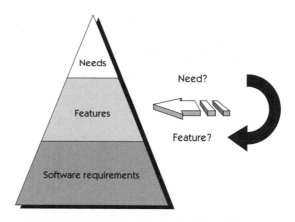

Figure 8–1   Needs and features are closely related

Features are a convenient way to describe functionality without getting bogged down in detail.

However, there is a caveat to this discussion, which is: If the team leaves the discussion without an understanding of the need behind the feature, then there is a real risk. If the feature does not solve the real need for any reason, then the system may fail to meet the user's objectives even though the implementation delivered the feature that was asked for.

In any case, we find this high level of abstraction—these *features*—to be very useful and a convenient way to describe the functionality of a new system without getting bogged down in too much detail. Indeed, we will drive most of our requirements activities from this "feature" construct.

Earlier, we defined a feature as

> *a service the system provides to fulfill one or more stakeholder needs.*

With this definition, users' *features* can't be too far removed from their *needs*, and we have a handy way to start to define the system.

Our focus in understanding user needs is on eliciting and organizing the *needs* and *features* of the proposed system. Sometimes, we'll get all needs and no features. Sometimes, we'll get all features and no needs. Sometimes, we won't be able to tell them apart. But so long as we are careful about the distinction in our own minds, we should, all the time, be learning valuable information about what the system must *do*.

Table 8–1   Features examples

Application Domain	Example of a Feature
Elevator control system	Manual control of doors during fire emergency.
Inventory control system	Provide up-to-date status of all inventoried items.
Defect tracking system	Provide trend data to assess product quality.
Payroll system	Report deductions-to-date by category.
Home lighting automation system (HOLIS)	Vacation settings for extended away periods.
Weapon control system	Minimum of two independent confirmations of attack authorization required.
Shrink-wrap application	Windows 2000 compatibility.

Features are easily expressed in natural language and consist of a short phrase; some examples are shown in Table 8–1. Rarely, if ever, are features elaborated in more detail. Features are also very helpful constructs for early product scope management and the related negotiation and trade-off processes. The statement of features does not entail a great deal of investment, and they are easy to describe and list.

Managing Complexity by Picking the Level of Abstraction

A system of arbitrary complexity can be defined in a list of 25–99 features.

The number of features we permit ourselves to consider will effectively pick the level of abstraction of the definition. To manage the complexity of the systems we are envisioning, *we recommend that for any new system or for an increment to an existing system, capabilities be abstracted to a high enough level so that a maximum of only 25–99 features result, with fewer than 50 preferred.*

In this way, a relatively small and manageable amount of information provides a comprehensive and complete basis for product definition, communication with the stakeholders, scope management, and project management. With 25–99 features suitably categorized and arranged, we should be able to describe and to communicate the gestalt of the system, be it a space shuttle ("reentry and reuse") or a software tool ("automatic defect trending"). In Team Skill 5, these features will be elaborated into detailed requirements specific enough to allow for implementation. We will call those *software requirements* to differentiate them from the higher-level features. We'll deal with that need for additional specificity later. For now, however, we'll keep our thinking at the features level.

Once the set of possible features is enumerated, it will be time to start making such decisions as "defer to a later release," "implement immediately," "reject entirely," or "investigate further." This *scoping* process is best done at the level of features rather than at the level of requirements, or you will be swamped in detail. We'll cover scoping in Team Skill 4, Managing Scope.

Attributes of Product Features

In order to help us better manage this information, we introduce the notion of feature *attributes*, or data elements that provide additional information about the item. Attributes are used to relate the feature or requirements data to other types of project information. We can use attributes to track (name or unique identifier, state, history data, allocated from, traced-to, and so on), to prioritize (priority field), and to manage (status) the features proposed for implementation. For example, the attribute *priority* could be used to capture the results of the cumulative voting in a brainstorming session; the attribute *version number* might be used to record the specific software release in which we intend to implement a specific feature.

By attaching various attributes to the features, you can better manage the complexity of the information. Although there is no limit to the types of attributes you might find useful, experience has demonstrated that some common attributes for features apply to most project circumstances (Table 8–2). In the remainder of this book, we'll use these attributes to help us manage the complexity of the feature and requirements data and to manage the relationships, such as dependencies, among the various types of system requirements.

So, let's move on to some team skills that will help us get the information *we* need. We'll start with interviewing (Chapter 9).

Table 8–2   Attributes of features

Attribute	Description
Status	Tracks progress during definition of the project baseline and subsequent development. *Example:* Proposed, Approved, Incorporated status states.
Priority/Benefit	All features are not created equal. Ranking by relative priority or benefit to the end user opens a dialogue between stakeholders and members of the development team. Used in managing scope and determining priority. *Example:* Critical, Important, Useful rankings.
Effort	Estimating the number of team- or person-weeks, lines of code or function points, or just general level of effort helps set expectations of what can and cannot be accomplished in a given time frame. *Example:* Low, Medium, High levels of effort.
Risk	A measure of the probability that the feature will cause undesirable events, such as cost overruns, schedule delays, or even cancellation. *Example:* High, Medium, Low risk level.
Stability	A measure of the probability that the feature will change or that the team's understanding of the feature will change. Used to help establish development priorities and to determine those items for which additional elicitation is the appropriate next action.
Target release	Records the intended product version in which the feature will first appear. When combined with the Status field, your team can propose, record, and discuss various features without committing them to development.
Assigned to	In many projects, features will be assigned to "feature teams" responsible for further elicitation, writing the software requirements, and perhaps even implementation.
Reason	Used to track the source of the requested feature. For example, the reference might be to a page and line number of a product specification or to a minute marker on a video of an important customer interview.

Chapter 9

INTERVIEWING

Key Points

- Interviewing is a simple and direct technique.
- Context-free questions can help achieve bias-free interviews.
- Then, it may be appropriate to search for undiscovered requirements by exploring solutions.
- Convergence on some common needs will initiate a "requirements repository" for use during the project.
- A questionnaire is no substitute for an interview.

One of the most important and most straightforward requirements-gathering techniques is the *user interview*, a simple, direct technique that can be used in virtually every situation. This chapter describes the interviewing process and provides a generic template for conducting user and stakeholder interviews. However, the interviewing process is not easy, and it forces us to get "up close and personal" to the "User and the Developer" syndrome.

In addition, one of the key goals of interviewing is to make sure that the biases and predispositions of the interviewer do not interfere with a free exchange of information. This is a subtle and pernicious problem. Sociology (oops, another class we missed!) teaches us that it is *impossible* to relate to others without the world filter that is the result of our own environment and cumulative experiences.

In addition, as solution providers, we rarely find ourselves in a situation in which we have no idea what types of potential solutions would address the problem. Indeed, in most cases, we operate within a repetitive domain or context in which certain elements of the solution are obvious, or at least appear to be obvious. ("We have solved this type of problem before, and we fully expect that our experience will apply in this new case. After all, we are just building houses, and hammers and nails work just fine.") Of course, this is not all bad, because having context is part of what we get paid for. Our point is that we shouldn't let our context interfere with understanding the real problem to be solved.

The Interview Context

The Context-Free Question

A context-free question helps us gain an understanding of the real problem without biasing the user's input.

So, how do we avoid prejudicing the user's response to our questions? We do so by asking questions about the nature of the user's problem without any context for a potential solution. To address this problem, Gause and Weinberg (1989) introduced the concept of the "context-free question." Examples of such questions are

- Who is the user?
- Who is the customer?
- Are their needs different?
- Where else can a solution to this problem be found?

These questions force us to listen before attempting to invent or to describe a potential solution. Listening gives us a better understanding of the customer's problem and any problems behind the problem. Such problems affect our customer's motivation or behavior and must be addressed before we can deliver a successful solution.

Context-free questions also parallel the questions salespeople are taught to ask as part of a technique called "solutions selling." In solutions selling, the salesperson uses a series of questions focused on first gaining a real understanding of the customer's problem and what solutions, if any, the customer already envisions. The intent of these questions is to allow the salesperson to fully understand the customer's real problem, so that effective solutions can be suggested and weighed on their specific merits. This process illustrates the value of the salesperson's wares as an element of a complete solution to the customer's real problem.

Value-Added Context

In our search for undiscovered requirements, it may also be appropriate to move the questions to a domain wherein solutions are explored after the

After the context-free questions are asked, suggested solutions can be explored.

context-free questions have been asked and answered. After all, most of us are not typically rewarded for simply understanding the problem but rather for providing solutions appropriate to the problems being solved. This addition of solution context may give the user new insights and perhaps even a different view of problem. And, of course, our users depend on us to have context; otherwise, they would have to teach us everything they know about the subject.

As an aid to building this skill within the development team, we have combined these techniques into our "generic, almost context-free interview," a structured interview that can be used to elicit user or stakeholder requirements in most software application contexts. The template for this interview is provided in Figure 9–1. The interview consists of both context-free and non-context-free sections. It also provides questions designed to make certain that all aspects of requirements, including some of those "gotcha" requirements for reliability, supportability, and so on, are thoroughly explored.

The Moment of Truth: The Interview

With a little preparation and with the structured interview in one's pocket, any member of the team can do an adequate job of interviewing a user or customer. (But. it may be best to pick those team members who are most "outgoing.") Here are some tips for a successful interview.

- Prepare an appropriate context-free interview, and jot it down in a notebook for reference during the interview. Review the questions just prior to the interview.
- Before the interview, research the background of the stakeholder and the company to be interviewed. Don't bore the person being interviewed with questions you could have answered in advance. On the other hand, it wouldn't hurt to *briefly* verify the answers with the interviewee.
- Jot down answers in your notebook during the interview. (Don't attempt to capture the data electronically at this time!)
- Refer to the template during the interview to make certain that the right questions are being asked.

Part I: Establishing Customer or User Profile

Name:

Company

Industry:

Job Title:

(The above information can typically be filled in in advance.)

What are your key responsibilities?

What outputs do you produce?

For whom?

How is success measured?

Which problems interfere with your success?

What, if any, trends make your job easier or more difficult?

Part II: Assessing the Problem

For which "(application type)" problems do you lack good solutions?

What are they? (*Hint: Keep asking, "Anything else?"*)

For each problem, ask:

- Why does this problem exist?
- How do you solve it now?
- How would you like to solve it?

Part III: Understanding the User Environment

Who are the users?

What is their educational background?

What is their computer background?

Are users experienced with this type of application?

Which platforms are in use?

What are your plans for future platforms?

Are additional applications in use that are relevant to this application? If so, let's talk about them a bit.

What are your expectations for usability of the product?

What are your expectations for training time?

What kinds of user help (for example, hard copy and online documentation) do you need?

Figure 9–1   The generic, almost context-free interview

Part IV: Recap for Understanding

You have told me:

(List customer-described problems in your own words.)

-
-
-

Does this adequately represent the problems you are having with your existing solution?

What, if any, other problems you are experiencing?

Part V: Analyst's Inputs on Customer's Problem

(validate or invalidate assumptions)

(*If not addressed*) Which, if any, problems are associated with: (*List any needs or additional problems you think should concern the customer or user.*)

-
-
-

For each suggested problem ask,

- Is this a real problem?
- What are the reasons for this problem?
- How do you currently solve the problem?
- How would you like to solve the problem?
- How would you rank solving these problems in comparison to others you've mentioned?

Part VI: Assessing Your Solution (if applicable)

(Summarize the key capabilities of your proposed solution.)

What if you could

-
-

How would you rank the importance of these?

Figure 9–1   The generic, almost context-free interview (*continued*)

Part VII: Assessing the Opportunity

Who in your organization needs this application?

How many of these types of users would use the application?

How would you value a successful solution?

Part VIII: Assessing Reliability, Performance, and Support Needs

What are your expectations for reliability?

What are your expectations for performance?

Will you support the product, or will others support it?

Do you have special needs for support?

What about maintenance and service access?

What are the security requirements?

What are the installation and configuration requirements?

Are there special licensing requirements?

How will the software be distributed?

Are there labeling and packaging requirements?

Part IX: Other Requirements

Are there any legal, regulatory, or environmental requirements or other standards that must be supported?

Can you think of any other requirements we should know about?

Part X: Wrapup

Are there any other questions I should be asking you?

If I need to ask follow-up questions, may I give you a call? Would you be willing to participate in a requirements review?

Part XI: Analyst's Summary

After the interview, and while the data is still fresh in your mind, summarize the three highest-priority needs or problems identified by this user/customer.

1.

2.

3.

Figure 9–1   The generic, almost context-free interview (*continued*)

It is OK to wander off course a bit, just as long as the interviewer keeps the goal in mind.

The interviewer should make sure that the script is not overly constraining. Once rapport has been established, the interview is likely to take on a life of its own. The customer may well launch into a stream-of-consciousness dialogue, describing in gory detail the horrors of the current situation. *This is exactly the behavior you are striving for.* If this happens to you, do not cut it off prematurely with another question; rather, write everything down as quickly as you can, letting the user exhaust that particular stream of thought! Ask follow-up questions about the information that has just been provided. Then, after this thread has run to its logical end, get back to other questions on the list.

After even a couple of such interviews, the developer/analyst will have gained some knowledge of the problem domain and will have an enhanced understanding of both the problem being solved and the user's insights on the characteristics of a successful solution. In addition, the developer can summarize the key user needs or product features that were defined in the interview. These "user needs" live near the top of our requirements pyramid and serve as the driving force for all of the work that follows.

Compiling the Need Data

Your problem analysis will have identified the key stakeholders and users you will need to interview to gain an understanding of the stakeholder's needs. Typically, it does not take many interviews to get a pretty solid feel for the issues.

The Analyst's Summary: 10 + 10 + 10 ≠ 30

The last section of the interview form, Analyst's Summary, is used for recording the "three most important needs or problems" uncovered in this interview. In many cases, after just a few interviews, these highest-priority needs will start to be repeated. This means that you may be starting to get convergence on some common needs. This is to be expected, especially among those users or stakeholders who share a common perspective. So, ten interviews will often create only 10–15 *different* needs. This is the start of your "requirements repository," a set of assets you will build and use to good advantage over the course of your project. This simple, inexpensive data, even by itself, will help you and your team build a more solid foundation with which to initiate your project.

The Case Study

HOLIS
user needs

The HOLIS team decided to have the marketing team (Eric and Cathy) develop the questions for the interview but wanted everyone on the team to experience the process and to have the opportunity to meet customers face to face and thereby "see" the problem and a potential solution from the customer's perspective. So, the team divided up the customer and distributor list and had each team member interview two people. The team used the Analyst's Summary to summarize the needs that were provided and weeded out the duplicates. After fifteen interviews, the team had identified 20-some needs to fill in the top of their requirements pyramid.

From the homeowner's perspective:

- Flexible and modifiable lighting control for entire house
- "Futureproof" ("As technology changes, I'd like compatibility with new technologies that might emerge.")
- Attractive, unobtrusive, ergonomic
- Fully independent and programmable or (reconfigurable) switches for each room in the house
- Additional security and peace of mind
- Intuitive operation ("I'd like to be able to explain it to my 'techno-phobic' mother.")
- A reasonable system cost, with low switch costs
- Easy and inexpensive to fix
- Flexible switch configurations (from one to seven "buttons" per switch)
- Out of sight, out of mind
- 100% reliability
- Vacation security settings
- Ability to create scenes, such as special housewide lighting settings for a party
- No increase in electrical or fire hazard in the home
- Ability, after a power failure, to restore the lights the way they were
- Program it myself, using my own PC
- Dimmers wherever I want them
- Can program it myself, without using a PC
- Somebody else will program it for me
- If system fails, I still want to be able to turn some lights on
- Interfaces to my home security system
- Interfaces to other home automation (HVAC, audio/video, and so on)

From the Distributor's Perspective:

- A competitive product offering
- Some strong product differentiation

- Easy to train my salespeople
- Can be demonstrated in my shop
- High gross margins

A Note on Questionnaires

There is *no* substitute for an interview.

- Do it first!
- Do it for every new class of problem!
- Do it for every new project!

We are often asked whether the team can substitute a questionnaire for this interviewing process. In some cases, the need expressed is perhaps a simple desire for efficiency ("I could do 100 questionnaires in the time it takes to do one interview.") In other cases, the need itself may come under suspicion ("Do I really have to talk to these people? Couldn't I just send them a letter?")

No matter what the motivation, the answer is *no*. There is *no* substitute for the personal contact, rapport building, and free-form interaction of the interview technique. We are confident that after one or two interviews, your world view will have changed. Even more important, the vision for the solution will have changed along with it! Do the interview first. Do it for every new class of problem, and do it for every new project.

However, when used appropriately, the questionnaire technique can also play a legitimate role in gathering user needs. Although the questionnaire technique is often used and appears scientific because of the opportunity for statistical analysis of the quantitative results, the technique is not a substitute for interviewing. When it comes to requirements gathering, the questionnaire technique has some fundamental problems.

- Relevant questions cannot be decided in advance.
- The assumptions behind the questions bias the answers.

   Example: Did this class meet your expectations? Assumption: You had expectations, so this is a meaningful question.

- It is difficult to explore new domains (What you really should be asking about is . . .), and there is no interaction to explore domains that need to be explored.
- Unclear responses from the user are difficult to follow up on.

Indeed, some have concluded that the questionnaire technique suppresses almost everything good about requirements gathering, and therefore, we generally do not recommend it for this purpose.

Questionnaires *can* be used to validate assumptions and gather statistical preference data.

However, the questionnaire technique can be applied with good effect as a corroborating technique after the initial interviewing and analysis activity. For example, if the application has a large number of existing or potential users and if the goal is to provide statistical input about user or customer preferences among a limited set of choices, a questionnaire can be used effectively to gather a significant amount of focused data in a short period of time. In short, the questionnaire technique, like all elicitation techniques, is suited to a subset of the requirements challenges that an organization may face.

Chapter 10

REQUIREMENTS WORKSHOPS

Key Points

- The requirements workshop is perhaps the most powerful technique for eliciting requirements.
- It gathers all key stakeholders together for a short but intensely focused period.
- The use of an outside facilitator experienced in requirements management can help ensure the success of the workshop.
- Brainstorming is the most important part of the workshop.

Accelerating the Decision Process

One of the prioritization schemes that we've used is blindingly simple. Ask the stakeholder what *one* item they would pick if only one feature could be implemented for the next release. Like the thought of being hanged in a fortnight, this question focuses the mind wonderfully on what really matters.

Applying this technique, if we were to give only one requirements elicitation technique—one that we had to apply in every circumstance, no matter the project context, no matter what the time frame—we would pick the requirements workshop. The requirements workshop may well be the most powerful technique in this book and one of the few that, when mastered, can really help change project outcomes, even when it's the only elicitation technique applied.

The requirements workshop is designed to encourage consensus on the requirements of the application and to gain rapid agreement on a course of action, all in a very short time frame. With this technique, key stakeholders of the project are gathered together for a short, intensive period, typically no more than 1 or 2 days. The workshop is facilitated by a team member or, better yet, by an experienced outside facilitator and focuses on the creation or review of the high-level features to be delivered by the new application.

A properly run requirements workshop has many benefits.

- It assists in building an effective team, committed to one common purpose: the success of *this* project.
- All stakeholders get their say; no one is left out.
- It forges an agreement between the stakeholders and the development team as to what the application must do.
- It can expose and resolve political issues that are interfering with project success.
- The output, a preliminary system definition at the features level, is available immediately.

Many organizations have had great success with the workshop technique. Together, we have participated in hundreds of such workshops, and rarely, if ever, has the workshop been unsuccessful in meeting its desired goals. The workshop provides a unique opportunity for stakeholders from various parts of the organization to work together toward the common goal of project success.

In this chapter, you will learn how to plan and to execute a successful requirements workshop. At the end of the chapter, we'll apply the technique to our HOLIS case study.

Preparing for the Workshop

Proper *preparation* for the workshop is critical to success.

Selling the Concept

Proper preparation is the key to a successful workshop.

First, it may be necessary to sell the concept inside the organization by communicating the benefits of the workshop approach to prospective members of the team. This is typically not a difficult process, but it's not unusual to encounter resistance: "Not another meeting!"; "We can't possibly get all these critical people together for one day," "You'll never get [name your favorite stakeholder] to attend." Don't be discouraged; if you hold it, they will come.

Ensuring the Participation of the Right Stakeholders

Second, preparation also involves identifying stakeholders who can contribute to the process and whose needs must be met in order to ensure a successful outcome. These stakeholders will have already been identified if the team executed the problem analysis steps, but now is the time for one last review to make sure that all critical stakeholders have been identified.

Logistics

Third, a conscientious approach to logistics is necessary and will pay dividends in that a poorly organized workshop is unlikely to achieve the desired result. Logistics involve everything from structuring the proper invitation to travel arrangements to the lighting in the workshop meeting room. A literal belief in Murphy's law—"Whatever can go wrong will go wrong"—should be your guideline here. If you approach logistics with a high degree of professionalism, it will be obvious to the attendees that this is indeed an important event, and they will act accordingly. You'll also have a more successful workshop.

"Warm-Up Materials"

Fourth, send materials out in advance of the workshop to prepare the attendees and also to increase productivity at the workshop session. These materials set the attendees' frame of mind. We call this "getting their mind right." One of the messages we need to deliver is that *this is not yet another meeting. This may be our one chance to get it right.*

Warm-up materials should spur both in-context, and out-of-box thinking.

We recommend that you provide two separate types of warm up materials.

1. *Project-specific information,* which might include drafts of requirements documents, bulleted lists of suggested features, copies of interviews with prospective users, analyst's reports on trends in the industry, letters from customers, bug reports from the existing system, new management directives, new marketing data, and so on. Although it's important not to bury the prospective attendees in data, it's also important to make sure that they have the right data.

2. *Out-of-box thinking preparation.* Part of "getting the mind right" is encouraging attendees to think "out of the box." "Forget for a minute what you know and what can't be done due to politics." "Forget that we tried to get management buy-in last time and failed."

"Forget that we haven't yet solidified our development process." "Simply bring your insights on the features of this new project, and be prepared to think 'out of the box.' " As workshop leader, you can assist in this process by providing thought-provoking and stimulating articles about the process of creativity, rules for brainstorming, requirements management, managing scope, and so on. In this atmosphere, creative solutions will more likely result.

Tip: Do not send the data out too far in advance. You do not want the attendees to read it and forget it, and you don't want the long planning cycle to decrease their sense of urgency. Send the data out anywhere from 2 days to 1 week in advance. In all likelihood, the attendees will read on the plane or at the last minute, anyway. That's OK; it will help them be in the right frame of mind for the session.

To help you with your out-of-box thinking and to help set the context for the workshop activity, we've provided a memo template in Figure 10–1. Parenthetically, we'll also "read between the lines" a little bit to provide insights on some of the challenges you may already face in your project, and how the workshop is intended to address them.

Role of the Facilitator

To ensure success, we recommend that the workshop be run by an outsider who is also experienced in the unique challenges of the requirements management process. However, if this is simply not practical in your environment, the workshop could be facilitated by a team member *if* and *only if* that person

- Has received some training in the process
- Has demonstrated solid consensus-building or team-building skills
- Is personable and well respected by both the internal and external team members
- Is strong enough to chair what could be a challenging meeting

If possible, have a facilitator who is not a team member run the workshop.

However, if the workshop is to be facilitated by a team member, that person must *not* contribute to the ideas and issues at the meeting. Otherwise, the workshop is in grave danger of losing the objectivity that is necessary to get at the real facts, and it may not foster a trusting environment in which a consensus can emerge.

In any case, the facilitator has a pivotal role in making the workshop a success. After all, you have all of the key stakeholders gathered together, perhaps

Memo:

To: **Stakeholders in the _____ project**

Subject: **Upcoming Requirements Workshop**

From:

I am the product [project] manager for the _____ project. The project was [or will be] initiated on _____ and will be completed on its deadline of _____.

(We know it; we mean it, and we intend to complete it on time.)

As with most projects, it has been difficult to gain consensus on the new features of this application and to define an initial baseline release that meets the needs of our diverse group of stakeholders.

(It's harder than heck to gain agreement on anything with this group, so we're going to try something a little different, and here's what that is....)

In order to facilitate this process, we will be holding a requirements workshop on _____.

The goal of the workshop is to finalize the new features for the next baseline release of the product. In order to do so, it's important that all stakeholders' inputs be heard. The workshop will be facilitated by _____, who is an experienced requirements management facilitator.

(Since as stakeholders, we may also be biased, we will have someone from outside the team help us make sure that the workshop is managed in a fair and unbiased way.)

Results of the workshop will be available immediately and will be distributed to the development and marketing teams the next day. You are cordially invited to attend the workshop and to provide the input that is representative of the needs of your [team, department, customer]. If you are unable to attend, we strongly recommend that you send a team member who is empowered to make the decisions representative of your needs.

(We are going to initiate development the very next day; if you want your input to be heard on this project, be there, or send someone who can speak for you. In other words, speak now or forever hold your peace.)

Included with this memo is a brief description of the currently anticipated features of the product, as well as some reading material about the workshop and brainstorming process. The workshop will last until 5:30 P.M., and we will convene promptly at 8:30 A.M.

(This project, and this workshop, is going to be professionally run; to demonstrate this, we have provided some advanced reading material to help you be better prepared. We need you to be there, to contribute, and to help us get this project off to a proper beginning.)

We look forward to seeing you there.

Sincerely,

[Project Leader]

Figure 10–1 Sample memo for kickstarting a requirements workshop

for the first and last time on the project, and you cannot afford a misfire. Some of the responsibilities of the facilitator are to

- Establish a professional and objective tone for the meeting.
- Start and stop the meeting on time.
- Establish and enforce the "rules" for the meeting.
- Introduce the goals and agenda for the meeting.
- Manage the meeting and keep the team "on track."
- Facilitate a process of decision and consensus making, but avoid participating in the content.
- Manage any facilities and logistics issues to ensure that the focus remains on the agenda.
- Make certain that all stakeholders participate and have their input heard.
- Control disruptive or unproductive behavior.

Setting the Agenda

The agenda for the workshop will be based on the needs of the particular project and the content that needs to be developed at the workshop. No one agenda fits all. However, most structured requirements workshops can follow a fairly standard format. Table 10–1 provides a typical agenda.

Table 10–1   Sample agenda for requirements workshop

Time	Agenda Item	Description
8:00–8:30	Introduction	Agenda, facilities, and rules
8:30–10:00	Context	Project status, market needs, results of user interviews, etc.
10:00–12:00	Brainstorming	Brainstorm features of application
12:00–1:00	Lunch	Working through lunch avoids loss of momentum
1:00–2:00	Brainstorming	Continues
2:00–3:00	Feature definition	Write out 2- or 3-sentence definition for features
3:00–4:00	Idea reduction and prioritization	Prioritize features
4:00–5:00	Wrapup	Summary and action items, address "parking lot" items

Running the Workshop

Problems and Tricks of the Trade

You can see that the facilitator has a crucial role to play. To make matters even more exciting, these workshops are often characterized by a highly charged atmosphere. In other words, there are reasons why it is difficult to get consensus on these projects; nearly *all* of these reasons will be present at the workshop.

Indeed, the setting may even be politically charged, confrontational, or both. This is yet another reason for having a facilitator; let the facilitator take the heat and manage the meeting so as to not exacerbate any problems—past, present, or future—among stakeholders.

Many facilitators carry a "bag of tricks" with them to help manage this highly charged atmosphere. At RELA, we evolved a set of highly useful "workshop tickets." Although they seem pretty odd, and even juvenile at first, you can trust us that they have proved their worth in a variety of settings. The more difficult the workshop, the more valuable they become! They also tend to spur "out-of-box" thinking. What's more, they are fun and contribute to a positive tone for the session. Figure 10–2 provides a sample set of workshop tickets. Feel free to adapt them and use them, along with "instructions" for use.

Table 10–2 describes some of the problems that can occur in the workshop setting and also provides suggestions on how you can use the workshop tickets to address the problems. The facilitator must also introduce these rules at the beginning of the meeting and, ideally, reach a consensus that it's OK to use these silly tickets for this one day.

Brainstorming and Idea Reduction

The most important part of the workshop is the brainstorming process. This technique is ideally suited for the workshop setting, and it fosters a creative and positive atmosphere and gets input from all stakeholders. We'll cover brainstorming in the next chapter.

Production and Follow-Up

After the workshop, the facilitator distributes the minutes from the meeting and records any other outputs. Then, the facilitator's job is over, and responsibility for success is again in the hands of the development team.

Rule: Each participant initially receives one free coupon for being late. Thereafter, participant donates $1 to the penalty box.

Objective: Keep the momentum going.

Rule: Each participant initially receives one free coupon for a "ding" or "knock" on a person or department. Thereafter, participant donates $1 to the penalty box.

Objective: Have a little fun and make people aware of the political issues in the project.

Rule: Participant initials both coupons. Participant gives coupon to any participant who provides a great idea. Goal to spend your coupons.

Objective: Give incentive and reward creative thinking.

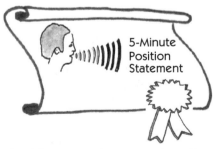

Rule: Participant spends coupon at any time. Facilitator gives podium to participant and sets timer. Everyone listens. No interruptions!

Objective: Allow for a structured process of ad hoc input. Assure everyone gets their say.

Figure 10–2   Workshop tickets

Table 10-2 Problems and solutions in the requirements workshop setting

Problem	Solution
Time management: ■ It's difficult to get restarted after breaks and lunch. ■ Key stakeholders may be late returning.	Facilitator keeps a kitchen timer for the meeting and times all breaks. Attendees who are late must contribute a late-from-break ticket while they have them or pay $1 to "charitable contributions" box.
Grandstanding, domineering positions	Facilitator enforces use of "5-Minute Position Statement" to regulate input. Also creates a "parking lot" list for later discussion of ideas that deserve discussion, but are not relevant to the agenda item.
Lack of input from stakeholders	Facilitator encourages attendees to use their "5-Minute-Position Statements" and their "That's a Great Idea" coupon. Make it clear that no one should leave the workshops not having used the tickets or having received a "That's a Great Idea" coupon from others. (Suggestion: Make a simple reward for use of 5-minute ticket and receipt of "That's a Great Idea" coupon).
Negative comments, petty behaviors, and turf wars	Use "Cheap Shot Tickets" until the participants don't have any more; thereafter, have them make charitable contributions to the box (group decides how much).
Flagging energy after lunch	Light lunches, midafternoon snack breaks, rearrange room, rearrange participants' seating, change lighting or temperature. Do whatever you can do to keep things moving.

Thereafter, the project leader has the responsibility to follow up any open action items that were recorded at the meeting and to organize the information for distribution to the attendees. Often, the output of the meeting will be a simple list of ideas or suggested product features which can be turned over immediately to the development team for further action. In some cases, additional workshops with other stakeholders will be scheduled, or additional elicitation efforts will be necessary to gain a better understanding of the ideas fostered at the workshop. The creation of these ideas is the crux of the entire workshop process. In the next chapter we'll look more closely at this portion of the workshop process.

Chapter 11

BRAINSTORMING AND IDEA REDUCTION

Key Points

- Brainstorming involves both idea generation and idea reduction.
- The most creative, innovative ideas often result from combining multiple, seemingly unrelated ideas.
- Various voting techniques may be used to prioritize the ideas created.
- Although live brainstorming is preferred, Web-based brainstorming may be a viable alternative in some situations.

Whether you are in the workshop setting of Chapter 10 or whenever you find yourself needing new ideas or creative solutions to problems, brainstorming is a very useful technique. It's simple, easy to do, and fun.

In the workshop setting, you probably already have a pretty good idea of the features of the new product. After all, few projects start out with a totally clean slate. However, in addition to reviewing the suggested features for the product, the workshop provides the opportunity to solicit new input and to mutate and combine these new features with those already under consideration. This process will also help us in our goal of "finding the undiscovered ruins" and thereby making sure that we have completeness of our input and that all stakeholder needs are addressed. Typically, a portion of the workshop is devoted to brainstorming new ideas and features for the application. Brainstorming is a collection of techniques that are useful when stakeholders are collocated.

This elicitation technique has a number of primary benefits.

- It encourages participation by all parties present.
- It allows participants to "piggyback" on one another's ideas.

- A facilitator or scribe maintains a written trail of everything discussed (so nothing is lost).
- It exhibits high bandwidth.
- Typically, it results in a broad set of possible solutions to whatever problem is posed.
- It encourages out-of-the-box thinking, that is, without being limited by normal constraints.

Brainstorming has two phases: idea generation and idea reduction. The primary goal during idea generation is to delineate as many ideas as possible; the goal is breadth of ideas, not necessarily depth. The primary goal during idea reduction is to analyze all of the ideas generated. Idea reduction includes pruning, organizing, ranking, expanding, grouping, refining, and the like.

Live Brainstorming

Although brainstorming can be approached in many different ways, the simple process we describe has proved effective in a variety of settings. First, all of the significant stakeholders are gathered into one room, and supplies are distributed. The supplies given to each participant can be as simple as a stack of large sticky notes and a thick black marker for writing on the notes. The sheets should be at least 3" × 5" (7 cm × 12 cm) and no larger than 5" × 7" (12 cm × 17 cm). Each participant should have at least 25 sheets for each brainstorming session. Post-Its or index cards work well. If index cards are used, push pins and a soft wall, such as a large cork board, are also needed.

Then the rules of brainstorming are explained (see Figure 11–1), and the objective of the session is clearly and concisely stated.

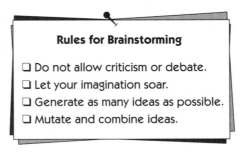

Rules for Brainstorming

❑ Do not allow criticism or debate.
❑ Let your imagination soar.
❑ Generate as many ideas as possible.
❑ Mutate and combine ideas.

Figure 11–1 Rules for brainstorming

The facilitator also explains the objective of the process. Although it may seem as though the objective that starts the process is rather straightforward, it is not. The way it is stated has an effect on the consequences of the session. For example, the following questions are a few ways to state the objective.

- What features would you like to see in the product?
- What services would you like to see the product provide?
- What things would you like the product to keep track of?

(Note that the objective also helps you to decide when the session is done. When the objectives are met and no one else has anything to add, *quit!*)

After the objective of the process has been stated, the facilitator asks participants to state their ideas aloud and to write them down, one per sheet. Ideas are spoken out loud to enable others in the room to piggyback on the ideas, that is, to think of related ideas and to follow rule 4, to mutate and combine ideas. In this process, however, the first rule—no criticism or debate—must be foremost in people's minds. If this rule is not enforced, the process will be squelched, and many bright folks who are sensitive to criticism will not feel comfortable putting forth more ideas, a tragic loss.

Tip: In our experience, the *most* creative and innovative ideas—those that truly revolutionized the product concept—were not the result of any one person's ideas but instead resulted from combining multiple, and seemingly unrelated, ideas from various stakeholders. Any process that fosters this result is a powerful process indeed.

As they are generated, ideas are written down by the idea generator on the supplied materials. This is important.

- To make sure that they are captured in that person's own words
- To make sure that they are not lost
- To enable them to be posted for later piggybacking
- To prevent delays in the creative process that could be caused by a single scribe trying to capture all ideas on a flip chart or whiteboard in front of the room

As ideas are generated, the facilitator simply collects them and posts them on a wall in the meeting room. Again, *no* criticism of ideas can be tolerated. It is inappropriate to say, "That's a stupid idea" or even "We already have that idea on the wall." The sole purpose is to generate ideas. Even a mildly negative remark can have the deleterious effect of suppressing further participation by the "victim." However, remarks such as "Great idea!" are appropriate and will often provide the award of a "That's a Great Idea Ticket," which can encourage further participation by all stakeholders. Idea generation should proceed until all parties feel that it has reached a natural end.

It is common for lulls to occur during idea generation. These are not times to stop the process. Lulls tend to correct themselves as soon as the next idea is generated. Longer lulls might be cause for the facilitator to re-ask the objective again or to ask similar questions. Most idea-generation sessions last around an hour, but some last 2–3 hours. Under no condition should the facilitator end a session that is going strong with a remark like "I know we're all doing great with this process, but we need to move on." To the participants, this remark says, "Your ideas are not as important as my schedule." The number of ideas generated will be a function of how fertile the subject being discussed is, but it is common to generate 100–200 ideas.

The process tends to have a natural end; at some point, the stakeholders will simply run out of ideas. This is typified by longer and longer gaps between idea submissions. At this point, the facilitator brings an end to the session, and it may well be a great time for a break.

Idea Reduction

When the idea-generation phase terminates, it is time to initiate idea reduction. Several steps are involved.

Pruning

The first step is to "prune" those ideas that are not worthy of further investment by the group. The facilitator starts by visiting each idea briefly and asking for concurrence from the group that the idea is basically valid. There is no reason for any participant to be defensive or to claim authorship for any idea; any participant may support or refute any idea.

Tip: The presence of ideas that can be easily pruned is an indicator of a quality process. The absence of a fair number of wild and crazy ideas indicates that the participants were not thinking far enough "out of the box."

The facilitator simply asks the participants whether each idea is worthy of further consideration and then simply removes an invalid idea, but if there is *any* disagreement among the participants, the idea stays on the list. If participants find two sheets with the same idea, group them together on the wall. (This is usually preferable to removing one; its author may feel insulted.)

Grouping Ideas

It may be helpful during this process to start grouping similar ideas. Doing so is most effective when participants from the session volunteer to go to the wall and do the grouping. Related ideas are grouped together in regions of the walls. Name the groups of related ideas. For example, the groups might be labeled

- New features
- Performance issues
- Enhancements to current features
- User interface and ease-of-use issues

Or, they may be specifically focused on capabilities of the system and the way they support various types of users. For example, in envisioning a new freight and delivery service, the features might be grouped by

- Package routing and tracking
- Customer service
- Marketing and sales
- Web-based services
- Billing
- Transportation management

Idea generation can be reinitiated now for any one of these groups if the participants feel that the grouping process has spurred development of new ideas or that some area of key functionality has been left out.

Feature Definition

At this point, it is important to take the time to write a short description of what the idea meant to the person who submitted it. This gives the contributor the opportunity to further describe the feature and helps ensure that the participants have a common understanding of the feature. This way, everyone understands what was meant by the idea, thus avoiding a fundamentally flawed prioritization process.

In this process, the facilitator walks through each idea that has not been pruned and asks the submitter to provide a one-sentence description.

Application Context	Brainstormed Feature	Feature Definition
Home lighting automation	"Automatic lighting settings"	Homeowner can create preset time-based schedules for certain lighting events to happen, based on time of day.
Sales order entry system	"fast"	Fast enough response time to not interfere with typical operations.
Defect tracking system	"Automatic notification"	All registered parties will be notified via e-mail when something has changed.

A welding robot feature, such as "automatic reweld," may already be sufficiently described, and no further work is required. However, it is important to not bog down in this process; it should take no longer than a few minutes per idea. You need capture only the essence of the idea.

Prioritization

In some situations, the generation of ideas is the only goal, and the process is complete. However, in most settings, including the requirements workshop, it will be necessary to prioritize the ideas that remain after pruning. After all, no development team can do "everything that anybody can ever think of." Once the groupings have stabilized and have been agreed to, it is time to move on to the next step. Again, a variety of techniques can be used; we'll describe two that we use routinely.

Results of cumulative voting:

Idea 1 $380

Idea 2 $200

Idea 3 $180

Idea 4 $140

Idea 5 . . .

.

.

.

Idea 27. . .

Cumulative Voting: The Hundred-Dollar Test. This simple test is fun, fair, and easy to do. Each person is given $100 of "idea money" to be spent on "purchasing ideas." (You may even wish to add a kit of "idea bucks" to the workshop ticket inventory.) Each participant is asked to write down on a sheet of paper how much of this money to spend on each idea. Then, after the participants have had a chance to vote, the facilitator tabulates the results and provides an order ranking. It may also be helpful to do a quick histogram of the result so participants can see the visual impact of their decision.

This process is straightforward and usually works just great. However, you should be aware of the following caveats. First, it will work only once. You cannot use the same technique twice on the project, because once the results are known, participants will bias their input the next time around. For example, if you're a participant and your favorite feature is first on the list but your second-favorite feature didn't even get honorable mention, you may put all of your money on the second feature. You're confident that other voters will see to it that your favorite feature still makes the cut.

Similarly, you may find it necessary to limit the amount anyone spends on one feature. Otherwise, a tricky participant, knowing full well that "other items" such as "Run faster" and "Easy to use" will make the cut to the top of the list, might put all of their money on "Runs on the Mac platform" and elevate it to a higher priority. On the other hand, you may wish to allow a higher limit, so long as you have the opportunity to understand where the really big votes came from. They may represent high-priority needs from a limited stakeholder community.

The "Critical, Important, Useful" Categorization   A colleague taught us another technique that has also been very effective, especially with a small group of stakeholders or even just one stakeholder, such as when you need your boss's opinion of your priorities. In this technique, each participant is given a number of votes equal to the number of ideas, but each vote must be categorized "critical," "important," or "useful." The trick in this technique is the rule that each stakeholder is given only one third of the votes from each category; therefore, only one third of the ideas can be considered critical.

- *Critical* means "indispensable," suggesting that a stakeholder would not be able to use a system without this feature. Without the feature, the system does not fulfill its primary mission, its role and is therefore not worth releasing.
- *Important* means that there will be a significant loss of customer utility or market share or revenue or new customer segments served. If the important items don't get implemented, some users would not like the product and would not buy it.
- *Useful* means nice to have. The feature makes life easier, makes the system more appealing, more fun, or delivers higher utility.

Note: With this scheme, all ideas that survived the pruning process get at least a "useful" vote, avoiding insult to those who submitted them.

In a larger group of participants, each item will have a mix of categories, but this is not really a problem. The facilitator has one more trick: Simply multiply "critical" votes times 9, "important" by 3, and "useful" by 1 and add up the score! This will tend to spread the results to heavily favor the "critical" votes, and thus every stakeholder's "critical" need will bubble to the top of the list.

Web-Based Brainstorming

So far, we have discussed a process for brainstorming that works very effectively when all stakeholders can be gathered together at the same time, are relatively proactive and not overly shy, the facilitator is experienced, and stakeholder politics is manageable. Indeed, there is *no* substitute for the developers and outside stakeholders spending this time together. Each will remember the various hot buttons and issues addressed by the others, and perspective and mutual respect are often byproducts of the process. Therefore, the requirements workshop and live brainstorming are by far our preferred approaches.

But sometimes, live brainstorming is not possible. In these situations, an alternative is to use the Internet or an intranet to facilitate the brainstorming process via the establishment of a discussion group. This technique may be particularly suited for developing advanced applications for which research is required or a long-term view is critical, the concept is initially fuzzy, and a wide variety and significant number of user and other stakeholders inputs are involved.

With this technique, the project leader sponsors a list server or Web page for recording and commenting on product features. The recording of ideas and comments can be done either anonymously or by crediting the author, based on the construct created by the administrator. An advantage of this technique is its persistence; ideas and comments can be circulated over a long period of time, with full recording of all threads for each idea. Perhaps most important, a unique advantage of this process is that ideas can grow and mature with the passage of time.

The Case Study: The HOLIS 2000 Requirements Workshop

Let's get back to our case study. While the interviewing process was under way, the development team met with marketing and decided to hold a requirements workshop for the HOLIS 2000 project.

Attendees

After thinking through the issues, the team decided not to bring in an outside facilitator but instead to have Eric, director of marketing, facilitate the workshop. The team also decided to have two development team members participate in the workshop: Cathy, the product manager, and Pete, the development manager. The team felt that both Cathy and Pete would speak for the team, as well as be able to contribute content, as they were both new homeowners. Other team members would not participate but would simply attend the workshop in order to observe the process, listen to the customers, and see the results immediately.

The team also decided to include representation from the four "classes" of customers and invited the following participants:

1. Distributors: John, CEO of the company's largest distributor, and Raquel, the general manager of the company's exclusive distributor in Europe
2. David, a local custom homebuilder with experience in purchasing and installing competitive systems in the marketplace
3. Betty, a local electrical contractor
4. Prospective homeowners, identified with the help of Betty, who were in the process of building, or were considering building a high-end residence.

The following list provides more detail on the participants.

Name	Role	Title	Comments
Eric	Facilitator	Director of Marketing	
Cathy	Participant	HOLIS 2000 Product Manager	Project champion
Pete	Participant	Software Development Manager	Development responsibility for HOLIS 2000
Jennifer	Participant		Prospective homeowner
Elmer	Participant		Prospective homeowner
Gene	Participant		Prospective homeowner
John	Participant	CEO, Automation Equip	Lumenations' largest distributor
Raquel	Participant	GM, EuroControls	Lumenations' European distributor
Betty	Participant	President, Krystel Electric	Local electrical contractor

Name	Role	Title	Comments
David	Participant	President, Rosewind Construction	Custom homebuilder
Various members	Observer	Development team	All team members who were available

The Workshop

Prior to the workshop, the team put together a warm-up package consisting of

- A few recent magazines articles highlighting the trends in home automation
- Copies of selective interviews that had been conducted
- A summarized list of the needs that had been identified to date

Eric brushed up on his facilitation skills, and Cathy handled the logistics for the workshop.

The Session

The session was held at a hotel near the airport and began promptly at 8 A.M. Eric introduced the agenda for the day and the rules for the workshop, including the workshop tickets. Figure 11–2 provides a perspective on the workshop.

In general, the workshop went very well, and all participants were able to have their input heard. Eric did a fine job of facilitating, but one awkward period occurred when Eric got into an argument with Cathy about priorities for a couple of features. (The team decided that for any future workshop, an outside facilitator would be brought in.) Eric led a brainstorming session on potential features for HOLIS, and the team used cumulative voting to decide on relative priorities. The results are shown in Table 11–1.

Analysis of Results

The results of the process turned out as expected, except for two significant items.

1. "Built-in security" appeared very high on the priority list. This feature had been mentioned in previous interviews but had not made it to the top of anyone's priority list. After a quick offline review, Cathy noted that built-in security, such as the ability to flash lights, an

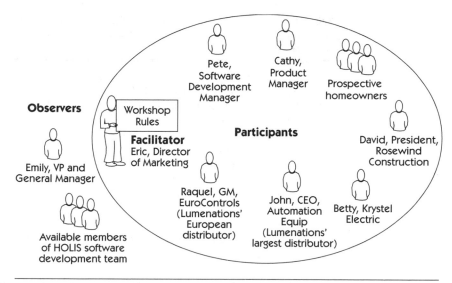

Figure 11–2 HOLIS 2000 requirements workshop structure

optional horn, and optional emergency call-out system, was apparently not offered by any competitive system. The distributors commented that although they were surprised by this input, they felt that it *would* be a competitive differentiation and agreed that this should be a high-priority feature. Krys and David agreed. Based on this conclusion, marketing decided to include this functionality and to position it as a unique, competitive differentiator in the marketplace. This became one of the *defining features* for HOLIS.

2. In addition, feature 25, "Internationalized user interface" did not get a lot of votes. (This seemed to make sense to the team, because the U.S.-based homeowners could not have cared less about how well the product sold in Europe!) The distributor, however, stated flatly that if the product was not internationalized at version 1.0, it would *not* be introduced in Europe. The team noted this position and agreed to explore the level of effort necessary to achieve internationalization in the 1.0 release.[1]

---

1. This issue demonstrates one of the problems with cumulative voting. Not all stakeholders are created equal. Failure to achieve internationalization, which had not been on the "radar screens" of the team prior to the workshop, would have been a strategic requirements misstep of significant proportions.

Table 11–1   Features from HOLIS workshop, sorted by priority

ID	Features	Votes
23	Custom lighting scenes	121
16	Automatic timing settings for lights, etc.	107
4	Built-in security features, e.g., lights, alarms, and bells	105
6	100% reliability	90
8	Easy to program, non-PC control unit	88
1	Easy to program control stations	77
5	Vacation settings	77
13	Any light can be dimmed	74
9	Uses my own PC for programming	73
14	Entertain feature	66
20	Close garage doors	66
19	Automatically turn on closet lights when door opened	55
3	Interface to home security system	52
2	Easy to install	50
18	Turn on lights automatically when someone approaches a door	50
7	Instant lighting on/off	44
11	Can drive drapes, shades, pumps, and motors	44
15	Control lighting, etc., via phone	44
10	Interfaces to home automation system	43
22	Gradual mode: slowly increase/decrease illumination	34
26	Master control stations	31
12	Easily expanded when remodeling	25
25	Internationalized user interface	24
21	Interface to audio/video system	23
24	Restore after power fail	23
17	Controls HVAC	22
28	Voice activation	7
27	Web site–user presentation	4

Chapter 12

STORYBOARDING

Key Points

- The purpose of storyboarding is to elicit early "Yes, But" reactions.
- Storyboards can be passive, active, or interactive.
- Storyboards identify the players, explain what happens to them, and describe how it happens.
- Make the storyboard sketchy, easy to modify, and unshippable.
- Storyboard early and often on every project with new or innovative content.

Perhaps no elicitation technique has been subject to as many interpretations as has "storyboarding." Nonetheless, most of these interpretations agree that the purpose of storyboarding is to gain an early reaction from the users on the concepts proposed for the application. In so doing, storyboards offer one of the most effective techniques for addressing the "Yes, But" syndrome. With storyboarding, the user's reaction can be observed very early in the lifecycle, well before concepts are committed to code and, in many cases, even before detailed specifications are developed. Human factors experts have told us for years that the power of storyboards should not be underestimated. Indeed, the movie industry has used the technique since the first flickers on the silver screen.

Effective storyboarding applies tools that are both inexpensive and easy to work with. Storyboarding

- Is extremely inexpensive
- Is user friendly, informal, and interactive
- Provides an early review of the user interfaces of the system
- Is easy to create and easy to modify

Storyboards are also a powerful way to ease the "blank-page syndrome." When the users do not know what they want, even a poor storyboard is likely to elicit a response of "No, that's not what we meant, it's more like the following," and the game is on.

Storyboards can be used to speed the conceptual development of many different facets of an application. Storyboards can be used to understand data visualization, to define and understand business rules that will be implemented in a new business application, to define algorithms and other mathematical constructs that are to be executed inside an embedded system, or to demonstrate reports and other hardcopy outputs for early review. Indeed, storyboards can and should be used for virtually any type of application in which gaining the user's reaction early will be a key success factor.

Types of Storyboards

Basically, a storyboard can be anything the team wants it to be, and the team should feel free to use its imagination to think of ways to storyboard a specific application. Storyboards can be categorized into three types, depending on the mode of interaction with the user: passive, active, or interactive.

- *Passive storyboards* tell a story to the user. They can consist of sketches, pictures, screen shots, PowerPoint presentations, or sample outputs. In a passive storyboard, the analyst plays the role of the system and simply walks the user through the storyboard, with a "When you do this, this happens" explanation.
- *Active storyboards* try to make the user see "a movie that hasn't been produced yet." Active storyboards are animated or automated, perhaps by an automatically sequencing slide presentation or an animation tool or even a movie. Active storyboards provide an automated description of the way the system behaves in a typical usage or operational scenario.
- *Interactive storyboards* let the user experience the system in as realistic a manner as practical. They require participation by the user in order to execute. Interactive storyboards can be simulations or mock-ups or can be advanced to the point of throwaway code. An advanced, interactive storyboard built out of throwaway code can be very close to a throwaway prototype (discussed in a later chapter).

As Figure 12–1 shows, these three storyboarding techniques offer a continuum of possibilities ranging from sample outputs to live interactive demos.

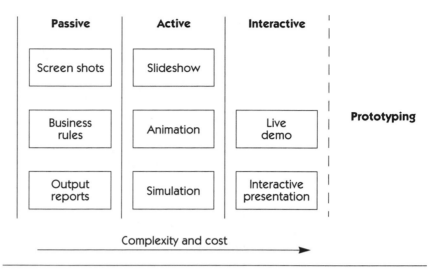

Figure 12–1 Storyboarding continuum

Indeed, the boundary between advanced storyboards and early product prototypes is a fuzzy one.

The choice of storyboarding technique will vary, based on the complexity of the system and the risk of the team's misunderstanding of what the system needs to do. An unprecedented and innovative system that has a soft and fuzzy definition may even require multiple storyboards, moving from passive to interactive as the team's understanding of the system improves.

What Storyboards Do

Disney's *Snow White and the Seven Dwarfs*, the first animated movie ever produced, used storyboards, and they are routinely used as an integral part of the creative process in movies and cartoons. Virtually all movies, animated features, and cartoons start out with storyboards. They represent the raw creative input that is used to develop the characters and the story line.

In software, storyboards are used most often to work through the details of the human-to-machine interface. In this area, generally one of high votality, each user is likely to have a different opinion of how the interface should work. Storyboards for user-based systems deal with the three essential elements of any activity:

1. Who the players are
2. What happens to them
3. How it happens

The *who* element defines the players, or the users of the system. In a software system, as we discussed earlier, the "who" are such players as users, other systems, or devices—the actors that interact with the solution system we are constructing. For users, the interaction is typically described via user input screens or data entry forms, outputs such as data or reports, or other types of input and output devices, such as buttons, switches, displays, and monitors. For devices and systems, interaction will be performed via a software or hardware interface, such as a communication protocol or motor controller drive signal.

The *what* element represents the behavior of the users as they interact with the system or, alternatively, the behavior of the system as it interacts with the user. The *how* element represents the states that the player or the system assumes during the interaction.

For example, we did a storyboard for an automated-vehicle amusement park ride.

- The *who* represented the guests who ride on the vehicle.
- The *what* represented the behavior of the vehicle as it provided various events for the guests.
- The *how* provided further descriptions of how this interaction happens—events, state transitions—and described both the guest states (surprised, scared) and the vehicle states (accelerating, braking, unloading).

Tools and Techniques for Storyboarding

Storyboards can be as varied as the imaginations of the team members will allow.

The tools and techniques for storyboarding can be as varied as the team members' and the system users' imaginations will allow. Passive-storyboarding constructs have been made out of tools as simple as paper and pencil or Post-It notes. More advanced passive storyboards can be built with presentation managers such as PowerPoint or Harvard Business Graphics. Passive and active user interactive storyboards have been built with HyperCard, SuperCard, and various packages that allow fast development of user screens and output reports. Interactive storyboards can be built with a variety of specialty software packages for interactive prototyping, such as Dan Bricklin's Demo It. Tools such as Macromedia's Director and Cinemation from Vividus Corp. can be used to create more complex animations and simulations.

In a simpler example, at RELA, Inc., one team member also dabbled in cartooning on the side. At the concept stage of a project, he would simply sketch a half dozen or so simple cartoons that showed the product in its typical use or various aspects of the product's interface. This was a quick and inexpensive way to gain a reaction from the potential users. Also, the cartoonlike nature of the output avoided some of the potential of problems of storyboarding, as we'll see later. Unfortunately, no other cartoonists were around when the designer left the company, leaving us to find alternative storyboarding techniques!

In our current efforts, which are focused mostly on ISV applications, we get along quite nicely by using only PowerPoint or other common desktop presentation managers, in combination with sample screen shots built by the same tools used to build the GUIs in the application. Interestingly, the greatest breakthrough in storyboarding technique may well have been the simple addition of the animation capability to PowerPoint. Suddenly, our ability to express dynamics and interactivity increased by an order of magnitude.

Tips for Storyboarding

Storyboarding is a powerful technique designed to gain early user feedback, using inexpensive tools. As such, storyboards are particularly effective at addressing the "Yes, But" syndrome. They also help address the "Undiscovered Ruins" syndrome by eliciting immediate user feedback as to what the system "doesn't appear to do." But as with any technique, certain caveats apply. Here are some tips to keep in mind as you practice your storyboarding technique.

- *Don't invest too much in a storyboard.* Customers will be intimidated from making changes if it looks like a real work product or they think they might insult you, a particularly difficult problem in some cultures. It's OK to keep the storyboard clunky and sketchy, even crude. (See the storyboarding story at the end of this chapter.)
- *If you don't change anything, you don't learn anything.* Make the storyboard easy to modify. You should be able to modify a storyboard in a few hours.

- *Don't make the storyboard too good.* If you do, the customers will want to "ship it." (In one real-world project, we suffered for years supporting an Excel/VB product that was never intended to be more than a storyboard.) Keep the storyboard sketchy; use tools and techniques that have no danger of making it into the field, especially for storyboards that are coded. (*Hint*: If the application is to be implemented in Java, write the storyboard in VB.)
- *Whenever possible, make the storyboard interactive.* The customer's experience of use will generate more feedback and will elicit more new requirements than a passive storyboard will.

Summary

In this chapter, we learned about a very simple and inexpensive technique for requirements elicitation. In a sense, a storyboard is anything you can build quickly and inexpensively that will elicit a "Yes, But" reaction from the user.

We can say with confidence that there has never been a time when we didn't learn a lot from a storyboard, and there has never been a case in which we left the storyboarding exercise with exactly the same understanding with which we entered it. So our advice to the development team is to

- Storyboard early.
- Storyboard often.
- Storyboard on every project that has new or innovative content.

By so doing, you will get the "Yes, Buts" out early, which in turn will help you build systems that do a better job of meeting the user's real needs. And perhaps you will do so more quickly and more economically than you have ever done before!

A Storyboarding Story

(Some facts have been changed to protect the innocent and the guilty in this very nearly true story.) This story occurred during the development of a complex electromechanical device for a hospital pharmacy. The customer was a Fortune 1,000 manufacturer; the vendor, our company, had been hired to develop this new, complex electromechanical optical and fluidics-handling system. The project was in trouble.

One day, the vendor's project manager's boss (we'll just call him "author") received the following call from the customer's upper management (a *Senior* VP, "Mr. Big," a powerful individual whom we had never before had the pleasure of meeting

Mr. Big: *Author, how goes our favorite project?*

Author: *Not particularly well.*

Mr. Big: *That's what I hear. Hey, no problem is so big it can't be solved. Just bring your entire team out for a meeting. How's Wednesday?*

Author: (hastily scrapping every appointment for the entire team for Wednesday) *Wednesday is perfect.*

Mr. Big: *Great. Come on out and bring your entire team. Hey, don't worry about the travel costs. We'll cover that. Heck, just buy those tickets "one way."*

Author.   (gulp) *Thanks, I think. We'll see you Wednesday.*

On the appointed day, we entered a large conference room with the customer's project team all seated at the far end. The team had clearly been at the meeting for some time. (Question: Why did the team feel the need to meet before the real meeting started?) Author, this not being his first such event, walked to the other end of the room and sat down next to Mr. Big (theory being that it's going to be difficult for Mr. Big to scream at him if he is sitting right next to him; also, if he hits Author, there's the chance to win a lawsuit and recover lost project profits!).

After a short discussion, Author noted that among many significant problems troubling the project, the problem of "lack of requirements convergence" is causing delays and cost overruns. Mr. Big said, "*Give me an example.*" Author gave an *excellent* example. The customer team members immediately started arguing among themselves, perhaps demonstrating that this was indeed a problem. Subcontractor breathed small sigh of relief. Mr. Big watched the team for a moment and then said, "*Very funny. Give me another example.*" Author's team pulled out five color renderings, each quite professionally done, of the proposed front panel and made the case that "*we presented all these design options weeks ago, and we can't get convergence on a design, and we are well into the necessary tooling lead times.*" Mr. Big said, "This can't be so difficult. "*Team, pick one.*" The customer team members then fell out among themselves again. The day passed in this fashion. There was no convergence. There was little hope.

The next morning, Author was asked to meet for an early breakfast with a project team member ("Team Member"). Team Member, also a seamstress, pulled out a pile of felt, shearing scissors, and colored markers and said "*I'd like to facilitate the user interface portion of the meeting, using these tools.*"

Author: "*Don't be silly; no way that would work. It will look silly and unprofessional.*"

Team Member: "*I understand, but how effective were you yesterday?*"

Author, being politically correct, did not speak the first word that comes to mind. The second word was "*OK.*"

The next day, the tone in the room was much different. The customer's team was again there early but this time was silent and morose rather than intemperate and excitable. (*Analysis: They now know they were as helpless as we were. They had been planning to kill us but now knew that we are all doomed.*)

To start the meeting, Team Member put a 3' by 5' (1 x 2 m) piece of felt on the wall, generating amusement but not disinterest on the part of the customer.

Team Member put large felt cutouts for power switch and various therapy-mode buttons on the front panel and said "*How would this design work?*"

Customer looked at the wall, and said "It won't, but why don't you move the emergency stop to the back?"

Team Member said: "*Here, why don't you do it,*" and gave the scissors to the customer.

The customer took the scissors, and Team Member retired to the back of the room. Customer proceeded to do an interactive design session with felt and scissors. One hour later, customer looked at the wall, and said, "*Good enough; build it.*"

Let's see if we can discover the moral to this story with a little reader Q&A.

Question: Why did the fuzzy felt work when the professional renderings did not?

Answers: There are two reasons.

- *Interactability:* What could the customer *do* with five drawings, of which it liked only a portion of each?
- *Usability:* How intimidating can it be to cut out a big piece of felt?

The customer, who had the domain but not necessarily the design, expertise, designed an adequate solution to its own problem.

We took the felt home with us and stuck it on the wall as a constant reminder of what we had learned. The user interface, although probably less than optimum, never changed again and was quite adequate for the intended purpose. But no, the project was not a huge success for the vendor, although the product did eventually go to market and achieve success. As we said before, that was only one of the problems on this particular project.

- **Lesson 1**: Understanding user needs is a soft and fuzzy problem. Use soft and fuzzy tools—storyboards and felt, if necessary—to address it.
- **Lesson 2**: Technology is difficult. Think twice before you start a medical device outsourcing business.

Chapter 13

APPLYING USE CASES

Key Points

- Use cases, like storyboards, identify the who, what, and how of system behavior.
- Use cases describe the interactions between a user and a system, focusing on what the system "does" for the user.
- The use-case model describes the totality of the system's functional behavior.

In Chapter 12, we described storyboarding and discussed how you can use storyboards to show the *who*, *what*, and *how* of system and user behavior. Use cases are another technique for expressing that behavior. We briefly introduced this technique in Chapters 2 and 5, where we used it to help us model the behavior of a business.

In this chapter, we'll develop the use-case technique further, describing how we can use it to understand the behavior of the system we are going to develop, as opposed to understanding the behavior of the business the system is going to operate within. In other words, we'll use use cases as an elicitation technique to understand the needed behavior of the application we are going to develop to solve a user's problem. Use cases are such an important technique for capturing and specifying system requirements that we'll be developing them further in Team Skill 5, Refining the System Definition, and Team Skill 6, Building the Right System.

The use-case technique is integral to the software methodology Object-Oriented Software Engineering, as described in the book *Object-Oriented Software Engineering, A Use Case Driven Approach* (Jacobson et al. 1992). This method for the analysis and design of complex systems is "use case driven," a way of describing a system's behavior from the perspective of how the various users interact with the system to accomplish their objectives. This user-centric approach provides an opportunity to explore system behaviors with early user involvement.

Also, as we mentioned earlier, use cases serve as the UML representation for the requirements of a system. In addition to capturing the requirements for the system, the use cases developed in the elicitation process will be of even further value during the analysis and design activities. Indeed, the use-case method is powerful throughout the software lifecycle, as the use cases can also play a significant role in the testing process. As later chapters develop the use-case technique more fully, for now we need understand only how we can apply use cases to capture the initial requirements for the system.

We'll start with a slightly more formal definition than we provided earlier.

> *A use case describes a sequence of actions a system performs that yields a result of value to a particular actor.*

In other words, use cases describe the interactions between a user and a system, and they focus on what the system "does" for the user. In addition, as the actions are described in a sequence, it's easy to "follow the action" and to gain an understanding of what the system does for the user. In the UML, the use case is represented by a simple oval icon that contains the name of the use case.

Use case

In requirements elicitation, use cases can elicit and capture system requirements. Each use case describes a series of events in which a particular actor, such as "Jenny the Model," interacts with a system, such as the "Ad Lib Modeling Agency Client Scheduling System," to achieve a result of value to Jenny, such as downloading directions to the next modeling assignment.

Building the Use-Case Model

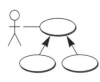

The *use-case model* for a system consists of all of the actors of the system and all of the various use cases by which the actors interact with the system, thereby describing the totality of the functional behavior of the system. The use-case model also shows relationships among use cases, which furthers our understanding of the system.

The first step in use-case modeling is to create a system diagram that describes the system boundaries and identifies the actors of the system. This nicely parallels steps 3 and 4 of the five steps in problem analysis, wherein we identified the stakeholders of the system and defined the system boundaries. We also know from Chapters 4, 5, and 6 how to identify the actors that will interact with the system.

For example, in a warehouse management system (Jacobson et al. 1992), the system boundary might appear as in Figure 13–1.

You can see that the system is used by a number of users, each of whom interacts with the system to achieve a specific operational objective.

Further analysis of the system determines that certain threads of system behavior are necessary to support the user's needs. These threads are the use cases, or the specific sequences by which the users interact with the system to accomplish a specific objective. Examples of use cases for this system could include

- Manual distribution of items within a warehouse
- Insertion of a new item in a warehouse
- Check items in a warehouse

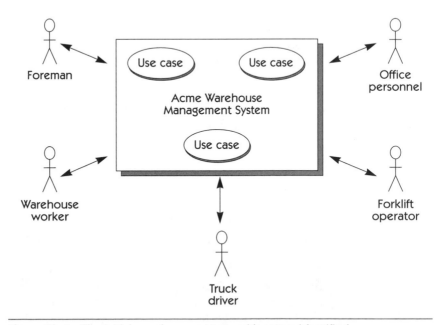

Figure 13–1   The initial warehouse system, with actors identified

Applying Use Cases to Requirements Elicitation

The notion of use cases can be described very simply to a prospective user of a system. Use cases are written in the user's natural language. They are easy to describe and to document. This provides a simple, structured format around which the development team and the user can work together to describe the behavior of an existing system or to define the behavior of a new system. And, of course, each individual user will naturally focus on the system capabilities needed in order to do the job better. If, in addition, behavior is fully explored with all potential users, the team has gone a long way toward the objective of complete understanding of desired system behavior. There should be few *undiscovered functionality ruins* left at the end of the process.

Also, to the extent that the use-case method explores the user interfaces directly, early feedback can be obtained on this important and volatile aspect of system specification and design.

However, we must also understand that the users of the system represent only one class of stakeholders, albeit an important class, and that we may need to apply other elicitation techniques to gather the requirements from other stakeholders, such as nonuser customers, management, subcontractors, and so on. In addition, use cases are not as helpful in identifying the nonfunctional aspects of the system requirements, such as the requirements for usability, reliability, performance, and the like. We'll rely on other techniques to address these issues.

After all of the use cases, actors, and objects in the system have been identified, the next step is to further refine the detailed functional behavior of each use case. These use-case specifications consist of textual and graphical descriptions of the use case, written from the point of view of the user.

The use-case specifications can be thought of as a container that describes a series of related events, which in turn can be used to imply other requirements that will be developed further at a later time. Thus, a use case specification might include the step "The maintenance technician enters his or her first name (16 characters maximum), last name, and so on."

As use cases define the user/system interaction, it may be an appropriate time to define, at least in concept, the screens, displays, front panels, and so on that the user interacts with. If a windowing system is used to present the information, a high-level graphical depiction of the data to be displayed may be appropriate; details of formal graphical user interface (GUI) design, such

---

Use Case: Redistribution of Items within a Warehouse

1. The foreman gives a command for redistribution with a warehouse.
2. The window in Figure xxx is presented to the foreman.
3. The items can be ordered a number of ways. Order is selected with the Order menu selection:

   Alphabetical order

   Index order

   Storing Order

4. In the "From place" table, we might choose to view either all Places within the current warehouse or, if we have selected an item, the places where that item exists.

Figure 13–2   Use-case specification for manual distribution between warehouses

as data definitions, colors, and fonts) should be left to later phases. Figure 13–2 shows portions of an example use-case specification.

Case Study: The Use Cases for HOLIS

Impressed by the power of use cases, the HOLIS development team decided to use this technique to describe the high-level system functionality of HOLIS. In order to do so, the team held a brainstorming session to define the significant use cases to be developed further in later activities. This "use-case model survey" identified 20 use cases to be elaborated in later activities, some of which are as follows.

Name	Description	Actor(s)
Create Custom Lighting Scene	Resident creates a custom lighting scene	Resident, Lights
Initiate Emergency	Resident initiates emergency action	Resident
Control Light	Resident turns light(s) on or off or sets desired dim effect	Resident, Lights
Program Switch	Change or set the actions for a particular button/switch	Homeowner/programmer

Name	Description	Actor(s)
Remote Programming	Lumenations service provider does remote programming based on request from resident	Lumenations Services
Go On Vacation	Homeowner sets vacation setting for extended away period	Homeowner/programmer
Set Timing Sequence	Homeowner programs time-based automated lighting sequence	Homeowner/programmer

Summary

Use cases provide a structured and reasonably formal notation for capturing a very important subset of the requirements information: how the system interacts with the user to deliver its functionality. In many applications, this subset represents the majority of the workload, so use cases can be applied to express the majority of the requirements for the system. Each identified use cases defines the needed behaviors of the system from the perspective of a particular class of user. As such, the technique is very useful in eliciting user needs and helps the development team represent these needs in a manner that is readily understandable by the user.

Also, as the use cases can be used later in the design and the testing processes, they provide a consistent representation and a consistent thread through the requirements, analysis, design, and testing activities. In this way, the technique builds early, reusable project assets, which helps improve the overall efficiency of the software development process. In addition, with the consistency of representation and the support provided within the UML and various application development tools, use cases can help in automating many elements of the requirements management activity. For these reasons, use cases are such an important notion that we will apply them from this point forward as an integral part of the team's requirements management activities.

Chapter 14

ROLE PLAYING

Key Points

- Role playing allows the development team to experience the user's world from the user's perspective.
- A scripted walkthrough may replace role playing in some situations, with the script becoming a live storyboard.
- Class-Responsibility-Collaboration (CRC) cards, often used in object-oriented analysis, are a derivative of role playing.

So far in Team Skill 2, we have discussed a variety of techniques to understand the needs of the stakeholder with respect to a new system we are building. We've *talked* one-on-one about *It* (interviewing); we've *discussed It* in a group format (workshops); we've *presented* our ideas about *It* (storyboard); and we've thought about how actors *interact* with *It* (use cases). These are all good things, and they add to the fabric of our understanding. But, we must also admit, we haven't *experienced It*.

In this chapter, we discuss role playing, which allows the development team to *experience* the user's world directly by playing the role of the user. The concept behind role playing is quite simple: Although it's true that observing and asking questions does aid understanding, *it is also naive to assume that, through observation only, the developer/analyst can gain a true, in-depth understanding of the problem being solved or, thereby, a clear understanding of the requirements of a system that would address the problem.*

This is one of the primary causes of the "Yes, But" problem. As sociology teaches us, we all see the world though our unique conceptual filters. Our life experiences and cultural biases are impossible to separate from the observations we make. For example, we can observe another culture partaking in a ritualistic ceremony as often as we want, but it will likely be impossible for us to *understand* what it means to them! What does this mean to our search for requirements understanding?

- We must understand that many users cannot articulate the procedures they follow or the needs that must be addressed. It is often not their job to do so, and they have never been asked to do so before. Also, it is more difficult than it looks! For example, try to describe the procedure by which you tie your shoe.
- Many users do not have the freedom to admit that they do not follow prescribed procedures; therefore, what they tell you may or may not be what they actually do.
- Individual users have patterns of work activity that are deeply ingrained and apply workarounds or unique paths of implementation that may mask real problems from the observer.
- It is impossible for any developer to anticipate every question that must be asked or for any user to know what questions the developer should be asking.

To address these particular causes, the simple act of "role playing" can be extremely effective. It is also cheap and usually quite quick. An hour or a half-day will typically do the trick.

How to Role Play

In the simplest form of role playing, the developer, the analyst, and, potentially, every member of the development team simply take the place of the user and execute the customer's work activity. For, example, in the case of the sales order entry problem in Team Skill 1, we became aware of the fact that inaccurate sales orders were a leading cost of scrap and thereby created profitability problems. When we look at the existing sales order process, we expect to find lots of different steps and sources for error. There are at least two ways to get at the root causes.

1. Use the fishbone technique that we described, together with user interviews, and analyze sales orders that were known to have errors. Quantify the errors by type, and address the most grievous contributors in the design of a new system. This would provide a quantitative understanding for the problem and probably be quite effective.

Still, it doesn't give you a qualitative "feel" for the problem, one that could, perhaps, change both your perception and your solution strategy. In order to get that, there may be a simpler and more efficient way to truly understand the problem.

2. The developer/analyst can experience the problems and inaccuracies inherent in the existing sales order entry system by simply *sitting down and entering a few sales orders.* The experience gained in 1 hour will forever change the team's understanding of the problem.

We can say from experience that the insights gained in role playing may even stay with the developer for a lifetime. Our personal world view has been changed by many such experiences, including the simple roles of "welding a complex part the way the robot is supposed to," "mixing a pharmaceutical compound in a laminar flow hood," "identifying a television commercial with only four compressed screen shots and a compressed audio track," "using immature requirements management tool software," and many others. We learned something every time, and we developed a much greater empathy for the user than we had before!

Try it!

Techniques Similar to Role Playing

Of course, role playing doesn't work in every situation. In many cases, the user role is minimal, and the problem to be solved is algorithmically, rather than functionally, intense. And, in many cases, it simply isn't practical. We wouldn't be the first to volunteer for the role of "patient" in an electrosurgery scenario or of "nuclear power plant operator on the night shift" or "747 pilot." In these cases, other techniques get us close to the user experience without having to "bleed" for the part.

Scripted Walkthroughs

A scripted walkthrough is a "play" on paper.

In the *scripted walkthrough*, each participant follows a script that defines a specific role in the "play." The walkthrough will demonstrate any misunderstandings in the roles, lack of information available to an actor or a subsystem, or lack of a specific behavior needed for the actors to succeed in their endeavor.

For example, we once built a scripted walkthrough that showed how students and teachers would interact with an automated test-scoring device used in the classroom. We used a prototype of the device and had team members and customer representatives play the roles of students and teacher. The walkthrough contained multiple scenes, such as "students scoring their own tests"

and "teacher scoring a large batch of tests during classroom time." The scripted walkthrough was very useful way to get a feel for the classroom environment, and the team learned a few new things in the process the experience. It was also fun.

One of the advantages of the scripted walkthrough is that the script can be modified and rerun as many times as necessary until the actors get it right. The script can also be reused to educate new team members. It may be modified and reused when the behavior of the system needs to be changed. In a sense, the script becomes the live storyboard for the project.

CRC (Class-Responsibility-Collaboration) Cards

A derivative of role playing is often applied as part of an object-oriented analysis effort. In this special case of a role play, each participant is given a set of index cards describing the class, or object; the responsibilities, or behavior; and collaborations, or who the object communicates with, of each entity being modeled. These collaborations may simply represent entities from the problem domain, such as users, push buttons, lights, and elevator cars, or objects that live in the solution domain, such as HallButton Indicator Lights, MDI Window, and ElevatorCar.

When an initiator actor starts a specific behavior, all participants follow the behaviors defined on their cards. When the process breaks down due to a lack of information or when one entity needs to talk to another and the collaboration is not defined, the cards can be modified and the roles run again.

For example, in the HOLIS case study, there is a time when the team will need to understand the interactions among the three subsystems in order to determine how the system cooperates to achieve the overall objective and to understand what derived requirements are created. One way to do this would be in a CRC-like role play. A team member would take the role of a subsystem, or actor, and then the team would walk through a use case, or scenario. Here's how one use case might be played out:

John (Control Switch): My homeowner just pressed a button that controls a light bank. He's still depressing the switch. I sent Bob a message just as soon as the switch was depressed, and I'm going to send Bob a message every second that the switch is pressed.

Bob (Central Control Unit):	When I received the first message, I changed the state of the output from Off to On. When I receive the second message, it becomes obvious that the homeowner is dimming a light bank, so for each message received, I'm going to change the brightness by 10 percent. By the way, Bob, don't forget to tell me which button is depressed.
Mike (Light):	I'm hardwired to the dimmer output. I'm feeling dimmer as we speak.

Note: In user needs elicitation, the CRC process is focused on external behaviors that are apparent to the actors, but this technique can also be used for designing object-oriented software systems. In this exercise, the focus is on understanding the internal workings of the software, not on the interaction with the external environment. However, even in this case, the technique will often cause the discovery of wrong or missing requirements for the system.

You may have also noticed an interesting side effect: The players invariably find out that there are weaknesses or deficiencies in the script, and correcting them usually results in improved understanding of the system.

Summary

Role playing is an excellent technique, although we don't see it used very often or not often enough. Why? The reasons are many. First, there is the discomfort factor. It's not particularly ego reinforcing to botch a simple sales order while our customer or a sales order entry person watches. Also, there's the soft and fuzzy factor: Being forced to interact with real people instead of a keyboard gets us out of our comfort zone—after all, we went to compiler theory classes while our peers participated in drama!

However, there can be no doubt that, if we can just push ourselves that extra little bit, role playing is one of the most useful and inexpensive techniques available to assist in requirements discovery.

PROTOTYPING

Software prototypes, as early incarnations of a software system, demonstrate a portion of the functionality of a new system. Given what we've discussed so far, we expect that it's become obvious by now that prototyping can be very effective at uncovering user needs. Users can touch, feel, and interact with a prototype system in a way that none of the other techniques can provide. Indeed, prototyping can be extremely effective at addressing both the "Yes, But" syndrome ("That is not exactly what I meant)" and the "Undiscovered Ruins" syndrome ("Now that I see it, I have another requirement to add").

Types of Prototypes

Prototypes can be categorized in many ways. For example, Davis (1995a) categorizes prototypes as throwaway versus evolutionary versus operational, vertical versus horizontal, user interface versus algorithmic, and so on. The type of prototype you pick depends on the problem you are trying to solve by building the prototype.

For example, if your project risk is based primarily on the feasibility of the technology approach—it's simply never been done this way before and you are uncertain whether the applicable technology can achieve the performance or throughput goals—you may wish to develop an *architectural prototype* that primarily demonstrates the feasibility of the technology to be used. An architectural prototype can still be *throwaway* versus *evolutionary*. "Throwaway" implies that the purpose of the effort is solely to establish feasibility, and you will use whatever shortcuts, alternative technologies, simulations, or whatever to achieve your goals. When you have done so, you simply throw away the result, keeping only the knowledge learned in the exercise. "Evolutionary" implies that you have implemented the prototype on the same architecture as you intend to use in the final system, and you will be able to build the final system by evolving the prototype.

If your primary project risk area is the user interface, by contrast, you will want to develop a *requirements prototype*, using whatever technologies allow you to prototype the user interface most quickly. Figure 15–1 shows a decision tree that you can use to select the kind of prototype that makes the most sense for your project.

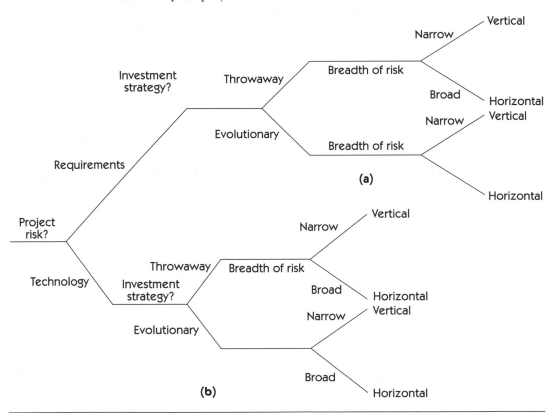

Figure 15–1 Decision tree for prototype selection: (a) requirements prototypes; (b) architectural prototypes

Requirements Prototypes

For purposes of requirements elicitation, we'll focus on the types of prototypes on the upper branch of this tree. We'll define a software requirements prototype as

a partial implementation of a software system, built to help developers, users, and customers better understand the requirements of the system.

For the purposes of requirements elicitation, we may often choose to build a "throwaway, horizontal, user interface" prototype. "Horizontal" implies that we will attempt to construct a wide range of the system's functionality; a vertical prototype, by contrast, constructs just a few requirements but does so in a quality manner. "User interface" implies that we will be constructing mostly the system's interface to its users rather than implementing the logic and algorithms that reside within the software or prototyping the interfaces to other devices or systems. As an elicitation tool, such a prototype serves its role in a number of ways.

- Built by the developer, it can be used to obtain customer confirmation that the developer understands the requirements.
- Built by the developer, it can be used as a catalyst to encourage the customer to think of yet more requirements.
- Built by the customer, it can help communicate requirements to the developer.

In all three cases, the goal is to construct the prototype in a manner that consumes the fewest resources. If it's too expensive to build, it might be more cost effective to just build the real system!

Many software prototypes tend to be requirements prototypes and are used primarily to capture aspects of the user interface of the system to be built. There are probably two reasons for this.

1. The emergence of a plethora of inexpensive, widely available tools that build user interfaces rapidly.
2. For user interaction–intensive systems, a prototyped user interface reveals many other requirements as well, such as what functions are provided to the user, when each function is available to the user, and what functions are missing to the user.

However, we need to be certain that the availability of these tools doesn't influence us to prototype the parts of the system that did not have the highest risk to begin with.

What to Prototype

How do we know what portion of the system we need to prototype? In a typical situation, our understanding of the user's needs will range from well understood and easy to verbalize to totally unknown (Figure 15–2).

Well-understood requirements may be obvious from the context of the application domain and the user's and team's experience with systems of that type. For example, if we are simply extending an existing system, it's clear what most of the new functionality needs to be. The well-known and well-understood requirements need not be prototyped unless they are necessary to help the users visualize the context of other user needs; building them will consume scarce resources, but since they are already well understood, little will be learned from seeing them.

The unknown requirements, however, are the "Undiscovered Ruins" that we are going to wish we knew later. Unfortunately, we can't really prototype those either, for if you could, they wouldn't be unknown! That leaves as the target for prototyping the "fuzzy" part in the middle. These requirements may be known or implied, but they are poorly defined and poorly understood.

Building the Prototype

The choice of technology used in building the prototype depends on further decisions on the right of the decision tree in Figure 15–1. For example, the choice for a throwaway GUI prototype is driven simply by whatever technology provides the fastest, cheapest way to implement the sample GUIs.

If an evolutionary prototype is selected, you must choose the implementation language and development environment that you will use in the production device. You will also have to invest a significant effort in designing the software architecture for the system, as well as apply whatever coding

Figure 15–2 Continuum of understanding user needs

standards or other software processes you will use to create the system. Otherwise, you will be attempting to evolve a system that is fundamentally flawed in one or more of these aspects. In that case, you may have created a throwaway prototype by accident! Or worse, the quality of the deployed system will be forever compromised by your well-intended requirements prototype.

Evaluating the Results

After the prototype is built, it should be exercised by its users in an environment that simulates as closely as possible the production environment in which the final system will be used. In this way, environmental and other external factors that affect the requirements for the device will also be obvious. Also, it will be important to have various types of users exercise the device, or the results may be biased.

The result of the prototyping process should be twofold.

1. Fuzzy needs become better understood.
2. Exercising the prototype inevitably elicits a "Yes, But" response from the user; therefore, previously unknown needs become known. Simply seeing a set of behaviors helps users understand other requirements that must be imposed on the system.

In any case, prototyping virtually *always* produces results. Therefore, you should typically prototype any new and innovative application. The trick is making sure that the return in requirements knowledge gained is worth the investment made. That's why we often want to prototype—or at least implement our earliest prototypes—in the quickest, cheapest techniques available. By limiting investment, we maximize return on investment in requirements knowledge gained.

Summary

Because software prototypes demonstrate a portion of the desired functionality of a new system, they can be effective tools that help refine the real requirements for the system. They are effective because users can *interact* with a prototype in their environment, which is as close to the real world as you can get without developing production software.

You should select your prototype technique based on the type of risk that is likely to be present in your system. Requirements prototypes are supposed to be inexpensive and easy to develop, and they can help you eliminate much of the requirements risk in your project.

On the continuum of investment possibilities, you should invest as little as possible in your prototype. The use of any of the prototyping techniques or, better, using a combination of a few prototyping techniques, has been shown to be extremely effective in helping project teams develop a much better understanding of the real needs of a software system.

Team Skill 2 Summary

Three "syndromes" increase the challenge of understanding the real needs of users and other stakeholders. The "Yes, But," "Undiscovered Ruins," and "User and the Developer" syndromes are metaphors to help us better understand the challenge ahead and provide a context for the elicitation techniques that we developed for understanding user needs.

But since teams are rarely given effective requirements specifications for the systems they are going to build, they have to go out and *get* the information they need to be successful. The term "requirements elicitation" describes this process, in which the team must play a more active role.

To help the team in this mission, a variety of techniques can be used to address these problems and better understand the real needs of users and other stakeholders:

- Interviewing and questionnaires
- Requirements workshop
- Brainstorming and idea reduction
- Storyboarding
- Use cases
- Role playing
- Prototyping

Although no one technique is perfect in every circumstance, each represents a proactive means of pushing knowledge of user needs forward and thereby converting "fuzzy" requirements to requirements that are "better known." Although all of these techniques work in certain circumstances, our favorite is the requirements workshop/brainstorming technique.

Team Skill 3

DEFINING THE SYSTEM

In Team Skill 1, we developed the skills that focus the team on analyzing the problem. In so doing, we came to fully understand the problem being solved before we invested any serious effort on the solution. We were focused fully on the problem domain.

In Team Skill 2, we described a set of techniques the team can use to understand user needs. These user needs live at the top of our requirements pyramid, representing the most critical information we must understand and driving everything that follows.

In Team Skill 3, we move from the problem space to the solution space, and we focus on *defining the system* that we can build to address our stakeholders' needs. As we move lower in the pyramid (see Figure 1), the amount of information increases. For example, a significant number of system features may be required to fulfill a single user need. We must also start to provide additional specificity to further define system behavior; thus, the amount of information we must manage increases.

The amount of information we must manage increases rapidly as we move lower on the pyramid.

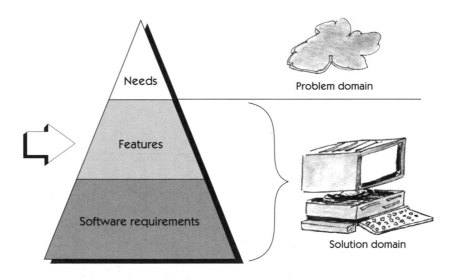

Figure 1 Features in the requirements pyramid

In addition, the team must now also be concerned with a variety of other issues that are unique to the solution space but that were of little concern in the problem domain. For example, if we are developing a software product for sale to the user, we must concern ourselves with packaging, installation, and licensing, each of which may be unique to the solution we are providing. If we are developing a system to address an in-house IS/IT need, we may need to concern ourselves with the requirements for deployment and maintenance, which were of little or no concern to a user not currently using such a system.

However, we must still remain at a fairly high level of abstraction, for if we sink too far into detail too quickly, we will not be able to see "the forest for the trees." In addition, it's important to pause for a second and to take the time to organize the requirements information ahead before moving into the software requirements section of the pyramid, in Team Skill 5, Refining the System Definition. For now, we'll cover organizing requirements information (Chapter 16), defining a vision (Chapter 17), and organizing *our team* to address the challenge of managing the requirements for the system (Chapter 18).

Chapter 16

ORGANIZING REQUIREMENTS INFORMATION

Key Points

- For nontrivial applications, requirements must be captured and recorded in a document database, model, or tool.
- Different types of projects require different requirements organization techniques.
- Complex systems entail requirements specification for each subsystem.

Requirements *must* be captured and documented. If you were the sole developer for a system on which you will also be the sole user and maintainer, you might consider designing and coding it immediately after identifying your needs. However, few system developments have such simplicity. More likely, developers and users are mutually exclusive, and stakeholders, users, developers, analysts, testers, architects, and other team members are involved. All parties must reach agreement about what system is being built.

Realities of budgets and schedules make it unlikely that all user needs are going to be satisfied in any particular release. Inevitable communication problems inherent in a multiple-person effort demand that a written document be produced to which all parties can agree and refer.

Documents that define the product to be built are typically called a requirements specification. The *requirements specification* for a system or application describes the external behavior of that system.

Note: For simplicity and to reflect historical usage, we'll use the term *document* generically in this section, but the requirements can be contained in a document, database, use-case model, requirements repository, or a combination of these elements. As we'll see in a later chapter, a "software requirements package" can be used to contain this information.

But requirements can rarely be defined in a single monolithic document, for a number of reasons.

- The system may be very complex.
- The customers' needs are being documented prior to documenting detailed requirements.
- The system may be a member of a family of related products.
- The system being constructed satisfies only a subset of all the requirements identified.
- Marketing and business goals need to be separated from the detailed product requirements.

In any of these cases, you will need to maintain multiple documents and, of course, to consider a number of special cases.

- One "parent" document defines requirements for the overall "system," including hardware, software, people, and procedures, and another defines requirements for just the software piece. Often, the former document is called a *system requirements specification*, whereas the latter is called a software requirements specification, or SRS for short.
- One document defines the features of the system in general terms, and another defines requirements in more specific terms. Often, the former document is called the *Vision document*, whereas the latter is called a *software requirements specification*.
- One document defines the full set of requirements for a family of products, and another defines requirements for just one specific application and for one specific release. The former document is often called a *product family requirements* document, or *product family Vision document*, whereas the latter is called a *software requirements specification* for a specific release of a specific application within the family.
- One document describes the overall business requirements and business environment in which the product will reside, and another defines the external behavior of the system being built. Often, the former document is called the *business requirements document*, or *marketing requirements document*, whereas the latter is called a *software requirements specification*.

The following sections describe what to do in each case. Any or all of these cases can be combined; for example, one document could contain the full set of requirements from which selected subsets are used for specific releases, as well as all business requirements.

Organizing Requirements of Complex Hardware and Software Systems

Although this book focuses primarily on software requirements, it's important to recognize that they are only one subset of the requirements management process in most system development efforts. As we described in Chapter 6, some systems are sufficiently complex that the only reasonable way to visualize and to build them is as *a system of subsystems*, which in turn are visualized as systems of subsystems, and so on, as shown in Figure 16–1. In an extreme case, such as an aircraft carrier, the system may be composed of hundreds of subsystems, each in turn having hardware and software components.

In these cases, a system-level requirements specification is created that describes the external behavior of the system, such as fuel capacity, rate of climb, or altitude ceiling, without knowledge of or reference to any of its subsystems. As we described in Chapter 6, once the requirements for the system are agreed on, a systems engineering activity is performed. *Systems engineering* refines a system into subsystems, describing the detailed interfaces among the subsystems, and allocating each of the system-level requirements to one or more subsystems. The resulting system architecture describes this partitioning and the interfaces among the systems.

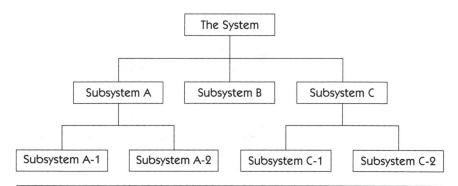

Figure 16–1   A system of systems

The system design process itself creates new classes of requirements.

Next, a requirements specification is developed for each subsystem. These specifications should describe the external behavior of the subsystem completely, without reference to any of its subsystems. This process causes a new class of requirements, derived requirements, to emerge. This type of requirement no longer describes the external behavior of the *system* except in the aggregate but instead describes the *exterior behavior* of the new subsystem. Thus, the process of system design creates new requirements for the subsystems of which the system is composed. In particular, the interfaces among these subsystems become key requirements: essentially, a contract between one subsystem and another, or a *promise* to perform as agreed to.

Once these requirements are agreed on, system design is performed again, if necessary, by breaking down each of the subsystems into its subsystems and developing requirements specifications for each. The result is a hierarchy of specifications, as shown in Figure 16–2.

At every level, requirements from the previous level are allocated to the appropriate lower-level specifications. For example, the fuel capacity requirement is allocated to the fuel control subsystem and to the fuel storage subsystem, and new requirements are discovered and defined as appropriate.

As seen in Figure 16–3, specifications that are themselves refined into additional subsystem specifications are termed system requirements specifications, or *system-level requirements specifications*. The lowest-level specifi-

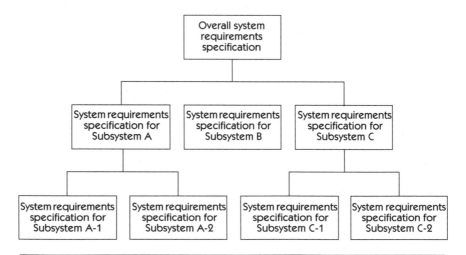

Figure 16–2   Hierarchy of specifications resulting from system design

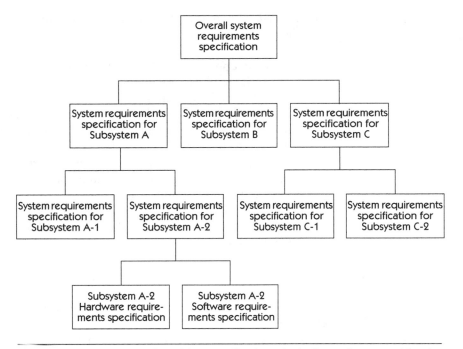

Figure 16–3   Hierarchy of resulting specifications, including software and hardware levels

cations, that is, those that are not further decomposed, usually correspond to software-only or hardware-only subsystems and are termed software requirements specifications or hardware requirements specifications, respectively. Further, any of the requirements specifications in Figure 16–3 may need to undergo an evolutionary process as details become better understood.

Organizing Requirements for Product Families

Many industries build sets of closely related products that have much functionality in common but with each containing some unique features. Such product families might be inventory control systems, telephone answering machines, burglar alarm systems, and so on.

For example, suppose that you are building a set of software products, each with some shared functionality, but that may need to share data or otherwise communicate with one another when in use. In such a case, you might consider the following approach:

- Develop a product-family *Vision document* that describes the ways in which the products are intended to work together and the other features that could be shared.
- To better understand the shared-usage model, you might also develop a set of *use cases* showing how the users will interact with various applications running together.
- Develop a *common software requirements specification* that defines the specific requirements for shared functionality, such as menu structures and communication protocols.
- For each product in the family, develop a *Vision document, software requirements specification*, and a *use-case model* that defines its specific functionality.

The resultant organization is shown in Figure 16–4.

The requirements specifications for the individual members may contain references—*links or "traced from"*—to the product-family documents or may reproduce all of the requirements from that document. The advantage of the former approach is that changes to requirements belonging to all family members can be made in just one place. However, you may need to use a

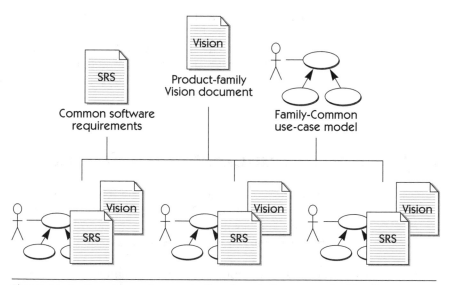

Figure 16–4 Requirements organization for a software product family

requirements tool to manage these dependencies, or it will be necessary to manually examine each specific member requirements document each time the parent document is changed.

On "Future" Requirements

Few development efforts have the luxury of either a stable set of requirements or being able to build a system that satisfies all known requirements. During any process of requirements elicitation, requirements will arise that are deemed inappropriate for the next release of the product being constructed.

It may not be appropriate to include such requirements in the requirements specifications; we cannot afford to create any confusion about what requirements are and are not to be implemented. On the other hand, it's inappropriate to discard them, because they represent value-added work products, and we will want to harvest requirements from them for future releases. More important, the system designers may well have designed the system differently had they know that future requirements of a certain type might be likely. The best thing is to record both types of requirements somewhere in the document but to *clearly identify those requirements that are planned for the current release*.

Business and Marketing Requirements versus Product Requirements

Planning for a new product does not occur in a technical world devoid of business considerations. Trade-offs must be made among market windows, target markets, product packaging, distribution channels, functionality, marketing costs, resource availability, margins, ability to amortize over large numbers of copies sold, and so on.

These considerations should be documented, but they do not belong in the requirements specifications. Some organizations use a *marketing requirements document* (MRD) to facilitate communication among management, marketing, and developers and to assist in making intelligent business decisions, including the all-important "go, no-go" decision. The MRD also provides customers and developers with early verification of communication, to foster understanding of the product in its most general terms, and to establish the general scope of the product. The MRD should answer the following questions:

- Who is the customer?
- Who is the user?
- What markets do we intend to sell to?
- How are these markets segmented?
- Are the requirements of the users in these segments different?
- What classes of users exist?
- What need does the product satisfy?
- What kind of product is it?
- What is the product's key benefits; why should someone buy it?
- Who is the competition?
- What differentiates the product from the competition?
- In what environment will the system be used?
- What will the development cost be?
- At what price do you want to sell the product?
- How will the product be installed, distributed, and maintained?

The Case Study

In Chapter 6, we performed some systems engineering on HOLIS, our home lighting automation system. At this point, we still don't know very much about HOLIS, but we probably know enough to establish a first cut at the organization for our requirements information. Figure 16–5 shows that the team is using the following elements to describe the requirements for HOLIS:

- The *Vision document* will contain the short-term and longer-term visions for HOLIS, including basic system-level requirements and the features that are being proposed.
- The *system-level use-case model* records the use cases by which the various actors in the system interact with HOLIS.
- After some debate, the team decided to document the hardware requirements—size, weight, power, packaging—for HOLIS's three subsystems in a single *hardware requirements specification*.
- As each subsystem of HOLIS is quite software intensive, the team decided to develop a *software requirements specification* for each of the three subsystems, as well as a *use-case model* for how each subsystem interacts with its various actors.

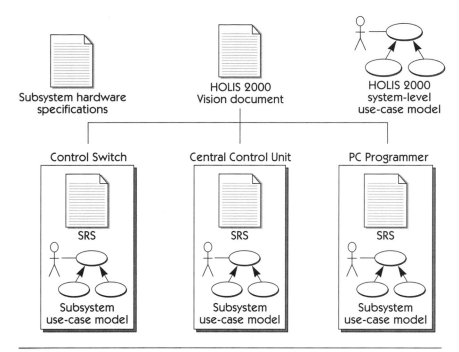

Figure 16–5   Organization of HOLIS requirements information

You'll have the opportunity to see these requirements artifacts develop further as we advance the case study in later chapters. A sample of each is included in Appendix A.

Summary

In this chapter, we examined a variety of requirements documents for systems of differing complexity. However, in most cases, requirements management eventually focuses on a single software subsystem, shrink-wrapped software product, or stand-alone application. This might be a software product, such as Microsoft Excel, Rational ClearCase, being developed by an independent software vendor, or the HOLIS lighting controls system.

In the next few chapters, we will "zoom in" on the process of requirements definition for a single software application so that we can demonstrate more clearly how the requirements management process works.

Chapter 17
THE VISION DOCUMENT

Key Points

- The Vision document describes the application in general terms, including descriptions of the target market, the system users, and the application features.
- The Vision document defines, at a high level of abstraction, both the problem and the solution.
- Virtually all software projects will benefit from having a Vision document.
- The Delta Vision document focuses on what has changed.

This chapter focuses on the Vision document. As our colleague Philippe Kruchten recently said, "If I were permitted to develop only one document, model, or other artifact in support of a software project, a short, well-crafted Vision document would be my choice."

Vision document for my project

The Vision document combines into a single document some modest elements of both a marketing requirements document and a product requirements document. We want to develop this particular document further, for two reasons.

1. Every project needs a Vision document.
2. It will help us demonstrate the requirements process further, as some key elements of this process will be recorded in this document.

The Vision document describes the application in general terms, including descriptions of the target market, the users of the system, and the features of the application. Over the years, we have found this document to be quite useful, and it has evolved to become a standard best practice for us when defining a software application.

Components of the Vision Document

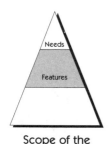

Scope of the
Vision document

The Vision document, perhaps *the* single most important document in a software project, captures the needs of the user, the features of the system, and other common requirements for the project. As such, the scope of the Vision document extends over the top two levels of the requirements pyramid, thereby defining at a high level of abstraction both the *problem* and the *solution*.

For a software product, the Vision document also serves as the basis for discussion and agreement among the three primary internal stakeholder communities of the project:

1. The marketing department, which serves as the proxy for the customer and the user, and which will ultimately be held accountable for the success of the product after release
2. The project team developing the application
3. The management team, which will be held responsible for the business outcome of the endeavor

The Vision document is powerful because it represents the gestalt of the product from all significant perspectives in a short, abstract, readable, and manageable form. As such, the Vision document is the primary focus in the early phases of the project, and any investment made in the process of gathering the information will pay handsome returns in later phases.

Because virtually all software projects will benefit from having a Vision document, we are going to describe it in some detail. Although our example is oriented toward a software product, it should be a fairly straightforward matter to modify it for your particular product context.

Figure 17–1 provides a briefly annotated outline of a sample Vision document. This outline has been used, with customizations, in hundreds of software products and a wide variety of software applications. A fully annotated version of this document appears in Appendix B.

In summary, the Vision document is a concise description of everything you consider to be most important about the product or application. The Vision

1. Introduction

This section should provide an overview of the entire Vision document.

1.1. Purpose of the Vision Document

This document collects, analyzes, and defines high-level user needs and features of the product.

1.2. Product Overview

State the purpose of the application, its version, and new features for delivery.

1.3. References

Provide a complete list of all documents referenced elsewhere in the Vision document.

2. User Description

Briefly describe the perspective of the users of your system.

2.1. User/Market Demographics

Summarize the key market demographics that motivate your product decisions.

2.2. User Profiles

Briefly describe the prospective users of your system.

2.3. User Environment

2.4. Key User Needs

List the key problems or needs as perceived by the user.

2.5. Alternatives and Competition

Identify any alternatives the user perceives as available.

3. Product Overview

3.1. Product Perspective

Provide a block diagram of the product or system and its interfaces to the external environment.

Figure continued on next page.

Figure 17–1   Template for a software product Vision document

3.2. Product Position Statement

Provide an overall statement summarizing, at the highest level, the unique position the product intends to fill in the marketplace. Moore (1991) recommends the following format:

For	(target customer)
Who	(statement of the need or opportunity)
The (product name)	is a (product category)
That	(statement of key benefit, that is, compelling reason to buy)
Unlike	(primary competitive alternative)
Our product	(statement of primary differentiation)

3.3. Summary of Capabilities

Summarize the major benefits and features the product will provide.

Customer Benefit	Supporting Features
Benefit 1	Feature
Benefit 2	Feature
Benefit 3	Feature

3.4. Assumptions and Dependencies

3.5. Cost and Pricing

4. Feature Attributes

Describe the feature attributes that will be used to evaluate, track, prioritize, and manage the features. The following are some suggestions.

Status	Proposed, Approved, Incorporated
Priority	Cumulative vote results; order ranking, or Critical, Important, Useful
Effort	Low, Medium, High; team-weeks; or person-months
Risk	Low, Medium, High
Stability	Low, Medium, High
Target release	Version number
Assigned to	Name
Reason	Text field

Figure 17–1   Template for a software product Vision document (*continued*)

5. Product Features

This section of the document lists the product features.

5.1. Feature #1

5.2. Feature #2

6. Key Use Cases

Describe a few key use cases, perhaps those that are architecturally significant or those that will most readily help the reader understand how the system is intended to be used.

7. Other Product Requirements

7.1. Applicable Standards

List all standards the product must comply with.

7.2. System Requirements

Define any system requirements necessary to support the application.

7.3. Licensing and Installation

Describe any installation requirements that also affect coding or that create the need for separate installation software.

7.4. Performance Requirements

Use this section to detail performance requirements.

8. Documentation Requirements

Describe the documentation that must be developed to support successful application deployment.

8.1. User Manual

Describe the purpose and contents of the product user manual.

8.2. Online Help

Requirements for online help, tool tips, and so on.

8.3. Installation Guides, Configuration, and Read Me Files

8.4. Labeling and Packaging

9.0 Glossary

Figure 17–1 Template for a software product Vision document (*continued*)

document is written at a level of detail, and in plain language, so as to be readily reviewable and understandable by the primary stakeholders of the project.

The "Delta Vision" Document

The development and management of the Vision document can play a key role in the success or failure of a software project, providing the locus of activity for the many stakeholders, customers, users, product management, and marketing management. Often, even the executive management of the company will be involved in its development and review. Keeping the Vision document understandable and manageable is an important team skill that will greatly benefit the overall productivity of the project.

To assist in this process, it is helpful to keep the Vision document as short, concise, and "to the point" as possible. This is not particularly difficult in the first release of the document, as nearly every item in the outline will be new to the project or at least must be restated in the context of this particular application.

However, in future releases, you may discover that it is counterproductive to repeat features that have been incorporated in prior releases and other information that has not changed in this particular project context, such as user profiles and markets served. We therefore introduce the "*Delta Vision*" document, which addresses these issues. Before we proceed however, let's look at the progression of the Vision document in the lifecycle of a new project.

Vision Document for Release 1.0

In the case of a new product or application, probably every element of the Vision document must be developed and elaborated. Otherwise, we would simply remove that element from the outline of the document, and you wouldn't have had to write about it! The Vision document must contain at least the following (see Figure 17–2):

- General and introductory information
- A description of the users of the system and markets served, features intended for release in version 1.0
- Other requirements, such as regulatory and environmental
- Future features that have been elicited but that are not to be incorporated in the 1.0 release

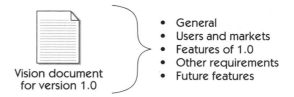

- General
- Users and markets
- Features of 1.0
- Other requirements
- Future features

Vision document
for version 1.0

Figure 17–2   Vision document v1.0

This document serves as the foundation for our 1.0 release and drives the more detailed software requirements and use cases that will more fully elaborate the system.

Vision Document for Version 2.0

Vision document
v2.0

As the project evolves, features become better defined; often, this means that they will be more fully elaborated in the Vision document. Also, new features will be discovered and added to the document. Thus, the document tends to grow, as does its value to the team. As we approach version 2.0, we certainly want to maintain this document that has served us so well. The logical next step in the evolution of the project and this document is to "mine" the future features that were included in v1.0 of the document but not implemented and to schedule them for v2.0. In other words, we want to find and "promote" some future features that will provide value in the 2.0 release. You may also wish to schedule a further requirements workshop or other elicitation process to discover new features that will be scheduled for 2.0 and some new future features that will need to be recorded in the document. Some of these features will already be obvious, based on customer feedback, others will come from the experience of the team. In any case, record these newly discovered features in v2.0 of the Vision document, either as scheduled for incorporation in 2.0 or as new future features.

You will also probably discover that some of the features implemented in version 1.0 did not deliver the intended value, perhaps because the external environment changed during the process and the feature was no longer needed or will be replaced by a new feature or perhaps because the customers simply didn't need the feature as they thought they would. In any case, you will likely discover that you will need to *remove* some features in the next release. How do you record these "anti-requirements"? Simply use the Vision document to record the fact that the particular feature must be removed in the next release.

As the team works its way through the process, it will discover that the document grows over time. That seems quite natural, as it is defining a system that is growing as well. Unfortunately, you may also discover that the document becomes more difficult to read and to understand over time. Why? Because it is now much longer and contains much information that has not changed since the previous release. For example, the product position statement and the target users are likely to be unchanged, as are the 25–50 features implemented in v1.0 that live on in the Vision document in v2.0.

Delta Vision
document v2.0

Therefore, we suggest the notion of the *Delta Vision document*. The *delta Vision document* focuses on only two things: *what has changed* and *any other information that must be included for context purposes.* This latter information is included either as a reminder to the team of the vision for the project or because new team members need the context for understanding.

The result is a Delta Vision document that now *focuses primarily on what is new and what is different* about this release. This *focus on only that which has changed* is a primary learning technique and is extremely beneficial in dealing with complex systems of information. With this model, we now have the model shown in Figure 17–3.

- Version 1.0 is our *comprehensive starting point*, telling us everything we need to know about our project.
- Version 2.0 defines that which is different in this release.
- Taken together, vision 1.0 plus delta vision 2.0 define the *"whole product definition."*

The two versions must be used together whenever the whole product definition is necessary, as for regulatory or customer requirements, for example,

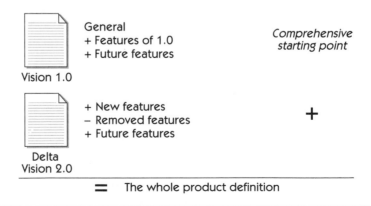

Figure 17–3 The Delta Vision document

and it is obviously valuable for new members of the team. However, in this case, you will read about features in v1.0 that do not appear in 2.0, as they were removed later, and it is necessary to follow this audit trail whenever you need to resurrect the whole definition.

If and when this becomes awkward, it is easy to remerge the contents of v1.0 and Delta 2.0 into a new Vision 2.0 document that represents a comprehensive and complete project picture.

Of course, we needn't be strict about this definition or what each document contains. In other circumstances, we have found it convenient to use the Delta Vision only for the minor release updates—such as v1.1 and v1.2—and to start with a clean slate and a revised "whole product" statement at each major release—such as v2.0 or 3.0. In any case, application of the Delta Vision document should help you manage the requirements process better by allowing your team to focus on "what really matters" at each specific time.

The Delta Vision Document in a Legacy System Environment

Rarely, if ever, is it practical to document the complete requirements of a large-scale legacy system.

One of the trickiest problems in requirements management is applying requirements management skills to the evolution of legacy IS/IT systems. Rarely, if ever, are there complete and adequate requirements specifications for the millions of lines of code and hundreds of person years of investment reflected in these systems. Nor is it practical to stop and redocument the past. By the time you have done so, the need may well be passed, and you may therefore fail in your mission by writing historical requirements when you should have been writing code!

So, if you're starting from scratch or with minimal documentation, you must proceed on a best-efforts basis, using whatever resources you can find around you—code, specifications, team members with a knowledge of history—to come to an understanding of what the system does now. Our recommendation in this case is to then apply the Delta Vision process and to define your features and use cases around the *changes* you are going to make to the legacy system. By following this process, you and your team can focus on *what's new* and *what's different* in this next release, and your customer and your team will gain the benefits of a well-managed requirements process. In addition, the requirements record you create will provide a documentation trail for others to follow behind you.

Chapter 18

THE CHAMPION

Key Points

- The product champion maintains the project vision.
- Every project needs an individual champion or a small champion team to advocate for the product.
- In software product environments, the product champion will often come from marketing.

In Chapter 1, we analyzed challenged projects and discovered a variety of root causes, with requirements management being near the top of the list. In Chapter 17, we defined the Vision document as a seminal document in a complicated software lifecycle; this document directly addresses the requirements challenge and is the one document you can look to, at any time, to see what the product, application, or system is and is not going to do. In total, the Vision document represents the essence of the product and must be defended as if the success of the project depends on it, for it *does*.

At some point, the question rightly becomes, "But who develops and maintains this all-important document? Who manages customer expectations? Who negotiates with the development team, the customer, the marketing department, the project manager, and the company executives who have shown such a keen interest in this project now that the deadline approaches?"

In virtually every successful project we've been involved in—from adventure ride vehicles that put butterflies in the stomach of every guest to life-supporting ventilators that sustain tens of thousands of lives without a single software failure—there was a *champion*. We can look back at these projects and point to one individual, and in the case of larger projects, a small team of a few folks, who played a "bigger-than-life" role. The champions kept the vision of the product (or system or application) in the front of their minds as if it was the single most important thing in their lives. They ate, slept, and dreamed about the vision for the project.

The Role of the Product Champion

The product champion may have a wide variety of titles: product manager, project manager, marketing manager, engineering manager, IT manager, project lead. But no matter the title, the job is the same. It's a big job. The champion must

- Manage the elicitation process and become comfortable when enough requirements are discovered
- Manage the conflicting inputs from all stakeholders
- Make the trade-offs necessary to find the set of features that delivers the highest value to the greatest number of stakeholders
- Own the product vision
- Advocate for the product
- Negotiate with management, users, and developers
- Defend against feature creep
- Maintain a "healthy tension" between what the customer desires and what the development team can deliver in the release time frame
- Be the representative of the official channel between the customer and the development team
- Manage the expectations of customers, executive management, and the internal marketing and engineering departments
- Communicate the features of the release to all stakeholders
- Review the software specifications to ensure that they conform to the true vision represented by the features
- Manage the changing priorities and the addition and deletion of features

This is the only person to whom the Vision document can be really be entrusted, and finding the right champion for this purpose is a key to project success or failure.

The Product Champion in a Software Product Environment

We once led a workshop for an online service provider confronting requirements challenges. When we got to the part of the tutorial emphasizing the notion of the product champion, the room got very quiet, and the mood changed noticeably. We asked the 25 people present, including developers and senior engineering and marketing managers, how these tough decisions were made in their environment. After a few tense moments, it became clear that no one made these decisions. After discussion among themselves, the best the group could describe was a "group grope," with input waxing and waning like the tides. *No one* had accountability for the tough decisions. *No one* decided when it was good enough.

Eventually, the team looked back at the senior marketing executive for answers, perhaps because that individual had the most input in the process. He looked around for a moment and then said: "*You know what scares me the most about this team? I can ask for any new feature to be added at any time in the process, and no one ever says no. How can we ever expect to ship a product?*"

It's probably clear from this vignette that the customer *had not* been able to ship a product for some time. It's also true that history demonstrates that that was an extremely painful "nonability" for that customer. The company had evolved from a traditional IT background and had moved to providing online services over the years. The notion of an application as a *software product* was new. The team members had no precedents to guide them though the process.

Although there is no one right way to organize and assign a product champion, perhaps we can look to our case study for a suggestion. After all, we did model it on a true-life and effective project team.

In Figure 18–1, it is Cathy, the *product manager*, who takes on the role of product champion. Note that, in this case, the product manager reports through marketing rather than though the engineering organization. This is fairly typical for software product companies since, in theory at least, product managers are closest to the customer, who will ultimately determine the success or failure of the project.

Perhaps more important, product managers report to the marketing management because marketing management ultimately has responsibility for "The Number," that is, the revenue associated with the product release. This is as it should be; marketing is ultimately accountable for sales and must be correspondingly responsible for making the hard decisions; otherwise, accountability will be lost.

How do you sort out the roles and responsibilities in a mix of requirements, technologies, customers, and developers? Imagine the following conversation,

Lumenations, Ltd.
Lighting Automation Division
Software Team Organization

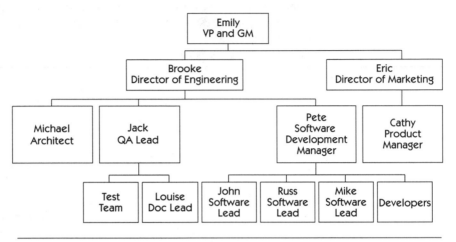

Figure 18–1 Case study: Software team organization

a variant of which occurred recently in a new organization that was sorting out its roles.

Product Manager (Champion):	It should have features A, B, and C, and you should build it using technology X.
Development Manager:	I think it should have feature D and not C, and we'll base it on technology Y.
Product Manager:	I say it has to have A, B, and C. After all, I'm accountable for meeting the sales quota, and that's what I need to meet my customers' needs. If you are willing to sign up for the number, you can add feature D, so long as you still meet the schedule
Development Manager:	hmmm (*thinking through what it means to spend her time helping their team meet the quota*). I'm not sure that's a good idea. We'll make it do A, B, and C. But do you want to be responsible for whether it actually works or not?

Product Manager:	(*envisioning learning how to write code in the next 48 hours rather than preparing for market launch*) Ummm, no, I don't think that's such a good idea. You can build it on whatever technology is most appropriate.
Development Manager:	Agreed. You decide on the features, and we'll pick the technology; that seems like the best mix for our skills and responsibilities.
Product Manager:	It's a deal.

This seem like a simple scenario and just plain common sense, but it is amazing how often, as in the case of the online services provider, that this responsibility is not clear.

In some ways, the independent software vendor (ISV) environment is easy: The customer is external, and we typically have a reasonably sophisticated marketing organization that we can leverage to elicit the requirements and determining who is accountable for balancing all of the conflicting needs. A customer whose needs are not met is simply *not* a customer. Although that may not be a good thing, at least they aren't hanging around to raise heck about it.

The Product Champion in an IS/IT Shop

Such is not the case in an IS/IT shop. There is no marketing department, your customers all work with you, and they will certainly be hanging around after this release to make their feelings known.

Where do we find our champion in such an environment? Perhaps we can again learn from an example. In one shop, a new enterprise support system was being developed to provide global 24-hour-a-day access to customer records for sales support and license management. The problem analysis exercise identified the following stakeholders: corporate marketing, tele-sales, licensing and support, business unit marketing, business unit financial management, order fulfillment, and collateral fulfillment. Each of these departments was quite vocal in its needs, yet it was clear that not all needs could possibly be met. The question "Who owns the Vision document" looked like a metaphor for the question "Who would like to make a great CLM (career-limiting move) by attempting to manage this project?"

Question: What is

Champion
+ Change control
  board

equal to?

On analysis, it was clear that none of the leads in the development team had the authority to make such hard decisions, and yet a champion must be assigned. In this case, the team decided to name Tracy, the current project lead, as the product champion and empowered her to elicit and to organize the requirements. She *owned* the Vision document. She interviewed the users, established their relative priorities, and collected the data into a feature-oriented format. But a special steering committee, or project change control board (CCB), was also immediately established for the project. The change control board consisted of three senior executives, each with the responsibility in a functional area.

Initially, Tracy facilitated a decision-making process whereby the CCB established the relative priorities for the initial release. Thereafter, the CCB, *and only the CCB*, had the requisite authority to add or to delete features, with recommendations coming from the product champion. In this way, there was only one champion, Tracy, and the results of elicitation and the vision of the project lived in her head and in the Vision document, but the responsibility for the hard decisions was given to the CCB. The CCB would take the heat for the hard decisions. The champion had "only" to see that the agreed-on features were properly elaborated on and communicated to the development team.

Answer:
A fighting chance

Once Tracy was empowered to drive the process and with the CCB, including members of upper management, backing her up and taking most of the heat, the project was successful and was used as an organizational model for new projects. Each new project used differing project champions. This provided an opportunity for personal growth and development for these individuals. It became an empowered role within the company. And, of course, we can't forget the CCB. For each new project, the makeup of the CCB was established, based on the themes of each new release and the organizations that would be most directly affected.

Although there is no prescription that you can follow to create a project champion, it is extremely important for your team to identify one, to promote one, or to empower the one who seems to already be leading the process. Then it is the team's responsibility to assist that champion in every way possible in managing the requirements of the applications. This will help ensure a successful outcome. Besides, if you don't help make that person successful, he or she might ask *you* to be the project champion on the next project.

Team Skill 3 Summary

In Team Skill 3, we moved from understanding the needs of the user to starting to define the solution. In so doing, we took our first baby steps out of the problem domain, the land of the user, and into the solution domain, wherein our job is to define a system to solve the problem at hand.

We also learned that complex systems require comprehensive strategies for managing requirements information, and we looked at a number of ways to organize requirements information. We recognized that we really have a hierarchy of information, starting with user needs, transitioning through features, then into the more detailed software requirements as expressed in use cases or traditional forms of expression. Also, we noted that the hierarchy reflects the level of abstraction with which we view the problem space and the solution space.

We then zoomed in to look at the application definition process for a stand-alone software application and invested some time in defining a Vision document for such an application. We maintain that the Vision document, with modifications to the particular context of a company's software applications, is a crucial document and that *every* project should have one.

We also recognized that without a champion—someone to champion the requirements for our application and to support the needs of the customer and the development team—we would have no way to be certain that the hard decisions are made. Requirements drift, delays, and suboptimum decisions forced by project deadlines are likely to result. So we decided to appoint one, or anoint one: someone to own the Vision document and the features it contains. In turn, the champion and the team will empower a change control board to help with the really tough decisions and to ensure that requirements changes are reasoned about *before* being accepted.

With a requirements management organizational strategy in hand and a champion at the helm, we are now better prepared for the work ahead. But first, we must take a look at the problem of *project scope*, the subject of Team Skill 4.

MANAGING SCOPE

So far in this book, we have been introduced to the Team Skills of analyzing the problem, understanding user needs, and defining the system. These three Team Skills all focus on a primary root cause of software development problems: the team's forging off into the solution space without having an adequate understanding of the problem to be solved. Although team members will need to practice these skills in order to develop them, doing so does not take great effort. We strongly recommend spending a little more time in these early lifecycle activities; the entire set of activities described so far should consume only a small fraction of the project budget, perhaps only 5 percent or so of the total costs. Although the issues are complex, only a few team members—analysts, project manager, technical lead, product manager/project champion—need to be heavily involved up to this point.

Hereafter, however, the game changes dramatically as the team size will be increased significantly. Each of these additional team members must participate in a coordinated team effort, and everyone must communicate effectively with one another. In addition, the investment, or "burn rate," of the project increases dramatically. We create documents for test plans, build design models and refine requirements, elaborate the use cases, develop the code, and thereby create momentum and a body of work that must be changed if the definition is not well understood or if the external requirements environment changes.

The requirements pyramid, by its very shape—wider at the bottom—correctly suggests that much more work is ahead of us. Team Skill 4 develops a strategy for a most crucial activity: managing scope. According to the Standish Group (1994) data, *"53% of the projects will cost 189% of estimates."* Data from our own experience is even worse: Almost all software projects will be late by a factor of 50%–100%. Assuming that the other root causes in software development will not be solved overnight, it seems clear that our industry is either incompetent or trying to do too much with too little resources, skills, and tools. We are trying to stuff ten pounds of desired functionality into a five-pound bag. Although the physics of software development are not clear, it should be obvious that this element of our strategy is heading for trouble and that the quality of both our work products and our reputation is about to suffer.

So, *before* we increase the team size, *before* we develop the more detailed specifications, *before* we commit our technology ideas to designs, and *before* we build the test scripts, we must pause and learn how to *manage the scope of the project*. Part psychology, part technology, and part just good project management, mastery of this Team Skill will dramatically improve the probability of a successful project.

Chapter 19

THE PROBLEM OF PROJECT SCOPE

Key Points

- Project scope is a combination of product functionality, project resources, and the time available.
- Brooks's law states that adding labor to a late software project makes it even later.
- If the effort required to implement the system features is equal to the resources over the time available, the project has an achievable scope.
- Over scoped projects are typical in industry.
- In many projects, in order to provide a reasonable probability of success, it will be necessary to reduce the scope by as much as a factor of *two*.

Components of Project Scope

As with any professional activity, meeting commitments in application development involves making realistic assessments of project resources, time lines, and objectives before the activity begins. For software development, these factors combine to create the "scope" of the project. Project scope is a function of:

- The functionality that must be delivered to meet the user's needs
- The resources available to the project
- The time available in which to achieve the implementation

Figure 19–1 provides a perspective of the "box" we can use to represent project scope.

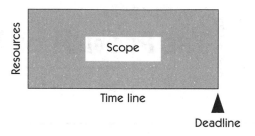

Figure 19–1 Project scope

In Figure 19–1, the area of the box represents the achievable scope of the project. Project scope derives from the following elements:

- *Resources*, consisting primarily of the labor from developers, testers, tech writers, quality assurance personnel, and others.

    As early as the 1970s, Fred Brooks (1975) had demonstrated that adding resources to a software project in order to increase the work output is a risky proposition at best. Indeed, Brooks' law states that adding labor to a late software project makes it even later.

    OK, if the time scale is long enough, work output can indeed go up, but it will not go up proportionally to the resources added, and the overall efficiency of the project thereby decreases. Adding resources may even slow a project because the need for training and supporting the new people decreases the productivity of those already on the project. As the competitive marketplace forces us to shorten our time lines, adding resources during a project becomes less and less practical. In addition, as development budgets are stretched and real years become Internet years, adding resources is simply not an option in many environments.

    For the purpose of analyzing scope, let's assume that resources, on the *y*-axis of Figure 19–1, are constant over the duration of the project.
- *Time*, perhaps here we have a "soft" boundary that is subject to change if the available resources are inadequate to achieve the desired functionality. For purposes of our scope analysis, time on the *x*-axis, is a fixed factor.

    Certainly, history would demonstrate that delivering software late is typically "par for the course." On the other hand, many applications have hard, fixed deadlines. Examples include a new tax program to be delivered in time for tax season, a new-product introduction timed for a trade show, or a contractually fixed customer deadline. In addition, if as a profession we want to ensure our credibility and to gain the confidence of our customers, it is important that we not slip the schedule for a change.

The total functionality we can deliver is obviously limited to the available time (fixed) and the available resources (also fixed) we have to apply, so the achievable scope is the area of the box.

In this book, we have used the notion of "features" to represent the value-added functionality we must deliver to the user. *If the effort required to implement the features required by the system is equal to the resources over the time we have available, the scope of the project is achievable, and we have no problem.* Barring unforeseen circumstances, the software team will deliver on time without sacrificing quality.

However, experience has shown that there is often a poor match between these factors in the scope equation. Indeed, in requirements classes that we teach, we always ask: "*At the start of the project, what amount of scope are you typically given by your management, customers, or stakeholders?*" In response, only a few trainees have ever answered "under 100 percent." The others have responded with numbers that vary from 125 percent to 500 percent. The median and the average for each session tend towards the same conclusion: approximately 200 percent. This data correlates remarkably well with the Standish Group finding stated earlier, namely, that more than half of all projects will cost close to double their estimates. Perhaps we now understand why.

A Short Story on Project Scope

We once had a student who had recently moved into a new role as product manager for a new software product. Her background included many aspects of product development and product marketing, but she had no direct experience in software development. After hearing the responses to our question about scope, she appeared incredulous. She looked around the room and said, "Do you people really mean to tell me that you routinely sign up for approximately two times the amount of work that can reasonably be accomplished in the available time period?[1] What kind of profession is this? Are you people crazy?" The developers looked at one another sheepishly and by consensus answered, "Yup."

---

1. Many students have commented that it is *management* that signed up, often committing them before they volunteered!

What happens when a project proceeds with a 200 percent initial scope?

- If the features of the application were completely independent, which is unlikely, only half of them will be working when the deadline passes. The product is limping but provides only half of the intended utility. And it's not a holistic half. The features don't work together, and they don't produce any useful aggregate functionality. A drastically reduced-scope application is quickly patched together and shipped. Consequences include seriously unhappy customers whose expectations have not been met, marketing commitments that have been missed, and inaccurate manuals and promotional materials that must be quickly reworked. The entire team is frustrated and demotivated.
- At deadline time, only 50 percent of each feature works. Moreover, since there are certainly interdependencies within those features, in this even more typical case, *nothing useful works when the deadline passes*. The deadline is missed badly. All commitments are missed; a new deadline is scheduled, and a new death march often begins. In the worst case, the entire team is fired, after working overtime for months on end; the final "phase" of this first attempt at the project, the phase called "promotion of the nonparticipants," is declared, and a new manager is added to the project.

What happens to software quality during either of these outcomes? The code, which is rushed to completion near the end, is poorly designed and bug-ridden; testing is reduced to an absolute minimum or skipped entirely; and documentation and help systems are eliminated. Customers take on both the testing and the quality assurance functions. Soon, the customers react to our extraordinary efforts as follows: *"Although we were initially disappointed by how late you were (or how little is working compared to our expectations), now we are really unhappy because we just discovered that what you shipped us is junk."*

The Hard Question

Clearly, in order for the project team to have any hope of success, scope must be managed before and during the development effort. Given the typical scenario, however, the task is daunting: *For if we truly begin the development effort with an expectation of 200 percent scope, it will be necessary to reduce the project scope by as much as a factor of 2 in order to have any chance of success.*

The team's dilemma in addressing this problem leads to perhaps the toughest question faced by the team: *How does one manage to reduce scope and keep the customers happy?* Well, all is not lost. We'll cover ways of dealing with this issue in the next two chapters.

Chapter 20

ESTABLISHING PROJECT SCOPE

Key Points

- The first step in establishing project scope is to establish a high-level requirements baseline, an itemized set of features intended to be delivered in a specified version of the product.
- The second step is to establish the rough level of effort required for each feature of the baseline.
- Next, estimate the risk for each feature, or the probability that implementing it will cause an adverse impact on the schedule and the budget.
- Using this data, the team establishes the baseline in such a way as to ensure the delivery of those features that are critical to project success.

The Requirements Baseline

The purpose of scope management is to establish a high-level requirements baseline for the project. We'll define the baseline as

the itemized set of features, or requirements, intended to be delivered in a specific version of the application.

See Figure 20–1. This baseline for the next release must be agreed to by both the customer and the development team. In other words, the baseline must

- Be at least "acceptable" to the customer.
- Have a reasonable probability of success, in the team's view.

The first step in creating the baseline is to simply list the features that have been defined for the application. Controlling the level of detail in this process

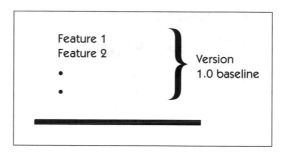

Figure 20–1   Requirements baseline

is an important key to success. In Team Skill 3, we suggested that any new system, no matter how complex, can be described by a list of 25–99 features. With any more than that, you are viewing the project at a level of detail that is too high to communicate effectively with the customers and the development team. With fewer than that, the level of detail may be too low to provide a sufficient understanding of the application and the associated level of effort necessary for implementation.

If we followed the requirements workshop process (Chapter 10) or any process that creates a similar outcome, we will have at our disposal a list of 25–99 features. This list provides an itemized, high-level description of the capabilities of a new or revised system. This features list is the primary project artifact we will use to manage the scope of the project *before* significant investments are made in requirements refinement, design, code, testing, or other project activities.

For example, let's consider a shrink-wrapped software product with a list of the following eight features:

Feature 1: External relational data base support

Feature 2: Multiuser security

Feature 3: Ability to clone a project

Feature 4: Port to new operating system (OS) release

Feature 5: New project wizard

Feature 6: Import of external data by style

Feature 7: Implement tool tips

Feature 8: Integrate with version-manager subsystem

Setting Priorities

As we discussed in Team Skill 2, Understanding User Needs, establishing the relative priorities for the feature set is integral to scope management. During prioritization, it is important that the customers and users, product managers, or other representatives—not the development team—set the priorities from your in-house marketing department. Indeed, this initial prioritization should be done without too much influence from the technical community; otherwise, the level of difficulty in implementing the features will influence customer priorities, and the result of the process will be compromised such that the application may not meet the real customer needs. There will be adequate opportunity for technical input at later phases of the prioritization process. In our project example, let's assume that we vote on the priority of each feature, using a critical-important-useful scale; the results of this exercise are shown in Table 20–1.

Table 20–1   Prioritized features

Feature	Priority
Feature 1: External relational database support	Critical
Feature 4: Port to new OS release	Critical
Feature 6: Import of external data by style	Critical
Feature 3: Ability to clone a project	Important
Feature 2: Multiuser security	Important
Feature 5: New project wizard	Important
Feature 7: Implement tool tips	Useful
Feature 8 : Integrate with version-manager subsystem	Uscful

Assessing Effort

Prioritization is only one piece of the scope puzzle. After all, if we could do all of the work, the prioritization would be unnecessary. If we can't do all of the work, we still haven't figured out how much we can do, and therefore, we do not yet know where to draw the baseline for the project.

The next step is to establish the rough level of effort implied by each feature of the proposed baseline. Doing so is tricky, as little useful information is available yet on which to estimate the work; we have no detailed requirements or design output on which to base an estimate. The best we can do is to determine a "rough order of magnitude" of the level of effort for each feature.

Estimating effort at this early time is a learned Team Skill. The engineering team will be naturally reluctant to provide estimates before feasibility and requirements are fully understood, and yet the first cut at scope management must happen before this next level of detail is known.

Let's assume that the product or project manager is the champion for our project and has the following dialogue with the developers for the project:[1]

Product Manager:	*How difficult is this feature to do?*
Development Team:	*We don't know. We don't have any requirements or design yet.*
Product Manager:	*I respect that, but is it the easiest thing we've ever done?*
Development Team:	*No.*
Product Manager:	*OK, is it the most difficult feature on the list?*
Development Team:	*No.*
Product Manager:	*On a scale of low-medium-high, we'll give it a medium. OK?*
Development Team:	*OK. Medium it is.*
Product Manager:	*OK, on to the next feature.*

Why can we not allow for a process that creates detailed requirements and design information for each feature so that we can create more meaningful estimates? Isn't that the professional way to approach the problem? If the schedule provides time for more detailed estimating at this time, by all means do it!

However, we believe that it is crucial to be able to make some quick decisions about the scope of the activity without a more detailed estimate. Why? Because to do otherwise invests resources in what will later be determined to be "wasted inventory," including requirements specifications for features that will not be implemented, design information for those features, test

---

1. The team may wish to use "team-weeks" or "team-months" as a gross estimate of the total impact of a feature on the project. This rough heuristic serves as a substitute for a more detailed estimate and is arguably better than the result of this dialogue. Then, using these totals and the total time available for the project, the team can determine where to initially draw the baseline. If it is past the critical-features set, all is well; if not, the project is out of scope, and a new, smaller project must be defined.

Table 20–2   Features list with effort added

Feature	Priority	Effort
Feature 1: External relational database support	Critical	Medium
Feature 4: Port to new OS release	Critical	High
Feature 6: Import of external data by style	Critical	Low
Feature 3: Ability to clone a project	Important	High
Feature 2: Multiuser security	Important	Low
Feature 5: New project wizard	Important	Low
Feature 7: Implement tool tips	Useful	Low
Feature 8: Integrate with version-manager subsystem	Useful	High

scripts for requirements that will be scope-managed out of the project later, a false determination of the critical path for the project, and so on. We cannot afford to invest any resources in these scrap-producing activities, or we will fail to optimize the resources invested. In other words, scope management will reduce the number of features that will be developed in the initial release, and since resources are extraordinarily scarce, we cannot afford any additional investment in features that are not going to be implemented in the current baseline. Table 20–2 illustrates the addition of effort information to our feature list.

Adding the Risk Element

Another aspect of managing scope is estimating the "risk" associated with each feature. In this context, we'll consider risk to be the probability that the implementation of a feature will cause an adverse impact on the schedule and the budget. Risk gives us a relative measure of the potential impact of including a particular feature within the project baseline. A high-risk feature has the potential to negatively impact the project, even if all other features can be accomplished within the allotted time.

The development team establishes risk, based on any heuristic it is comfortable with, using the same low-medium-high scale used to assess effort. Table 20–3 shows the revised features list for the example.

Strategies for mitigating risk vary from project to project, and we won't cover that topic here. For the purposes of scope management, it is adequate to simply be aware of the risk associated with each feature so that intelligent decisions can be made early in the project. For example, if a feature has a

Table 20–3 Features list with risk added

Feature	Priority	Effort	Risk
Feature 1: External relational database	Critical	Medium	Low
Feature 4: Port to new OS release	Critical	High	Medium
Feature 6: Import of external data by style	Critical	Low	High
Feature 3: Ability to clone a project	Important	High	Medium
Feature 2: Multiuser security	Important	Low	High
Feature 5: New project wizard	Important	Low	Low
Feature 7: Implement tool tips	Useful	Low	High
Feature 8: Integrate with version-manager subsystem	Useful	High	Low

benefit of *critical* and a risk of *high*, then an effective mitigation strategy is mandatory. If priority is *important* and the feature hovers around the baseline, the item may be dropped or simply developed "if time is available." There's no harm in the process, so long as no commitment was made to include the item in the release. If the benefit of a *high* risk item is only *useful*, consider skipping it entirely.

Reducing Scope

We have made substantial progress. We now have a prioritized features set with associated relative effort and risk. Note that there is often little correlation between priority and effort or with risk. Indeed, many critical items are low effort; many items that are only useful are very difficult. This can help in the team's prioritization of the features. For example, a feature that is critical, medium effort, and low risk may be a candidate for immediate resourcing. Between these extremes, we can find the "sweet spot," wherein we can apply our fixed resources so as to maximize the benefit to the customer. Table 20–4 provides a few guidelines for prioritizing the development of critical features based on these attributes.

A Reasonable First Estimate

If the team uses even a rough, labor-based estimate, it can determine the baseline by simply adding the labor estimates until the time limit has been met; the team will have established the project baseline. Often, however, the team will not have even this data available and yet must make a first cut at

Table 20–4 Scope prioritization techniques

Attributes	Consider
Priority: Critical *Effort:* High *Risk:* High	Alarm! Establish immediate risk-mitigation strategy; resource immediately; focus on feasibility with architecture
Priority: Critical *Effort:* High *Risk:* Low	A likely critical resource-constrained item; resource immediately
Priority: Critical *Effort:* Low *Risk :* Low	Resource as a safety factor, or defer until later

project scope. In this case, we still do not know where to draw the baseline, but if it is the team's gut feel that scope is greater than 100 percent, the list will likely have to be cut.

The next step is the trickiest. If we assume, for example, that the features add up to 200 percent scope, the baseline must be chopped in half or more. How do we go about this process?

The first consideration is whether we can do only the *critical* items on the list. Ask the project manager, "If all else fails, can we be certain of achieving at least the *critical* items by the deadline?" After all, if we applied the prioritization scheme well, only one third or so of the items on the list will be *critical* to the release. Unless some of the critical features represent a highly disproportionate level of effort, the answer should be yes, even if we have 200 percent scope. If the answer is yes, *and in our experience it is almost always yes,* even at this first early cut, we have the beginnings of a plan. If the answer is no, the project is way out of scope (300%–400% or more), and a smaller-scope project must be defined and the prioritization process repeated.

Since our estimating process was crude at best, we cannot say for sure how many items beyond *critical* can be achieved. A further estimating effort, based on more detailed requirements and appraisal of technical feasibility, can be used to further refine the baseline. (Also, this is the time to do the detailed project plan to validate the assumptions that have been made.)

In our experience, however, it is sufficient in many real-world projects to draw the baseline at the *critical* requirements, perhaps including one or two *important* items, leaving the development team to make further decisions about the inclusion of *important* items, based on project progress. No, it isn't scientific. But yes, it does work.

If expectations are properly set and managed, anything that can be accomplished beyond the baseline will be a bonus. Table 20–5 applies this simple heuristic to the baseline for our sample project.

Features below the baseline are now future features and will be considered in later releases. Such features may be later promoted to a higher priority, based on what is accomplished in the near-term release and on future customer input.

Of course, the features are not always independent. In many cases, one of the features below the baseline is integral to one of the features above the baseline or can be implemented more readily as a result of having accomplished another feature. Or, perhaps the project team is good or lucky and gets ahead of schedule (now a conceivable notion!) or finds a class library that makes a below-the-baseline feature easy to implement. In these cases, the team should be empowered to bring that feature into the baseline and include it in the release and to reprioritize and to reset the baseline, subject to proper communication processes, of course.

In this fashion, the team should be able to create a project plan, at least at the first order of approximation. However, in all likelihood, many of the desired features did not make the first cut, and there will be expectations to be managed, both inside and outside the company. We'll cover that topic in the next chapter. But first, look at the case study and see what the team came up with for the HOLIS v1.0 release.

Table 20–5 Prioritized feature list

Feature	Priority	Effort
Feature 1: External relational database support	Critical	Medium
Feature 4: Port to new OS release	Critical	High
Feature 6: Import of external data by style	Critical	Low
Feature 3: Ability to clone a project	Important	Medium
Baseline (features above this line are committed features)		
Feature 2: Multiuser security	Important	Low
Feature 5: New project wizard	Important	Low
Feature 7: Implement tool tips	Useful	Low
Feature 8: Integrate with version-manager subsystem	Useful	High

The Case Study

After holding the requirements workshop, the HOLIS team was chartered with the responsibility of assessing the level of effort for each feature and coming up with a first draft of the v1.0 baseline. Rigorous scope management had to be applied because of the constraints on the team, including the "drop dead" date of having a prototype available at the trade show in December and the (even tougher) date of a release to manufacturing in January.[2] The team estimated the level of effort for each feature via the high-medium-low heuristic and then added the risk assessment for each feature. Table 20–6 shows the full features list, with these attributes added.

For the next step, the team provided rough estimates for each feature and developed a detailed project plan showing certain interdependencies and critical milestones. Also, after negotiation with marketing, which, in turn did some negotiating with Raquel (its international distributor), the team determined that, at release 1.0, it was adequate to internationalize only the CCU user interface, which reduced the scope of this feature immensely. The final internationalization of the optional PC Programmer interface software could wait until v2.0. This caused the team to change feature 25 from "internationalize user interface" to "internationalize CCU interface" and to add a new feature, "internationalize PC programmer," to the futures list.

Then, based on revised labor estimates, the team proposed the baseline as shown in Table 20–7. This baseline proposal was sent all the way to the executive team, where Emily, the VP, made the final decision. Before doing so, however, she had the team walk her through the project plan so she could "see the dependencies." (The team was suspicious that she really wanted to see whether it had "done its homework" or if it was just "sandbagging" to get some slack in the schedule.) In the end, the decision was *yes*, but Emily's caveat was, "We accept this proposal for the 1.0 release of HOLIS, but you should be aware that the CEO, Mark, told my boss, Jason, who told me that 'thou shall not fail to release the product in January as you have committed.'" Emily commented further, "I'm not sure

---

2. Although it was given manufacturing lead times, the team decided that they actually had until the end of February for the final 1.0 software release. This was a crucial additional 6 weeks that the team was convinced it would need for final modifications, based on feedback from the trade show.

Table 20–6   HOLIS 2000 features, sorted with effort and risk attributes added

ID	Feature	Votes	Effort	Risk
23	Create custom lighting scenes	121	Med	Low
16	Automatic timing settings for lights, etc.	107	Low	Low
4	Built in security features: lights, alarms, and bells	105	Low	High
6	100% reliability	90	High	High
8	Easy-to-program, non-PC control unit	88	High	Med
1	Easy-to-program control stations	77	Med	Med
5	Vacation settings	77	Low	Med
13	Any light can be dimmed	74	Low	Low
9	Uses my own PC for programming	73	High	Med
14	Entertain feature	66	Low	Low
20	Close garage doors	66	Low	Low
19	Automatically turn on closet lights when door opened	55	Low	High
3	Interface to home security system	52	High	High
2	Easy to install	50	Med	Med
18	Turn on lights automatically when someone approaches a door	50	Med	Med
7	Instant lighting on/off	44	High	High
11	Can drive drapes, shades, pumps, and motors	44	Low	Low
15	Control lighting, etc., via phone	44	High	High
10	Interfaces to home automation system	43	High	High
22	Gradual mode—slowly increase/decrease illumination	34	Med	Low
26	Master control stations	31	High	High
12	Easily expanded when remodeling	25	Med	Med
25	Internationalized user interface	24	Med	High
21	Interface to audio/video system	23	High	High
24	Restore after power fail	23	N/A	N/A
17	Controls HVAC	22	High	High
28	Voice activation	7	High	High
27	Web site–like user presentation	4	Med	Low

what he meant by that. I think he meant that if we fail, he's going to have *me* committed, but I don't ever want to find out. Do you?"

Hearing Emily's words very clearly, the team members committed *themselves* to the delivery date and proceeded with the next phase. The next milestone in the project plan was to be an elaboration iteration, which would include a rapid prototype of HOLIS that would be available for demonstration by August 1.

Table 20–7 V1.0 baseline for HOLIS

ID	Feature	Votes	Effort	Risk	Marketing Comments
23	Create custom lighting scenes	121	Med	Low	As flexible as possible
16	Automatic timing settings for lights, etc.	107	Low	Low	As flexible as possible
4	Built-in security features: lights, alarms, and bells	105	Low	High	Marketing to do more research
6	100% reliability	90	High	High	Get as close to 100% as possible
8	Easy-to-program, non-PC control unit	88	High	Med	Provide dedicated controller
1	Easy-to-program control stations	77	Med	Med	As easy as feasible with measured effort
5	Vacation settings	77	Low	Med	
13	Any light can be dimmed	74	Low	Low	
9	Uses my own PC for programming	73	High	Med	Only one configuration supported in 1.0
25	**Internationalized CCU user interface**	24	Med	Med	Per agreement with European distributor
14	~~Entertain feature~~	~~66~~	~~Low~~	~~Low~~	(Not applicable, included in 23)
7	Instant lighting on/off	44	High	High	Make intelligent investments

V1.0 Mandatory Baseline: Everything above the line must be included or we will delay release.

ID	Feature	Votes	Effort	Risk	Marketing Comments
20	Close garage doors	66	Low	Low	May be little impact on software
2	Easy to install	50	Med	Med	Level of effort basis
11	Can drive drapes, shades, pumps, and motors	44	Low	Low	May be little impact on software
22	Gradual mode: slowly increase/decrease illumination	34	Med	Low	Nice if we can get it

V1.0 Optional: Do as many of the preceding as you can (Cathy)

Future Features: Below this line, no current development

ID	Feature	Votes	Effort	Risk	Marketing Comments
29	**Internationalize PC Programmer interface**	N/A	**High**	**Med**	**Will become mandatory for version 2.0**
3	Interface to home security system	52	High	High	Can we at least provide a hardware interface? (Eric)
19	Automatically turn on closet lights when door opened	55	Low	High	
18	Turn on lights automatically when someone approaches a door	50	Med	Med	
15	Control lighting, etc., via phone	44	High	High	
10	Interfaces to home automation system	43	High	High	
26	Master control stations	31	High	High	
12	Easily expanded when remodeling	25	Med	Med	
25	Hand-held remote controls	24	Med	High	

Table continued on next page.

Table 20–7   V1.0 baseline for HOLIS (*continued*)

ID	Feature	Votes	Effort	Risk	Marketing Comments
21	Interface to audio/video system	23	High	High	
24	Restore after power fail	23	N/A	N/A	
17	Controls HVAC	22	High	High	
28	Voice activation	7	High	High	
27	Web site-like user presentation	4	Med	Low	

Chapter 21
MANAGING YOUR CUSTOMER

Key Points

- Managing your customers means engaging them in managing *their* requirements and *their* project scope.
- Customers who are part of the process will own the result.
- Getting the job done right means providing enough functionality at the right time to meet the customer's real need.
- Negotiating skills are an invaluable aid to the scope management challenge.

Engaging Customers to Manage *Their* Project Scope

Reducing project scope to within shouting distance of available time and resources has the potential to create an adversarial relationship between the project team and its customers, whose needs we must meet. Let's be honest. We've all been there. Fortunately, it does not have to be so. Instead, *we can actively engage our customers in managing **their** requirements and **their** project scope to ensure both the quality and the timeliness of the software outcomes.*

This conclusion is based on some important insights:

- It is in our customers' best financial interests to meet their external commitments to their marketplaces. Therefore, delivering a high-quality and, if necessary, scope-reduced application—on time and on budget—is the highest overall benefit that the team can provide.
- The application, its key features, and the business needs it fulfills all belong to the customers, *not* to the application development team.

We need customers' input to make the key decisions, and only the customers can really determine how to manage scope and achieve a useful deliverable. We are their humble technological servants. It is *their* project.

Communicating the Result

If the project scope must be reduced, make sure that the customer is a direct participant. A customer who is part of the process will own the result. A customer who is excluded from the process will be unhappy with the result and will naturally tend to blame the developers for not trying hard enough.

Engaging the customer in this dialogue helps lay the problems of scope management ever so gently on the customer's doorstep. And with the philosophy we've described in the previous chapter, smart customers will make commitments to their external marketplaces only for the critical items included in the baseline. The embarrassment of missed schedules and missing features is avoided. Any extra features accomplished beyond the baseline will be perceived positively as exceeding expectations.

Sometimes, the discovery of the scope management problem occurs outside of the customer engagement process; then, in all likelihood, some bad news is about to be delivered. Delivering this message to our customers and/or management is a delicate process requiring both negotiation skills and a total commitment to the schedule and scope that results. After we deliver the bad news, we cannot afford to fail to deliver on the new promise lest *all* credibility be lost.

Negotiating with the Customer

Almost all business processes require negotiation. Consider negotiating with a customer for a delivery date for ball bearings, negotiating price on a large order, negotiating your annual increase with your manager, negotiating an achievable quota for your sales team, or negotiating additional resources for your project.

On behalf of both your project and your customer's business objective, you may need to negotiate the scope commitment for your team. The team should also keep in mind that, in many cases, the customer may already have developed the skills of negotiation and will naturally use them in their discussions with you and your team. Therefore, if you are a team leader, project manager, or project champion, you should *develop these skills* as well. Negotiation is a professional business activity. It is not a particularly difficult process, and it can be done with integrity, grace, and style. Take the opportunity to gain some training in this process; your human resources department can probably help, or you may want to take an external seminar. Failing that, you should at least familiarize yourself with some of the rules of the game. For example, a good overview of the negotiating process can be found in Fisher, Ury, and Patton's (1983) *Getting to Yes*, which can be read in a few hours. They recommend a few helpful guidelines for every negotiating session.

- Start high but not unreasonable.
- Separate the people from the problem.
- Focus on interests, not positions.
- Understand your walk-away position.
- Invent options for mutual gain.
- Apply objective criteria.

The guiding principle for scope management: *"underpromise and overdeliver.*

As you negotiate with your customer, your guiding principle in establishing the baseline should be: *Underpromise and overdeliver*. Doing so ensures that the inevitable vagaries of software development, unanticipated technological risks, changing requirements, delays in availability of purchased components, a key team member's unanticipated leave, and so on, can be accommodated within your project schedule. If you should happen to run the one project in a thousand free of these unfortunate circumstances, it's OK: at worst, you will embarrass yourself by delivering early! Even that would provide at least some entertainment value within your company!

Managing the Baseline

Successful development managers create margins for error in estimating effort and allow for time to incorporate legitimate change during the development cycle. These managers also resist feature creep, which author Jerry Weinberg (1995) notes can increase scope by as much as 50%–100% after the start of a project. Focusing the development effort on the customer's critical priorities can mitigate even hostile political environments. With scope negotiated to an achievable level, and with development focused almost exclusively on the customer's "must haves," the team will establish credibility by meeting schedules with quality and, occasionally, with utility that could not have been predicted in advance.

However, your customers, be they internal or external, naturally want as much functionality as possible with each release of a software system. After all, it's the functionality that delivers the added value they need to meet their business objectives. Indeed, we must have a healthy respect for customers who are demanding, for they are the ones who will ultimately be the most successful in the marketplace. Demanding, competent customers are the only ones really worth having.

Left unchecked, however, the demand for more and more functionality can compromise the quality and the overall viability of the project. *More* becomes the enemy of *adequate*. *Better* becomes the enemy of *good enough*.

If we were operating in a business sector where the physics are better defined, where the industry had a few hundred years of experience in reliably delivering the goods, things would be different. But we operate in the software world; the physics are indeterminate, the processes are immature, and the technology changes with every application. Let's first focus on learning how to get the job done right: *enough functionality at the right time to meet the customer's real need*. We can tune our process later to see if we can exceed expectations, but for now, let's focus on just *meeting* them! In order to do so, we need to manage the baseline.

Once established, the baseline provides the center of focus for many project activities. The features baseline can be used to realistically assess progress. Resources can be adjusted, based on progress relative to the baseline. The features within the baseline can be refined into further detail suited for code development. Requirements traceability can be applied from user needs to the features in the baseline. Traceability can be further extended from features into additional specifications and implementation.

Perhaps most important, the high-level baseline can be used as a part of an effective change management process. Change is an integral part of every application development activity. Managing change is so critical that we have devoted Chapter 34 to this topic. For now, we'll look at how we can apply the features baseline to this important aspect of software management.

Official Change

The features baseline provides an excellent mechanism for managing high-level change. For example, when the customer requests a new system capability (an official change) and that capability is not part of the features baseline, the impact of the change must be assessed before including the new feature in the baseline. If the project team has done a good job of defining the baseline to begin with, the assumption must be that *any change to the base-*

line must affect the resources, the schedule, or the features set to be delivered in the release.

If the resources are fixed and the schedule cannot be changed, the project team must engage the customer in a decision-making process that prioritizes the new feature relative to the other features scheduled for the release. If the new feature is *critical*, it must, by definition, be included in the release, and the customer and the project team should jointly determine which features will be excluded from the release or at least lowered in priority, with accompanying lower expectations. If the feature is *important* but not *critical*, the project team can proceed with the implementation of the feature on a best-efforts basis, allowing progress to dictate whether the feature makes the release.

Unofficial Change

Paradoxically, the problem of customer-initiated change may be the easiest scope management challenge to handle. It is externally focused, we can establish certain safeguards, and the impact of change can be assessed and made clear to this external stakeholder.

However, experience shows that another class of change threat is even more subversive to the development process. In Chapter 34, we will discuss the hidden dangers of change and gain additional ammunition with which to address the scope management challenge.

Chapter 22

SCOPE MANAGEMENT AND SOFTWARE DEVELOPMENT PROCESS MODELS

Key Points

- The team's development process defines *who* is doing *what*, *when*, and *how*.
- In the waterfall model, software activities proceed through a sequence of steps, with each step based on the activities of the previous step.
- The spiral model begins with a series of risk-driven prototypes, followed by a structured waterfall-like process.
- The iterative approach, a hybrid of the waterfall and spiral models, decouples the lifecycle phases from the software activities that take place in each phase.
- No matter what model you use, you must develop at least one early prototype to get customer feedback.

So far, we have not talked much about the overall software development process and its relationship to the team's ability to achieve the results it desires. However, effective requirements management cannot occur without the context of a reasonably well-defined software process that defines the full set of activities that your team must execute to deliver the final software product. Some software processes are relatively formal, and some are informal, but always, a process is at work, even though it may not be rigorous or documented.

Your team's software development process *defines who (which member of the team) is doing what (what activity is being performed, when (that activity is done in relation to other activities), and how (the details and steps in the activity) in order for your team to reach its goal.* Software processes have a material effect on your team's ability to develop software on time and on budget. In this chapter, we look at some of the higher-level aspects of various types of software processes, namely, the time-dependent phases and major types of activities in those phases, and we then analyze how the various software processes affect the scope management challenge.

The Waterfall Model

Boehm (1988a) points out that, as early as the 1950s, the software industry, recognizing the cost of discovering software defects late in the cycle, adopted a logical, stepwise process model, which progressed from a requirement phase to a design phase to a coding phase, and so on. This was a major improvement over the earlier, two phase "code and fix" model, whereby programmers first wrote the code and then fixed it until it couldn't be fixed any more.

In the 1970s, Winston Royce (1970), working at TRW, defined what became known as the "waterfall model" of software development. The waterfall model improved on the strictly stepwise model by

- Recognizing the need for feedback loops between stages, thereby acknowledging that design affects requirements, that coding the system will cause the design to be revisited, and so on.
- Developing a prototype system in parallel with requirements analysis and design activities

As shown in Figure 22–1, in the waterfall model, software activities proceed logically through a sequence of steps. Each step bases its work on the activities of the previous step. Design logically follows requirements, coding follows design, and so on. The waterfall model has been widely followed over the past two decades and has served successfully as a process model for a variety of medium- to large-scale projects.

Note that as commonly applied, Figure 22–1 does not reference the prototyping activity prescribed. This is an unfortunate mistake in history that we'll return to shortly.

The waterfall model has been somewhat successful in reinforcing the role of requirements as the necessary first step in software development, the basis for design and coding activities. However, this strength became a source of difficulty, as it tended to emphasize fully elaborated requirements and design documents as a barrier to exit from each phase. Also, through perhaps its misapplication by overzealous development teams, *this model has come to represent a fixed, rigid approach to development, wherein requirements are "frozen"*

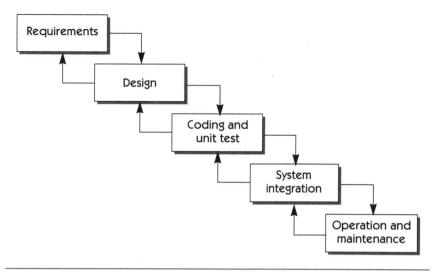

Figure 22–1 Waterfall model of software development

for the life of the project, change is anathema, and the process of development takes on a life of its own. In this case, over time, the team may be completely disengaged from the real world that the project was originally based on.

The waterfall model comes under additional pressure when it is aligned to the scope management challenge (Figure 22–2). Specifically, if the waterfall model is applied to a project that is initiated with 200 percent scope, the results can be disastrous. At deadline time, nothing really works, unit test and system integration are forced or abandoned, and significant investments have been made in the specification, design, and coding of system features that are never delivered. The result: nothing deliverable, chaos, poor quality, and software scrap.

Primarily for these reasons, the waterfall model has become less popular. One unfortunate result has been the tendency to leap right into code, with an inadequate understanding of the requirements for the system, which was one of the main problems the waterfall model was trying to solve!

The Spiral Model

Barry Boehm's pivotal study (1988a) recommended a different framework for guiding the software development process. His "spiral model" of software

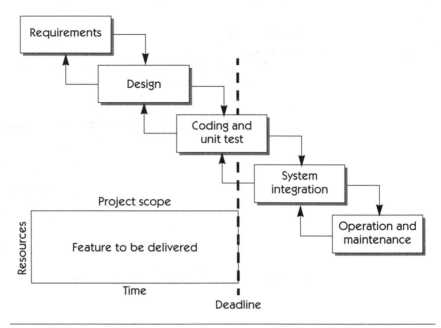

Figure 22–2 Applying the waterfall model to a project with 200% scope

development is a role model for those who believe that success follows a more risk-driven and incremental development path (Figure 22–3).

In the spiral model, development is initially driven by a series of risk-driven prototypes; then a structured waterfall-like process is used to produce the final system. Of course, when misused, the spiral model can exhibit as many problems as the misused waterfall model. Projects sometimes fall into a cut-and-try approach, providing incremental deliverables that must be expanded and maintained with the addition of bubble gum and baling wire, of what some refer to as the process of creating instant legacy code, progress being measured by our newfound ability to create nonmaintainable and nonunder-standable code two to three times as fast as with earlier technology!

When you look at the spiral model more carefully, however, it provides a sensible road map that helps address some of the requirements challenges noted in this book. Specifically, the spiral model starts with requirements planning and concept validation, followed by one or more prototypes to assist in early confirmation of our understanding of the requirements for the system. The main advantage of this process is the availability of multiple feedback opportunities with the users and customers, which is intended to get the "Yes, Buts" out early. Opponents of this rigorous approach note that

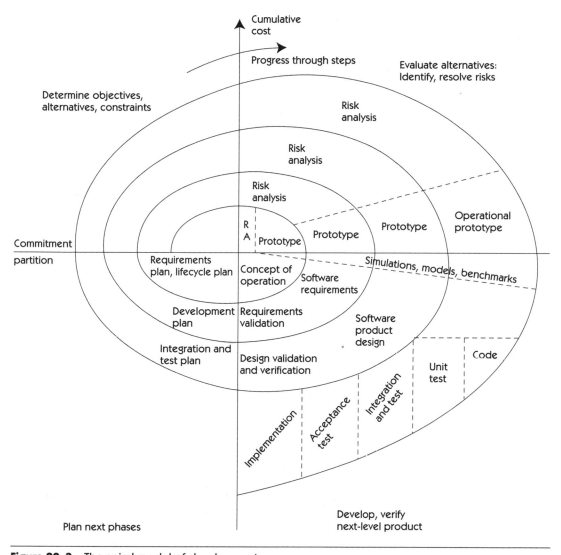

Figure 22–3 The spiral model of development

in today's environment, the luxury of time implied by full concept validation, two or three prototypes, and then a rigorous waterfall methodology is simply not available.

Again, what happens in the spiral model when a project is initiated with 200 percent scope? Figure 22–4 illustrates the result. One might argue that the result is not much better than a disastrous waterfall plan; others might note

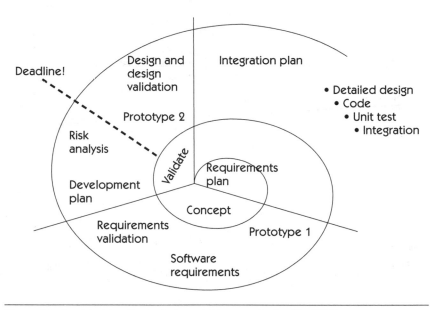

Figure 22–4   Applying the spiral model to a project with 200% scope

that at least a prototype or two is operational and that one has customer feedback at the deadline time. (Of course, a lot of this feedback will focus on the lack of availability of any production-deployable software!)

The Iterative Approach

In the past decade, many teams have migrated to a new approach, one that combines the best of waterfall and spiral models and is a hybrid of the two. This new approach also incorporates some additional constructs from the advancing discipline of software process engineering. The "iterative approach" that was introduced in Kruchten (1995) has now been well described in a number of texts, including Kruchten (1999) and Royce (1998). This approach has proved effective in a wide variety of project types and can exhibit a number of advantages over the waterfall and the spiral models of development.

In the traditional software development process models, time moves forward through a series of sequential activities, with requirements preceding design, design preceding implementation, and so on. This seems quite sensible. In the iterative approach, the lifecycle phases are decoupled from the logical software activities that occur in each phase, allowing us to revisit various activities, such as requirements, design, and implementation, at various iterations of the project. In addition, like the spiral model, each iteration is designed to mitigate whatever risks are present in that stage of development activity.

Lifecycle Phases

The interactive approach consists of four lifecycle phases: inception, elaboration, construction, and transition, corresponding to fairly natural "states" of the project at these times. (See Figure 22–5.).

1. In the *inception* phase, the team is focused on understanding the business case for the project, the scope of the project, and the feasibility of an implementation. Problem analysis is performed, the Vision document is created, and preliminary estimates of schedule and budget, as well as project risk factors, are defined.
2. In the *elaboration* phase, the requirements for the system are refined, an initial executable architecture is established, and an early feasibility prototype is typically developed and demonstrated.
3. In the *construction* phase, the focus is on implementation. Most of the coding is done in this phase, and the architecture and design are fully developed.
4. Beta testing typically happens in this *transition* phase, and the users and the maintainers of the system are trained on the application. The tested baseline of the application is transitioned to the user community and deployed for use.

Iterations

Within each phase, the project typically undergoes multiple iterations (Figure 22–6). An *iteration* is a sequence of activities with an established plan and evaluation criteria, resulting in an executable of some type. Each iteration builds on the functionality of the prior iteration; thus, the project is developed in an "iterative and incremental" fashion.

Figure 22–5 Lifecycle phases in the iterative approach

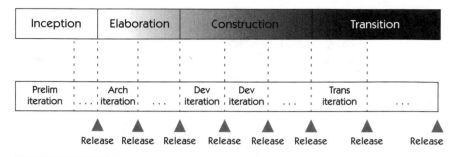

Figure 22–6   Phase iterations, resulting in viable releases

Iterations are selected according to a number of criteria. Early iterations should be designed to evaluate the viability of the chosen architecture against some of the most important and risk-laden use cases.

Workflows

In the iterative approach, the activities associated with the development of the software are organized into a set of *workflows*. Each workflow consists of a logically related set of activities, and each defines how the activities must be sequenced to produce a viable work product, or "artifact." Although the number and kind of workflows can vary, based on the company or project circumstances, there are typically at least six workflows, as Figure 22–7 illustrates.

During each iteration, the team spends as much time as appropriate in each workflow. Thus, an iteration can be regarded as a miniwaterfall through the activities of requirements, analysis and design, and so on, but each miniwaterfall is "tuned" to the specific needs of that iteration. The size of the "hump" in Figure 22–7 indicates the relative amount of effort invested in a workflow. For example, in the elaboration phase, significant time is spent on "refining" the requirements and in defining the architecture that will support the functionality. The activities can be sequential (a true miniwaterfall) or may execute concurrently, as is appropriate to the project.

From the requirements management perspective, the iterative approach has two significant advantages

1. *Getting the "Yes, Buts" out early.* Each iteration produces an executable release such that, very early in the project, the customers have the opportunity to see the work product. And, of course, their reaction

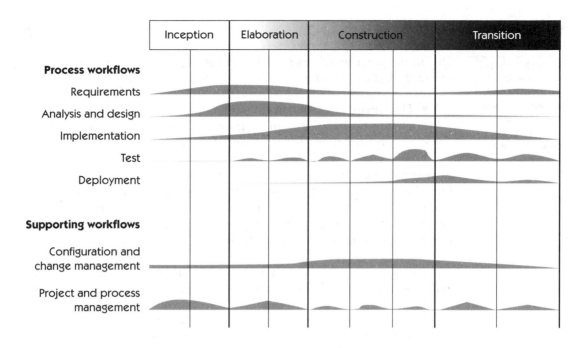

Figure 22–7   Workflows of the iterative approach

will be "Yes, But," but at this early stage, only a minimal investment has been made. With each successive iteration, the size of the "Yes, But" should decrease, and you and your customer will eventually converge on the right system.

2. *Better scope management.* If the first iteration is missed by 30 percent, that's an indicator that the project may be badly scoped, and adjustments can be made. Even if scope is not well managed, multiple executable iterations have been developed by the time the deadline is reached, and the last may even be deployed. Even though it lacks some functionality, the release will deliver value to the user, if the features have been picked and prioritized carefully, allowing your customer to meet objectives, at least in part, as you continue with further development iterations. And, if the architecture is robust and addresses the key technical issues, your team will have a solid platform on which to base the additional functionality.

What to Do, What to Do . . .

No matter what model you use, the team must *provide at least one* robust, evaluation prototype for early customer feedback.

One of the premises of this book is that getting the "Yes, Buts" out early is one of *the* highest-leverage activities of the software process.

- How many times do you have to do it?
- Do the customer's demands change at each and every prototype?
- Are we doomed no matter what process we follow?

Answers: at least once, yes, and no. Yes, customers will ask for change every time they see it. No, you are not doomed. The reason is that the *amount* of change that occurs after a customer has the opportunity to see, touch, and interact with the intended implementation is small compared to the customer's response to the first tangible artifact of the process.

So, although we prefer the iterative model in our development projects, no matter what software development process model you use, it is mandatory that the development activity *provide at least one robust evaluation prototype* for customer feedback before the majority of the design and coding activity is performed. (Remember the prototype activity that Royce (1970) suggested in the initial waterfall model?) By reducing the amount of change to a manageable level, the developer succeeds by making incremental changes, typically in user interfaces, reports, and other outputs, to a robust and high-quality design and implementation. Thereafter, a rigorous process of finalizing design, coding, unit tests, and system integration activities will provide a solid foundation for the product while simultaneously greatly assisting the quality assurance and test activities.

Team Skill 4 Summary

In Team Skill 4, Managing Scope, we learned that the problem of project scope is endemic. Projects typically are initiated with approximately twice the amount of functionality that the team can reasonably implement in a quality manner. This shouldn't surprise us, as it is the nature of the beast: customers want more, marketing wants more, and we want more, too. We just need to make sure that we put ourselves on a diet sufficient to make sure that we can deliver *something* on time.

We looked at various techniques for setting priorities, and we defined the notion of the baseline—an agreed-to understanding of what the system will do—as a key project work product—our touchstone and reference point for decisions and assessment. We learned that if scope and the concomitant expectations exceed reality, in all probability, some bad news is about to be delivered. We decided on a philosophy of approach that engages our customer in the hard decisions. After all, we are just the resources, not the decision makers; it's the customer's project. So the question is, What exactly *must* be accomplished in the next release, given the resources that are available to the project?

Even then, we expect to do some negotiating; all of life, and certainly all of business, is a negotiation in a sense, and we shouldn't be surprised by this either. We briefly mentioned a few negotiation skills and hinted that the team may need to use these skills on occasion.

We cannot expect that this process will make the scope challenge go away, any more than any other single process will solve the problems of the application development world. However, the steps we have outlined can be expected to have a material effect on the scope of the problem, allowing application developers to focus on critical subsets and to incrementally deliver high-quality systems that meet or exceed the expectations of the user. Further, engaging the customer in helping solve the scope management problem increases commitment on the part of both parties and fosters improved communication and trust between the customer and application development teams. With a comprehensive definition of the product (Vision document) in hand and scope managed to a reasonable level, while it's too early to start bragging, we at least have the *opportunity* to succeed in the next phases of the project.

Team Skill 5

REFINING THE SYSTEM DEFINITION

The previous Team Skills were focused on the processes of analyzing the problem, eliciting user needs, and collecting, documenting, and managing the desired product features. Once the product features have been specified, the next task is to refine the specification to a level of detail suitable to drive the design, coding, and testing processes. We have now arrived at the heart of the requirements pyramid, the "specification level," as shown in Figure 1.

In Team Skill 5, we will examine an organized method for elaborating, organizing, and communicating the software requirements. We will end Team Skill 5 with a look at one of the more perplexing issues: how to state the requirements in a clear, concise manner.

Regardless of the method you use to collect the requirements, it is *crucial* that you adopt a philosophy that the collected requirements and only those requirements will drive the project. If they are discovered to be insufficient or just wrong, they must be quickly and officially changed so that the rule remains true. In this way, the entire team has an unambiguous target, and its efforts can be focused on discovering and implementing requirements, minimizing the time spent "in the weeds." We will start by examining the nature of the requirements themselves.

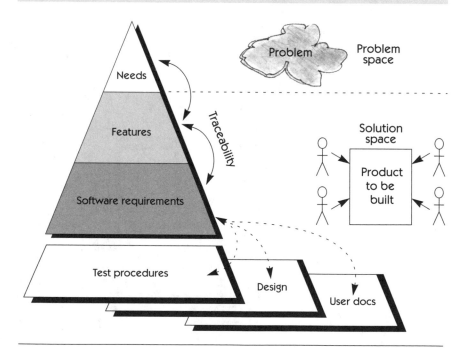

Figure 1   The requirements pyramid

Chapter 23

SOFTWARE REQUIREMENTS

Key Points

- A complete set of requirements can be determined by defining the system inputs, outputs, functions, attributes, and attributes of the system environment.
- Requirements should exclude project-related information, such as schedules, project plans, budgets, and tests, as well as design information.
- The requirements/design process is iterative; requirements lead to the selection of certain design options, which in turn may initiate new requirements.
- Design constraints are restrictions on the design of the system, or the process by which a system is developed.

In the prior Team Skills, the features that were defined for the system were purposely left at a high level of abstraction so that:

- We can better understand the shape and the form of the system by focusing on its features and how they fulfill user needs.
- We can assess the system for completeness and consistency and its fit within its environment.
- We can use this information to determine feasibility and to manage the scope of the system before making significant investments.

In addition, staying at a high level of abstraction kept us from making overly constraining requirements decisions too early, that is, before the people closest to the system implementation have their opportunity to add their perspective and value to the system definition. In Team Skill 5, Refining the System Definition, our discussions transition to elaborating the system features in detail sufficient to ensure that the design and coding activities result in a system that fully conforms to the user needs. In so doing, we drive to the next level of specificity and detail, and we create a richer, deeper requirements model for the system to be built. Of course, we also create more information to be managed, and we will have to be better organized to handle this additional detail.

The level of specificity needed in this next step depends on a number of factors, including the context of the application and the skills of the development team. In high-assurance software systems for medical equipment, aircraft avionics, or online trading, the level of specificity is appropriately high. The refinement process may include formal mechanisms for quality assurance, reviews, inspections, modeling, and the like. In systems with less catastrophic consequences of failure, the level of effort will be more modest. In those cases, the work involved is simply to make certain that the system definition is precise enough so as to be understood by all parties and yet provide an efficient development environment and a "high enough" probability of success. The focus is on pragmatics and economics, doing just enough requirements specification to make certain that the software developed is what the user wanted.

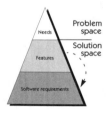

Just as there is no one right programming language for every application, there is no one right way to develop the more detailed specifications. Different environments call for different techniques, and the requirements managers and requirements writers will probably need to develop a mix of skills suited to various circumstances. We have applied a variety of techniques in a variety of circumstances, from fairly rigorous requirements documents, custom databases, or requirements repositories to use-case models and more formal methods. However, the locus of the effort has typically been on a natural-language specification, written clearly enough to be understandable by all stakeholders, customers, users, developers, and testers but specific enough ("Axis 4 shall have a maximum traverse speed of 1 meter/second") to allow for verification and demonstration of compliance. Before we begin to collect the system requirements, we will first consider the nature of the requirements you will need to discover and to define.

Definition of Software Requirements

In Chapter 2, we started with this straightforward definition for a requirement, which is one of the following.

- A software capability needed by the user to solve a problem to achieve an objective
- A software capability that must be met or possessed by a system or a system component to satisfy a contract, standard, specification, or other formally imposed documentation

Software requirements are those things that the software does on behalf of the user or device or another system. The first place to look for software requirements is around the boundary of the system for the things that go "into" and "out of" the system: the system interactions with these users.

To do this, it's easiest to first think of the system as a black box and to think about things that you would have to define to fully describe what the black box does.

In addition to the inputs and outputs, you will also need to think about certain other characteristics of the system, including its performance and other types of complex behavior, as well as other ways in which the system interacts with its environment (Figure 23–1).

Using a similar approach, Davis (1999) determined that we need five major classes of things to fully describe the system:

1. *Inputs to the system*—not only the *content* of the input but also, as necessary, the details of input devices and the form, look, and feel—protocol—of the input. As most developers are well aware, this area can involve significant detail and may be subject to volatility, especially for GUI, multimedia, or Internet environments.

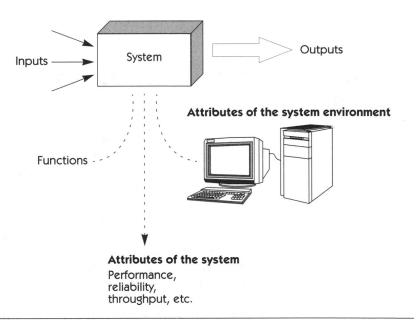

Figure 23–1   System elements

2. *Outputs from the system*—a description of the output devices, such as voice-output or visual display, that must be supported, as well as the protocol and formats of the information generated by the system.

3. *Functions of the system*—the mapping of inputs to outputs, and their various combinations.

4. *Attributes of the system*—such typical nonbehavioral requirements as reliability, maintainability, availability, and throughput, that the developers must taken into account.

5. *Attributes of the system environment*—such additional nonbehavioral requirements as the ability of the system to operate within certain operating constraints, loads, and operating system compatibility.

We have worked with this categorization for a number of years and have found that it works quite well, as it helps one think about the requirements problem in a consistent and complete manner. Accordingly, we can determine a complete set of software requirements by defining

- Inputs to the system
- Outputs from the system
- Functions of the system
- Attributes of the system
- Attributes of the system environment

In addition, we'll be able to evaluate whether a "thing" is a software requirement by testing it against this elaborated definition.

Relationship between Features and Software Requirements

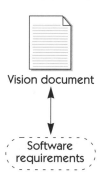

Vision document

↕

Software
requirements

Earlier, we spent some time exploring the "features" of a system. The features are simple descriptions of a desired and useful behavior. We can now see that there is a mapping relationship between features and software requirements. The Vision document cites features in the user's language. The software requirements, in turn, express those features in more detailed terms, using one or more specific software requirements that must be fulfilled by the developers in order to provide the features to the user. In other words, features help us understand and communicate at a high level of abstraction, but we probably can't describe the system and write code from those descriptions. They are at too high a level of abstraction for this purpose.

Software requirements, however, are specific. We can code from them, and they should be specific enough to be "testable"; that is, we should be able

Table 23–1 Requirements associated with particular Vision document features

Vision document	Software Requirements
Feature 63: The defect-tracking system will provide trending information to help the user assess project status.	SR63.1 Trending information will be provided in a histogram report showing time on the x-axis and the number of defects found on the y-axis. SR63.2 The user can enter the trending period in units of days, weeks, or months. SR63.3 An example trend report is shown in attached Figure 1.

to test a system to validate that it really does implement the requirement. For example, suppose we are developing a defect-tracking system for an assembly-line manufacturing organization or for a software development organization. Table 23–1 shows the relationship between one of the features identified in the Vision document and an associated set of requirements. This mapping, and the ability to trace between the various features and requirements, will form the backbone of a very important requirements management concept known as "traceability," a topic we'll discuss later.

The Requirements Dilemma: What versus How

As we have seen, requirements tell the developers what their system must do and must cover the issues of the system inputs, outputs, functions, and attributes, along with attributes of the system environment. But there's a lot of other information that the requirements should *not* contain. In particular, they should avoid stipulating any unnecessary design or implementation details, information associated with project management; and they should avoid information about how the system will be tested. In this way, the requirements focus on the *behavior* of the system, and they are volatile only to the extent that the behavior is volatile or subject to change.

Exclude Project Information

Project-related information, such as schedules, configuration management plans, verification and validation plans, budgets, and staffing schedules, are sometimes bundled into the set of requirements for the convenience of the project manager. In general, this must be avoided, since changes in this information, such as schedule changes, increase volatility and the tendency for the "requirements" to be out of date. (When the requirements are dated, they become less trustworthy and more likely to be ignored.) In addition, the inevitable debates about such things should be well separated from the discussion of what the *system is supposed to do*. There are different stakeholders involved, and they serve different purposes.

The budget could be construed as a requirement too; nevertheless, this is another type of information that doesn't fit our definition and therefore doesn't belong with the overall system or software requirements. The budget may turn out to be an important piece of information when the developers try to decide which implementation strategies they'll choose, because some strategies may be too expensive or may take too long to carry out. Nevertheless, they are not requirements; in a similar fashion, information describing how we'll know that the requirements have actually been met—test procedures or acceptance procedures—also don't meet the definition and therefore don't belong in the specs.

We usually find it convenient to "push the envelope" a little bit here. In many cases, it is probably useful for the requirement writer to give a "hint" as to a suitable test for the requirement. After all, the requirement writer had a specific behavior in mind for the requirement, and it's only reasonable to give as much help as possible.

Exclude Design Information

The requirements should also not include information about the system design or architecture. Otherwise, you may accidentally have restricted your team from pursuing whatever design options make the most sense for your application. ("Hey, we have to design it that way; it's in the requirements.")

Whereas the elimination of project management and testing details from the list of requirements is fairly straightforward, the elimination of design/implementation details is usually much more difficult and much more subtle. Suppose, for example, that the first requirement in Table 23–1 had been worded like this: "SR63.1 Trending information will be provided in a histogram report written in Visual Basic, showing major contributing causes on the *x*-axis and the number of defects found on the *y*-axis" (see Figure 23–2).

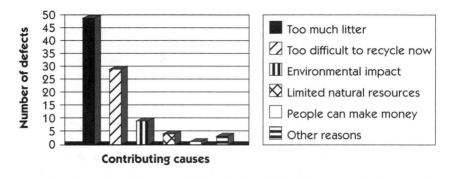

Figure 23–2   Pareto diagram

Although the reference to Visual Basic appears to be a fairly blatant violation of the guidelines we've recommended (because it doesn't represent any input, output, function, or behavioral attribute), it's useful to ask: "Who decided to impose the requirement that the histogram be implemented in Visual Basic, and why was that decision made?" Possible answers to that question might be:

- One of the technically oriented members of the group defining the Vision document decided that Visual Basic should be specified because it is the "best" solution for the problem.
- The user may have specified it. Knowing just enough about technology to be dangerous, the user, worried that the technical people may adopt another technology, one that's more expensive or less readily available, knows that VB is readily available and relatively cheap and wants that technology to be used.
- A political decision within the development organization may have mandated that all applications will be developed with Visual Basic. In an effort to ensure compliance and to prevent its policies from being ignored, management insists that references to Visual Basic be inserted whenever possible into requirements documents.

If a technical developer decides to insert a reference to Visual Basic because of an arbitrary preference for the language, it obviously has no legitimate place in the list of requirements. If the user provided the requirement, things get a little stickier. If the customer refuses to pay for a system unless it's written in Visual Basic, the best course of action is to treat it like a requirement, *although we will place it in a special class, called design constraints, so that it is separated from the normal requirements, which influence only the external behavior.* Nevertheless, it's an implementation constraint that has been imposed on the development team. (By the way, if you think that this example is unrealistic, consider the common requirement imposed by the U.S. Defense Department on its software contractors until the late 1990s to build systems using Ada.)

Meanwhile, the discussion of Visual Basic in this example may have obscured a more subtle and perhaps more important requirement analysis: Why does the trending information have to be shown in a histogram report? Why not a bar chart, a pie chart, or another representation of the information? Furthermore, does the word "report" imply a hard-copy printed document, or does it also imply that the information can be displayed on a computer screen? Is it necessary to capture the information so that it can be imported into other programs or uploaded to the corporate extranet? The feature described in the Vision document can almost certainly be fulfilled in various ways, some of which have very definite implementation consequences.

In many cases, the description of a problem from which a requirement can be formulated is influenced by the user's perception of the potential solutions that are available to solve the problem. The same is true of the developers who participate with the user to formulate the features that make up the Vision document and the requirements. As the old adage reminds us, "If your only tool is a hammer, all your problems look like a nail." But we need to be vigilant about unnecessary and unconscious implementation constraints creeping into the requirements, and we need to remove such constraints whenever we can.

More on Requirements versus Design

So far, we have treated software requirements, design decisions, and design constraints as if they were distinct entities that can be clearly differentiated. That is, we have stated or implied that

- Requirements precede design.
- Users and customers, because they are closest to the need, make requirements decisions.

- Technologists make design decisions because they are best suited to pick, among the many design options, which option is best suited to meet the need.

This is a good model, and it is the right starting point for a requirements management philosophy. Davis (1993) calls this the "what versus how" paradigm, where "what" represents the requirements, or "what" the system is to do, and "how" represents the design that is to be implemented to achieve this objective.

We've presented the story in this fashion for a reason. It is best to understand requirements before design, and most design constraints ("use XYZ class library for database access") are important design decisions recorded in the requirements assets so that we can ensure that we achieve them for a contractual or, perhaps quite legitimate, technical reason.

If we couldn't make these classifications at all, the picture would be very muddled, and we couldn't differentiate requirements from design. Further, we would no longer know *who* is responsible for *what* in the development process. Even worse, our customers would dictate design, and our designers would dictate requirements.

But a subtle and yet serious complication underlies this discussion and belies the simple paradigm we've presented. Returning to our case study for example, if the team makes a design decision, such as selection of a PC technology to run in the HOLIS CCU subsystem, it's likely to have some external impact on the user. For example, a prompt or log-on screen will show up somewhere in the user's world. Better yet, we will probably want to take advantage of some user input capabilities of the OS, and those class libraries will certainly exhibit external behaviors to the user. (Note to the techies among you: Yes, we could hide it, but that's beside the point.)

Given the definitions we've provided in this chapter, the question becomes: Once the impact of a design decision causes external behavior seen by the user, does that same decision, which now clearly affects "input or output from the system," now become a requirement? One could argue that the correct answer is "yes," or "no," or even "it doesn't really matter," based on your individual interpretation of the definitions and analysis we've provided so far. But that makes light of a very important matter, as an understanding of this issue is critical to an understanding of the nature of the iterative process itself. Let's take a closer look.

Requirements:
What the
system needs
to do

Design:
How the
system is
to do it

Iterating Requirements and Design

In reality, the requirements versus design activities must be iterative. Requirements *discovery*, definition, and *design decisions* are circular. The process is a continual give and take, in that

current requirements cause us to consider selecting certain design options,

and

selected design options may initiate new requirements.

Occasionally, discovery of a new technology may cause us to throw out a host of assumptions about what the requirements were supposed to be; we may have discovered an entirely new approach that obviates the old strategy. ("Let's throw out the entire client/data access/GUI module and substitute a browser-based interface.") This is a prime, and legitimate, source of requirements change.

This process is as it should be; to attempt to do otherwise would be folly. On the other hand, there is grave danger in all of this, for if we do not truly understand the customer's needs *and* the customer is not engaged actively in the requirements process—and yes, in some cases, even understanding our *design-related activities*—the *wrong* decision might be made. When properly managed, this "continual reconsideration of requirements and design" is a truly fantastic process, as technology drives our continually improving ability to meet our customer's real needs. *That's the essence of what effective and iterative requirements management is all about.* But when improperly managed, we continually "chase our technology tail," and disaster results. We never said it would be easy.

A Further Characterization of Requirements

The preceding discussions on requirements suggested that various "kinds" of requirements exist. Specifically, we have found it useful to think about three "types" of requirements, as shown in Figure 23–3:

- Functional software requirements
- Nonfunctional software requirements
- Design constraints

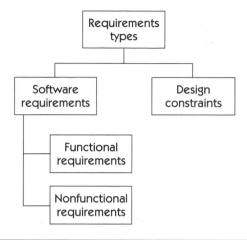

Figure 23–3   Types of requirements

Functional Software Requirements

As you might expect, functional requirements express how the system behaves. These requirements are usually action oriented ("When the user does *x*, the system will do *y*.") Most products and applications, conceived to do useful work, are rich with software functional requirements. Software is used to implement the majority of the functionality.

When you are defining functional requirements, you should seek a good balance between being too specific in stating a requirement and being too general or too ambiguous. For example, it is not usually helpful to have a general functional requirement stated in the form "When you push this button, the system turns on and operates." On the other hand, a requirement statement that takes up several pages of text is probably too specific, but it may be the right thing to do in very special cases. We'll return to this matter in Chapter 26.

We have found that most functional requirements can be stated in simple declarative statements or in the use case form we'll describe in the next chapter. Experience has shown us that a one- or two-sentence statement of a requirement is usually the best way to match a user need with a level of specificity that a developer can deal with.

Nonfunctional Software Requirements

So far in this chapter, most of the examples for requirements have involved *behavioral*, or *functional*, requirements of a system, focusing on inputs, outputs, and processing details. The functional requirements tell us how the system must behave when presented with certain inputs or conditions.

But that's not enough to fully describe the requirements of a system. We must also consider things that Grady (1992) called "*nonfunctional requirements*":

- Usability
- Reliability
- Performance
- Supportability

These requirements are used most typically to express some of the "attributes of the system" or "attributes of the system environment" elements of our elaborated definition. This convenient classification helps us to understand more about the system we are to build. Let's look at each in further detail.

Usability   It's important to describe the ease with which the system can be learned and operated by the intended users. Indeed, we may have to identify various categories of users: beginners, "normal" users, "power" users, illiterate users, users who are not fluent in the native language of the "normal" users, and so on. If you expect your customer to review and to participate in these discussion—and you'd better—you should realize that whatever requirements you write in this area will be written in a natural language; you shouldn't expect to see a finite state machine description of usability!

Since usability tends to be in the eye of the beholder, how do we specify such a fuzzy set of requirements? Some suggestions follow.

- Specify the required training time for a user to become marginally productive—able to accomplish simple tasks—and operationally productive—able to accomplish the normal day-to-day tasks. As noted, this may need to be further described in terms of novice users, who may have never seen a computer before, normal users, and power users.
- Specify measurable task times for typical tasks or transactions that the end user will be carrying out. If we're building a system for order entry, it's likely that the most common tasks carried out by end users will be entering, deleting, or modifying an order and checking on the status of an order. Once the users have been trained how to perform those tasks, how long should it take them to enter a typical order? A minute? Five minutes? An hour? Of course, this could be affected by performance issues in the technical implementation (such as modem speed, network capacity, RAM, and CPU power, that collectively

determine the response time provided by the system, but task-performance times are also strongly affected by the usability of the system, and we should be able to specify that separately.

- Compare the usability of the new system with other state-of-the-art systems that the user community knows and likes. Thus, the requirement might state, "The new system shall be judged by 90 percent of the user community to be at least as usable as the existing XYZ system." Remember, this kind of requirement, like all other requirements, should be verifiable; that is, we must describe the requirement in such a way that the users can test and verify the usability against the criteria we've established.

- Specify the existence and required features of online help systems, wizards, tool tips, user manuals, and other forms of documentation and assistance.

- Follow conventions and standards that have been developed for the human-to-machine interface. Having a system work "just like what I'm used to" can be accomplished by following consistent standards from application to application. For example, you can specify a requirement to conform to common usability standards, such as IBM's CUA (Common User Access) standards, or the Windows applications standards published by Microsoft.

Examples of usability breakthroughs in the computer world include the difference between command line interfaces, exemplified by DOS (shudder!) and UNIX systems, versus the GUI interfaces, exemplified by Macintosh and Windows systems. It is clear that the GUI interfaces were instrumental in making computers easier to use by the great masses of nontechnical users. Another example is the Internet browser, which gave a "face" to the World Wide Web and radically accelerated the adoption of the Internet for the average user.

User's Bill of Rights

Several interesting attempts to strengthen the somewhat fuzzy notion of usability have been made. Perhaps the most interesting effort has resulted in the "User's Bill of Rights" (Karat 1998). A recent version of the bill contains ten key points:

1. The user is always right. If there is a problem with the use of the system, the system is the problem, not the user.
2. The user has the right to easily install and uninstall software and hardware systems without negative consequences.
3. The user has a right to a system that performs exactly as promised.
4. The user has a right to easy-to-use instructions (user guides, online or contextual help, error messages) for understanding and utilizing a system to achieve desired goals and recover efficiently and gracefully from problem situations.

5. The user has a right to be in control of the system and to be able to get the system to respond to a request for attention.
6. The user has the right to a system that provides clear, understandable, and accurate information regarding the task it is performing and the progress toward completion.
7. The user has a right to be clearly informed about all system requirements for successfully using software or hardware.
8. The user has a right to know the limits of the system's capabilities.
9. The user has a right to communicate with the technology provider and receive a thoughtful and helpful response when raising concerns.
10. The user should be the master of software and hardware technology, not vice versa. Products should be natural and intuitive to use.

Note that some of the topics covered in the Bill of Rights are essentially unmeasurable and are probably not good candidates for requirements per se. On the other hand, it seems clear that the bill should be useful to you as a starting point in developing questions and defining requirements for the usability of the proposed product.

Reliability Of course, nobody likes bugs, defects, system failures, or lost data, and in the absence of any reference to such phenomena in the requirements, the user will naturally assume that none will exist. But in today's computer-literate world, even the most optimistic user is aware that things do go wrong. Thus, the requirements should describe the degree to which the system *must* behave in a user-acceptable fashion. This typically includes the following issues:

- *Availability.* The system must be available for operational use a specified percentage of the time. In the extreme case, the requirement(s) might specify "nonstop" availability, that is, 24 hours a day, 365 days a year. It's more common to see a stipulation of 99 percent availability or a stipulation of 99.9 percent availability between the hours of 8 A.M. and midnight. Note that the requirement(s) must define what "availability" means. Does 100 percent availability mean that all of the users must be able to use all of the system's services all of the time?
- *Mean time between failures (MTBF).* This is usually specified in hours, but it also could be specified in days, months, or years. Again, this requires precision: The requirement(s) must carefully define what is meant by a "failure."
- *Mean time to repair (MTTR).* How long is the system allowed to be out of operation after it has failed? A range of MTTR values may be appropriate; for example, the user might stipulate that 90 percent of all system failures must be repairable within 5 minutes and that 99.9 percent of all failures must be repairable within 1 hour. Again, preci-

sion is important: The requirement(s) must clarify whether "repair" means that all of the users will once again be able to access all of the services or whether a subset of full recovery is acceptable.

▪ *Accuracy.* What precision is required in systems that produce numerical outputs? Must the results in a financial system, for example, be accurate to the nearest penny or to the nearest dollar?

▪ *Maximum bugs, or defect rate.* This is usually expressed in terms of bugs/KLOC (thousands of lines of code), or bugs per function-point.

▪ *Bugs per type.* This is usually categorized in terms of minor, significant, and critical bugs. Definitions are important here, too: The requirement(s) must define what is meant by a "critical" bug, such as complete loss of data or complete inability to use certain parts of the functionality of the system.

In some cases, the requirements may specify some "predictor" metrics for reliability. A typical example of this is the use of a "complexity metric," such as the cyclomatic complexity metric, which can be used to assess the complexity—and therefore the potential "bugginess"—of a software program.

Performance Performance requirements usually cover such categories as

▪ Response time for a transaction: average, maximum
▪ Throughput: transactions per second
▪ Capacity: the number of customers or transactions the system can accommodate
▪ Degradation modes: what is the acceptable mode of operation when the system has been degraded

If the new system has to share hardware resources with other systems or applications, it may also be necessary to stipulate the degree to which the implementation will make "civilized" use of such scarce resources as the CPU, memory, channels, disk storage, and network bandwidth.

Supportability Supportability is the ability of the software to be easily modified to accommodate enhancements and repairs. For some application domains, the likely nature of future enhancements can be anticipated in advance, and a requirement could stipulate the "response time" of the maintenance group for simple enhancements, moderate enhancements, and complex enhancements.

For example, suppose that we are building a new payroll system; one of the many requirements of such a system is that it must compute the government withholding taxes for each employee. The user knows, of course, that the government changes the algorithm for this calculation each year. This change involves two numbers: instead of withholding X percent of an employee's gross salary up to a maximum of P, the new law requires the payroll system to withhold Y percent up to a maximum of Q. As a result, a requirement might say, "Modifications to the system for a new set of with-holding tax rates shall be accomplished by the team within 1 day of notification by the tax regulatory authority."

But suppose that the tax authority also periodically introduced "exceptions" to this algorithm: "For left-handed people with blue eyes, the withholding tax rate shall be Z percent, up to a maximum of R." Modifications of this kind would be more difficult for the software people to anticipate; although they might try to build their system in as flexible a manner as possible, they would still argue that the modification for left-handed employees falls into the category of "medium-level" changes, for which the requirement might stipulate a response time of 1 week.

But suppose that at the outset of the project, the manager of the payroll department also said, "By the way, it's possible that we'll expand our operation overseas, in which case, the withholding tax algorithm would have to be adjusted to reflect the current laws in France and Germany and maybe Hong Kong, too." Assuming that such a "requirement" made any sense at all, it could probably be stated only in terms of goals and intentions; it would be difficult to measure and verify such a requirement.

What the requirement statement *can* do, in order to increase the chances that the system will be supportable in the manner just described, is stipulate the use of certain programming languages, database management system (DBMS) environments, programming tools, maintenance routines, programming styles and standards, and so on. (In this case, these really become design constraints, as we'll see.) Whether this does produce a system that can be maintained more easily is a topic for debate and discussion, but at least we can get closer to the goal.

Design Constraints

The third class of requirements, *design constraints*, typically impose limitations on the design of the system or the processes we use to build a system. For example,

- Usually, a requirement allows for more than one design option; a design is a conscious choice among options. Whenever possible, we want to leave that choice to the designers rather than specifying it in the requirements, for they will be in the best position to evaluate the technical and economic merits of each option. Whenever we do not allow a choice to be made ("Use Oracle DBMS"), the design has been constrained, and a degree of flexibility and development freedom has been lost.

■ A requirement that is imposed on the process of building software ("Program in VB," or use "XYZ class library") is a design constraint.

As illustrated with the preceding Visual Basic example, there may be many such sources and rationales, and the designers may have to accept them whether they like them or not. But it's important to distinguish them from more conventional requirements, for many of the constraints may be arbitrary, political, or subject to rapid technological change and might thus be subject to renegotiation at a later point.

We'll define design constraints as

restrictions on the design of a system, or the process by which a system is developed, that do not affect the external behavior of the system but that must be fulfilled to meet technical, business, or contractual obligations.

Design constraints can also be found in the developmental infrastructure immediately surrounding the system to be developed. These usually include

■ Operating environments: *"Write the software in Visual Basic."*
■ Compatibility with existing systems: *"The application must run on both our new and old platforms."*
■ Application standards: *"Use the class library from Developer's Library 99-724 on the corporate IT server."*
■ Corporate "best practices" and standards: *"Compatibility with the legacy data base must be maintained." "Use our C++ coding standards."*

Another important source of design constraints is the body of regulations and standards under which the project is being developed. For example, the development of a medical product in the United States is subject to a significant number of Food and Drug Administration (FDA) standards and regulations, imposed on not only the product but also the process by which the product is developed and documented. Typical regulatory design constraints might include regulations and standards from the following:

■ Food and Drug Administration (FDA)
■ Federal Communications Commission (FCC)
■ Department of Defense (DOD)

- International Organization for Standardization (ISO) (No, this is not an error. ISO is a short, language-independent form, not an acronym.)
- Underwriters Laboratory (UL)

Typically, the body of regulation imposed by these types of design constraints is far too lengthy to incorporate directly into your requirements. In most cases, it is sufficient to include the design constraints *by reference* into your package. Thus, your requirements might appear in the form: "*The software shall fail safely per the provisions of TüV Software Standard, Sections 3.1–3.4.*"

Incorporation by reference has its hazards, however. Where necessary, you should be careful to incorporate specific and relevant references instead of more general references. For example, a single reference of the form "*The product must conform to ISO 601*" effectively binds your product to *all* of the standards in the entire document. As usual, you should strive for the "sweet spot" between too much specificity and not enough.

Almost all projects will have some design constraints. Generally, the best way to handle them is to follow these guidelines.

- Distinguish them from the other requirements. For example, if you identified other software requirements with a tag, such as "SR," you might consider using "DC" for design constraints. You might be tempted to distinguish between true design constraints and regulatory constraints, but we have found that this distinction is seldom useful, and it can impose an unacceptable maintenance burden.
- Include all design constraints in a special section of your collected requirements package, or use a special attribute so that they can be readily aggregated. That way, you can easily find them and review them when the factors that influenced them change.
- Identify the source of each design constraint. By doing so, you can use the reference later to question or to revise the requirement. "Oh, this came from Bill in marketing. Let's go see if we can talk to him about this constraint." This would be a good time to supply a specific bibliographic reference in the case of regulatory standard references. That way, you can find the standard more easily when you need to refer to it later.
- Document the rationale for each design constraint. In effect, write a sentence or two explaining why the design constraint was placed in the project. This will help remind you later as to what the motive was for the design constraint. In our experience, almost all projects eventually ask, "Why did we put this constraint in there?" By documenting the rationale, you will be able to more effectively deal with the

design constraints in the later stages of the project when it (inevitably) will become an issue.

Are Design Constraints True Requirements?

You could argue that design constraints are not true software requirements because they do not represent one of the five system elements in our elaborated definition. But when a design constraint is elevated to the level of legitimate business, political, or technical concern, it does meet our definition of a requirement as something necessary to "satisfy a contract, standard, specification, or other formally imposed documentation."

In those cases, it's easiest to treat the design constraint just like any other requirement and to make certain that the system is designed and developed in compliance with that design constraint. However, we should always strive to have as few design constraints as possible, since their existence may often restrict our options for implementing the other requirements, those that directly fulfill a user need.

A Cautionary Tale:

We were working with a Fortune 500 company well known in the industry for its adherence to process and procedure. Imagine our surprise when we found that the company was totally paralyzed in its current requirements-collection activities because the team could not agree on whether certain requirements were functional requirements, nonfunctional requirements, or design constraints. In effect, the team's ability to move ahead with its project was stalled on various semantic quibbles! We told the team that it didn't matter, just move on with *something*!

The point is, the value of the classification is simply to spur your thinking, to assist you on your search for "Undiscovered ruins," and to help you think about these things in different ways. But in a very real sense, the classification doesn't matter, so long as you understand that the requirement is something that you, or the system, will be measured against. Moving ahead with some sort of organized effort is superior to not moving ahead while preparing the perfect requirements categorization plan.

Using Parent-Child Requirements to Increase Specificity

We have found that many projects will benefit from the use of *parent-child requirements* as a tool for augmenting certain basic requirements. We view a parent-child requirement as *an amplification of the specificity expressed in a parent requirement.*

Let's consider an example. This time, we'll use a hardware example to illustrate the point. Suppose that you are developing an electronic device intended to work off standard electrical power. That is, the user is expected to plug the device into a wall outlet. The question arises, "How shall we specify the power requirements of the device?"

A perfectly natural response might be to include a product requirement that says, "The device shall operate off standard North American electrical power." But what does this mean? Your engineers will immediately besiege you for details on voltages, currents, frequencies, and so on. Of course, you could rewrite the requirement to include all of the needed details, but you will probably find that including all of the engineering details has obscured the original intent of the requirement. After all, you just want the device to work when it's plugged into a wall outlet!

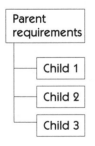

In this case, you might wish to create some requirements to specify voltage, current, frequency, and so on. These requirements should be thought of as "children" of the parent requirement; indeed, we will frequently refer to parent-child relationships in a hierarchical requirement structure. Thus, you might find that specifying the electrical power needs for the device will appear as follows:

Parent: The device shall operate off standard North American power.

> *Child 1:* The device shall operate in a voltage range of *xxx–yyy* volts AC.

> *Child 2:* The device shall require not more than *xxx* AC amperes for correct operation.

> *Child 3:* The device shall operate within specification over an input power frequency range of *xx–yy* hertz.

Parent-child requirements give you a very flexible way to enhance and to augment your specification while simultaneously controlling the depth of detail presented. In our example, it becomes straightforward to present the top-level specification in a way that is easily understandable by the users. At the same time, the detailed "child" specification can be easily inspected by the implementers to make sure that they understand all of the implementation details.

You can extend this notion for cases that require further amplification. For example, it is easy to imagine a case in which the "child" requirement becomes the "parent" requirement to a further level of detail. That is, you might wish to extend the hierarchy further and to detail the product needs as follows:

Parent:

  Child 1:

    Grandchild 1:

    Grandchild 2:

But we want to insert a note of caution here. Although we have found the concept of parent-child requirement to be extremely useful, you must guard against adding too many hierarchical levels of detail, simply because you get bogged down in so many microscopic details that you lose sight of the main user objective. We have found that most projects work quite well with only one sublevel of detail. On occasion, you might find it useful to move to two sublevels of detail—the "child" and the "grandchild"—but rarely is it useful to go below that level of detail.

Organizing Parent-Child Requirements

On balance, we have found that the best plan is to consider the child requirements to be no different from the parent requirements, and you should plan on including them in the main requirements package.

Requirements readers can most easily relate the requirements back to the parent requirement if the identification of child requirements follows a logical pattern of identification based on the parent requirement's identification. For example, suppose that software requirement SR63.1 from Table 23–1 has one or more child requirements. A natural identification scheme for the child requirements would be to identify them as SR63.1.1, SR63.1.2, SR63.1.3, and so on. A hierarchical view of Table 23-1 might then appear as follows:

Feature 63

  SR63.1

    SR63.1.1

    SR63.1.2

    SR63.1.3

  SR63.2

When managing a mixed software requirement/child requirement environment, a helpful feature is the ability to expand/collapse the total set of requirements so that you can view either the parents alone or the parents with the children.

Looking Ahead

Now that we have examined the nature of requirements, we will turn to techniques for *capturing* and *organizing* them. Our next chapter will focus on a powerful technique to capture requirements. Subsequent chapters will focus on the issue of organizing the collection.

Chapter 24

REFINING THE USE CASES

Key Points

- To support the design and coding activities, the use cases developed in the elicitation activities must be more fully elaborated.
- Use cases are most appropriate when the system is rich in functionality and must support differing types of users.
- Use cases are not as effective when applied to systems with few or no users and minimal interfaces, those with mostly nonfunctional requirements, and design constraints.

In Team Skills 1 and 2, we introduced use cases, another technique for expressing requirements for a system. This technique has achieved a degree of popularity and common use.

It can be argued that the use-case technique has certain inherent advantages over the traditional approach to defining individual, discrete (declarative) software requirements.

- Use cases are relatively easy to write.
- Use cases are written in the language of the user.
- Use cases provide related, cohesive threads of behavior, or scenarios, that can be understood by both the user and the developer.
- Because of the "thread of behavior" characteristic and the fact that the UML includes certain specialized elements and notations for use in modeling, use cases provide additional added value by linking the requirements activities to design and implementation. (We'll discuss this further in Chapter 30.)
- The graphical representation of use cases within the UML and support by various modeling tools provide a visual means of expressing

the relationships among use cases, which can improve understandability of a complex software system.

▪ A scenario described by a use case can be used almost directly as a test script at validation time.

Questions to Ask

When Should I Use the Use-Case Methodology?

You should consider using them for capturing the majority of the requirements for the system if either or both of the following aspects apply to your application

▪ The system is functionally oriented, with both varied types of users and functional behavior. Since use cases describe the behavior of the system *for each type of user*, they are most powerful when there are many types of system users and the system needs to deliver different types of functionality for each type of user.

▪ Your project team is implementing the system, using the UML and object-oriented (OO) methods. Certain OO concepts, such as inherited behavior among actors and use cases, abstract actors, lend themselves well to the use-case method and deliver additional utility to the analyst or modeler. The UML notation for use cases also supports visual modeling of the system and provides a modeling paradigm that supports the representation of the needed behavior of the system (the use case) and how that behavior is implemented within the software (via use-case realizations).

When Are Use Cases Not the Best Choice?

However, use cases are not well suited for certain types of systems and some types of requirements. Specifically, you may need to augment or perhaps even abandon the use cases for systems with the following characteristics.

Systems with Few or No Users and Minimal Interfaces Many classes of systems are functionally rich but have few external interfaces and few users and therefore do not lend themselves as well to the use-case technique. Consider, for example, systems designed primarily to perform scientific calculations or simulations, embedded systems, process control systems, a virus-checking system that runs without operator interaction, and software utilities such as compilers and memory management programs. Again, although you can apply use cases in these applications, and although they will probably be useful in augmenting the traditional approach, there may be easier ways to express the majority of the requirements.

Systems Dominated Primarily by Nonfunctional Requirements and Design Constraints As mentioned earlier, use cases can be poor containers for nonfunctional requirements—the attributes of the system and of the system environment, special requirements, and design constraints we discussed earlier. In fact, use cases have a "special requirements" pigeonhole for inserting these types of requirements. This works well when you are applying these types of requirements to one or a few use cases, but in general, not all such requirements relate well to a specific use case.

Other, global nonfunctional requirements are generally not good candidates for use-case capture: legal and regulatory compliance requirements, operating environments, and software development standards. (For example, at Rational, one specification is used solely to define the requirements for globalization of software products. These requirements consist almost entirely of constraints that govern the design of the software so as to make translations into other languages feasible and cost-effective. Use cases are needed only to describe the limited patterns of usage implied, such as a "French-speaking person using the German OS.")

The Redundancy Problem

Use cases can also lead to a significant redundancy of expression that increases the size of the requirements documentation. The reason is that many use cases are very similar yet distinct enough to require separate expression. In addition, maintenance can then be a challenge when the common behavior, expressed in many use cases, must be changed. In this latter case, there are additional use-case relationships, such as generalization, include-relationships, and extends-relationships that you can use to reduce redundancy (Booch 1999).

However, the use of these relationships adds complexity in its own right, and there may be a point of diminishing returns if the behavior can be readily expressed in other ways. And yes, some relatively complex behaviors can be expressed more simply in natural language (for example, "When the system is in the ready state, and two officers each depress the launch button and hold it for more than 1 second, the missile will launch"). Yes, you can hammer the use cases into submission in these cases, but the goal is to pick the best technique for the circumstances, one that provides ease of expression and understandability, not to use them because you think you have to. In most projects, you will probably want to use a mix of use cases and traditional methods to create the optimum approach.

Refining Use-Case Specifications

In this chapter, we'll build on what we learned in Chapters 2 and 13 and apply the use-case technique again to refine the system specification. This is convenient, as the use cases derived in the earlier activities can be revisited and elaborated on here. Depending on the level of specificity achieved in the elicitation process, the use cases developed earlier may be sufficiently detailed to drive design and implementation. It's more likely, however, and it is recommended, that an appropriately high level of abstraction in the elicitation process was maintained so you don't become bogged down in detail at that stage of the process. Also, you probably didn't define all of the use cases that would be needed or detail the exception conditions, state conditions, and other special conditions that are of less interest to the user but that may materially affect the design of the system. The time to add this additional level of specificity is now.

Note: It is not the intention of this book to provide a full course on use cases. If you are interested in becoming more fully versed in the methodology and its supporting tool technologies, two good books on the subject are Schneider and Winters (1998) and Jacobson (1999). Nevertheless, we will review a few basic principles of the use-case methodology.

To add specificity, we'll need to take a more rigorous approach to the use-case technique so you can gain a better understanding of some of the nuances. Let's look at the definition of use cases one last time, focusing on what the UML has to say about them: "*A use case is a description of a set of actions, including variants, that a system performs that yields an observable result of value to a particular actor*" (Booch 1999).

Whew! That looks like a bunch of lawyers wrote the definition![1] As we've described earlier, the use-case methodology identifies two elements that will be present in all use-case instances.

---

1. It was actually a bunch of methodologists. Ivar Jacobson tells the following joke: Question: Do you know what the difference is between a methodologist and a terrorist?
Answer: You can negotiate with a terrorist.

Use case

Actor

1. *Use case.* The UML represents the use case with an oval. Even though the use case is a textual description, the icon serves as a shorthand aid that helps us model the system visually and show interactions between use cases and other modeling elements.
2. *Actors.* An actor is some*one* or some*thing* that interacts with our system. There are only three types of actors: users ("Bill the technician"), devices ("the robot arm motor controller"), and other systems ("the HOLIS CCU controller"). Actors are not part of the system being described but live outside of the system boundary.

Let's look at some of the other the key phrases in the UML definition: "A use case is a description of a *set of actions*, including *variants*, that a *system performs* that yields an *observable result of value* to a particular actor."

- *Variants.* A use case describes a basic flow, or thread, as well as variants, or alternative flows.
- *A set of actions.* The set of actions describes a function performed or perhaps an algorithmic procedure that produces a result; the set is invoked when the actor initiates the use case by providing some input to the system. An action is atomic; that is, it is performed either entirely or not at all. By the way, the atomicity requirement is a strong determinant in selecting the level of granularity of the use case. You should examine the proposed use case, and if the action is not atomic, then the level of granularity should be reduced to a finer level of detail.
- *System performs.* This means that the system provides the functionality described in the use case. It's what the system does, based on the input it is given.
- *An observable result of value.* It is important to note that the result of the use case must be "of value" to a user. Therefore, "the resident pushes the light button" is not a valid use case; (the system didn't do anything for the user.) But "the resident pushes the light button and the system turns the light on" is a meaningful use case and is more likely to motivate the resident to interact with the system!
- *A particular actor.* The particular actor is the individual or device (Linda the resident; the signal from the emergency button) that initiates the action (toggle the light or activate security alarm).

How Use Cases Evolve

In the early iterations of Team Skill 3, Defining the System, most of the major use cases have been identified, but only a few—perhaps those considered architecturally significant or particularly descriptive of the system behavior—are well described. These use cases might typically be done as an elaboration of the Vision document, which describes how the features expressed are intended to be used.

The refining process completes all use cases needed to define the system. The test for "enough" use cases is that the complete collection of use cases describes all possible ways in which the system can be used, at a level of specificity suitable to drive design, implementation, and testing.

It's worth pointing out that use case elaboration is *not* system decomposition. That is, we don't start with a high-level use case and decompose it into more and more use cases. Instead, we are searching for more and more detailed actor's interactions with the system. Thus, use-case elaboration is more closely aligned with refining a series of actions rather than hierarchically dividing actions into subactions. Your model will often have use cases that are so simple that they do not need a detailed description of the flow of events; a simple outline is quite enough. The criteria for making this decision are that users don't disagree on what the use case means and that designers and testers are comfortable with the level of detail provided by the simple format.

The Scope of a Use Case

It is often difficult to decide whether a set of user system interactions, or dialog, is one or several use cases. Consider the use of a recycling machine: The customer inserts cans and bottles into the recycling machine, presses a button, and received a printed receipt that can be exchanged for money.

Is it one use case to insert a deposit item and another use case to require the receipt? Or is it all one use case? Two actions occur, but one without the other is of little value to the customer. Rather, it is the complete dialog, with all of the insertions and getting the receipt, that is of value and makes sense to the customer. Thus, the complete dialog—from inserting the first deposit item, pressing the button, and getting the receipt—is a complete instance of use, a use case.

Additionally, you want to keep the two actions together, to be able to review them at the same time, modify them together, test them together, change them together when necessary, write user documentation that describes them, and, in general, manage them as a unit. This becomes particularly important in larger systems.

The Case Study: Anatomy of a Simple Use Case

Let's look at a step-by-step procedure for defining a use case. We'll use a simple HOLIS example: a resident activating a light in a house, using the HOLIS home automation lighting system.

Define the Actor(s)

We first need to decide and to define exactly who is to interact with the use case. In many systems designed for users, we should first look to identifying the humans who will use the system. In our use case, the homeowner interacts with the system to control the light in a room. So only one actor is discovered, the user (Resident) pressing the switch.

Tip: As you work your way through the determination of actors in the project, it will be helpful to maintain an "actor list" so that you can readily refer to actors already defined and avoid accidentally creating an actor again, using a different name.

Define the Use Case by Naming It

Each use case should have a name indicating what is achieved by its interaction with the actor(s). The name may have to be several words to be understood. No two use cases can have the same name.

You should consider the name carefully. It should be unique and easily distinguishable among the use cases defined for the project. Use-case names often begin with an action verb to indicate the intent of the use case. We will name our use case Control Light.

Also, you may want to structure the name in a formal method so as to group similar use cases into similarly named groupings. Or, you may want to incorporate a "serial number" or other unique identifier into the use-case name to facilitate managing a list of the use cases. For example, a designer might specify the name of this use case as "031 Control Light." But, although the spirit of this approach is laudable, our experience has shown that proper use-case naming, and perhaps application of tools that allow us to search, sort, and analyze use cases, are usually adequate to the task.

Write a Brief Description

A brief description of the use case should reflect its role and purpose. As you write the description, refer to the actors involved in the use case and the glossary. If you need to, define new concepts.

This description is intended as an informal overview of the functionality. A later section, Flow of Events, will be the spot where you can write a detailed description of the full functionality. The use-case description is intended to give a "quick look" and nothing more. In our use case, we might describe the use case as follows:

Use Case Description for Control Light

This use case prescribes the way in which lights are turned on or off or are dimmed by how long the user presses a light switch in various manners.

Define a Flow of Events

The heart of the use case is the event flow, usually a textual description of the operations by the actor and the system's various responses. Therefore, the event flow describes what the system is supposed to do, based on the actor's behavior. By the way, it is not required that the flow be described textually. You can use UML interaction diagrams for this purpose, and many of the formal methods discussed in Chapter 28 might apply equally well to your use-case documentation, so be sure and select an appropriate technique. Remember, the goal is to convey *understanding*, and there is no "one-size-fits-all" approach. However, in most cases, you'll find that natural language works just fine.

The flow of events conveys the meat of the use case's purpose and is intended for viewing by a variety of audiences:

- Customers, who approve the result and bless the functions
- Users, who are the intended target for the system's actions
- Use-case designers, who are interested in accurately capturing the system's intended behavior
- Reviewers, who provide third-party perspective
- Designers, who dissect the use cases, looking for design classes, objects, and so on
- Testers, who need to construct test cases
- Project manager, who needs to understand the entire project
- Technical writer, who needs to document the system's functions in a user-friendly manner
- Marketing and sales people, who need to understand the features of the product and explain its wonders to the outside world

You're probably saying to yourself, "I almost never find situations in which I can describe a simple flow of events that works every time. Many times, I need a way to describe some alternative flows." Fear not. The determination of a use-case flow allows for alternative flows. But first, let's create a basic flow for our example.

Basic Flow for the Control Light Use Case Note that the following flow of events does not specify *how* the system does any of those things. It specifies only *what* happens.

> Basic flow begins when Resident presses any button on the Control Switch. If Resident removes pressure on the Control Switch within the timer period, the system "toggles" the state of the light.
>
> - If the light was on, the light is turned off, and there is no illumination.
> - If the light was off, the light is turned on to the last remembered brightness level.
>
> End of basic flow.

Alternative Flow of Events: In many cases, the use case may have different flows, depending on conditions present. In some cases, these flows deal with error conditions detected during processing, or they may record optional ways of handling certain conditions. For example, a use case that prints a receipt for a credit card transaction may discover that the printer has run out of paper. This special case would be described within the use case as an alternative flow of events. When you record the alternative flows, don't forget to document the conditions giving rise to the flows. There is no set limit on alternative flows, so be sure and document all alternative flows, including possible error conditions.

In our example, an alternative flow of events will occur when Resident holds a button on the Control Switch down for more than 1 second. So, we need to add an alternative flow to the use case.

> **Alternative Flow of Events: Dimming**
>
> If Resident keeps pressure on the Control Switch for more than 1 second, the system initiates a dimming activity for the indicated Control Switch button.
>
> While Resident continues to press the Control Switch button,
>
> 1. The brightness of the controlled light is smoothly increased to a system-wide maximum value at a rate of 10 percent a second.
> 2. When the maximum value is reached, the brightness of the controlled light is smoothly decreased to a systemwide minimum value at a rate of 10 percent a second.
> 3. When the minimum value is reached, processing continues at subflow step 1.

When Resident ceases to press the Control Switch button,

4. The system ceases to change the brightness of the light.

Identify Pre- and Postconditions

In some cases, you will need to identify preconditions that affect the behavior of the system described in the use case and to describe postconditions, such as system state or persistent data that is left when the use case is complete. However, you need to use pre- and postconditions only when necessary to clarify the behavior expressed in the use case.

It is important to distinguish between events that start the use-case flows and preconditions, which must be met before the use-case flow can be initiated. For example, a precondition to the Control Light use case is that the homeowner (Resident) has enabled a specific bank of lights for the dimming action. Another precondition is that the selected Control Switch (CS) button must be preprogrammed to control a light bank. (Presumably, other use cases describe how these preconditions are accomplished.) So we'll need to state the preconditions.

Preconditions for Control Light Use Case
- The selected Control Switch button must be "Dim Enabled."
- The selected Control Switch button must be preprogrammed to control a light bank.

Similarly, you will often need to identify and include postconditions in your documentation. Postconditions allow you to specify the exact state that on use case exit *must* be true even if alternative paths are taken.

In order for the brightness to come on to the proper level when Resident uses the switch the next time, the system must remember the previous brightness level that was set for a selected Control Switch button after a dimming action has occurred. So, this is a postcondition that we'll record in the use case.

Postconditions for Control Light Use Case
- On leaving this use case, the current brightness level for the selected Control Switch button is remembered.

Now let's put it all together. Table 24–1 outlines what we have after filling in all of the important pieces of our use case. (Although many other pieces can be defined for a use case, they are not important to our needs now.) This use case is documented in the narrative style and may be found in the HOLIS artifacts in Appendix A.

Table 24–1 Defining a use case

Item	Value
Use case name	*Control light*
Brief description	This use case prescribes the way in which lights are turned on or off or are dimmed by the user's pressing a light switch in various manners.
Flow of events	Basic flow for the use case begins when Resident presses a button on the Control Switch (CS). If Resident removes pressure on the CS within the timer period, the system "toggles" the state of the light. This means: ▪ If the light was on, the light is turned off, and there is no illumination. ▪ If the light was off, the light is turned on to the last known brightness level.
Alternative flow of events	If Resident keeps pressure on the CS for more than 1 second, the system initiates dimming for the indicated light. The following actions occur while Resident continues to press the CS button: **1.** The brightness of the light is smoothly increased to a systemwide maximum value at a rate of 10% a second. **2.** When the maximum brightness is reached, the brightness of the light is smoothly decreased to a systemwide minimum value at a rate of 10% a second. **3.** When the minimum value is reached, the use case's sequences back to subflow step 1. When Resident ceases to press the CS button: **4.** The system ceases to change the brightness of the light.
Preconditions	▪ The selected CS button must be "Dim Enabled." ▪ The selected CS button must be preprogrammed to control a light bank.
Postconditions	On leaving this use case, the brightness of the light is remembered by the system.
Special requirements	The systemwide minimum light level cannot be 0. It should be an acceptably low value such that the controlled lights are adequate for night use.

Looking Ahead

When all use cases have been discovered and elaborated at about this level of detail, the refining process is complete for those portions of the system that we decide to elaborate in use cases. In the next chapter, we'll look at organizing the specifications.

Chapter 25

A MODERN SOFTWARE REQUIREMENTS SPECIFICATION

Key Points

- The Modern SRS Package is a collection of artifacts describing the complete external behavior of the system. It creates a conceptual model of the system to be built.
- The Vision document serves as input to the Modern SRS Package. The former is a broad statement of user needs, goals and objectives, target markets, and system features; the latter focuses on the details of implementing those features.
- The "right balance" of techniques is typically a mix of use-case modeling and traditional requirements specification.

N ow that we have refined our understanding of the system, it's time to develop a strategy to organize and document the requirements. Although much of the effort involved in this process does center on organizing the software requirements, documents, use cases, and models that have been elicited and refined, the most important part of this process is that *the collection of these artifacts, in the whole, represents a complete conceptual model of the system to be built.* After all, if we had already built it, we wouldn't be doing this part.

In short, for the first time, we have the pieces of a relatively complete and conceptual framework with which we can reason about the future system. Perhaps we can't touch it yet, though we might have seen some storyboards and prototypes along the way, but we can start to analyze it and to test our understanding of it while it still lives only in the realm of paper and models. In a sense, we have reached a major milestone: a conceptual model, or *proxy*, for the system to be built.

The Modern SRS Package

Historically, the most popular technique for documenting requirements was to use natural language and to simply write them all down in an organized fashion. This technique was revised and improved over the course of many projects, and eventually a number of standards developed for these documents, including IEEE (Institute of Electrical and Electronics Engineers) 830: Standard for Software Requirements Specification (1994).

However, with today's tools and techniques, we prefer to think of the software requirement specification, or SRS, as a *logical structure* rather than a physical document. The elaboration of the various requirements for the system is embodied in a package we call the *Modern Software Requirements Specification Package* as distinct from earlier forms, which will simply call the SRS. The Modern SRS Package is related to the Vision document, which serves as the input to the Modern SRS Package. But the two artifacts serve different needs and are typically written by different authors. At this stage in the project, the focus moves from the broad statement of user needs, goals, and objectives, target markets, and system features to the details of how these features are going to be implemented in the solution. Figure 25–1 shows an overview of the elements that make up the package.

What we need now is a package of information that describes the complete *external* behavior of the system: a collection of artifacts that says, specifically, "Here is what the system has to do to deliver those features." That's the Modern SRS Package.

There is no strong reason to focus on the differences between the tools used. After all, you are collecting requirements and should focus on the efficient collection and organization of the requirements, without regard to the tools at hand. Therefore, we will assume that the collection of requirements constitutes a *package* of information. Thus, Figure 25–1 shows not only the elements of the package but their relationships.

The Modern SRS Package is not a frozen tome, produced to ensure ISO 9000 compliance and then buried in a corner and ignored as the project continues. Instead, it is an active, living package, playing a number of crucial roles as the developers embark on their implementation effort.

- It serves as a basis of communication among all parties: among the developers themselves and between the developers and the external groups, users, and other stakeholders with whom they must communicate.
- Formally or informally, it represents an agreement among the various parties: If it's *not* in the package, the developers shouldn't be working

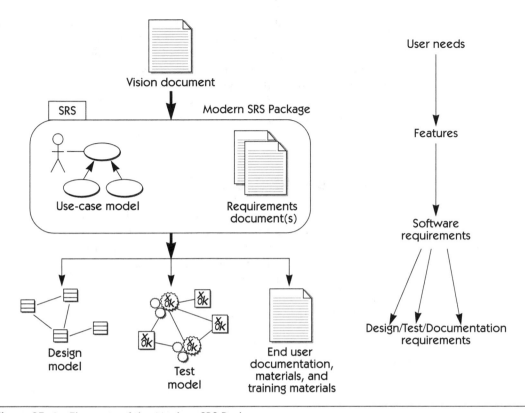

Figure 25–1 Elements of the Modern SRS Package

on it. And if it *is* in the package, they are accountable to deliver that functionality.

■ It serves as the software manager's reference standard. The manager is unlikely to have the time, energy, or skills to read the code being generated by the developers and to compare that directly to the Vision document; the manager must use the package as the standard reference for discussions with the project team.

■ As noted earlier, it serves as input to the design and implementation groups. Depending on how the project is organized, the implementers may have been involved in the earlier problem-solving and feature-definition activities that ultimately produced the Vision document. But it's the Modern SRS Package they need to focus on for deciding what their code must do.

■ It serves as input to the software testing and QA (quality assurance) groups. These groups should also have been involved in some of the earlier discussions, and it's obviously helpful for them to have a good understanding of the vision laid out in the Vision document. But their charter is to create test cases and QA procedures to ensure that the developed system does indeed fulfill the requirements laid out in the Modern SRS Package, which also serves as the standard reference for their planning and testing activities.

- It controls the evolution of the system throughout the development phase of the project; as new features are added or modified in the Vision document, they are elaborated within the package.

Who Owns the SRS Package?

It doesn't really matter who writes the package. What really matters is that there *is* a Modern SRS Package and that it is the basis for the remaining development and testing activities.

The question naturally arises, "Who is responsible for creating and maintaining components within the Modern SRS Package?" Usually, the developer team members themselves take on this task. The development team has a significant stake in fully understanding the package and all of its requirements and can appropriately influence many system decisions by taking ownership. After all, who better to write the software requirements than the people who will end up being responsible for adherence to them? Often, the system analyst will take on this task as a refinement of the Vision document; in other cases, the testers will work hand in hand with the project team and will take responsibility for the requirements.

Each approach has its pluses and minuses, and each project team will decide for itself what the best strategy will be. In our experience, if the package is taken seriously, it doesn't really matter who writes it, although we have a slight preference for the development lead or development team to take ownership. What really matters is that there *is* a Modern SRS Package and that it is the basis for the remaining development and testing activities.

Of course, the SRS authors don't write requirements in a vacuum. We have found that reviews of this package are the most productive step that can be taken to ensure that the developers, marketers, users, and other stakeholders are all singing from the same music. Remember, the Modern SRS Package is a living artifact and will need updating as the project evolves and various user features become better understood. It *should never* be the case that the package is written once and then ignored.

Organizing the Modern SRS Package

The Modern SRS Package for a large system could be voluminous, perhaps running to hundreds of pages (or more!) of text and use-case diagrams, and it contains a great deal of detailed information to which the developers must pay close attention. However, if the package is properly written and well focused, its size is not a valid argument against having one; it just speaks to the relative complexity of the system you are about to build.

This raises the question of how the package should be organized. For example, if a new developer is assigned to a project and told that he will be working on the XYZ feature, where should he expect to find the relevant details about XYZ? Or, suppose that the project manager resigns midway through the project; how can the new manager assigned get "up to speed" on the details that govern the day-to-day development activities of the project team?

Of course, the package should be organized in a fashion that suits the nature of the application and the organization; a package for the development of a shrink-wrapped word processor in a Silicon Valley software company probably won't look exactly the same as one for an air traffic control system. We don't really care whether an air traffic control expert can visit the Silicon Valley software firm and figure out what its SRS really means; what we *do* care about is that the developers and the users within a particular organization *can* make sense of the SRS they've constructed, for it's a package they'll have to live with throughout the development lifecycle and on into the maintenance of the system after it's in production.

To the extent that an organization wants to qualify for higher levels on the SEI-CMM scale or to achieve ISO 9000 certification, the interest is more likely to be in *standardizing* the organization and format of its package. Even without the influence of the CMM and ISO, the examples we've mentioned illustrate the benefits: the opportunity to "ramp up" more quickly when (not if) there is turnover or when (not if) new people join the project team. It also ensures that critical information doesn't fall through the cracks and that everyone knows where to look for information.

Also, remember that the Modern SRS Package is not intended to be read like a novel, from cover to cover; it's primarily a reference item, and each developer will typically look at only the specific information they need. Thus, it's useful to have an SRS organizational format that's familiar and easy to "navigate" rather than one with an unfamiliar format that forces people to read sequentially until they find the information they need.

Of course, the package has to have some organizing concept. We have found that the following organizational outline is a good match to almost any type of project. This outline, along with commentary that provides some of the details of the structure, is provided in Appendix C.

Overview

Revision History

Table of Contents

1.0 Introduction

    1.1 Purpose

    1.2 Scope

    1.3 References

    1.4 Assumptions and Dependencies

2.0 Use-Case Model Survey

3.0 Actor Survey

4.0 Requirements

    4.1 Functional Requirements

    4.2 Nonfunctional Requirements

        4.2.1 Usability

        4.2.2 Reliability

        4.2.3 Performance

        4.2.4 Supportability

5.0 Online User Documentation and Help System Requirements

6.0 Design Constraints

7.0 Purchased Components

8.0 Interfaces

    8.1 User Interfaces

    8.2 Hardware Interfaces

Date	Issue	Description	Author

First Special Requirement

Second Special Requirement

Preconditions

   Precondition 1

Postconditions

   Postcondition 1

Extension Points

   Name of extension point

Other Use-Case Material

Documenting Functional Requirements

Let's review where we are.

- We've promoted the idea that the documentation of the system's requirements should be contained in a *package* of artifacts.
- These artifacts can consist of textual documents, tables and charts, use cases, and many other things to help the developers understand what the customer wants.
- We've outlined a template for the organization of the Modern SRS Package. The template allows you to organize and to categorize all sorts of elements, but the primary focus is on *textual* elements, such as natural-language specifications of some requirements and *use case* elements, which include the graphical use-case model and textual representations of the use cases.

The good news is that both traditional requirement specification techniques and use-case techniques are well suited for the task of gathering requirements, and each has been used exclusive of the other technique in thousands of successful projects. But how can we optimize our work? Which technique should we apply in each case?

When it comes to specifying functional requirements for the system, we've found that combining use-case modeling and the traditional requirements

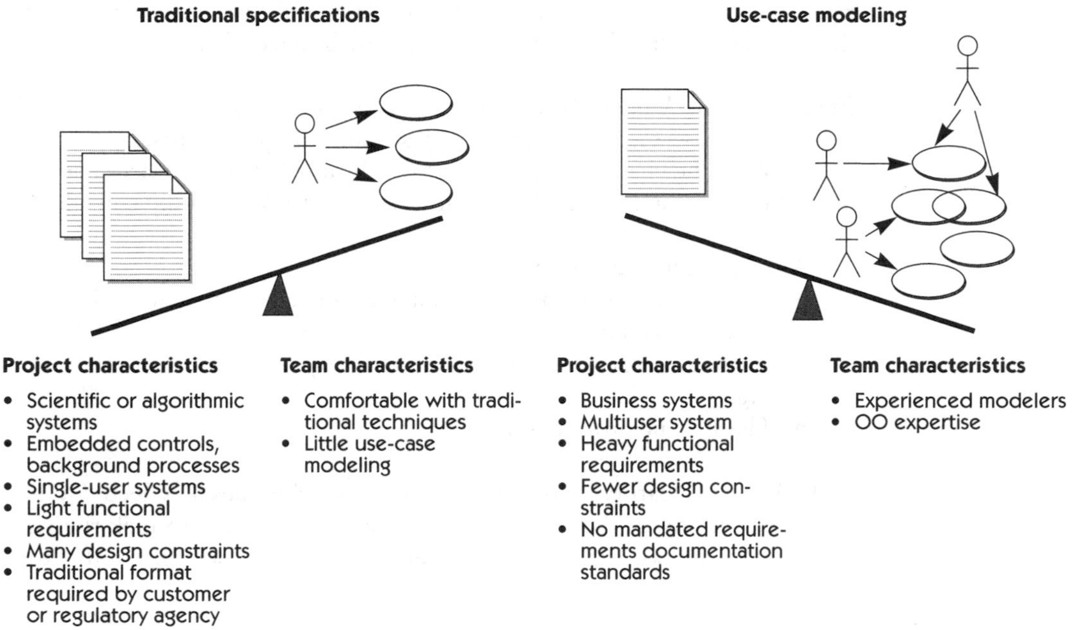

Traditional specifications   **Use-case modeling**

Project characteristics
- Scientific or algorithmic systems
- Embedded controls, background processes
- Single-user systems
- Light functional requirements
- Many design constraints
- Traditional format required by customer or regulatory agency

Team characteristics
- Comfortable with traditional techniques
- Little use-case modeling

Project characteristics
- Business systems
- Multiuser system
- Heavy functional requirements
- Fewer design constraints
- No mandated requirements documentation standards

Team characteristics
- Experienced modelers
- OO expertise

Figure 25–2   The requirements balance

specification is the best approach. Consider the "requirements balance" as shown in Figure 25–2.

In this view, we note that there is a *continuum* of possibilities. Some projects are characterized by a small, if any, amount of specification that can be accomplished via the functional representation power of the use-case technique. These projects tend to be highly computational, internal, and algorithmic, such as weather calculations or scientific systems. At the other end of the functional spectrum are projects that are heavily focused on satisfying user functional needs. These projects are typically focused on *doing a lot of things* for the user. In addition, you may need to handle *many types of users*, a real strength of the use-case technique.

Also, we consider the skill set of the project team itself. Some development teams have had little or no experience in use case and OO methods. Other teams have mastered these techniques.

To use this "balance view," simply fill in the appropriate set of check boxes for your project's characteristics and your team's skills and predilections. The resultant "tilt," or balance, offers you a plan for how to capture the requirements. To a first approximation, you should create a requirements documentation plan that depends on how the balance tilts.

In any case, the Modern SRS Package allows you to combine the best qualities of both use-case modeling and traditional requirements specification techniques. The challenge is to find the right mix for your project and your team. We have found that all of the following must be carefully considered:

- The organization's abilities
- The trend in software development processes and methods within the organization
- Outside factors such as regulatory requirements and other constraints
- The specific project context

Only then can a particular technique or mix of techniques be selected. Given an understanding of these factors, your team will be able to pick the right balance that works and to then migrate to a more powerful combination where applicable.

Looking Ahead

The Modern SRS Package is a powerful tool for communicating the needs of the project. However, those packages are not particularly easy to write. Like everything else, writing good software requirements specifications is a learned skill. In the next chapter, we will explore some of the problems involved in writing a clear, unambiguous set of specifications.

Chapter 26

ON AMBIGUITY AND SPECIFICITY

Key Points

- The requirement "sweet spot" is the balance point of the greatest amount of understandability and the least amount of ambiguity.
- A learned skill, finding the sweet spot will depend on the team members' abilities, the application context, and the level of surety you must provide that your system works as intended.
- If the risk of misunderstanding is unacceptable, more formal requirements techniques may need to be applied.

Finding the "Sweet Spot"

One of the *most* difficult challenge we face in the requirements process is making the requirements detailed enough to be well understood without overconstraining the system and predefining a whole host of things that may be better off left to others downstream in the process. (*"Do we really have to specify Pantone 287 as the background color in our GUI spec? No? How do you like the color they came up with last time?"*)

Time after time, our students pose the following question, which represents one of their biggest concerns: *"To what level of specificity must I state the requirements in order to avoid any chance of being misunderstood?"* Although many students are hoping for a simple answer, unfortunately, there isn't one. As if we were consultants about to sell the customer more services, the only answer we can truthfully provide is, *"It just depends."* For example, as an exercise in requirements writing, we often use the "light box" exercise shown in Figure 26–1.

The goal of the exercise is to write clear and simple requirements, using natural language or the use-case technique to describe the behavior of this device. In the exercise, the user is available for interview, so that the requirements writer can refine the specification with clear user input. As an example

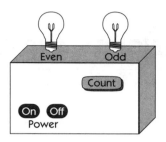

Features

- Microprocessor controlled
- Keeps track of whether count button has been pressed even or odd number of times
- Burned-out-bulb detector flashes remaining bulb

Figure 26–1   Light box

of a reasonably good effort in the natural language style, let's look at the following requirements specification (Davis 1993).

> After On pushed but before Off pushed, system is termed "powered on."
>
> After Off pushed but before On pushed, system is termed "powered off," and no lights shall be lit.
>
> Since most recent On press, if Count has been pressed an odd number of times, Odd shall be lit.
>
> Since most recent On press, if Count has been pressed an even number of times, Even shall be lit.
>
> If either light burns out, the other light shall flash every 1 second.

This specification is fairly tight and would be quite adequate for most purposes. More important, it reflects the way the device user intended that it work!

However, a programmer who has the task of writing a program to simulate this behavior will discover at least one ambiguity in this exercise almost immediately: *What does it mean to flash the bulb every 1 second?* Still seem obvious? Let's take a look at the duty cycles in Figure 26–2.

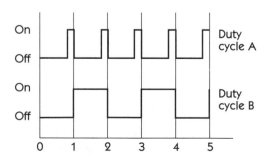

Figure 26–2   Possible lamp duty cycles

If you were the programmer, would you pick duty cycle A or duty cycle B? Although most pick duty cycle B, it becomes clear that the requirement is ambiguous. Now, a requirements-sensitized programmer will recognize this ambiguity and will attempt to resolve it by asking the customer, *"Which duty cycle should I use?"* But if the programmer is not so savvy or does not recognize the ambiguity or thinks, *"I know what you meant because I know how this thing should work,"* the behavior of the device when delivered may deviate perceptibly from the customer's stated requirements. Your project may be at risk.

In most potential applications, it probably doesn't matter whether the bulb flashes on for 1 second or 0.25 second. But if this were an electrosurgical device, it would matter *a lot*. The power delivered to the electrode would be 100 percent higher in duty cycle B than in A, with perhaps unfortunate results.

So, the answer to "What level of specificity must I provide?" is: *"It depends on the context of your application and how capable those doing the implementation are of making the right decisions or of at least being certain to ask questions where there is ambiguity."*

In the case of the even and odd counting device, the specification as stated is probably adequate. In the case of the electrosurgical device, more investment in describing the requirement would be needed. A timing diagram would be needed, and the spec would probably also have to define such issues as the rise time on the upslope of the "on" current, the precision with which the "on" time must be controlled ($\pm x$ msec), and other factors; otherwise, the power delivered will not be right, and the device will operate incorrectly. Figure 26–3 summarizes this dilemma.

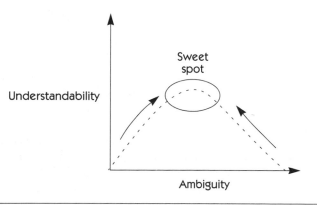

Figure 26–3 Ambiguity versus specificity

The goal is to find the "sweet spot," or the balance point wherein the investment in requirements provides "just the right amount" of specificity and leaves just the "right amount of ambiguity" for others to resolve further downstream.

As you move to the left from the sweet spot on the curve in Figure 26–3, you lower both ambiguity and understandability. For example, if we provided timing diagrams to an unsophisticated user, complete with timing tolerances indicated and if we maintained that level of specificity throughout, the user may well *not* be able to understand the spec at all or might even be unwilling to take the time to read it. Worse, due to your apparent thoroughness, the user might trust you too much and not take the time for a careful review. You are also at the risk of the customer's being unable to see the forest for the trees ("*I didn't want a light bulb; I wanted you to turn on the emergency light at the end of the production line*").

As you move to the right of the sweet spot, ambiguity goes up, but understandability again goes down. For example, at the extreme limit, you might simply say, "*Build me an even/odd counting device*," and no one could possibly understand what you mean.

Finding the sweet spot is a learned skill. It will depend on the abilities of the team members, the context of the application, and the level of surety that you must provide so that your system "works as intended."

Mary Had a Little Lamb

Let's have a little fun with the issue of ambiguity and also see whether we can find some more tips that will help us "disambiguate" whenever and wherever it's necessary to do so. (If you are a fairly formal sort, without much use for the "softer" side of this problem space, you may wish to move directly to Chapter 28, Technical Methods.)

For the rest of us, let's have a little fun, courtesy of Gause and Weinberg (1989), whose book leads us through a fun exercise that illustrates the ambiguity problem and also provides some serious insights as to possible solutions.

Consider the familiar nursery rhyme: "Mary had a little lamb." Although it's unlikely that anyone will build an information system based on this sentence, it's nevertheless interesting to ask, What does it mean? In order to disambiguate, we can perhaps use the *keyword*, or dictionary, technique. In this technique, we focus on the keywords in the statement and look at the options, based on various meanings for each. Here we'll focus on the words "had" and "lamb." "Had" is the past tense of "have," so we'll have to use the definition of "have"; we can use "lamb" directly. Here's what we find for "have":

> **have 1a:** *to hold in possession as property . . .* **4a:** *to acquire or get possession of: to obtain (as in "the best to be had") . . .* **4c:** *ACCEPT; to have in marriage . . .* **5a:** *to be marked or characterized by (to have red hair) . . .* **10a:** *to hold in a position of disadvantage or certain defeat . . .* **10b:** *TRICK, FOOL (been had by a partner or friend) . . .* **12:** *BEGET, BEAR (have a baby) . . .* **13:** *to partake of (have dinner) . . .* **14:** *BRIBE, SUBORN (can be had for a price)*[1]

And here's what we have for "lamb":

> **lamb 1a:** *a young sheep esp. less than one year old or without permanent teeth . . .* **1b:** *the young of various other animals (e.g., smaller antelopes) . . .* **2a:** *a person as gentle or weak as a lamb . . .* **2b:** *DEAR, PET . . .* **2c:** *a person easily cheated or deceived, esp. in trading securities . . .* **3a:** *the flesh of lamb used as food*[2]

Accordingly, we could interpret the phrase "Mary had a little lamb" to mean any one of the following:

Lambic Interpretations		
"Have"	**"Lamb"**	**Interpretation**
1a	1a	Mary owned a little sheep under one year of age or without permanent teeth.
4a	1a	Mary acquired a little sheep under one year of age or without permanent teeth.
5a	1a	Mary is the person who owned a little sheep under one year of age or without permanent teeth.
10a	1a	Mary held a little lamb under one year of age or without permanent teeth.
10b	1a	Mary tricked a little sheep under one year or age or without permanent teeth.
12	1b	Mary gave birth to a young antelope.
12	2a	Mary is (or was) the mother of a particular small, gentle person.

---

1. Adapted from *Webster's Seventh New Collegiate Dictionary* (Springfield, MA: Merriam Co., 1967).
2. Ibid.

Lambic Interpretations		
"Have"	"Lamb"	Interpretation
13	3a	Mary ate a little of the flesh of lamb.
14	2c	Mary bribed a small person trading in securities who was easily cheated.

For people who grew up with this nursery rhyme and who read the rhyme to their children each night, this discussion might sound preposterous: "How could any reasonable person interpret such a familiar phrase in so many bizarre, outlandish ways?" But such a complaint is neither fair nor realistic if we expect someone from a different background, and perhaps even a different nationality and culture, to attempt an interpretation based strictly on the dictionary definition of the two keywords. If it can happen with nursery rhymes, surely it can happen with complex software systems the likes of which have never yet been created.

Techniques for Disambiguation

One way of coping with ambiguity is to use not natural language but rather "formal" requirements specification techniques, which we'll discuss in Chapter 28. For obvious reasons, the user and the stakeholders outside the development group typically prefer natural language, and even computer people manage to carry on most of their day-to-day communication in natural language. But even though both groups have some facility for communication in a natural language, they do come from very different cultures; they have a different focus, orientation, and set of assumptions.

Although it may be impossible to eliminate ambiguity entirely, we can attack it in a variety of different ways. Gause and Weinberg (1989) provide some techniques we can use when faced with this all-too-common situation.

- *Memorization heuristic:* Ask several individuals, both from the development group and from the user/stakeholder group, to try recalling, from memory, the customer's real requirement. Parts that are not clear and cannot be easily remembered are likely to be the most ambiguous. Focus on them and try to restate them with more clarity, so that they can be remembered.
- *Keyword technique:* As illustrated with Mary's lamb, it often helps to identify the key operational words in a statement and to list all of their definitions, using an authoritative source that the various mem-

bers of the project environment will accept. Then mix and match to determine different interpretations, as was done with Mary and her lamb. As a quick test on this technique, you may also note that interpretation 1(a) and 1(a) above, "Mary owned a little sheep under one year of age or without permanent teeth," is probably closest to the meaning in the fairy tale.

- *Emphasis technique:* Read the requirement aloud and emphasize individual words until as many different interpretations as possible have been discovered. If only one of the interpretations is correct, restate the requirement appropriately; if multiple interpretations are correct, additional requirements may need to be generated accordingly. We'll illustrate this point with another investigation of Mary and her lamb.
- *Other techniques:* If appropriate, try using pictures, graphics, or formal methods to flush out the ambiguity and eliminate it.

Suppose that we saw the phrase "Mary had a little lamb" in our requirement set and were trying to ensure that we understood what the user was really driving at. Saying the sentence aloud and emphasizing individual words might help us elicit any one of the following:

- *Mary* had a little lamb; if this is the case, perhaps the user is telling us that it was Mary's lamb, not Richard's or anyone else's.
- Mary *had* a little lamb; perhaps she no longer has it. Perhaps it's the tense of the statement that's significant.
- Mary had *a* little lamb; thus, the key point may be that Mary had only one lamb, not an entire flock.
- Mary had a *little* lamb; indeed, it was one of the littlest lambs you ever saw.
- Mary had a little *lamb*; the emphasis here reminds us that Mary didn't have a pig, a cow, or even a grown-up sheep. But we might still be misled into thinking she had a baby antelope.

What to Do?

No one technique will work in every circumstance. Achieving the right balance of ambiguity and specificity will be a practiced skill that you will need to develop within your organization and project context. The amount of specificity you need to provide may even vary over time, based on the changing skills of those downstream in the process and their understanding of the domain in which you operate.

Here are our recommendations to find the "sweet spot" in your project context.

- Use natural language wherever possible.
- Use pictures and diagrams to further illustrate the intent.
- When in doubt, *ask*! When you're not in doubt, consider asking anyway.
- Augment your specifications with more formal methods when you cannot afford to be misunderstood.

Train your people to recognize both the problem of ambiguity and the solutions that can be applied.

Chapter 27

QUALITY MEASURES OF SOFTWARE REQUIREMENTS

Key Points

- Having a set of requirements is the primary quality goal; in addition, those requirements must themselves meet nine measures of quality.
- Checklists can be used to ensure the quality of requirements, the use-case model, and use-case specifications and actors.
- A high-quality Modern SRS Package has a good TOC, a good index, a revision history, and a glossary.

Quality, like art, is tough to measure. "I know good art when I see it." Nevertheless, we have to establish a way to measure and to improve the quality of our specifications. Of course, one measure of the quality is whether we get a good product at the end of the development project. But that's not very helpful, because lots of other factors also contributed to the end result.

So, we will break down the "quality" measurement of the overall specification into a series of major elements:

- The quality of each individual specification
- Technique-specific quality measures, such as assessing the quality of a use-case specification, an actor specification, and so on
- The quality of the collected package containing all of the individual specifications

Let's start by considering the quality of the individual specifications. Of course, to measure anything, we need to have a way of conducting the measurements.

Nine Quality Measures

We've already suggested what constitutes "good" requirements: items that meet the definition provided and those that avoid design and implementation details, as well as software process or project management issues. But how can we distinguish between a high-quality set of requirements and a low-quality set? Taking our lead from the IEEE 830 standard, which identifies eight "quality measures" for evaluating an SRS, we'll add one of our own and explore how they can help us develop a quality set of requirements. A Modern SRS package is of high quality if it is:

- Correct
- Unambiguous
- Complete
- Consistent
- Ranked for importance and stability
- Verifiable
- Modifiable
- Traceable
- Understandable

We added the ninth measure, understandability, because we strongly believe that *communication* is an important key to a project's success.

Although having a high-quality set of requirements is second to *having* a set of requirements, we'll discuss each of these nine elements in more detail because they bring additional insights to the requirements process, as well as give us insight into the nature of "good" requirements.

Correct Requirements

As Davis (1993) states and illustrates (see Figure 27–1), "An SRS [set of requirements] is correct if and only if every requirement stated therein represents something required of the system to be built."

If the universe of user needs is represented by the circle on the left and the requirements by the circle on the right, the portion of correct requirements is area B, the area of overlap.

Of course, by simply writing some information in a document, we can't guarantee that it's correct; nor can any automated design tool provide a guarantee that it will be so. If the user's *true* requirements in a payroll system

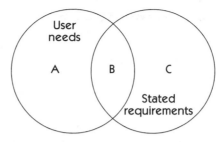

Figure 27–1   Needs/requirements universe

are that all employees should be given an automatic 5 percent salary increase and the project team inadvertently creates a requirement stipulating a 10 percent salary increase, it's certainly not correct. This form of correctness will be verified only by review and acceptance by the user.

Of course, this is not a new and unfamiliar phenomenon; it's been an issue ever since project teams first began developing software systems, as well as all other kinds of engineering and development projects. But in a software project, what often happens is the *omission* of information represented by area A and the undesirable inclusion of information represented by area C. The information represented by area C may be the design/implementation details that we warned about earlier, but it may also consist of requirements that the user never asked for. Sometimes, this information is introduced by enthusiastic marketing or technical people who say, "We're sure the user will really love this feature once they see it." (We will revisit the issue of spurious requirements in Team Skill 6.)

Unambiguous Requirements

A requirement is unambiguous *if and only if it can be subject to only one interpretation*. (IEEE 830-1993, § 4.3.2, 1994). Although correctness is obviously a key concern in any requirement, ambiguity often turns out to be a larger problem. If a statement of requirements can be interpreted differently by developers, users, and other stakeholders in the project, it's quite possible to build a system that's completely different from what the user had in mind. This is, of course, an insidious problem whenever requirements are written in natural language, as well as because different cultures and groups within an organization are so accustomed to their interpretation of a word or phrase that it never occurs to them that others might interpret the word differently, a problem we discussed in Chapter 26.

Completeness of the Requirements Set

A set of requirements is complete *if and only if it describes all significant requirements of concern to the user, including requirements associated with functionality, performance, design constraints, attributes, or external interfaces* (IEEE 830-1993, §4.3.3, 1994). A complete set of requirements must also define the required response of the software to all realizable classes of inputs—both valid and invalid—in all realizable classes of situations. Further, it must provide complete references and labels for all of the figures, tables, and diagrams within the requirement set, as well as definitions of all terms and units of measure.

Ensuring Completeness Some aspects of completeness can be judged by any competent reviewer who critically assesses the requirement set package to ensure that the figures, labels, and diagrams have proper references and labels. Also, some aspects of completeness can be assessed even by a developer with no special understanding of the application. For example, if the requirement set says, "The system shall accept a single numerical input from the user and return the square root of that number, accurate to three decimal places," the obvious question is, "What happens if the user tries to input a negative number?"

$$\sqrt{-1} = ?$$

In fact, there's nothing illegal about attempting to compute the square root of a negative number, as long as it's meaningful within the application domain to return an imaginary number as the output from the system. But it does usually require an understanding of the problem domain to differentiate between the valid and invalid inputs; this is an especially common problem when specifying the upper and lower limits of numerical input parameters, the length of character strings, and so on. And because these details are often ignored in the requirements, they're left for the developer to decide, either consciously or unconsciously, and we end up with systems that refuse to accept a customer name more than 25 characters long or that produce bizarre results when erroneous inputs are entered by the user.

Reviewing the realizable classes of inputs to ensure that the complete requirement set properly describes the system behavior for valid and invalid inputs is something that every developer knows about, even though we still make mistakes in writing such requirements. It's more common for users to overlook this area and to express surprise and annoyance when it's brought up: "But why would any reasonable person try to enter a negative number when the system asks for age?" The veteran developer knows that it could happen because of a simple typographical mistake or because the end user is deliberately trying to "break" the system or for various other obscure reasons.

Completeness in Nonfunctional Requirements It's more common to overlook aspects of performance and design constraints or assumptions about external interfaces to other systems. Our advice is to create a simple checklist that follows the guidelines we've provided in the areas of usability, reliability, performance, and supportability and that also covers the right questions to ask in the search for design constraints; that way, the developers and the users can at least be sure that they've asked the appropriate questions while composing the requirements. Again, the novice user might complain, "Well, of course I want the system to have good performance; that's so obvious that I don't see why I need to specify it." The veteran developer knows that it's usually important to specify performance requirements in terms of maximum response time or average response time or perhaps a statement that "90 percent of all transactions will have a response time less than 3 seconds."

Completeness of Functional Requirements The issue of missing functionality is more difficult; without a great deal of expertise in the application domain, it's very difficult for the technical developers to know whether the set of requirements has omitted an important area of functionality. After all, since all the functionality is new, how do you know how much more there should be?

Sometimes, the functionality is so deeply ingrained and "obvious" that the user is not even consciously aware of it. "Of *course* we run the payroll system on the day before the normal payday if it falls on a holiday. We've always done that! How else could you possibly have imagined that things would work?")

The use-case techniques should help you out here.

Completeness through Prototyping Storyboarding, requirements reviews, and prototyping the system by using an iterative development approach will catch many to most of these problems. The closer we get to real use, and the more experience our users have with the system we will be deploying, the more likely we are to see the problems with our definition.

However, even then, the development team must go one step further in its analysis to ensure completeness by asking all of the "what-if" questions. These questions should focus on boundary conditions, exceptions, and unusual events.

For example, the functionality sometimes involves situations that are so rare that they've never occurred in the user's normal business experience, and no one thinks to specify the requirements for that situation. The payroll system user, for example, might complain that the required behavior of the system is "obvious" if the normal payday falls on a holiday, but what if an official national holiday, state holiday, and city holiday fall on three consecutive business days? "It's never happened," the user might complain; perhaps so, but the developer may be able to demonstrate that it *could* happen sometime within the next 5 years.

This kind of issue is not as far-fetched as it sounds. The commotion about the year 2000 bug graphically illustrates the consequences of short-sighted decisions based on "reasonable" expectations as to future events.[1]

Consistency in the Requirements Set

A requirement set is internally consistent *if and only if no subset of individual requirements described within it are in conflict with one another* (IEEE 830-1993, §4.3.4.1, 1994). The conflicts can take various forms and are visible at various levels of detail; if the set has been written in a reasonably formal fashion and if it is supported with appropriate automated tools, the conflicts can sometimes be identified through a mechanical analysis. But it's likely that a manual review of the set by developers and nondevelopers alike will be necessary to weed out all of the potential conflicts.

Sometimes, the conflicts are blatant and obvious; one part of the requirements might say, "When X occurs, carry out action P," whereas another part of the requirements might say, "When X occurs, carry out action Q." Sometimes, it's unclear whether the problem is a conflict or an instance of ambiguity; for example, one part of the requirements in a payroll system might say, "All employees who are 65 or older at the end of the calendar year shall receive a bonus of $1,000," whereas another part of the requirements might say, "All employees with 10 years or more of service at the end of the calendar year shall receive a bonus of $500." What about employees who satisfy both conditions?

Although prototypes are often successful at spotting missing functionality and are enormously useful for validating the user's requirements about input/output details, it's unusual to see either the user or the testing/QA professionals exercise the prototype thoroughly enough to uncover the more subtle

---

1. It's well known that decision makers made trade-off decisions that resulted in the Y2K commotion. Other cases abound. For example, an early Gemini space mission incorporated flawed code, based on a conscious decision to shortcut certain physical laws of motion in the interest of efficiency. This decision resulted in a spacecraft landing that was several hundred miles off course.

conflict errors. These have to be identified through careful manual review and analysis of the complete set of requirements, supported by the skills of the development team and whatever automated tools are appropriate.

Requirements Ranked for Importance and Stability

In a high-quality set, the developers and the customers and other stakeholders have ranked the individual requirements by importance to the customer and in terms of stability (IEEE 830-1993, §4.3.5, 1994). This ranking process is particularly important for scope management. If resources are insufficient to implement all of the requirements within the allotted schedule and budget, it's extremely helpful to know which requirements are volatile and which requirements the user deems critical.

Indeed, one can assign additional attributes to each requirement, just as we recommended for requirements described in the Vision document: cost, risk, difficulty, and other descriptors could be enormously useful. However, much of this is likely to be based on an assessment of the implementation strategies. For example, after looking at a requirement, a developer might say, "Hmmm, I think it's going to be really tough to implement this requirement, and I'm not even sure we know how to do it at all." Although that might be a valuable piece of information for managing the scope and prioritizing decisions, it can usually be done at the higher level of abstraction represented by the Vision document; for reasons discussed earlier, such items typically should *not* be included in the requirement set.

But the attributes of "importance" and "stability" are more likely to be associated with the user's perception of the world. The user might say, "This requirement is not very stable, because we're expecting a change next month in the government regulations that affect this requirement. On the other hand, it's *very* important to us because it affects our ability to operate in a competitive fashion." Even before the development team begins developing strategies based on technology opportunities, it would be helpful to have a ranking that shows, for example, two columns of requirements:

Requirements Ranked by Importance	Requirements Ranked by Stability
SR103	SR172
SR172	SR103
SR192	SR063
SR071	SR071
SR063	SR192

Given this information, and if all other factors were equal, a prudent software development manager would be prepared to invest a proportionately higher percentage of resources in SR103 and SR172; the manager would be more likely to deemphasize SR071, since it has been judged relatively unimportant *and* relatively volatile in nature.

Verifiable Requirement

Requirements must be verifiable, or "testable."

A requirement is verifiable in the aggregate *if and only if each of the component requirements contained within it is verifiable. And the requirements can be deemed verifiable if and only if there exists a finite, cost-effective process with which a person or a machine can determine that the developed software system does indeed meet the requirement* (IEEE 830-1993, §4.3.6, 1994). Heavy stuff. In short, we realize, as a *practical* matter, that it is necessary to define requirements so that we can later test them and determine whether they were achieved.

It's unlikely that we can provide a rigorous scientific proof of the verifiability of each requirement, but that's not usually necessary. It's the responsibility of the testing and quality assurance personnel to create the appropriate test cases and test procedures to carry out the verification once the software has been developed. Of course, they need reasonably well-defined and reasonably unambiguous requirements in order to be able to do so. It's common to see a review meeting in which everyone in the meeting turns to the testing specialist and asks, "Are you confident that you can create a test script to verify that this requirement has been met?"

The following are examples of requirements and typical reactions from the developers and/or the testing professionals in terms of the likely verifiability:

- "*The system shall support up to 1,000 simultaneous users.*" "Well, that depends on what those users are capable of doing when they're logged in. If the users have 'open-ended' capabilities and could, in theory, enter a transaction that causes the application program to scan sequentially through every record in the database, it will be very difficult to verify that the system can handle a 1,000-user load; there's a tiny but nonzero probability that all 1,000 users will decide to enter such a transaction at the same time. But if the users are constrained in the kinds of transactions they can enter, and if we can determine a typical, modestly resource-expensive transaction they can enter, we can verify that the requirement has been met to within a reasonable degree of certainty, although we'll have to use our load-testing tool to simulate 1,000 active terminals."

■ *"The system shall respond to an arbitrary query in 500 milliseconds."* "Well, that depends on what we mean by 'arbitrary.' If the range of possible queries is finite and if we can identify the most complex query, we can verify the system's behavior."

■ *"The time display shall have a pleasing shape for the digits."* "Don't even bother with this one. Beauty is in the eye of the beholder."

■ *"The system shall be user friendly."* "This is even worse than 'pleasing shape.' But without some very carefully defined terms and details, 'user friendly' is just an invitation for arguments."

■ *"The system shall export view data in comma-separated format."* "Well, I'd like to pin down the details; for example, what happens if the 'view data' is null? But in principle, yes, we can verify that the system does produce the desired behavior in this area."

Verification and validation are important issues in developing high-quality software. We will return to this topic again later, in Team Skill 6.

Modifiable Requirements Set

A requirement set is modifiable *if and only if its structure and style are such that any changes to the requirements can be made easily, completely, and consistently, while retaining the existing structure and style of the set* (IEEE 830-1993, §4.3.7, 1994). This requires that the containing package have minimum redundancy and that it be well organized, with a proper table of contents, index, and cross-referencing capabilities. It may or may not imply that the package is maintained and supported by an automated tool, although that usually becomes a practical necessity in large systems, which may have thousands requirements.

Requirements *will* be modified, whether anyone likes it or not; the alternative is a "frozen" requirements package, which is tantamount to a nonexistent package and a commensurately failed project. But if the requirement (or the containing package) is nonmodifiable, then it effectively becomes non-existent after a few weeks or months, because the project team gradually abandons its effort to change the requirements and keep them up to date.

Every software manager likes to think that his or her requirements set is modifiable, and every tool vendor brags that one of its primary virtues is that its product *does* promote modifiability. All of this sounds great, but the proof is in the pudding: you have to *do* it in order to see whether it works. And you have to do it on the same "scale" of size and complexity that you'll be encountering in the project itself.

Traceable Requirements

A requirement is traceable *if and only if the origin of each of its component requirements is clear, and if there is a mechanism that makes it feasible to refer to that requirement in future development efforts* (IEEE 830-1993, §4.3.8, 1994). As a practical matter, this usually means that the requirements are identified with unique numbers or labels. Sometimes, it means that you may wish to use a keyword, such as "shall," to articulate a requirement, to distinguish it from other nonessential statements—comments, introductory statements, and so on—that may also exist in the requirement set. With requirements tool automation, this identification requirement can be handled automatically by the system.

Some components will need to be traced to other components within the same project and possibly within the same package. For example, some components will be dependent on other components; if one is changed, the other will be affected. And some requirements statements may be further described by "sub" or "child" requirements, for which traceability is an obvious concern. But in addition, we need the ability to trace *backward* from the current stages to the previous stages of definition or development, particularly the product Vision document discussed in Team Skill 3. In Table 23–1, for example, we saw that SR63.1, SR63.2, and SR63.3 could all be traced to Feature 63 in the product requirements (Vision) document. That's obviously essential in case we need to add or delete features; it's also essential if we run into trouble with the requirements and need to go back to the user to renegotiate the budget or schedule for the affected feature. We also need *forward* traceability from the current requirement to all of its subordinate requirements, regardless of the package containers—design documents, flowcharts, code, test cases, and so on—spawned by the current container.

Traceability is a Big Deal. We have found that developers can use traceability in a number of ways to better understand their project and to provide a higher degree of assurance that all requirements are fulfilled by the implementation. For example, we have used full traceability to connect *all* of the elements of a medical project, including Vision document elements, SRS elements, testing elements, coding elements, and the project review elements that occurred throughout the life of the project. By having all of these elements interconnected, the project developers were much better equipped to handle interactions among project elements.

Traceability also allows the project team to handle "what-if" questions, such as "What if we change this requirement right here? Does that interact with the software development and, if so, which elements? Does that force us to revise the test plans and, if so, which ones?"

In that same project, traceability was used to create the *trace matrices* that were required by the FDA to ensure that the product complied with its own requirements. Trace matrices are an invaluable way to "check off" the development activities and to make sure you are doing everything needed for the development (and not doing things that don't need doing). We will conduct a major examination of traceability in Team Skill 6.

Understandable Requirements

Finally, a requirement set is *understandable* if both the user and the developer communities are able to fully comprehend the individual requirements and the aggregate functionality implied by the set. The documents described in earlier chapters of this book tend to focus on general descriptions and features of the system and are usually not as difficult to understand. But as we refine the system definition, that is, produce detailed requirements, things become more specific and more detailed, and there is a temptation to begin using more technical terms. Thus, the people who write the requirements must understand the vocabulary, the buzzwords, and the cultures of *both* audiences. In addition, it's important that the users of the requirement set be able to understand the behavior of the system in the whole. This can also be done by providing storyboards, scenarios, or illustrative use cases that show how the system is intended to be used in its operating environment.

Quality Measures for the Use-Case Model

Note: In this section of the chapter, we discuss a broad spectrum of use case matters. Sometimes, the checklist item will refer to specific use case issues that were not discussed in this book because they were not of major importance to the requirements management points being made. If you wish to follow up on these issues, please consult an appropriate use case reference. Two books you might find useful are Booch (1999) and Jacobson, Booch, and Rumbaugh (1999).

- Have you found all of the use cases? Those you have found must be able to perform all system behaviors; if not, some use cases are missing.
- Do the use cases meet all of the functional requirements? If you have intentionally left any requirements to be dealt with in the object models, such as nonfunctional requirements, you must mention this somewhere. If a requirement of this type concerns a specific use case, state this in the Special Requirements section of the use case.
- Does the use-case model contain any superfluous behavior; that is, does it present more functions than were called for in the requirements?
- Does the model need all of the identified include-, extend-, and generalization-relationships? If not, they might be redundant, and you should probably remove them.
- Do the relationships in the model depend on one another? It is essential that they do not, so you must check this point.
- Is the division of the model into use-case packages appropriate? Does the packaging make the model more simple and intuitive to understand and to maintain?
- By studying the use-case model, can you form a clear idea of the system's functions and how they are related?
- Does the Introduction section of the use-case model contain all of the necessary information?
- Does the Survey Description of the use-case model contain all of the necessary information; for example, does it describe the most common sequences of use cases?

Use-Case Specifications

- Is each concrete use case involved with at least one actor? If not, something is wrong; a use case that does not interact with an actor is superfluous, and you should remove it.
- Is each use case independent of the others? If two use cases are always activated in the same sequence, you should probably merge them into one use case.
- Do any use cases have very similar behaviors or flows of events? If so—and if you wish their behavior to be similar in the future—you should merge them into a single use case. This makes it easier to introduce future changes. Note: You must involve the users if you decide to merge use cases, because the users who interact with the new, merged use case will probably be affected.
- Has part of the flow of events already been modeled as another use case? If so, you can have the new use case use the old one.

- Is part of the flow of events already part of another use case? If so, you should extract this subflow and have it be used by the use cases in question. Note: You must involve the users if you decide to "reuse" the subflow, because the users of the existing use case will probably be affected.
- Should the flow of events of one use case be inserted into the flow of events of another? If so, you model this with an extend-relationship to the other use case. (We didn't discuss this, as it wasn't important to the overall concepts of use cases.)
- Do the use cases have unique, intuitive, and explanatory names so that they cannot be mixed up at a later stage? If not, you should change their names.
- Do customers and users alike understand the names and descriptions of the use cases? Each use-case name must describe the behavior the use case supports.
- Does the use case meet all of the requirements that obviously govern its performance? You may want to include any nonfunctional requirements to be handled in other portions of your Modern SRS Package.
- Does the communication sequence between actor and use case conform to the user's expectations?
- Is it clear how and when the use case's flow of events starts and ends?
- Behavior might exist that is activated only when a certain condition is not met. Is there a description of what will happen if a given condition is not met?
- Are any use cases overly complex? If you want your use-case model to be easy to understand, you might have to split up complex use cases.
- Does a use case contain disparate flows of events? If so, it is best to divide it into two or more separate use cases. A use case that contains disparate flows of events will be very difficult to understand and to maintain.
- Is the subflow in a use case modeled accurately?
- Is it clear who wishes to perform a use case? Is the purpose of the use case also clear?
- Are the actor interactions and exchanged information clear?
- Does the brief description give a true picture of the use case?

Use-Case Actors

- Have you found all of the actors? That is, have you accounted for and modeled all of the roles in the system's environment? Although you should check this, you cannot be sure until you have found and described all of the use cases.

- Is each actor involved with at least one use case? Remove any actors not mentioned in the use case descriptions or without communicates-associations with a use case. However, an actor mentioned in a use-case description is likely to have a communicates-association with that particular use case.
- Can you name at least two people who would be able to perform as a particular actor? If not, check to see whether the role the actor models is part of another role. If so, you should merge the actor with another actor.
- Do any actors play similar roles in relation to the system? If so, you should merge them into a single actor. The communicates-associations and use-case descriptions show how the actors and the system interrelate.
- Do two actors play the same role in relation to a use case? If so, you should use actor-generalizations to model their shared behavior.
- Will a particular actor use the system in several completely different ways, or does the actor have several completely different purposes for using the use case? If so, you should probably have more than one actor.
- Do the actors have intuitive and descriptive names? Can both users and customers understand the names? It is important that actor names correspond to their roles. If not, change them.

Quality Measures of the Modern SRS Package

Over and above the individual quality measures, some other quality features are specific to the containing package. We will now turn to the measures that help to ensure that the package itself is of the highest understandability and quality.

One of the most frustrating things about documentation is *finding something*. How many times have you said, "I know the fail-safe requirement is in here somewhere," but you just can't find it? All too often, we assume that simply getting the requirement captured is the entire game. It's not.

We have found that a Modern SRS Package not only organizes and captures the requirements but *also is easy to use*. A great SRS contains the following simple features.

A Good Table of Contents

An absolutely mandatory feature of a good SRS is a good table of contents (TOC). We have found that a TOC provides more benefits than you might first imagine. For example, the prospect of a good TOC nudges the author to use helpful headings that will subsequently appear in the SRS TOC. Look at the TOC in this book and note that the TOC heading themselves can "tell a story" and guide the reader. In effect, the TOC is like a condensed version of the actual package.

With today's tools, there is no excuse for not having a TOC. Creation of TOCs is easy and automatic and allows the author to select the level of detail and formatting to be used in the TOC. We believe that TOCs that record the third- or fourth-level headings are usually an appropriate level of detail for a Modern SRS Package. Also, adequate use of white space to break the TOC into major elements is always useful.

One frequently encountered problem is a TOC that has not been updated to reflect the current package. You should ensure that part of the SRS publication process *always* includes an update of the TOC to ensure the pagination markers are correct. A TOC is rendered useless if it is not updated. This has the unfortunate aspect of making the reader wonder about other things that may be wrong with the SRS. It's difficult enough to do the project without such pointless distractions.

Another problem that may arise is that TOCs are difficult to prepare if you need to go outside the document being processed. For example, suppose that you are preparing an SRS package containing several Word documents, several use-case specifications prepared by another tool, and a few Excel charts tossed in. You are not likely to find a good tool that can examine all of this input simultaneously and prepare a good TOC. In such cases, you may want to consider a multivolume TOC that uses the top level to indicate major groupings, such as Word documents, use-case model files, and Excel spreadsheets. Then, you can use the individual TOC tools to prepare file-oriented TOCs.

A Good Index

Indexes should be an important element of every SRS. Unlike TOCs, the creation of an index is more difficult because the authors must identify key elements for indexing. Of course, once they are identified, creation of the index is straightforward.

Part of the indexing problem stems from the varying views that the project team maintains. For example, the requirements for the medical device's fail-safe error recovery may be viewed as a "fail-safe" element by some team members and as an "error recovery" element by other members. If both views are valid, requirements that deal with this element should be indexed under both terms.

Frankly, indexing is work, but it is usually required only one time for each requirement added to the SRS. Once added, the index elements ride along with the package and become a useful part of the understanding of the project.

You should use the indexing features to move beyond simple TOC-like access to the package. That is, it serves no purpose to prepare an index whose only elements already appear in the TOC. Instead, you should use the indexing features to point the reader to *concepts* rather than to *titles*. As with TOCs, the index should always be updated as part of the publication process to ensure a consistent package.

A Revision History

It's very frustrating to discover that you have been looking at an older, obsolete version of an SRS. Every SRS should include a revision history page that captures the relevant changes to each version of the elements within the package. As a minimum, the revision history page should include

- The revision number or code for each change to the published information
- The date of each revision to the published information
- A short summary of the revisions made to the published information
- The name of the person responsible for the changes to the published information

You might also find it helpful to provide revision markers on each changed element within the SRS. Typically, the use of revision bars in the margins is very helpful when readers are trying to find changes.

Most modern documentation and requirements tools provide powerful revision control and automated version history. Use them!

A note of caution: Do not install revision control too early. (See Chapter 34, Managing Change.) Otherwise, while you are in the heat of battle over a set of revisions, you may wash over a specific requirement several times before you finally "get it right" prior to publication. There is no advantage in recording all of the twists and turns; don't put the package under revision control until you reach a reasonably stable point in your software development process. On the other hand, don't wait too long, or you will be overrun by uncontrolled development!

A Glossary

As the nature of each application domain is unique and, typically, quite technical, projects tend to develop a special language, or at least a shorthand, over time. The shorthand typically includes mnemonics, such as "SRS": avoid wherever possible, and eschew term usages that are meaningful only in the context of the situation. A good SRS has a glossary of such terms to help all users understand the language of the specific application domain. You should think in terms of including and defining all project-specific terms, all acronyms, all abbreviations, and any special phrases.

Chapter 28

TECHNICAL METHODS FOR SPECIFYING REQUIREMENTS

Key Points

- Technical methods for specifying requirements are appropriate when the requirement description is too complex for natural language or if you cannot afford to have the specification misunderstood.
- Technical methods include pseudocode, finite state machines, decision trees, activity diagrams, entity-relationship models, object-oriented analysis, and structured analysis.

Throughout this book, we have assumed that most requirements will be written in the team's natural language, be it in the form of a traditional statement or via the use-case method. We also suggest that requirements be augmented with diagrams, tables, or charts or other techniques to help clarify the meaning of a user requirement. But sometimes the ambiguity of natural language is simply not tolerable, particularly when the requirements deal with life-and-death issues or when the erroneous behavior of a system could have extreme financial or legal consequences. *If the description of the requirement is too complex for a natural language and if you cannot afford to have the specification misunderstood, you should consider writing that portion of the requirements with a "technical methods" approach.*

You can choose from a variety of technical specification methods:

- Pseudocode
- Finite state machines
- Decision trees
- Activity diagrams (flowcharts)
- Entity relationship models
- Object-oriented analysis
- Structured analysis

We won't attempt to teach you any of these techniques in detail, as each is worthy of an entire book of its own. Here, we will simply provide some "overview" training.

Technical methods should be used sparingly and consistently in a Modern SRS Package, and common sense should guide the decision as to *which* formal technique will be used. If you're building a nuclear reactor control system, perhaps *every* aspect of the system is critical; in most systems, however, it's unlikely that more than 10 percent of the requirements will require this degree of formality.

If possible, only one of these technical methods should be used for all requirements within the system. This will simplify the nontechnical reviewers' task of reading and understanding the package elements. And if all of the systems developed by an organization fall into one application domain, such as telephone switching systems, perhaps the same technical method can be used for all of the systems. But in most organizations, it's unrealistic to mandate a single technique for all requirements in all systems; the requirements writers need to pick the approach that best suits the situation.

Pseudocode

As the term implies, pseudocode is a "quasi" programming language, an attempt to combine the informality of natural language with the strict syntax and control structures of a programming language. In the extreme form, pseudocode consists of combinations of

- Imperative sentences with a single verb and a single object
- A limited set, typically not more than 40–50, of "action-oriented" verbs from which the sentences must be constructed
- Decisions represented with a formal IF-ELSE-ENDIF structure
- Iterative activities represented with DO-WHILE or FOR-NEXT structures

Figure 28–1 shows an example of a pseudocode specification of an algorithm for calculating deferred service-revenue earned within a given month in a business application. Note that the text of the pseudocode is indented, in an outline-style format, in order to show "blocks" of logic. The combination of the syntax restrictions and the format and the layout of the text greatly reduces the ambiguity of what could otherwise be a very difficult and error-prone requirement. (It certainly was before we wrote the pseudocode!) At the same time, it should be possible for a nonprogramming person (Rhonda, our bookkeeper) to read and to understand the requirement in the form

The algorithm for calculating deferred-service revenue earned for any month is:

Set SUM(x)=0

FOR each customer X

  IF customer purchased paid support

    AND ((Current month) >= (2 months after ship date))

    AND ((Current month) <= (14 months after ship date))

  THEN Sum(X)=Sum(X) + (amount customer paid)/12

Figure 28–1 Pseudocode example

shown in Figure 28–1. You don't have to be a rocket scientist to understand pseudocode, and you don't have to know C++ or Java.

Finite State Machines

In some cases, it's convenient to regard the system or a discrete subset of the system as a "hypothetical machine that can be in only one of a given number of 'states' at any specific time" (Davis 1993). In response to an input, such as data entry from the user or an input from an external device, the machine changes its state and then generates an output or carries out an action. Both the output and the next state can be determined solely on the basis of understanding the current state and the event that caused the transition. In that way, a system's behavior can be said to be deterministic; we can mathematically determine every possible state and, therefore, the outputs of the system, based on any set of inputs provided.

Hardware designers have used finite state machines (FSMs) for decades, and a vast body of literature describes the creation and analysis of such machines. Indeed, the mathematical nature of the FSM notation lends itself to formal and rigorous analysis, so that the problems of consistency, completeness, and ambiguity described earlier in this Team Skill can be largely mitigated, using this technique.

A popular notation for FSMs is the state-transition diagram shown in Figure 28–2. In this notation, the boxes represent the state the device is in, and the arrows represent actions that transition the device to alternative states. Figure 28–2 illustrates state transitions for the light box described in

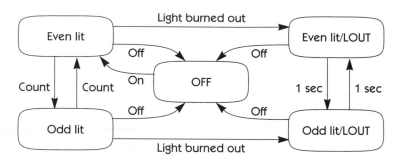

Figure 28–2   State transition diagram

Chapter 26. In that example, the natural-language expression "the light will flash every 1 second" was somewhat ambiguous. The state-transition diagram in Figure 28–2 is not ambiguous, as it illustrates that duty cycle B was indeed the right choice. If a bulb burns out, the device alternates between attempting to light the even light and attempting to light the odd light, each for a period of one second.

Here's an interesting exercise to try. Consider using the FSM technique to restate the HOLIS Control Light use case. You should immediately notice that the Dim alternative flow in the use case lends itself nicely to the FSM style of representation.

An even more precise form of representing a finite state machine is the state-transition matrix, which is represented as a table, or matrix, that shows every possible state the device can be in, the output of the system for each state, and the effect of every possible stimulus or event on every possible state. This ensures a higher degree of specificity because every state and the effect of every possible event must be represented in the table. For example, Table 28–1 defines the behavior of our light box in the form of a state-transition matrix.

With this technique, we can resolve additional ambiguities that may have been present in our attempt to understand the behavior of the device.

- What happens if the user presses the on switch and the device is already on? *Answer*: Nothing.
- What happens if the both bulbs are burned out? *Answer*: The device powers itself off.

FSMs are very popular for certain categories of systems programming applications, such as message-switching systems, operating systems, and process con-

Table 28-1   State-transition matrix for on/off counting device

	Event					
State	**On press**	**Off press**	**Count press**	**Bulb burns out**	**Every second**	**Output**
Off	Even lit	—	—	—	—	Both off
Even lit	—	Off	Odd lit	LO/Even lit	—	Even lit
Odd lit	—	Off	Even lit	LO/Odd lit	—	Odd lit
Light out/Even lit	—	Off	—	Off	LO/Odd lit	Even lit
Light out/Odd lit	—	Off	—	Off	LO/Even lit	Odd lit

trol systems. FSMs also are an elegant way of describing the interaction between an external human user and a system—consider, for example, the interaction between a bank customer and an ATM machine when the customer wants to withdraw money. However, FSMs can become unwieldy, particularly if we need to represent the system's behavior as a function of *several* inputs. In such cases, the required system behavior is typically a function of all current conditions and stimuli rather than the current stimulus or a history of stimuli.

Decision Trees and Decision Tables

It's common to see a requirement that deals with a combination of inputs; different combinations of those inputs lead to different behaviors or outputs. Suppose, for example, that we have a system with five inputs—A, B, C, D, and E—and we see a requirement that starts with a pseudocode-like statement: "If A is true, then if B and C are also true, generate output X, unless E is true, in which case the required output is Y." The combination of IF-THEN-ELSE clauses quickly becomes tangled, especially as in this example, it involves *nested* IFs. Typically, nontechnical users are not sure that they understand any of it, and nobody is sure whether all of the possible combinations and permutations of A, B, C, D, and E have been covered.

The solution, in this case, is to enumerate all of the combinations of inputs and to describe each one explicitly in a table. In our example, if the only permissible values of the inputs are "true" and "false," we have 2^5, or 32, combinations. These can be represented in a table containing 5 rows—one for each input variable—and 32 columns.

Graphical Decision Trees

Alternatively, a *decision tree* can be drawn to portray the information. We used this pictorial technique in Chapter 15 when we had to understand what

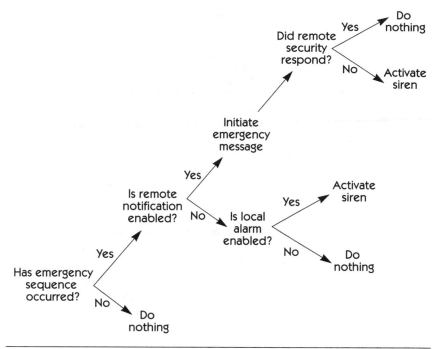

Figure 28–3 Graphical decision tree

kind of a prototype to build. Figure 28–3 shows a decision tree used to describe the HOLIS emergency sequence.

Activity Diagrams

Flowcharts and their new incarnation, the UML activity diagram, have the advantage of reasonable familiarity: Even people with no computer-related training or background know what a flowchart is. For example, a local newspaper recently had a flowchart describing an algorithm by which the brain processes the decisions involved in purchasing a SAAB convertible. For reasons that are pretty clear, all paths through that particular flowchart ended up at the same activity: "Buy the Saab." There must have been a logic error in there somewhere but we couldn't find it. But we sure are enjoying the car!

Figure 28–4 shows a typical activity diagram in UML notation. Although the same information could have been presented in pseudocode form, the UML notation provides a visual representation that may be easier to understand.

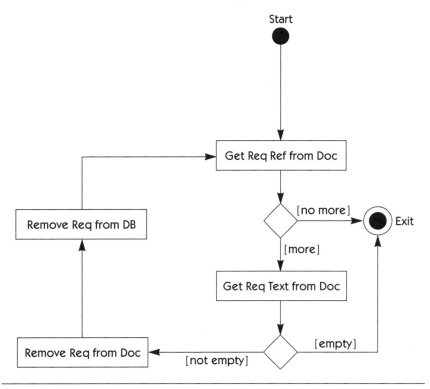

Figure 28–4   Activity diagram

The problem with activity diagrams, as the technical computer community has learned over the past 30 years, is that they are a nuisance to keep up to date. Of course, it can be a nuisance to keep any visual representation of a requirement up to date without automated tools; nobody wants to redraw a state-transition diagram or a decision tree, either.

Entity-Relationship Models

If the requirements within a set involve a description of the structure and relationships among *data* within the system, it's often convenient to represent that information in an entity-relationship diagram (ERD). Figure 28–5 shows a typical ERD.

Note that the ERD provides a high-level "architectural" view of the data represented by customers, invoices, packing lists, and so on; it would be further augmented with appropriate details about the required information to

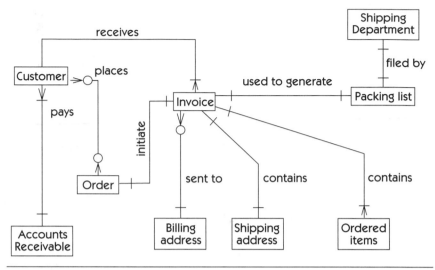

Figure 28–5   Entity-relationship diagram

describe a customer. The ERD does correctly focus on the external behaviors of the system and allows us to define such questions as "Can there be more than one billing address per invoice?" *Answer:* no.

Although an ERD is a powerful modeling technique, it has the potential disadvantage of being difficult for a nontechnical reader to understand. As you can see in Figure 28–5, the lines connecting "customer" to "order" and "order" to "invoice" are annotated with circles and "crows-feet" indicators. The obvious question is: What does all of this mean? Attempting to answer such a question within this book would be a major digression, which we have decided to avoid, but avoiding the question in the review of a requirements set is likely to mean that some users simply won't understand what's going on. The alternatives are to send the appropriate users to a 2-day training course in ERD notation, which they may or may not appreciate, or to use the notation as a "technical" form of documentation within the development group.

Object-Oriented Modeling

If the requirements that must be refined involve a description of the structure and relationships among *entities* within the system—for example, paycheck stubs, employees, payroll clerks and the like—it may be beneficial to

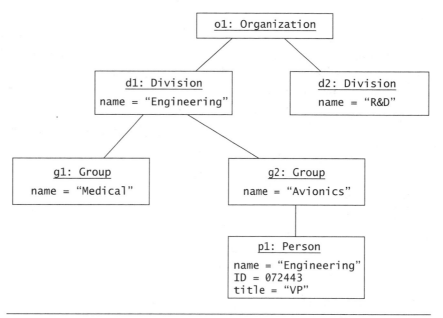

Figure 28–6 Object-oriented model

use object-oriented models to more fully describe the behavior of a system. With the popularity of OO and the rapid adoption of the UML, these diagrams are now starting to turn up in specifications and, even more appropriately, in the implementation models used to realize the functionality of the system.

There is some convenience to this in that the adoption of the UML standard will provide everyone with a common understanding of what these representations mean and will, therefore, reduce ambiguity by having everyone "speak the same language," albeit a technical one.

In Figure 28–6, for example, the "object" known as "Person" would be described in terms of the data-oriented "attributes" it contains, such as name and title, and also in terms of the "services" it can provide, such as add a new person, delete a person, and search for a particular instance of a person.

Data Flow Diagrams

Our discussion of requirements earlier in this chapter implied that we were dealing with "atomic-level" requirements. Although this is what we find in

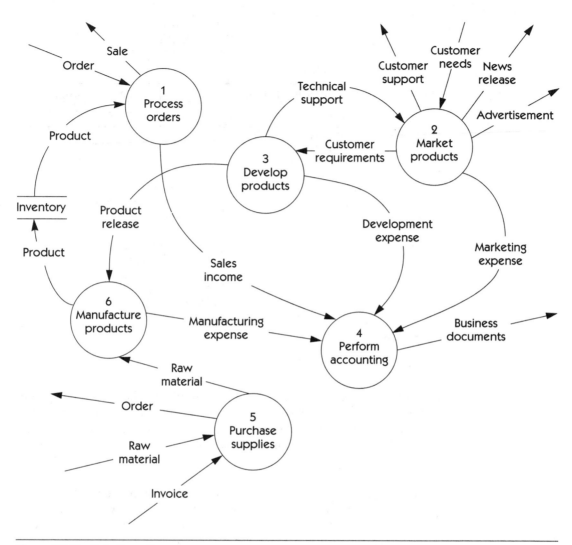

Figure 28–7   Data flow diagram

a typical document, it's often useful to provide a visual representation that shows the structure and the organization of those atomic-level requirements and also the input/output relationships between them. A popular notation for presenting this kind of information is the *data flow diagram* (see Figure 28–7).

Data flow diagram (DFD) models run the same risk as ERD models, although it's usually somewhat easier for a nontechnical reader to understand the meaning of a DFD without any formal training. Indeed, some organizations have had great success with DFDs as the basis for communication between nontechnical users and technical developers; other organizations have found, though, that their users balk at any such "technical" notation. If the DFD *can* be used, each of the "bubbles" in Figure 28–7 can be further decomposed into lower-level DFDs; thus, the requirements for bubble 5 ("purchase supplies") in Figure 28–7 could be further elaborated with a lower-level diagram that shows the appropriate details. This decomposition process continues until the bubbles are truly "atomic," at which point the requirements associated with that bubble could be described with the pseudocode, FSM, decision tree, or flowchart techniques discussed earlier. (In fact, there is a larger danger in using DFDs in today's world; the OO folks will think that you are a "functionally decomposing data modeler" and thereby fossilized matter and will ignore everything further you have to say on any subject.)

Maintenance of Specifications

From a requirements perspective, we use these technical methods only sparingly, and then *only* to illustrate the behavior of the system. This reduces the maintenance headache considerably. In addition, the newest generation of software development tools is starting to provide meaningful support for roundtrip engineering, that is, the ability to keep the code automatically synchronized with the representation in the model. As these tools mature, we'll have the opportunity to see requirements change as decisions that affect the external behavior of the system are made during the coding process.

> When it comes to the matter of maintenance, let common sense prevail.

A common maintenance problem occurs when the code or the specifications are revised and the related technical specifications are not revised in lockstep. Indeed, one body of theory states that "the code is the specification." We are not prepared to state that it is an absolute rule that the technical specifications *must* be updated as the project evolves. However, many pitfalls lurk for those who accidentally refer to outdated documentation. We've been guilty of this ourselves during the writing of this book, when we have said that "we don't need to update this drawing" and then later used an outdated version by accident.

With regard to the matter of updating, let common sense prevail. Update as appropriate, based on the critical nature of the information. If it's not vital, you might find it useful to not update it. One technique we have used is to stamp outdated documents with an "Outdated" label when we have made a conscious decision to let the documents lapse. That way, we at least know we are not looking at the most recent information.

We view stale models as the lesser of two evils. Having a stale model is far better than having no specification model at all!

Case Study

All of these techniques were considered by the HOLIS project team as they prepared the HOLIS SRS Package. The first incarnation of the package is shown in the HOLIS artifacts found in Appendix A.

Team Skill 5 Summary

In Team Skill 5, we learned that requirements are *the* key communication technique to completely and concisely capture the user's needs in such a way that the developer can build an application to meet those needs. In addition, requirements need to have sufficient specificity so that we can tell when they have been met. We needn't be alarmed by this. Often, it is our team—after all, we are closest to the project—that can provide this specificity; this is one of our opportunities to make sure that the right system gets defined.

Various ways of organizing and documenting these requirements exist; we focused on what we called a Modern SRS Package, a logical construct that allows us to document requirements in use cases, documents, database forms, or other requirements repositories. Although we made some suggestions about how to organize this package, we don't really care what form it takes, so long as it contains the right things.

All development should flow from the requirements specified in the Modern SRS Package, and all specifications in the package should be reflected in the development activities. Since these are the governing elements, it follows that all activities, such as regulatory constraints, should reflect the package and vice versa. The Modern SRS Package is a living entity that should be reviewed and updated throughout the lifetime of the project. The package should specify *what* functions are to be accomplished, not *how* they are to be accomplished. The Modern SRS Package should be used to specify functional requirements, nonfunctional requirements, and design constraints.

We also provided a set of quality measures you can use to assess the quality of your package and the various elements contained therein. Where necessary, the requirements documentation may be supplemented by one or more formal, or more structured, methods of specification.

The Modern SRS Package provides the detail you need to proceed to *implement*, or *build*, the right system. We'll discuss this part of the project next, in Team Skill 6, Building the Right System.

Team Skill 6
BUILDING THE RIGHT SYSTEM

Team Skill 5 led us through some useful techniques for collecting, organizing, and documenting the requirements for your development project. We also considered various techniques for specifying the needs of the project, noting that the single most important success factor is *to collect all of the requirements for the project and to help the stakeholders understand and agree on the requirements.*

In this Team Skill, we'll focus on moving from the definition of a solution system to finally building a system that meets stakeholder needs. This next step is the most difficult and it will consume many times the resources that have been expended to date. To help you accomplish this, in the next few chapters we will examine a method to move from the specifications (via use cases) to designing and implementing the system.

Many projects quickly evolve into a flurry of development activities with lots of favorable progress being made. However, at the end of the day, it turned out that the mighty dust cloud of development obscured the fact that the client did not get the system they wanted. In this Team Skill, we also want to look beyond the development activities and ask, "How do you know you are building the right system?"

Two strong determinants that help you answer that question are verification and validation. We will look more closely at how these two techniques can be integrated into your implementation activities so as to sharpen your development focus onto those things that really matter to the project.

And of course, no development is immune to changes in the project as time passes. Accordingly, this Team Skill will investigate the nature of change and will discuss ways of embracing change and controlling it so that your project does not run out of control.

Chapter 29

BUILDING THE RIGHT
SYSTEM RIGHT: OVERVIEW

Key Points

- Building the right system right depends on continually confirming that the development is on track and that the results are correct, as well as being able to deal with change during development.
- Verification is the process of ensuring that the development activities continually conform to the customer's needs.
- Validation demonstrates that the product conforms to its requirements and gains customer acceptance of the final result.
- Since change happens, plan for it, and know how to manage it.

As we have stressed throughout this book, it is *vital* that everyone on the team understands the project requirements. However, it's not practical to wait around until absolutely everyone is totally with the program. That's why we have described iterative development techniques that allow you to progressively refine your understanding as you go along.

But even then, we have seen projects that have done a good job up to this point but still ruin those efforts by diving into disorganized development activities. This is yet another potential project failure mode: when the team *does understand* the requirements but is still not able to build a system that *meets* those requirements. In this chapter, we'll focus on a few more key concepts you can master to ensure that you are building the right system right.

- Continually confirm that the development is on track.
- Confirm that the development results are correct.
- Learn how to deal with change during development.

Continually Confirm that the Development Is on Track

As the design and implementation evolve, the team must be able to continually reassure itself that the project hasn't inadvertently "run off the rails." That is, the team needs to be able to continually verify that the development results conform to the customer's needs.

We'll use the term *verification* to describe an ongoing process that will help ensure that every step of the development is correct, meets the needs of the next activity, and is not superfluous to the needed activities. Unfortunately, there is a lot of confusion in the industry as to just exactly what verification is. So, we'll discuss this important and powerful concept in more detail.

Principles of Software Verification

The IEEE (1994) defines verification as

> *"the process of evaluating a system or component to determine whether the products of a given phase satisfy the conditions imposed at the start of that phase"* (IEEE 1012-1986, §2, 1994).

That is, verification is largely an analysis-based activity that requires you to confirm that each stage of the development—for example, a software implementation of one or more requirements—conforms to the requirements defined in the previous stage.

At a minimum, we will want to verify that

- The features we expressed really meet the needs
- The use cases and requirements we derive from the features truly support the features
- The use cases are implemented in the design
- The design supports the functional and nonfunctional aspects of the system's behavior
- The code really does conform to the design and the design objectives
- Our tests provide full coverage for the requirements and use cases that have been developed.

So, how do we know what the whole project is? We need some kind of method to make sure that we have verified everything that needs verifying—and no more than that.

In order to do this, you'll need a verification plan, and you'll benefit from some tools to help execute this plan. But most important, the team will need to understand what verification is, and you'll need a commitment to the verification activities. Verification is *not* just an activity handled by the project's QA team, which may nonetheless be of great assistance during this process.

One method for continually checking up on your verification activities is *traceability*. We've made passing mention of traceability in Team Skill 5, and Chapter 31 will discuss how we can use traceability to help us organize our verification activities.

Regardless of how we organize it, we must remember that the essence of verification is to reassure ourselves that the step we are working on has the proper antecedents and that it is performed in a consistent and reliable way. Furthermore, we must verify that every activity that we decide to do is needed and that no necessary steps are omitted.

We gain reassurance of these issues largely by effective software processes and by analysis. For example, we can examine the requirements and reassure ourselves that they correctly, completely, and concisely express the higher-level user needs. We can examine the design to reassure ourselves that it is driven by the requirements and use cases, that it is complete, and that it has no extra elements. In some cases, the analysis boils down to *inspections* and *reviews*. In other cases, we can use our models and tool automation to assist with checking completeness, semantics, and so on. Remember, we are not trying to ensure that things are working; we'll get to that later. Instead, we are focused on the issue of making sure that we've done the things we need to do and that they follow a logical development progression.

OK, so much for the digression. Now let's get back to discussing some implications of verification.

The Cost of Verification

The dark side of the verification issue is that we can go "verification happy" and spend time in verification activities that do not give us a satisfactory payback. So, we need some way of computing an economic "return on investment" (ROI) for our verification activities.

We will need to have an approach to help us make the *right* investments in checking our activities. We don't want to overdo the checking, and we don't want to skimp on crucial checking aspects. Chapter 33 considers an overview of the techniques of risk assessment and hazard analysis and offers insights as to how these techniques can be used to get the most out of your development dollars during system review activities.

The team must be able to design and to implement a system that conforms to the requirements. That is, the team must be able to verify that the implementation plans conform to the project needs.

But the previous point begs a significant question: How do we get from requirements to design to implementation? After all, you don't just hold the requirements up to a computer and expect a design and implementation to occur! In Chapter 30, we will examine ways in which you can move from requirements to design, and we'll provide an overview of how you can use artifacts of the requirements process to drive the design and implementation of your system.

Verification at All Levels

You can apply the verification throughout the lifecycle of the project; the technique is not confined to any particular phase. You can and should verify requirements elements, design elements, implementation elements, testing elements, and any other elements that are deemed important to your project, based on your ROI analysis. In general, you will be invoking some amount of verification activity at *every* stage of the project. You will be invoking verification to ensure the correctness of the

- User needs to product features
- Product features to requirements
- Requirements to architecture
- Architecture to design model
- Design model to implementation
- Implementation to test planning

(*Note*: We'll cover testing as part of validation.)

Again, we stress that verification is extremely important in the design stages of the project because errors introduced in the design stage are extremely costly to remove after implementation is under way.

The Reason for Verification

We recommend that all projects incorporate a verification process that begins at project inception and continues throughout the life of the project.

If you are working on a project whose software development process is regulated, you will likely be forced to do verification, whether you want to or not. If you are developing high-assurance systems—safety-critical systems or those for which the cost of failure is unacceptably high—you will have to do verification, or you will be taking unacceptable risks or perhaps imposing unacceptable risks on others. But every project of any reasonable scope will benefit by the right amount of verification.

Confirm that the Development Results Are Correct

As important milestones, such as executable iterations, are reached, it will be important to validate the functionality that has been developed—that it works correctly and conforms to the requirements. After all, there is little point in achieving a particular milestone if the pieces don't work the way they are supposed to, although even then we learn something.

A very special milestone is the completion of the project. In an effective process, the completion milestone is simply one more step in ensuring that the system is designed and implemented in compliance with the customer's needs. In addition, at the completion milestone, we must show that the system really works as it is supposed to.

The final checkpoint is achieved when the system is shown to work in the customers environment.

There's one final and *very* important checkpoint in the development process. The product has to be demonstrated to work within the customer's environment, and the customer has to like the product enough to accept the result. The bottom line is that the customer must be happy when the project is over, or at least not too unhappy!

Validating the development work has *two* important aspects: (1) to show that the product conforms to its requirements and (2) to focus on customer acceptance of the final result. Although, in theory, these would be the same thing, in practice, the final acceptance testing will often demonstrate how well we've handled requirements or user need "drift" from the earlier project activities. Chapter 32 will discuss system validation from both of these perspectives, as well as the varying opinions as to what validation means.

Just as for verification, we also need a way to make sure that our validation, or testing, time and resource investments are cost effective. Once again, an ROI review may prove beneficial.

Learn How to Cope with Change that Occurs during the Development Process

Finally, of course, we have to consider the impact of changing requirements. Have you ever worked on a system that *never* changed its requirements from day 1?

We must plan for change and know how to manage it. Chapter 34 will discuss the potentially devastating impact of uncontrolled change and will offer an organized way to recognize change, estimate its impact, and incorporate changes in an orderly manner.

Looking Ahead

Let's begin by considering the issue of how you can move from the requirements for the project into designing and implementing a solution to the problem at hand. That is the focus of the next chapter.

Chapter 30

FROM REQUIREMENTS TO IMPLEMENTATION

Key Points

- Many requirements map well from design to implementation code.
- Other requirements have little correlation to design and implementation; the form of the requirement differs from the form of the design and implementation: the problem of orthogonality.
- Object orientation and use cases can help alleviate the problem of orthogonality.
- Use cases drive design by allowing all stakeholders to examine the proposed system implementation against a backdrop of system uses and requirements.
- Good system design is not necessarily optimized to make it easy to see how the requirements are implemented within the implementation.

We have been building complex software systems for over 40 years. And yes, our industry has struggled and had its share of failures, as well as an extraordinary degree of success: online trading, word processing, desktop productivity, life-saving medical equipment, and safe power plants, to name a few.

It's clear that we have somehow managed to move from the world of requirements to the world of design and implementation. We have implemented many complex systems that conform to their requirements. However, when it comes to building complex systems that require a high degree of design assurance, it's not always been a pretty, or at least a rigorously scientific, matter. The reason is that requirements do not lend themselves to being readily exposed for inspection within the implementation. Proving that the requirement is fulfilled in the code is a nontrivial effort.

Mapping Requirements to Design and Code

Fortunately, for a significant percentage of our requirements, it is a relatively easy matter to design the software so that it is fairly straightforward to follow our requirements into design and then into code. This also means that we can test a significant portion of our code, using a requirement-to-module test, as there will be a reasonable degree of correlation between the statement of a requirement and the code that implements it. For example, it's probably fairly straightforward to find, inspect, and validate the code that fulfills the requirement "Support up to an eight-digit floating-point input parameter," or "Indicate compilation progress to the user," as we can see in Figure 30–1. Depending on the type of system we are building, this approach may work for a substantial portion of our code, so the requirements to design to implementation process is not so difficult in these cases.

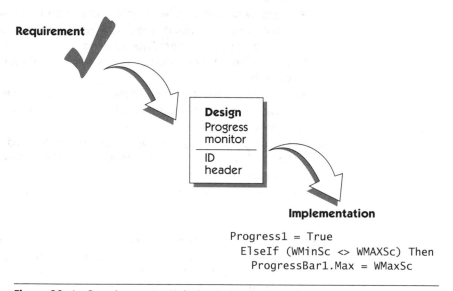

Requirement

Design
Progress
monitor

ID
header

Implementation

```
Progress1 = True
  ElseIf (WMinSc <> WMAXSc) Then
    ProgressBar1.Max = WMaxSc
```

Figure 30–1   Requirements to design to implementation

The Orthogonality Problem

Requirement:
"100,000 trades
an hour"

Code

However, when it comes to such requirements as "The system shall handle up to 100,000 trades an hour" or "The system shall allow editing, based on security set up by the system administrator," things get a little trickier. In these cases, there is little correlation between the requirement and the design and implementation; they are orthogonal, or nearly so. In other words, the *form* of our requirements and the *form* of our design and implementation are different. There is no one-to-one mapping to make implementation and validation easier, for a number of reasons.

- Requirements speak of real-world items, such as engines and paychecks, but code speaks of stacks, queues, and computation algorithms. The two are different languages.
- Certain requirements, such as performance requirements, have little to do with the *logical* structure of code but lots to do with the *process* structure, or how various pieces of code interact, how fast a particular piece of code runs, how often we get interrupted while in module A, and so on. When you can't physically map to the logical structure, there is no place to "point" your requirement *to* within the implementation.
- Other functional requirements require that a number of system element's interact to achieve the functionality. Looking at a part is not the same as looking at the whole, and the implementation of the requirement is distributed throughout the code.
- Perhaps most important, good system design is often not driven by optimizing the ease with which we can prove that a requirement is met but instead by many more important issues. We may be optimizing for scarce resources, using an architectural pattern that has been proven in other applications but that is not the exact paradigm of our current application, reusing code, or applying purchased components that bring their own overhead and functional behaviors, and so on.

For those of us who have been building high-assurance systems and/or have been forced by political or contractual considerations into being able to demonstrate on paper the direct correlation between requirements and code, we managed to get by. But, we admit, the formulation consisted of one part real-and-deadly-serious-requirements traceability mechanisms and one part pixie dust.

Object Orientation

In many ways, this problem of orthogonality—lack of direct relationship between requirements reflecting the problem space and the code we implemented—was substantially improved with the advent of OO technology. In applying OO, we tended to build code entities that were a better match to the problem domain, and we discovered that an improved degree of robustness resulted. This was due not only to the OO principles of abstraction, information hiding, inheritance, and so on, but also to the fact that the real-world entities simply changed less often than the transactions and the data we used to model our system after. Therefore, our code changed less often, too. (For example, people still get paychecks today, just like they did 40 years ago, although the form of delivery—electronic versus paper—has changed dramatically.)

With OO, we did start to find engine objects and paycheck objects in the code, and we used this to good advantage to decrease the degree of orthogonality in requirements verification. We could look at the requirements for "paycheck stub" and see whether the implied operations and attributes were supported in the design model.

However, we must be careful because a purposeful attempt to provide a one-to-one mapping from requirements to code can lead to a *very non-OO* architecture, one that is functionally organized. The basic principles of OO drive the designer to describe a small number of mechanisms that satisfy the key requirements of the system, resulting in a set of classes that collaborate and yield behavior that's bigger than the sum of its parts. This "bigger behavior" is intended to provide a more robust, more extensible design that can deliver the current and, ideally, future requirements in the *aggregate*, but it is not a one-to-one mapping from requirements. Therefore, even with OO, some degree of orthogonality with requirements will always remain.

The Use Case as a Requirement

As we mentioned earlier, the "itemized" nature of the requirements can further compound the problem of orthogonality. Each requirement by itself may not present a huge problem, but it makes it difficult to look at system behavior in the aggregate to see whether it does all the right things. Also, how could we examine the system to determine whether requirement 3 (display progress bar) immediately followed requirement 7 (during compilation, the algorithm is . . .)?

- Client inserts ATM card.
- System prompts for PIN.
- Client enters PIN.

The use case, which provides a sequence of actions between the system and the user instead of an itemized individual requirement, improves this problem significantly. Now, the requirements themselves, in the form of the use cases, do a better job of providing the behavior of the system in sequential fashion, complete with alternatives and exceptions. Use cases simply "tell a better story" about what the system is to do. And, as we will see, they also give us a head start on the design, since use cases are handy constructs for collecting requirements and starting the design process.

Managing the Transition

So, although we haven't solved the problem of orthogonality, we do have a number of existing assets and a few new techniques that can help us deal with the problem. If we can use these assets to increase the parallels between requirements and code, it seems likely that we can logically use our understanding of the requirements to more easily drive the design of the system. In so doing, it should also be easier to translate between these dissimilar worlds, to improve the design of the system, and to improve the overall quality of the system that results. Before we do so, however, we need to make a small digression into the world of modeling and software architecture.

Modeling Software Systems

Nontrivial software systems today are extraordinarily complex undertakings. It is not uncommon to find systems and applications that are composed of *millions* of lines of code. These systems or applications may, in turn, be embedded in other systems that also have an extraordinary complexity in their own right, not to mention the complex interactions that may occur between the systems. We take it as a given that no one person or even group of persons can possibly understand the details of each of these systems and their planned interactions.

In the face of this complexity and to keep our wits about us, a useful technique is to abstract the system into a simplified *model*, removing the minutia of the system in order to have a more understandable version. The purpose of modeling is to simplify the details down to an understandable "essence" but to not oversimplify to the point that the model does not adequately represent the real system. In this way, we can think about the system without being buried in the details.

Selection of the model is an important issue. We want the model to help us understand the system in the proper way, but we don't want the model to mislead us because of errors or abstractions in the model. You've undoubtedly seen pictures of drawings and machines that helped the early philosophers, astronomers, and mathematicians understand the workings of the solar system. Many of these models, based on a *geocentric* view of the solar system with Earth at the center of the universe, thus led to many blind alleys and incorrect theories. Only when sun-centered, or *heliocentric*, models were proposed did a better understanding of our solar system emerge.

Indeed, the heliocentric models of the universe opened up many new possibilities and ideas regarding the universe at large (very large). Early scientists were able to reason from the model and to propose refined mathematical theories relating motion, gravity, and so on. But it's important to note that the model was *not* the reality. In some cases, the mechanical views of the universe, as exemplified by the model, did not exactly match the observed realities. For example, one of the early confirmations of Einstein's relativity theory was observed in some previously unexplained anomalies of the planet Mercury's orbit.

Models provide a powerful way to reason about a complex problem and to derive useful insights. However, we must be aware that *the model is not the reality*. We must continually check and assure ourselves that the model has not led us astray.

Remember, the model is not the reality.

Many different aspects of a system can be modeled. If you are interested in concurrency, you may model that. If you are interested in the system's logical structure, you may model that. Also, these models need to interact in some way, and that aspect too can be modeled. Each of these mechanisms contributes to our understanding of the system in the aggregate, and taken together, they allow us to consider the *system architecture* in the whole.

The Architecture of Software Systems According to Shaw and Garlan (1996), software architecture involves the

> *"description of elements from which systems are built, interactions amongst those elements, patterns that guide their composition, and constraints on those patterns."*

According to Kruchten (1998), we use architecture to help us

- Understand *what* the system does
- Understand *how* the system works
- Be able to think and work on pieces of the system
- Extend the system
- Reuse part(s) of the system to build another one

Architecture becomes the tool by which decisions are made about what and how the system will be built. In many projects, we know at the start how we are going to put the pieces together because we, or others, have developed such systems before. The easy starting decisions are reflected in the "dominant architecture" notion, which is just a fancy way of saying that "everyone knows how to build a payroll system."

Dominant architecture helps us kickstart the decision process and minimizes risk through the reuse of pieces of a successful solution. If you're going to build a payroll system, it would be silly to start from scratch and invent the entire concept of FICA, check writing, medical deductions, and so on. Start by looking at models of existing systems, and use them to start your thinking.

Different stakeholders need different perspectives of the system.

But, different groups of stakeholders may need to consider your architectural models and may want to view the proposed architecture from different perspectives. The parallel to our "building a house" metaphor holds: If you were building a house, you'd want to have views of the house that were suitable for the framers, the roofers, the electricians, the plumbers, and so on. It's all the same house, but our *view* of it may differ, depending on the need.

4+1 Views of Architecture   There is usually a small set of common needs for viewing the system architecture. The views that best illustrate these needs are discussed by our colleague, Philippe Kruchten (1995), as the "4+1" view shown in Figure 30–2. The figure identifies a number of stakeholders (programmers, management, users) and positions them near the types of views that they would normally need to consider.

1. The *logical view* addresses the functionality of the system. This abstraction of the design model represents the logical structure of the system in terms of subsystems and classes, which in turn are the entities that deliver the functionality to the user.

2. The *implementation view* describes the bits and pieces that are relevant to the implementation of the system: source code, libraries,

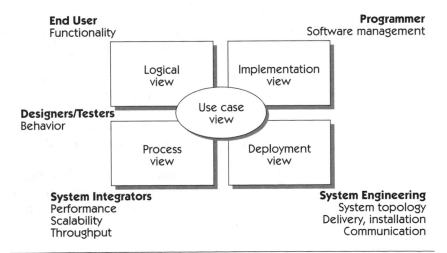

Figure 30–2   The 4+1 architectural view

object classes, and so on. This view represents the static view of these pieces, not how they interact.

3. *Process views*, generally more useful to describe operations of the system, are extremely important for systems that have parallel tasks, interfaces with other systems, and other interactions that occur during execution. Since many modern systems exhibit high degrees of parallelism and multithreading, this view allows the reviewer to determine potential problems, such as race conditions or deadlocks. You should also use the process view to examine throughput issues and other performance issues that the user specified in the nonfunctional requirements.

4. Because the project modules rarely exist in a vacuum, the *deployment view* allocates the implementation elements to the supporting infrastructure, such as operating systems and computing platforms. This view is not especially concerned with *what* the interactions are but rather with the fact that there *are* interactions and constraints where the two systems meet.

Role of the Use-Case Model in Architecture

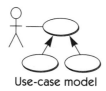
Use-case model

Finally, we return to our problem of orthogonality. Within the architecture, the *use-case view*, as the holder of requirements, plays a special role in the architectural model. This view presents key use cases of the use-case model and thereby is used to drive design, and it also ties all of the various views of the architecture together. We favor this view because it allows all stakeholders to examine the proposed system implementation plans against a backdrop of actual uses and requirements of the system. So, the use-case view, which represents the functionality of the system, is the "tie that binds," that is, the one view that binds the other views together.

For example, the HOLIS use case Initiate Emergency Sequence would impact the design of the system in each of the four views as follows.

1. The *logical view* would describe the various classes and subsystems that implemented the behaviors called for by the emergency sequence functionality.

2. The *process view* would demonstrate how the multitasking capability of HOLIS was always available to initiate an emergency sequence, even when it was being programmed or was busy doing other tasks.

3. The *deployment view* would show that the functionality of HOLIS was distributed across the three HOLIS nodes, or subsystems: Control Switch, Central Control Unit, and Homeowner's PC.

4. The *implementation view* would describe the various code artifacts for HOLIS, including source and executable files.

Realizing Use Cases in the Design Model

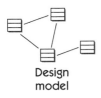

Design model

This notion of "use-case-driven design" is a key theme in the Unified Modeling Language and the associated book *Unified Software Development Process* (Jacobson, Booch, and Rumbaugh 1999). The technique we describe here is the means by which the UML and the process help the design team transition from an understanding of the *requirements* to the design and implementation of the solution.

Further, the UML contains specific modeling constructs that support *realizing* the use case in the implementation. Specifically, use cases are realized via *collaborations*, which are societies of classes, interfaces, subsystems, or other elements that cooperate to achieve some behavior. The UML stereotype, *use-case realization*, is used for this purpose and is simply a special form of collaboration, one that is used to show how the functionality of a specific use case is achieved in the design model.

Collaborations, then, are key modeling constructs within our area of concern, for it is within the collaborations that you see the systematic and aggregate behavioral aspects of the system, or how the system achieves its overall goals. These key constructs deliver some of the "bigger-than-the-sum-of-its-parts behavior" through the activities of participating classes and other logical elements. The graphical symbol for a collaboration is a simple dotted line ellipse with a name inside, as shown in Figure 30–3. (The UML authors have commented that the similarity to use case notation is intentional.)

Collaborations have another useful aspect. With collaborations, we can trace from the use-case model into the design model as can be seen in Figure 30–4.

Figure 30–3 Collaboration

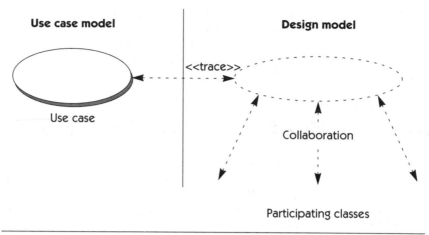

Figure 30–4   A use case collaboration in the design model

Structural and Behavioral Aspects of Collaborations

Collaborations have two aspects: a structural part that specifies the static structure of the system—the classes, elements, interfaces, and subsystems on which the implementation is structured—and a behavioral part that specifies the dynamics of how the elements interact to accomplish the result. However, a collaboration is not a physical thing; it is just a description of how cooperating elements of the system work together. To know more about how the collaboration is affected, you must look inside.

Inside the collaboration, the structural aspects can be represented by a class diagram. Figure 30–5 shows a class diagram for the HOLIS Emergency Message Sequence collaboration. For behavioral aspects, you might choose to model its behavior, using an interaction diagram such as the one shown in Figure 30–6.

Using Collaborations to Realize Sets of Individual Requirements

Although use cases show how requirements can drive design, it's also true that we can model the implementation of any individual requirement, or any set of requirements, as a collaboration (see Figure 30–7). Although the use

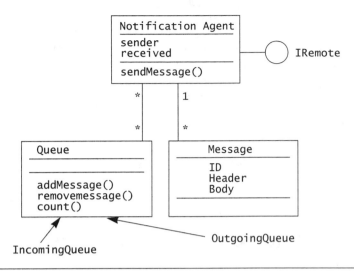

Figure 30–5   Class diagram for HOLIS emergency message sequences

case does have some special properties, namely, the sequence of events, we can often arrange our itemized requirements so as to accomplish the same objective. With this slight extension, we have a meaningful way to use requirements, of all types, to drive design and implementation.

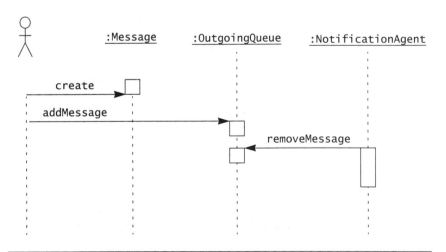

Figure 30–6   Behavioral aspects of collaboration: "HOLIS Emergency Message Sequence"

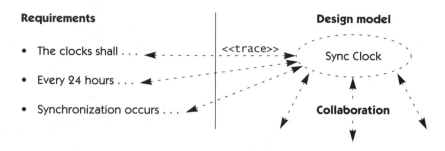

Figure 30–7   Model of requirements implementation as a collaboration

From Design to Implementation

By modeling the system this way, we can ensure that the significant use cases and requirements of the system are properly realized in the design model. In turn, this helps ensure that the software design conforms to the requirements, and we have achieved a major step in the process of *design verification*.

The next step follows quite logically, although admittedly not easily. The classes and the objects defined in the design model are implemented in terms of the physical software components—source files, binaries, executables, and others—that will be used to create the executable software. But even this mapping has its complications. For example, the decisions that lead you to a certain componentization of the logical models will often be driven by such requirements as the need for resilience, performance requirements, constraints on the system's deployed topology, and so on. The point is that every view of a system's architecture is, or at least should be, influenced by the system's requirements. But if we keep these factors in mind, we should be able to complete this process of the transition requirements to design to implementation.

Summary

It would be nice if you could go directly from the requirements to the code. Unfortunately, that's impractical. The best that modern practice can offer is a series of constructs that will help you move closer to the direct translation goal.

One of these techniques, use-case realization, takes advantage of the unique characteristics of the use case and the UML's modeling constructs to help drive design. This has many advantages in shortening the path from requirements to implementation.

Other modern practices have offered us the clarity of viewing our efforts in the "4+1 view" architectural views construct, and we have found that this helps provide a separation of concerns. This makes it easier for the various stakeholders in the implementation process to develop and to assess the design as it evolves.

Looking Ahead

We admit it. We've only skimmed the top layer of implementation. In reality, you are well aware, as are we, that implementation is a *huge* topic in its own right. Fortunately, this is *not* a book on implementing software systems, so we don't have to get involved with that problem. For now, we'll leave the topic of implementation and move on to the glue that binds the whole thing together, verification and validation (V&V). In the next few chapters, we'll show a number of approaches designed to minimize the undetected introduction of bugs into the project and testing and validation techniques that will help ensure that the system meets its overall objectives.

V&V plays an important role in the overall goal of developing quality software. Specifically, verification activities keep us from falling into the trap of "testing quality into the product." We have seen many projects fall short of expectations due to the erroneous notion that "we will find all the bugs during testing." That's just not possible. Finding and correcting bugs is vastly more expensive than simply not introducing the bugs in the first place.

To put this into a V&V context, we will use the next two chapters to show that traceability is a powerful approach to help you verify and minimize the undetected introduction of bugs into the project. Validation is a different technique to help ensure that the testing is on target to find the bugs that do find their way into the system.

Chapter 31

USING TRACEABILITY TO SUPPORT VERIFICATION

Key Points

- Traceability is an effective technique which supports the verification activity.
- Software requirements are traced from one or more product features identified in the Vision document.
- Traceability tools enable you to inspect the traceability relationships to ensure that no verification relationships have been omitted and that no excess verification relationships are present.
- Tools alone can't do the job; verification requires thinking.

Verification is the ongoing process we recommend to ensure that each step of the development is correct, meets the needs of the next step, and is not superfluous to the needed activities. This chapter examines traceability techniques you can use to support all stages of verification of the project, right from the start.

The Role of Traceability in Requirements Verification

A significant factor in quality software implementation is the ability to trace the implementation through the stages of specification, architecture, design, implementation, and testing. The ability to track relationships and to relate them when change occurs forms a key thread throughout many modern high-assurance software processes, particularly in life-critical medical products or business or mission-critical activities. The reason is that historical safety data has shown that the impact of change is often missed and that small changes to a system can create significant safety and reliability problems.

For example, the latest U.S. Food and Drug Administration (FDA) guidance for traceability in medical software development activities is contained in the FDA Office of Device Evaluations (ODE) Guidance Document (1996b). In addition, the Design Controls section of the new medical Current Good Manufacturing Practices (CGMP) document (FDA 1996a), Subpart C of the CGMP, defines the obligations of the system designers to be able to trace relationships between various work products within the lifecycle of the product's development.

IEEE (1994) provides two working definitions of traceability:

- "The degree to which a relationship can be established between two or more products of the development process, especially products having a predecessor-successor or master-subordinate relationship to one another; for example, the degree to which the requirements and design of a given software component match." (IEEE 610.12-1990 §3)
- "The degree to which each element in a software development product establishes its reason for existing; for example, the degree to which each element in a bubble chart references the requirement it satisfies." (IEEE 610.12-1990 §3)

A key element of traceability is the "traceability relationship." We find it convenient to define the relationship in terms of a simple "traced-to" and "traced-from" model. For example, we can easily imagine that one or more software requirements are created in the system in order to support a given feature specified in the Vision document. Thus, we can say that a software requirement is traced from one or more features (see Figure 31–1).

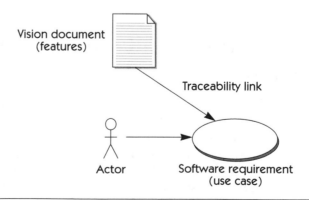

Figure 31–1   Traceability link from Vision document to software requirement

Additional meaning can be placed on the relationship from the context of the requirement types that are created. For example, a software requirement that is traced to a test case would suggest that the software requirement is "tested by" the test case that it is "traced to." An object description that is traced from a software requirement would imply that the requirement is "implemented by" the referenced object. Indeed, your project is likely to have one-to-many, many-to-one, and many-to-many interrelationships among these project elements.

Building on what we've learned about the various means of expressing requirements and the requirements organization we discussed in Chapter 25, your project might be structured with the full set of relationships as shown in Figure 31–2.

Implicit versus Explicit Traceability

In Figure 31–2, we observe that your project team explicitly adds the relationships between the elements. That is, we define *explicit traceability* as the

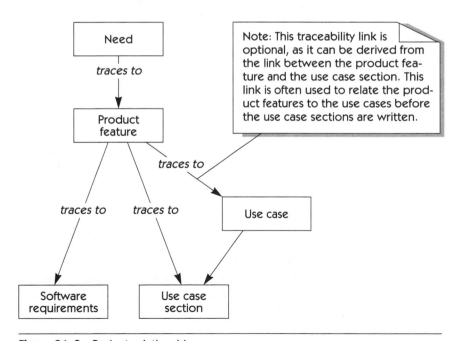

Figure 31–2   Project relationships

development of relationships stemming from external considerations supplied by your team. So, for example, the linkage, or relationship, between a product feature and a use case that supports that feature is determined solely by the team's deciding that such a relationship has meaning. There is no intrinsic relationship between the elements; only external decisions can establish the relationships.

The structure of the model itself may provide implicit traceability relationships.

On the other hand, the methodology and the structure of the model may provide *implicit traceability* relationships. For example, Team Skill 5 discussed the notion of parent-child requirements that exhibited a formal parent-child hierarchical relationship. In the case of hierarchical requirements, there is an implicit traceability between the parent requirements and the related child requirements. This implicit relationship need not be explicitly stated as an explicit relationship; indeed, it should *not* be stated explicitly, because of possible confusions that may arise.

Other cases of implicit traceability may arise from the modeling paradigm used. For example, the modeling tools used in the development process may automatically provide other traceability relationships among the modeling elements. If, for example, your modeling tool provides implicit links between use-case modeling elements and the actors that interact with the use case, you have a significant opportunity to exploit those implicit traceability relationships. You can further extend the traceability into the implementation by tracing the use-case collaborations that trace to the implementation objects.

In summary, we make little distinction between the two classes of traceability. The only caution we offer is to make sure that you are aware of all of the forms of traceability your modeling tools offer. If the tools *do* provide certain forms of implicit traceability, use them. If the tools *do not* offer implicit traceability in areas of interest to you, you will need to generate explicit traceability linkages as required to support your development efforts.

Additional Traceability Options to Consider

Traceability can frequently help in understanding other parts of a project. We have often added less traditional elements to a project and included them in the traceability processes because they add value to our understanding of the project.

For example, you might find it useful to define a new element called an "issue" and to keep all of your running, unresolved issues as part of your project elements. By using traceability techniques, you can link your issues to the items they are referring to. For example, if you have an unresolved issue about the product's functionality, you can link that issue to the product features and the software requirements related to that issue. By maintaining the "issue" links, you have an easy way to go back into your project and find all of the elements related to an issue you may have just resolved. Other nontraditional elements you may want to incorporate into your project traceability processes include

- Assumptions and rationales
- Action items
- Requests for new/revised features
- Glossary and acronym terms
- Bibliographic references

The key point is that you can use traceability to help you understand the relationships among "things" in your project. Let your imagination roam over the possibilities and add "things" that will help your team understand the project better. Feel free to trace all of useful relationships among "things." For example, there may be unresolved issues with a particular definition of a glossary item. In such cases, linking an issue with a glossary element (and, perhaps, other features) may be a useful aid to reminding the team that unresolved matters still exist in the project. A typical traceability structure might be augmented with additional traceability items, as shown in Figure 31–3.

Always look for a good *balance* between tracing elements and the cost of doing so.

A caution: Do not go overboard with this notion. We have found that adding too many "things" to the traceability process becomes a maintenance burden. As always, you should strive for a good *balance* between the value of the extra elements you wish to trace and the cost of maintaining them.

Using Traceability Tools

Powerful software development tools offer a simple user-guided procedure to "point and click" through the relationships that may exist between two elements of the lifecycle. We have had extensive experience with the RequisitePro tool offered by Rational Software and have chosen to use that tool for all of the tool illustrations in this book. Your choice of tool may differ, but the end results should be similar to our examples. (Refer to Appendix A for a more detailed view of the HOLIS project artifacts that we will be using in the following examples.)

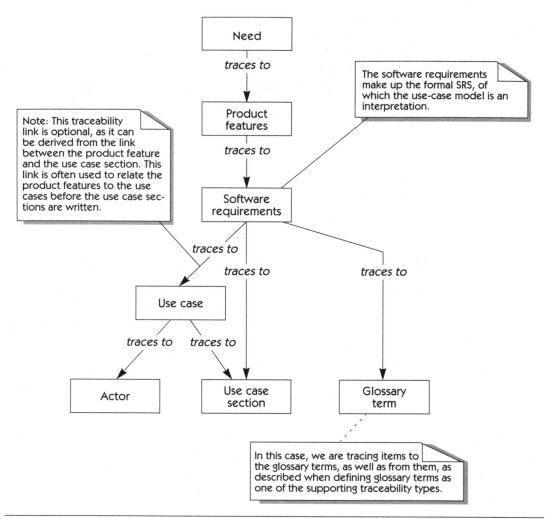

Figure 31–3 Augmented traceability relationships

Using a tool offers you many ways to obtain additional insights into your project. For example, after we have defined the relationships between the features and the software requirements on our HOLIS project, we can display a matrix version of those relationships, as shown in Figure 31–4.

Interpreting the traceability matrix in Figure 31–4 is straightforward. For example, consider the intersection of FEA1 ("Easy to program control . . . ") and SR3 ("HOLIS shall support up to . . . .") At the intersecting cell, the

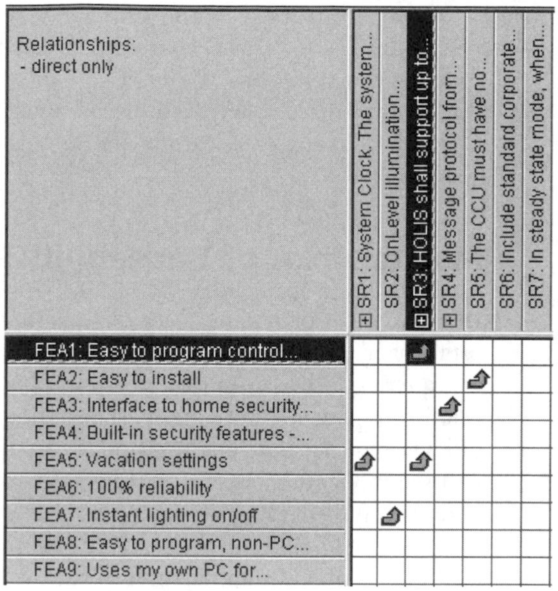

Figure 31–4 Matrix version of traceability relationships

arrow indicates that a relationship traces from FEA1 to SR3, meaning that SR3 in some way satisfies the feature defined as FEA1.

After using a tool to establish all known relationships, an instructive requirements management activity—strongly supported by not only governmental regulatory guidance but also our own experiences—is to examine a traceability matrix for two potential indications of error:

1. If inspection of a *row* fails to detect any traceability relationships (no "arrows"), a possibility exists that no software requirement is yet defined to respond to a feature required in the Vision document. This may be acceptable if, for example, the feature is not software ("The case shall be of nonbreakable plastic"). Nevertheless, empty rows are potential red flags and should be checked carefully. Modern requirements management tools should have a facility to automate this type of inspection.

2. If inspection of a *column* fails to detect any traceability relationships, a possibility exists that a software requirement has been included for which there is no known product feature that requires it. This may indicate a misunderstanding of the role of the software requirement,

or a weakness in the original Vision document, or it may indicate dead code or code that is not in support of the system requirement or a programmer's "Easter Egg," in which case it should be weeded out immediately. (We will discuss Easter Eggs in more detail in Chapter 34.) In any case, careful checking is required.

Maintenance of Traceability Relationships

In addition to providing a set of tools to query the relationships you have established, your development tool should provide a simple means to store the queries and to recall them later. This feature allows you to revisit the relationships at a later time, perhaps after changes have been made, and to quickly requery the relationships to detect potential trouble spots. As you will see in Chapter 34, this virtually guaranteed occurrence arises from the continual project changes.

Simple and obvious application of such techniques will enable you to relate many elements of your project. You should consider linking and relating

- Software requirements and use cases to test plans/test specs/test results
- User needs to product features
- Product features to software requirements and use cases
- Software requirements and use cases to implementation units such as functions, modules, objects, and collaborations
- Implementation units to test plans/specs/results

After linking the various elements of the various documents, you should have a relationship setup similar to that shown in Figure 31–5.

Your requirements management tool should also be able to display the full set of traceability relationships within a project. Figure 31–6 shows such a "tree" view. Note that the (partial) tree view allows you to view simultaneously all of the currently established relationships in your project. You should use the tree view to help you comprehend the overall relationships within your project. For example, Figure 31–6 reveals that FEA5 ("Vacation settings") links to SR1, SR3, and UC1.

Once you have linked the elements, your tool should maintain those linkages. You may then use the full power of the tool to examine relationships among the project elements as you desire. You've probably already figured out that we can use the traceability relationships to support our verification efforts.

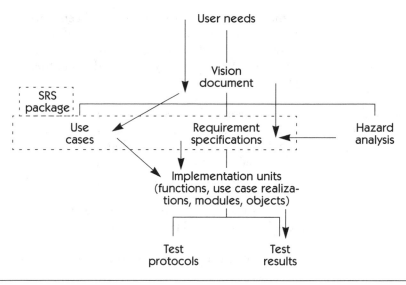

Figure 31–5   Document/element relationships

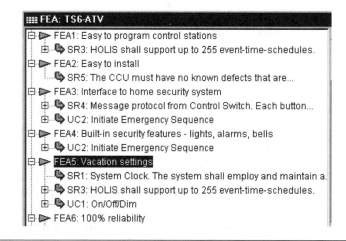

Figure 31–6   Abbreviated tree view

Proceeding without Traceability Tools

Of course, you may not have a tool specifically constructed to support the types of operations identified in the preceding section. Without such a tool, how should you proceed?

In the pretool days, we used spreadsheets and databases to maintain the traceability relationships. After all, many of the matrix relationships could be easily handled with a simple spreadsheet. We used spreadsheets extensively during the 1980s and early 1990s and found them to be a useful aid in managing projects.

Spreadsheet and databases can be used to implement traceability.

The problem with spreadsheets, however, was maintenance, especially in extensive hierarchies of relationships. For instance, we found that changing a single linkage could have far-flung impacts in the relationships at issue, as well as other relationships in other parts of the hierarchy. Truth to tell, it was usually a nightmare if extensive changes to the linkages had to be made.

Since it was so difficult to manually keep track of the changes and their "ripple effects," we found that we either

- Fell into a pattern of resisting any discussions to change the relationships, or
- Abandoned the matrices as the work became too overwhelming.

Of course, we *always* came to regret both of these behaviors, as they inevitably led to subsequent problems in the project. Imagine our excitement when modern tools began to arrive and to help in this activity!

The other alternative was to use a database. We used relational databases extensively and found it fairly easy to construct them and to input the data. Indeed, in the pretool days, we used such tools to run human-critical medical device development projects. Relational databases worked pretty well. Even though it was more difficult to expand the database application to include tracking ripple effects from changes, it could be done. The problem, however, was that we ended up spending disproportionate amounts of time improving the tool's capability. Good for the ego but bad for the project resources who should have been doing something else.

So, although you *can* use spreadsheets or databases to maintain the traceability relationships, it won't be easy. If you have a small project, the pain and suffering will be minimal, and it *might* be worth considering simpler alternatives. On the other hand, we do *not* recommend tackling larger projects without the use of specialized requirements management tools.

Omitted Verification Relationships

In this case, you are looking for cases in which the *rows* of the traceability matrix show you that a particular feature is *not* linked to some software requirements/use cases. For example, inspection of the matrix in Figure 31–7 shows that Product Feature 4 (FEA4) is not linked to any Software Requirement. And, although we didn't show it, there are no links to any use case (UC) either.

Upon detecting a "hole" in the relationships, you should review the original set of product requirements and the related software requirements/use cases.

- You may find that a link was accidentally missed in establishing the traceability. In such cases, simply adding a new link and recomputing the trace matrix will solve the problem. This type of omission frequently occurs in the early stages of a project.
- On the other hand, you might find that the development of the software requirements simply failed to consider the needs of one of the required product features. In this case, a project review may be necessary to consider the addition of suitable requirements to respond to the product feature. Or, the project review may determine that the omitted feature should be moved to a "future" category or removed entirely.

In any event, the important facet of verification is to ensure that no linkages have been left out and that all lower-level elements, such as the software requirements/use cases, have been properly related to the higher-level product requirements.

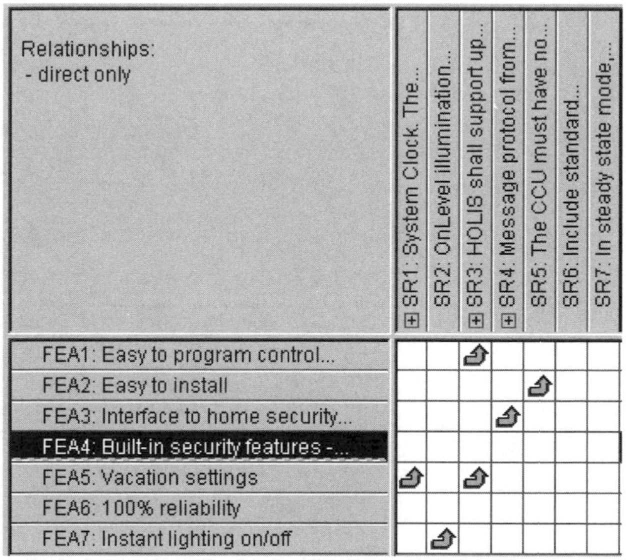

Figure 31–7 Using traceability to detect missing relationships

Excess Verification Relationships

Verification may also uncover the opposite issue. That is, inspection of the *columns* of the trace matrix may reveal a column that is not linked to any row elements. In Figure 31–8, for example, use case 3 (UC3) is not linked to any product feature (FEA).

This type of situation indicates that you have created a use case (or requirement) for which there was no related product feature. That is, the requirement appears to be superfluous to the product features. As before, you should review the trace relationships

- You may find that a link was accidentally missed in establishing the traceability. In such cases, simply adding a new link and recomputing the trace matrix will solve the problem.
- On the other hand, you might find that the determination of the product features simply failed to consider the needs of one of the required software requirements. This situation may occur if, for example, you have certain design constraints that are required in the implementation but that change the features of the product. Here, a project review may be necessary to consider the feasibility and need

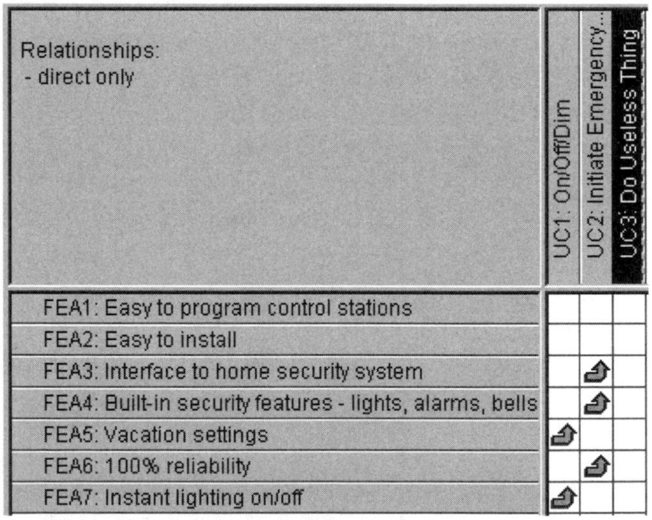

Relationships: - direct only	UC1: On/Off/Dim	UC2: Initiate Emergency...	UC3: Do Useless Thing
FEA1: Easy to program control stations			
FEA2: Easy to install			
FEA3: Interface to home security system		☝	
FEA4: Built-in security features - lights, alarms, bells		☝	
FEA5: Vacation settings	☝		
FEA6: 100% reliability		☝	
FEA7: Instant lighting on/off	☝		

Figure 31–8   Omitted use case relationship

for the requirements. You might wish to remove the requirement(s) or place them on a "future" list. Or, the project review may determine that the omitted feature should be moved to a "future" category or added now. In our example, we have reviewed the project and have determined that UC3 was a superfluous specification that should not have been in the project.

This type of verification inspection focuses on ensuring that gratuitous elements have not crept into the project. Experience has shown that such elements typically increase the project scope and rarely contribute to the overall quality of the result.

Thinking about Verification and Traceability

The problem with considering omitted/excess relationships is that it is very mechanical. That is, it is all too tempting to say, "Well, we looked at all of the rows and columns, and everything looks OK. So, we're verified. Let's move on."

The fallacy in this argument is that we have not considered whether or not we've *correctly and completely* considered all of the links that should (and should not) be established. We have found that deeper consideration of the initial traceability linkages always leads to some revisions in the linkages. New linkages may be added, and existing linkages may be revised or removed.

We urge you to consider the initial linkages as merely a starting point in verification. Formal or informal reviews should be held after the initial linkages have been established and the initial row/column inspections completed. After at least one full-scale review is completed and changes posted, *then* you may consider that verification for the current phase is valid.

Linkages, like requirements themselves, will evolve over time.

Of course, change happens. Thus, you will need to treat all linkages as living linkages that will be revised as the project matures and evolves. You should consider verification reviews whenever it becomes apparent that future, current, or past phases have had significant changes in the traceability linkages. Retrospective reviews are frequently needed whenever new understandings of the project cause old linkages and relationships to be reconsidered. The crucial point is that verification requires *thinking*, and you should not fall into the trap of rote mechanical processing.

Looking Ahead

Verification is an important technique your team can apply in the struggle to help ensure that you are designing and implementing the right systems. To our amazement, we continue to find many projects that don't use a verification strategy to make sure that the project is heading in the right direction. Inevitably, those projects "fall off the rails," and the team members *don't even know it*. Of course, they eventually find it out but, by then, it is very late in the game, and bad feelings and desperate measures ensue. Projects that undergo frequent verification challenges are much less subject to such surprises.

But all the verification in the world will not guarantee that the final result works as intended. So, we need to include another concept to help us ensure that the right system is being built. That concept is called validation and is the subject of our next chapter.

Chapter 32

VALIDATING THE SYSTEM

Key Points

- Validation is the process of confirming that the implemented system conforms to the requirements established for it.
- Acceptance testing validates the system within the customer's environment and usage scenarios.
- Quality can be achieved by testing not simply against implementation but must include testing against requirements and actual customer usage.

The IEEE (1994) defines validation as

"the process of evaluating a system or component during or at the end of the development process to determine whether it satisfies specified requirements" (IEEE 1012-1986, §2, 1994).

In other words, use validation to confirm that the implemented system conforms to the requirements we've established.

But this definition doesn't go far enough. Although testing to the requirements is certainly an important step, there is still a chance that the system we deliver may not be what the customer wanted. We've seen projects on which much time and effort were expended on making sure that the customer's needs were collected and understood, followed by an implementation effort that prepared a system shown (by validation tests) to correctly meet all of the collected requirements, followed by delivering the final product to the customer, who balked and said that the product was not what was wanted.

What went wrong? Simple. The project failed to move the nebulous "cloud" of the user's problem into alignment with the proxy represented by the requirements. However, this is of small comfort to the project team that has just made heroic sacrifices to deliver the product. Performing acceptance tests at each iteration will minimize this syndrome.

Validation

Acceptance Tests

Acceptance tests include the customer in the final validation activity.

Acceptance tests bring the customer into the final validation process in order to gain assurance that "the product works the way the customer really needs it to." In an outsourcing environment, acceptance testing may be developed and executed as part of the contract provisions. In an IS/IT or ISV environment, the value provided by acceptance tests is more typically accomplished by the customer alpha or beta evaluation process.

Acceptance tests are typically based on a specific number of "scenarios" that the user specifies and executes in the usage environment. Thus, the customer has freedom to think "outside the box" and has license to construct interesting ways to test the system in order to gain confidence that the system works as needed. If we've done our job right, the acceptance test will be based on certain key use cases that we've already defined and implemented. But the acceptance test should also apply these use cases in interesting combinations and under the types of system load and other environmental factors—interoperability with other applications, OS dependencies, and so on—that are likely to be present in the user's environment.

In an iterative development process, generations of acceptance tests should be run at the various construction milestones, so the final acceptance test should not bring any significant surprises to the development team. In a more waterfall-like model, this is often not the case, and major surprises are routine. In any model, it's never too late to discover at least a few "Undiscovered Ruins" that will still need to be addressed. In Chapter 34, we'll talk about how to manage changes that this may occasion.

Validation Testing

The primary activities in validation are testing activities. But what does a good test plan look like? For one answer, the IEEE 829-1983, *IEEE Stan-*

dard for Software Test Documentation (IEEE 1994) provides eight document templates that offer guidance on the establishment of a test methodology, conducting tests, reporting results, and resolving anomalies. Other guidelines (Rational 1999) have somewhat different approaches, but most agree on a few key elements.

- Your development process must include *planning for test activities.* (In the iterative model, most test planning is done in the elaboration phase.)
- Your development process must also provide time and resources to *design the tests.* It helps to have an overall template designed so that each individual test design can be largely a matter of plugging in the individual test details.
- Your development must also provide time and resources to *execute the tests*, both at the unit test level (as required) and at the overall system level. The test documents form part of the implementation documentation. Allowing for test documents, the implementation documentation tree should appear as in Figure 32–1.

We recommend that you maintain an audit trail between the validation/testing activities and the specifications for that implementation. This audit trail is provided by traceability.

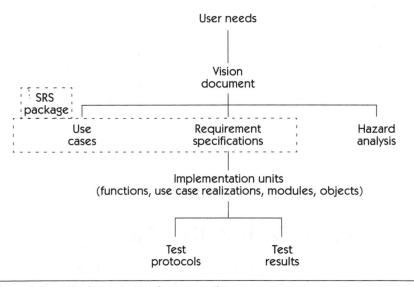

Figure 32–1 Implementation documentation

Validation Traceability

Validation traceability gives you confidence that two important goals have been addressed.

1. Do we have enough tests to cover everything that needs testing?
2. Do we have any extra or gratuitous tests that serve no useful purpose?

Validation focuses on whether the product works as it is supposed to. We are no longer inspecting the relationships of the various specification and design elements but instead are considering the relationships between the tests (and test results) and the system being tested. As in verification, the object is to ensure that all relevant elements are tested for conformance to the requirements.

Requirements-Based Testing

But what is a "relevant element"? What do you test? One common approach is to test the product against its *implementation*. That is, many projects approach testing with a mind set that says, "Here is an implementation feature, say, the database manager, so let's test it by banging away on the database manager interfaces." Although this may be an appropriate test, it covers only half the job.

Quality can be achieved only by testing the system against its requirements.

Quality can be achieved only by testing the system against its *requirements*. Yes, it may be useful to perform *unit tests* against various project elements such as the database manager, but we have found that unit tests rarely give you the needed assurance that the *entire system* works as required. Indeed, many complex projects are often found to pass all of the unit tests but to fail as a system. Why? Because the units interact in more complex behaviors, and the resulting system has not been adequately tested against the governing system requirements.

Let's examine how we can use the techniques we developed for verification in the execution of the system validation activities. We'll turn again to our case study.

Case Study: Testing Use Cases

Writing test cases, like collecting requirements, is both an art and a science. Although we won't examine the matter too deeply, it is instructive to get at least a top-level view of how the test cases can be derived from the functionality expressed by the use cases and the requirements we collected to define the system. For this example, we'll return to our case study and use the Control Light use case that we developed in Team Skill 5.

Test Case 1 Description

Table 32–1 is a sample test case for the Control Light use case. Test Case 1, used to test instances of the use case Control Light, is used only to test Control Switch buttons that have been preassigned to a light bank that is dim-enabled.

Test Case 1 focuses on testing interactions with the system that closely mimic the real-world flow of events that we spelled out in the Control Light use case. So, the use case served as a template for how to test the system. This is one of the major benefits of the use-case technique.

The unabbreviated version of this test case appears in Appendix A with the other HOLIS ᵖartifacts. Test Case 2 in Appendix A is an example that tests an aggregate set of discrete requirements rather than a single use case test. We'll visit Test Case 2 and its relationship to the software requirements shortly. Both Test Case 1 and Test Case 2 are the subjects of the following traceability discussion.

Tracing Test Cases

Traceability helps confirm that test cases cover the required functionality.

Traceability techniques allow us to easily confirm that the test cases cover the required functionality of the system. We simply need to construct a series of test plans that we can link back to the original system requirements and use cases.

For example, suppose we had a traceability matrix that compared tests to the use cases (see Figure 32–2). Just as in the verification activities, we can examine the matrix to ensure proper coverage of the test cases versus the system specifications. Similarly, we can compare use cases against test cases, as shown in Figure 32–3.

Table 32–1   Test Case 1 (simplified)

Test Case ID	Event Description	Input 1	Input 2	Expected Result
			Basic flow	
2001	Resident presses Control Switch (CS).	Any enabled button	Light was on before button was pressed (tester must record level).	Light is turned off.
2002			Light was off before button was pressed.	Light is turned on to OnLevel.
2003	Resident releases button in less than 1 second.	Light on		Stays off.
2005	Resident releases button in less than 1 second. (This ends path 1 through use case.)	Light off		Stays on at OnLevel.
2006	Resident presses button again and releases it in less than 1 second.	Same enabled button as in 2003	Light off before	Light is turned on to same illumination level as in 2002.
	Resident presses button again and releases it in less than 1 second.		Light on before	Light is turned off.
			Alternative flow	
2007	Button held longer than 1 second.	Enabled button	Light off before	Light turned on. Brightness increases 10% to maximum level for each second held, then decreases 10% for each second held until minimum reached, then increases again. Cycles continuously while held.
2008	Resident releases button.			Brightness held at last reached level.

Note: Run test case multiple times and with different lengths of hold-button time to verify that system is restoring OnLevel properly.

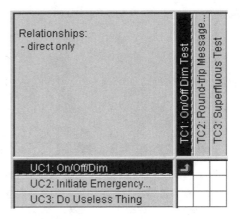

Figure 32–2   Tests versus use cases

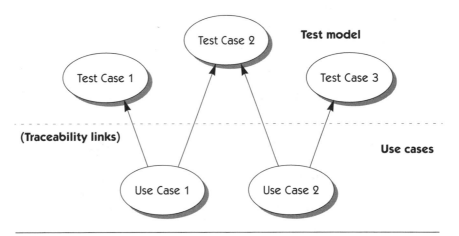

Figure 32–3   Use cases and test cases

Testing Discrete Requirements

In the same way that we used traceability relationships to relate use cases to test cases, we can use traceability to manage relationships between discrete, or itemized requirements and to then associate them with test cases. Figure 32–4 shows a fragment of a test case specification traceability matrix. Note that Test Case 2 ("TC2: Round-trip message") has appeared and is linked to the software requirements of the HOLIS SRS package. Note also

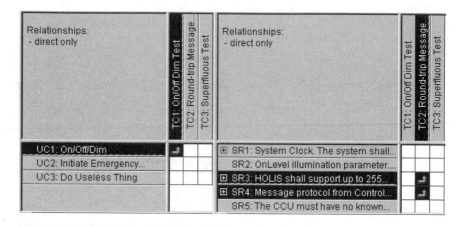

Figure 32–4 Test case fragment of traceability

that we treat test cases no differently from the other types of elements we have traced in our verification and validation activities.

So far, we have linked the test cases into the traceability matrices. Now it's time to examine the linkages as we did it in the verification inspections.

Omitted Validation Relationships

Once again, you are looking for cases in which the *rows* of the traceability matrix show you that a particular feature or requirement is not linked to a software test. In Figure 32–5, for example, Use Case 2 (UC2) is not linked to any test case (TC). (UC3 links are missing also, but our verification activities already decided that the use case should never have been in there at all.)

Having detected this "hole" in the relationships, you should review the original set of product requirements and the related test cases.

- If you find that a link was accidentally missed in establishing the traceability, simply add a new link and recompute the trace matrix. This type of omission frequently occurs in the early stages of establishing validation traceability.
- If you find that the development of the software test cases simply failed to test one of the required product features, you may need a project review to consider the addition of suitable tests to respond to the product feature. Unlike the similar case in verification activities,

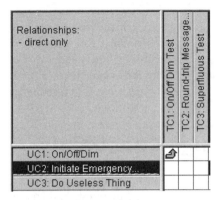

Figure 32–5 Missing test case

we do *not* recommend marking the missing test case as a "future" activity. If there is an untested feature, you may be assured that your customer will test it, often with grievous consequences! Also, regulated developments, such as FDA regulation of a medical product, will not accept the postponement of necessary tests.

Validation traceability helps ensure that no linkages have been left out and that all product tests have been properly related to the higher-level product requirements. Of course, it also helps if the product passes the tests!

Excess Validation Relationships

As with verification, validation may also uncover the opposite issue. That is, inspection of the *columns* of the trace matrix may reveal a column that is not linked to any row elements. In Figure 32–5, for example, Test Case 3 (TC3) is not linked to any use case. We also know from Figure 32–4 that it is not linked to any software requirement. This type of situation indicates that you have created a test for which there was no related product feature. That is, the test appears to be superfluous to the product features. As before, you should review the trace relationships.

- Perhaps a link was accidentally missed in establishing the traceability. If so, simply add a new link and recompute the trace matrix. This type of omission frequently occurs in the early stages of establishing validation traceability.
- Or, you might find that the development of the product features simply failed to consider the needs of one of the required software tests.

This case may occur if, for example, certain nonfunctional requirements for the implementation in fact change the features of the product. In this case, a project review may be necessary to consider the feasibility and need for the requirements. As in verification, your team will need to resolve whether the test is required at all and, if it is, what traceability linkages are needed.

Testing Design Constraints

OK, so you know how to collect and manage the tests for the use cases and requirements. The question then arises, "How do you test design constraints?"

In Team Skill 5, we discussed the fact that although design constraints are unique, the easiest way to treat them is to simply consider them requirements. That is, we trace their linkages in the same way, and we verify them in the same way. Therefore, it is appropriate to include design constraints as part of the validation effort. When it comes to testing, you should test design constraints just as you would anything else. Many design constraints will yield to a simple test by inspection. For example, a design constraint that requires the software to be written in Visual Basic (VB) can be tested by simply looking at the source code.

Since many design constraints will yield to simple inspections, you should consider having an abbreviated test procedure for such inspection matters. There is no need to have a complicated form listing the calibrated equipment needed, setup procedures, environmental setups, and so on. Instead, just have a simple form saying that you have inspected the code or other artifact and found it to be in conformance with the design constraint. Some sample approaches to testing design constraints are shown in Table 32–2.

Table 32–2   Design constraint validation approaches

Design Constraint	Validation Approach
"Write the software in VB 5.0"	Inspect source code.
"The application must be based on the architectural patterns from the Fuji Project."	Identify patterns in Fuji design models; compare with current project design.
"Use the Developer's Library 99-724 class library from XYZ Corporation."	Inspect ordering and receiving records, product documentation supplied, and revision numbers; inspect that libraries are properly loaded and properly used.

Looking Ahead

Verification is an analytical process that works throughout the project to ensure that you are doing the right things. *Validation* ensures that the system works as it is supposed to, both in conforming to the customer's documented requirements and in the actual usage scenario. Together, verification and validation help assure the team that they are indeed "Building the Right System Right."

But, we've left something out. You might be wondering, "How do I decide on how much V&V work to do?" Let's look at that question in the next chapter.

Chapter 33

USING ROI TO DETERMINE THE V&V EFFORT

Key Points

- *Depth*, the level of detail selected to verify a system element, may range from examination (minimal) to walkthrough and independent review to black-box testing (simulation) to white-box testing (exercising every line of code).
- Coverage refers to the extent to which system elements are verified and validated.
- Selective V&V is viable as long as you know why you are doing it and what the risks are.
- The key to using hazard analysis is to decide what errors must be prevented and the scope of the V&V activities needed to ensure that they do not occur.

As in all aspects of the development project, it costs money to initiate and maintain the V&V activities. The question naturally arises, "How do we do cost/benefit analyses to see whether this V&V stuff is really worth it?" This chapter will help you plan your V&V activities, using some quasi-economic concepts to answer the cost/benefit question. We'll plan our V&V activities on the basis of the answers to two questions.

1. What are the social or economic consequences of a failure of our system?

2. How much V&V do we need to do to ensure that we do not experience these consequences?

Of course, it's not very useful to find out *after* the project is completed that there was way too much V&V that yielded results of minimal value to the project. It's even more painful to find out that you didn't do enough checking.

This is the sort of problem that product recalls stem from. ("What? We have to recall the first 10,000 HOLIS switches that are already installed in peoples' homes?") Therefore, we will use an analytic approach to guide us in selecting the proper amount of V&V activities *before* we commit to them. Let's start by considering some "depth" versus "coverage" issues.

Depth versus Coverage

V&V Depth

Depth defines the level of V&V effort to be applied to a system element.

Depth refers to the level of detail that we select to verify or to evaluate a system element. In general, the greater the depth, the more resources are consumed in performing the activity. Thus, it is to your advantage to ensure that a proper depth of inspection is selected for each element selected. And, no, you don't get to say, "Let's just do a once-over-lightly." It is important to match the depth of the review to the importance of the element.

Not all elements need to be inspected to the same depth of detail. For example, minor elements on the periphery of the project may be adequately served by an inspection, or simple system test, but critical elements at the heart of the project may require extensive white-box testing.

In Chapter 26, On Ambiguity and Specificity, we said that the level of specificity you pick will determine both the depth and the number of requirements you define. Picking the right level of specificity (depth) will be a primary determinant in your V&V depth of review. In addition to your requirements methods, you can apply a variety of additional techniques to ensure that the requirements are reviewed to the appropriate depth. Let's look at several strategies and relate them to the depth of review they offer.

- *Examination*. We review the code or take some measurements. The essence of examination is that a prescribed and minimally invasive look is taken at the element under test. This is usually considered to be the minimal depth of review of an element.
- *Walkthrough*. A peer group "walks the element through" its paces. In a sense, this process is a structured inspection performed by a wider audience, one that is searching for weaknesses, oversights, and so on, in the code. This type of review provides more depth than a simple examination.
- *Independent reviews*. This strategy, similar to the two preceding ones, has an unrelated but knowledgeable group examine the element and

search for weaknesses. This type of review may provide additional insights that were not in the "mind set" of the project group.

- *Black-box test.* Black-box testing treats the element as a module that cannot be internally inspected. Thus, you can supply inputs to the box and observe the box's outputs to ensure that the element is working to the required standards. These tests are usually performed via instrumented code or with system emulators and other tools to simulate and to record the system operation.
- *White-box test.* White-box testing allows you to "open the box" and to examine the internal workings of the element. Most modules of code have way too many combinatorial pathways to test in a reasonable amount of time, so some sort of reasonable test concept has to be applied to white-box testing to keep it from becoming prohibitively time consuming. A common white-box test compromise is to exercise every line of code but not every possible *combination* of code pathways. This type of review often requires significant project personnel and resources.

V&V Coverage

Coverage defines the extent of coverage of system elements to be verified and validated.

Coverage means the extent of coverage of the system elements we will consider for our V&V efforts. As we described in the previous two chapters, you can apply traceability techniques to a number of different elements as part of your V&V activities. For example, you can trace requirements to test cases, features to use cases, use cases to implementation, and so on. The *amount* of traceability that you do, and the corresponding level of specificity in the requirements that you provide, is a primary factor in your V&V coverage.

That is, we ask questions about which requirements—both textual and use cases—need to be considered, which implementation units need consideration, which test units need consideration, and so on. In addition, it may be necessary to examine, verify, and validate software provided by others, such as purchased components and the operating system the application runs on. In effect, this is the "what should we do V&V on" issue. Fortunately, this question has some reasonably straightforward answers.

What to Verify and Validate

The obvious question in creating the V&V plan is, What elements should be verified and validated? You are trying to ensure a high-quality product, but you are also trying to minimize the overall development cost of the project. There are several ways to address this question.

Option 1: Verify and Validate Everything

In smaller projects that require a reasonable degree of delivered quality, you might want to consider invoking your V&V processes on essentially everything in the application This approach has the advantages of being simple and easy to understand and treating the project elements uniformly. It also bypasses the step of analyzing the project before it is started and making your best guesses as to the cost elements for V&V.

Selective V&V can be appropriate if you know what the risks are.

If you adopt this policy, you will soon arrive at areas in which the team consensus is, "We don't need to do V&V on this element, because it is too trivial to worry about." This may be appropriate, but, of course, this attitude will usually become more common as the budget runs out and the deadlines approach!

Selective V&V is often appropriate *as long as you know why you are doing it and what the risks are*. It is a perfectly viable approach, provided that the omitted elements are being omitted for good reasons, which do *not* include having run out of time or money.

When elements are to be omitted from V&V, however, it is important to document the rationale for doing so.

But a potential danger here is that you may, with the best of intentions, omit V&V activities on a project element that eventually proves to be more significant than you had originally imagined. Possible repercussions might include

- Embarrassment over an element's not conforming to the customer specification (and subsequent unpaid rework on your part)
- Elements not working per the specification (and subsequent expensive recalls from the field)
- The worst case: an unsafe product that can cause harm to its users

Thus, even in the informal case of selectively trimming your V&V activities, there is some probability that a "gotcha" may be looming on the horizon.

But if it is impractical to V&V everything on a significant project and yet a high degree of quality *must* be ensured, how do you decide which elements are important to the V&V process and which elements are not important? That brings us to option 2.

Option 2: Use a Hazard Analysis to Determine V&V Necessities

One organized way to consider the impact of important elements in the project is the hazard analysis and a related activity, risk assessment. Although we cannot delve deeply into these disciplines in this book, we will provide a brief overview of the concepts.

Regulatory agencies, such as the FDA, have shifted focus onto hazard analysis as a key technique in the improvement of product quality. Indeed, contemporary regulatory guidelines have devoted entire sections to the question of risk assessment and hazard analysis. Wood and Ermes (1993a) provide a useful definition of hazard analysis for a medical product:

> *Hazard Analysis is the detailed examination of a device from the user and patient perspectives. Its purpose is to detect potential design flaws—possibilities of failure that could cause harm—and to enable manufacturers to correct them before a device is released for use.*

Hazard analysis requires the designer to consider various classes and types of errors that may occur in the product yet to be constructed. As each potential hazard is documented and examined, the hazard analysis document allows the designer to document the potential hazard and to then suggest design strategies to alleviate each.

In subsequent stages of the product development lifecycle, the hazard analysis will serve to record both the potential hazards and the risk-mitigation strategies that have been defined to prevent the hazard from occurring. System validation will later refer to this document to confirm that all anticipated hazards have been completely addressed and resolved, and validation testing will be emphasized in these areas to gain a further degree of assurance.

Of course, hazard analysis needn't apply solely to medical systems (or even other systems, such as transportation and industrial equipment), in which human safety is at risk. You should do a hazard analysis that targets whatever you consider to be the greatest risks of failure in your system. For example, an online trading system might focus hazard analysis on "ensuring that the bid quote delivered is accurate" or "validating the number of shares entered by the user." A telecommunications company might focus on the risk of "catastrophic software failure of a switch."

In any case, a hazard analysis is used to decide what hazards you must prevent in your system and the scope of the V&V activities necessary to ensure that you prevent them. For those design issues are important to the overall safety, efficacy, and success of the project, as documented in the hazard analysis, you should provide a full set of V&V activities. For elements that are revealed to be of lesser or inconsequential impact, you may consider omitting or reducing the V&V activities, although comprehensive testing must still be done.

Hazard analysis guides the selection of project elements for V&V.

It's important to realize that the hazard analysis can be used to guide the selection of the project elements that need verification. Independently of verification, the hazard analysis can also guide the selection of tests and test coverage for the validation activities. No rule states that verification must faithfully track validation, so your team can feel free to use the hazard analysis results to independently develop plans for verification as well as validation.

Hazard Analysis as Return on Investment (ROI)

Another way of looking at a hazard analysis and a risk assessment is to interpret them as a standard cost/benefit analysis; use the hazard analysis results as input to a standard return on investment (ROI) analysis.

Thus, you would develop estimates on the costs—in terms of time, resources, and total dollars—for V&V activities on a particular element or segment of the project. These costs could then be input into standard ROI economic models to get an idea of the staged costs. Then, estimates could be made as to the potential impact of negative consequences as previously identified in the hazard analysis should a non-V&V element go wrong. After comparing the two analyses, you could then make an informed judgment as to whether the V&V activities should be performed and to what depth.

In many cases, the analysis will show that a clear-cut yes/no decision may be overly simplistic. For example, it is far more typical for the analysis to show that *portions* of the V&V for a segment may be very cost-effective and that other portions may not be. In such cases, it is probably worth considering a modified V&V strategy to optimize the return on the V&V investment.

Always perform a hazard analysis for human-critical safety issues.

We should be very clear that ROI calculations are on a different plane from safety and efficacy analysis. For example, your hazard analysis may show that a human-critical risk is at issue in a portion of the development and implementation of your software. In such cases, it is simply unacceptable to ignore the human-safety factors in lieu of a standard ROI calculation. You should *always* perform a full V&V on those segments of the project that involve human-critical safety issues. In other words, use ROI techniques if the only thing at issue is the financial costs of your project. Use hazard analysis and risk assessment if safety and efficacy issues are at stake. Use a combination of techniques, if appropriate.

Looking Ahead

Let's review where we are:

- We have established a way of looking at the requirements artifacts and using them as the basis for the design and implementation of the system.
- We have applied verification techniques to ensure that every step of the project is traced to the earlier steps.
- We described two validation processes—validation testing and acceptance testing—that together help ensure that the implementation produces workable systems.
- We have examined the techniques of risk assessment and hazard analysis to help us decide where to spend our project resources in the most cost-effective manner.

The only major issue left is the old bugaboo of *change*. We'll use the next chapter to learn how to manage change and to handle it responsibly in our project activities.

Chapter 34
MANAGING CHANGE

Key Points

- A process to manage requirements can be useful only if it recognizes and addresses the issue of change.
- Internal change factors include failing to ask the right people the right questions at the right time and failing to create a practical process to help manage changes to requirements.
- In order to have a reasonable probability of success, requirements leakage *must* be stopped or, at least, reduced to a manageable level.

Why Do Requirements Change?

If it were possible to define a set of requirements for a system once and only once, life would be much simpler, and there would be no need for this chapter. We could simply create a perfect Vision document, software requirements specification, and use-case model; freeze them for the duration of the development effort; and then declare everything past that point to be the responsibility of the maintenance team. Alas, things don't work that way; they never did in the past, and even with a more systematic approach to requirements management, they will not work that way in the future.

There are several reasons for the inevitability of changes to the requirements. Some of these reasons are internal factors and may be under our control, but many of them are external factors and are outside the control of the developers *and* the users.

External Factors

External factors are those change agents over which the project team has no control. No matter how we manage them, we must prepare ourselves technically, emotionally, and managerially to be able to address these changes as part of the "normal course of software development activity." Changes occur because:

- There was a *change to the problem* that we were attempting to solve with the new system. Perhaps a change occurred in the economy, in government regulations, or in the marketplace and consumer preferences. Because of the fast pace of technology change, it is now more and more likely that such changes will take place *before* we even finish solving the *original* problem that the user described.

- The users *changed their minds* or their perceptions about what they wanted the system to do. This, too, can occur for a number of reasons: not only because users are fickle, particularly when specifying the details of the human interface for their system, but also because their perceptions are based on the marketplace, the economy, the state of government regulations, and so on. Moreover, the identity of the users themselves sometimes changes; for example, if the user who described the requirements for the system leaves the customer's team, the replacement is likely to be someone with an entirely different set of opinions and perceptions.

- The external *environment has changed*, which creates new constraints and/or new opportunities. One of the most obvious examples of environmental change is the ongoing improvements in computer hardware and software systems: If tomorrow's computers are 50 percent faster, cheaper, and smaller and run more advanced applications than do today's computers, they will likely trigger a change in the requirements for a system. Back in the 1993–1994 time frame, hardly anyone anticipated the Internet and the World Wide Web. The requirements for a wide range of information systems—from word processors to customer information systems to banking systems—are clearly quite different today from what they were in the pre-Internet era.

- The *new system* comes into existence. One of the most insidious external factors, and a prime factor in the "Yes, But" syndrome, is that the *very existence of a new system causes the requirements for the system itself to change*. As the organizational behavior evolves around the new system, the old ways of doing things are no longer appropriate; the need for new types of information emerge, and new requirements for the system inevitably develop. Thus, the simple act of delivering a new system elicits requirements for the new system!

A requirements management process can be useful only if it recognizes and addresses the issue of change.

As a practical matter, a process to manage requirements can be useful only if it recognizes and addresses the issue of change. We can't prevent change, but we can manage it.

Internal Factors

In addition to the external factors, a number of internal factors can contribute to the problem of change.

- We failed to ask the right people the right questions at the right time during the initial requirements-gathering effort. If our process does not include *all* stakeholders or if we do not *ask* all the right questions of them, we contribute to the change problem by simply not understanding the true requirements for the system. In other words, there are far more "Undiscovered Ruins" than necessary, and we are making significant changes that could have been avoided had we developed a more comprehensive understanding up front.
- We failed to create a practical process to help *manage changes* to the requirements that would normally have happened on an incremental basis. We may have attempted to "freeze" the requirements; thus, the "latent," necessary changes piled up until they created such pressure that they inevitably exploded in the face of the developers and the users, causing rework and stress. Or, perhaps, we created no change process at all, thereby allowing, or even encouraging, people to change whatever they wished whenever they wished. In this case, at some point, almost everything is change, and you can no longer "see the forest for the trees."

Before we address these problems, however, let's look at a specific project and see what other factors we can discover.

"We Have Met the Enemy, and They Is Us"

Weinberg (1995) notes that change can be insidious. In one project postmortem, he compared the known requirements of the system at the end of the project to those known at the beginning of the project. In so doing, he discovered a variety of sources of requirements change. Some were "official," representing customer requests made through the appropriate channels of communications, but many were surprisingly "unofficial," or what Weinberg calls "requirements leakage":

- Enhancements mentioned by distributors who had been overheard by programmers at a sales convention
- Direct customer requests to programmers
- Mistakes that had been made and shipped and had to be supported
- Hardware features that didn't get in or didn't work
- Knee-jerk change-of-scope reactions to competitors

- Functionality inserted by programmers with "careful consideration" of what's good for the customer
- Programmers' "Easter Eggs"

In one project, half of the total work product of the system was invested in requirements leakage!

Each of these sources may contribute only a small amount of change, but in accumulation, *unofficial sources contributed up to half of the total scope of one project*! In other words, half of the total work product of the system was invested in requirements leakage, or requirements that entered the system without visibility to the team members responsible for managing to schedule, budget, and quality criteria.

How can a project manager accommodate change of this type and still meet the schedule and quality criteria? *It can't be done*! In order to have a reasonable probability of success, requirements leakage *must* be stopped or, at least, reduced to manageable levels.

Programmers' Easter Eggs

Programmers' Easter Eggs are a particularly pathological form of requirements leakage. An Easter Egg is a hidden behavior built into the system for debug purposes, for the "fun of it," or, occasionally, for worse motives. In our experience, Easter Eggs are extremely dangerous, and programmers must know that to insert them is completely unacceptable and that doing so will subject the offenders to dire consequences. Two painfully true cases follow.

1. A large military simulation system took a long time to execute, so the programmers built in a background game of "Battleship" to amuse themselves during the simulation. Unfortunately, they never took it out; nor did its existence appear on any of the verification and validation activities or reports. When it was discovered, the customer, having lost confidence in the contractor, canceled the entire program: a multimillion-dollar loss to the subcontractor and a serious detriment to future business opportunities.
2. A junior programmer contributing to the development of a shrink-wrapped software tool amused himself by building in derogatory error messages in early stubs of error-recovery code. One such message was accidentally left in and discovered by a customer in a formal product training session. The software had to be repaired and rereleased on an unplanned basis, causing the loss of critical team-weeks to the company.

A Process for Managing Change

Clearly, given the fact that change is a natural part of the process and that change will come from both external and internal sources, a process for managing change is needed. Such a process puts the *team* in control so that it can effectively discover change, perform impact analysis, and incorporate those changes that are deemed to be both necessary and acceptable into the system in a systematic manner. Building on Weinberg's recommendations, a process for more effectively managing change must include the following steps.

1. Recognize that change is inevitable, and plan for it.
2. Baseline the requirements.
3. Establish a single channel to control change.
4. Use a change control system to capture changes.
5. Manage change hierarchically.

We'll look at each of these elements in more detail.

Step 1: Recognize that Change Is Inevitable, and Plan for It

The first step is a simple one. The team must recognize that changing requirements for the system is inevitable and even necessary. Some amount of change will occur, and the team should develop an awareness of this issue and a corresponding *plan for managing change* that should include some allowance for change in the initial baseline.

As for the legitimacy of change, *all* (with the single exception of the Easter Egg), can be considered legitimate in that they originate from a stakeholder who has both a real need and the potential to add real value to the application.

For example, requests for changes from the development team are legitimate, as that team knows more about the system than anyone else. Clearly, we hope and expect that the developers will have a variety of suggestions on what the system should do. Some of the "best" requirements come from the implementers who are closest to the system; only they recognize what the system really can do. We should encourage their input to the process, since the result will be a better system for our users.

Step 2: Baseline the Requirements

Toward the end of the elaboration phase in the development cycle, the team should baseline all known requirements for the system. The baselining process may be as simple as putting version control on the pertinent artifacts—Vision document, software requirements, and use-case models—and publishing the baseline for the development team. The collection of itemized requirements in these documents creates a baseline of information about the requirements and anticipated use cases for the system.

This simple step gives the team the ability to distinguish between *known*, or "old," requirements and new requirements, or those being added, deleted, or modified and that can now be distinguished from the "baseline" of known requirements. Once the baseline has been established, new requirements can be more easily identified and managed. A request for a new requirement can be compared against the existing baseline as to where it will fit in and whether it will create a conflict with any other requirements; this is often something that users overlook in their haste to respond to a change in their environment. And, if the change is accepted, we can manage the evolution of that change from the vision to the software requirements, from the software requirements to the appropriate technical design documents and models, and then to the code and the test procedures.

If this is done in an orderly, efficient, and responsive manner, the user community is likely to be much more cooperative. In the past, users in many organizations felt that they were being "stonewalled" by the technical development community when they asked for a change; often, it was because the team had a chaotic, inefficient process for making the changes or because it was unable to describe the nature of that process to the users.

The fact that we can be responsive and efficient about making changes doesn't mean that we want to invite vast numbers of frivolous changes.

However, the fact that we can be responsive and efficient about making requirements changes doesn't mean that we want to invite vast numbers of frivolous changes. In the best of all worlds—from the perspectives of both the users *and* the developers—life would be a lot simpler if we could create a single set of stable, correct requirements. Even with a reasonably well-managed change control process, there's a limit to the number of such changes that the developers will be able to accommodate, especially during the design and implementation stages of the project. It's typical, for example, to see requirements change at the rate of 1%–4% a month during the course of development. However, when the change rate exceeds 2 percent a month, the phenomenon of "requirements churn" becomes a very serious risk to the customer's project.

Step 3: Establish a Single Channel to Control Change

Changes to a software system can be insidious. Although it should be obvious that the existence of a new feature can cause significant impact to software requirements, system architecture, test plans, and so on, all of us have also experienced the case in which a "simple change" to code causes unanticipated consequences, occasionally even catastrophic ones. In addition, one proposed new feature might obviate, or make more difficult, an important future system feature that is not even being implemented in this release. Also, there is that thorny issue of the schedule and the budget for a project, the responsibility of the management team. The customer's wish for a change cannot be assumed to officially change the schedule and the budget, and a negotiation or budget-reconciliation process must be initiated before a change can be approved.

The customer's wish for a change cannot be assumed to officially change the schedule and the budget.

Therefore, it is crucial that every change *go through a single channel* to determine its impact on the system and to make the official decision as to whether the change is going to be made in the system at all. In a small project, this official channel can be the project champion or manager: the "owner" of the Vision document and other requirements artifacts, someone who has an overall understanding of the system requirements and design. Or, it can be someone else.

In larger systems or ones that affect a variety of stakeholders, this official channel should consist of a few people (a Change Control Board, or CCB) who share the responsibility and who, together, have the requisite authority and technical competence to decide when a change request is officially approved. (We briefly introduced this concept in Chapter 18.)

In any case, a change in the system should not be initiated until the change control mechanism makes the change "official."

Step 4: Use a Change Control System to Capture Changes

In a sense, it may be easiest to focus on the external, customer-requested changes because they are most readily identified and will tend to naturally find their way into the project via the project management or change control function. However, during development, there will be a tremendous number and variety of other types of potential changes to the system.

Indeed, many of the proposed changes that occur during the design, coding, and testing of a system may appear be unrelated to requirements, involving corrections to code- or design-level bugs. However, the impact must still be assessed. And yes, as the deadline approaches, we must even make conscious decisions about which bugs will be allowed to remain in the system—due to the potential for the fix to destabilize the entire system and thereby jeopardize the release date—and which ones will be removed. Also, many bugs may affect the requirements, require interpolation between the requirements, or require disambiguation of a known requirement.

In some cases, it won't even be obvious what kind of change is being requested. This is particularly common when end users complain about problems after the system has been developed or when the members of the "help desk" team pass on their analysis of the user complaints to the technical developers. For example, suppose the end user calls the help desk and complains, "I'm trying to enter a new employee into my payroll system, but whenever I have an employee whose first name is more than 16 characters, the program crashes." The fact that the program crashes is presumably either a code-level bug or a design-level bug. (Perhaps the operating system or the DBMS package was being invoked in an illegal fashion.) But even if the program had produced a civilized error message for such names, there may be a bug in the requirements; they may need to be changed to allow employee names of up to 256 characters. In the extreme case, this may even involve a "feature," because the marketing department may decide that it can brag that its payroll system is the only one being marketed that will now be able to handle 256-character employee names.

In any event, an analysis of the situation is required, along with a decision as to *where* the change will be implemented in the hierarchy of documents that we've discussed. Therefore, as Figure 34–1 illustrates, the team should implement a formal method for capturing *all* requested changes to the system. This could be accomplished through a change request and defect tracking system that provides a centralized repository of such requests, web-based entry of items from any physical location, automatic status tracking and trending, automatic notification of affected parties, and a mechanism for promotion of change requests into the requirements management system when appropriate. (We use the "firewall" metaphor in Figure 34–1 to suggest that the process is controlled and attempts to prevent uncontrolled wildfires of change from sweeping through the system.)

The system should be used to capture *all* inputs and to transmit them to the authority of the change control board (CCB) for resolution. The CCB plays a key role in helping the project achieve success and should consist of no

---

We will have to make conscious decisions about which bugs will remain in the system.

The team should implement a system for capturing all change requests.

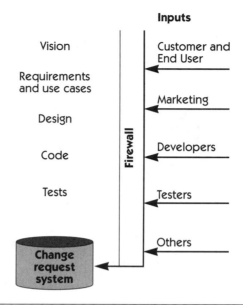

Figure 34–1 Change capture

more than three to five people who represent the key stakeholders for the project: customers, marketing, and program management.

When considering whether to approve a change request, the CCB must consider the following factors:

- The impact of the change on the cost and functionality of the system
- The impact of the change on customers and other external stakeholders not well represented on the CCB: other project contractors, component suppliers, and so on.
- The potential for the change to destabilize the system

When the decision is made, the CCB also has the responsibility to ensure that all those affected by the change are notified, even if the decision is made *not* to approve the change.

Once a change has been determined, the next step is to decide *where* to insert the change. (For example, we need to determine whether to change a requirement or to change a test being proposed.) Subsequent changes will ripple through in the hierarchy, as shown in Figure 34–2.

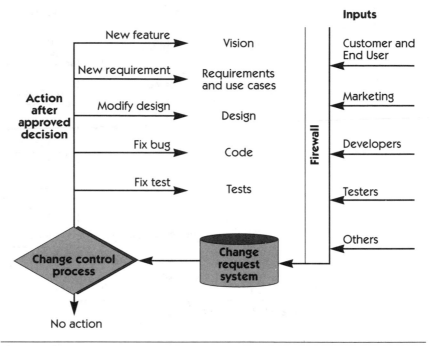

Figure 34–2   Change request flow

Step 5: Manage Change Hierarchically

The fact that all of these people are interested in making changes to the requirements is not intrinsically bad; aside from the Easter Egg phenomenon, we could even imagine that all of these changes are beneficial. But the fact that the changes might not be documented or analyzed *is* a problem, and if they're not managed carefully, disaster can occur. A change to one requirement can have a "ripple effect" in other related requirements, design, or other subsystems; further, this fact may not be obvious to the marketing representative, who casually asks the programmer to make a "quick and easy" change to the system.

But the problem is even worse, for without an explicit process, the changes typically occur in a "bottom-up" fashion. That is, if the change is envisioned while the code is being written for a new system, it's typically introduced directly into the code itself. If the developers are extremely disciplined, they *might* then ask themselves, "Hmmm, I wonder whether the changes we're making to the code will cause any changes in the design. And do the design-level changes have an impact on the requirements? And do the changes to the software requirements have any impact on the Vision document?"

(Meanwhile, nobody remembers to tell *any* of this to the testing team, whose members thought that they were supposed to be creating test plans for the original software requirements!)

A programmer doesn't have the authority to introduce new features and requirements directly into the code on the user's behalf.

In theory, it's possible to manage this "backward" ripple-effect phenomenon if all of the respective documents are under the control of a sophisticated software tools environment. But even if all the documents are kept synchronized, the kind of bottom-up changes to the requirements that we've been discussing here are still undesirable. To be blunt: *A programmer doesn't have the authority to introduce new features and requirements directly into the code on the user's behalf, no matter how well intentioned.* Similarly, the marketing representative who makes a casual request of the programmer for such a change, while they're both sipping a beer at the neighborhood brewpub, is not acting in an *official* capacity. *Every* new feature/requirement has an impact on the cost, schedule, reliability, and risk associated with the project.

In order to mitigate this ripple effect, changes to the requirements should be carried out in the top-down hierarchical fashion shown in Figure 34–3. As discussed earlier in this book, changes to a baseline Vision document can be

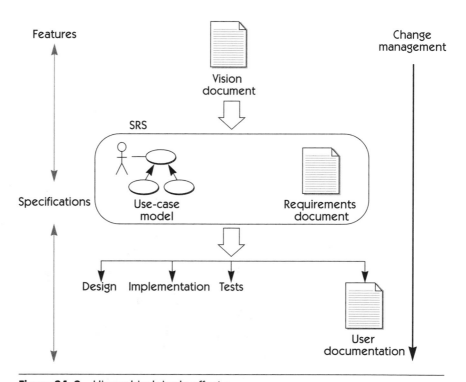

Figure 34–3 Hierarchical ripple effect

documented in a separate "Delta" document, which is normally a very small subset of the original document. However, since the Vision document changes may stipulate the *deletion* of features, we may need to regenerate a completely new baselined set of software requirements, and that can lead to appropriate changes in the design, the code, and the test plans.

If we have followed the processes in this book and have reasonable support from our tool environment, the downward "ripple effect" will be highlighted by the traceability mechanism we used in building our requirements pyramid. This allows us to work downward through the pyramid, making further changes as necessary. Each subsequent change, in turn, highlights additional "suspect links," or places lower in the pyramid where additional analysis needs to occur.

Thus, change is a controlled "brushfire," and we can proceed logically through the hierarchy. In addition, if we've done a good job of encapsulating the systems and subsystems and have used a well-structured requirements strategy, changes should be limited to the areas directly linked to the requirements that have changed.

For example, Figure 34–4 shows a traceability report for HOLIS that resulted when a change was made; two features, FEA3 and FEA5, indicate traceability links that the automated tool has marked as suspect. These suspected impacts resulted from proposed changes to the two features. You

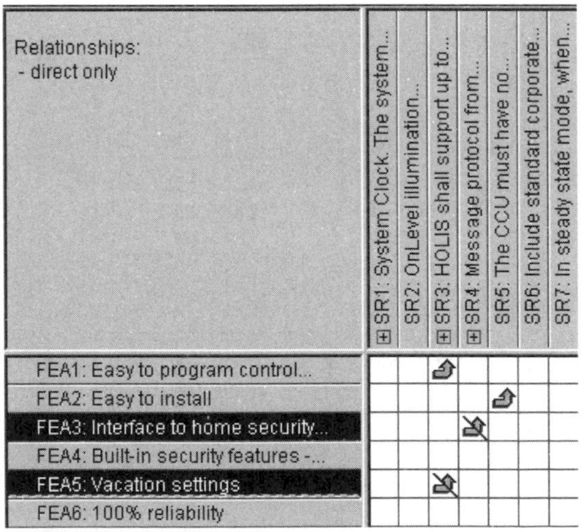

Figure 34–4 Impact analysis by traceability link

need to review SR3 and SR4 for possible interactions as a result of the changes proposed by FEA3 and FEA5. In turn, possible revisions to SR3 and SR4 may ripple down into the implementation, and so on. We will explore this issue again later in this chapter.

Requirements Configuration Management

Some elements of the preceding change review and approval process are referred to as "change control," "version control," or *configuration management* (CM) in some organizations. Interestingly, most organizations have a reasonably rigorous process for configuration management of the source code produced during the implementation lifecycle phase of a project, but no corresponding process for the project requirements. Even if the organization does have a formal process for generating the Vision document and software requirements, it often ignores the many requirements-oriented changes that creep into the project during the coding phase.

However, in today's modern tool environments, it's a reasonably straightforward matter to have all elements of the requirements hierarchy under configuration management (see Figure 34–5).

The benefits of a CM-based requirements management process should be obvious by now, but let's review them briefly. Such a process

- Prevents unauthorized and potentially destructive or frivolous changes to the requirements
- Preserves the revisions to requirements documents
- Facilitates the retrieval and/or reconstruction of previous versions of documents
- Supports a managed, organized baseline "release strategy" for incremental improvements or updates to a system
- Prevents simultaneous update of documents or conflicting and uncoordinated updates to different documents at the same time.

Tool-Based Support for Change Management

In this recap of previous sections, we offer a practical approach for change management, *assuming that you have a set of tools to support this effort*. If you choose to use your own manual techniques, portions of this section may not be applicable, but the overall ideas are worth reviewing nonetheless.

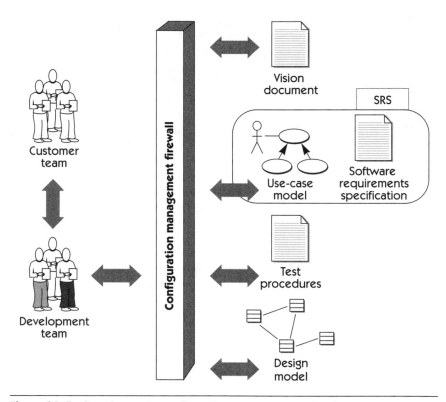

Figure 34–5   Requirements configuration management overview

Change management practices help you to understand and manage these important project development aspects:

- If a single product feature is proposed for a change, what are the work consequences of that change? In other words, change management helps you determine the amount of rework that may be required. The amount of work to effect a change may have significant impact on your project resource planning and workload planning.
- If an element is proposed for a change, what are the *other* elements of the system that may be impacted by the change? This topic is of key concern both to your project planning and to your customer.
- Active projects inevitably take wrong turns. It is certain that your project will arrive at a point at which you would like to be able to "roll back" a requirement and to examine a previous revision of the requirement. In addition, it would be helpful to remember how and why the requirement was changed. In other words, an audit trail of each requirement is valuable and may even be mandated by regulatory agencies as part of the design process.

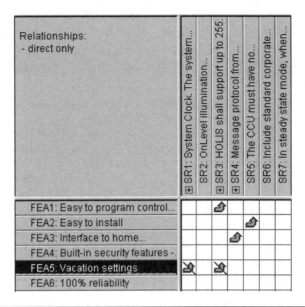

Figure 34–6   Abbreviated traceability matrix after FEA5 was altered

Elements Impacted by Change

After establishing the traceability relationships for your project, you should use the traceability linkages as a tool for change management. In the case of HOLIS, for example, suppose that we need to change the wording of FEA5 ("Vacation settings") in Figure 34–6 to reflect a revised statement of the product feature. Note the diagonal lines through the traceability arrows in the row for FEA5. These lines, the "suspect links," are intended to warn you that changing the feature may have an impact on SR1 and SR3 and that you should therefore review them.

As the project evolves, changes inevitably will be proposed for various aspects of the project: the top-level Vision document, through specification, implementation, and testing. Whenever a change occurs, you should use the suspect links to warn you of possible relationships affected by the change. Your change management activities usually will involve one of two steps.

1. If the change to the feature does not impact a requirement, you need only clear the suspect link. Note that subsequent later changes to the feature may again set the suspect link.

2. If the feature *does* impact a requirement, you may need to rework the affected element. For example, the proposed change to the feature may require a respecification of another requirement. After editing it, you will discover that additional suspect links now warn you of the potential interactions linked to changing it. Then, those interactions will need to be examined for changes, and so on.

Change management capability must exist throughout multiple levels of traceability relationships. That is, changing a feature entry in the Vision document may impact several software requirements in the SRS and/or selected use cases, which may, in turn, impact several implementation units, which may, in turn, impact one or more test plans. You should also track the traceability linkages bidirectionally. For example, changing a test plan specification may cause you to look back to the implementation units for potential impact. In turn, changing an implementation unit may require a reinspection of affected software requirements and may even require a reinspection of the top-level features, which are ultimately linked via the traceability relationships you established.

Audit Trail of Change History

You will also find it beneficial to maintain an audit trail of changes, especially changes made to individual requirements. With tool support, you should be able to manage each requirement separately, regardless of the document or model it's in. Thus, changes you make to each requirement will be captured automatically by your tool and can be recalled for later inspection and review.

The change history should capture the current statement of the requirement, including the current values of all of the requirement's attributes. By capturing all such parameters, you can use the history as a concise overview of the requirement.

The change history also allows you to view a chronological history of all prior changes to the requirement, including its attributes. The tool should automatically capture all changes to the text of the requirement, as well as changes to the values for the requirement's attributes.

Whenever the tool detects a change, the background for the change should be automatically captured. In addition, the tool should include an automatic capture of the change's author and the date and time of the change. Then, at any future time, the chronology of the change and the change author can be viewed as part of the history record.

The tool should also allow you to enter a change description to document the change. Typically, you might enter a sentence or two to explain why the change was made, make references to project memos regarding the change, and so on. Documenting the change will provide a satisfactory rationale and cross reference so that later inspection of the history can adequately recall the motivation for the change. This will be a key element in any regulatory or project review of those changes that affect the claims, efficacy, and safety of the device and its software.

Figure 34–7 shows a printout of a partial SRS requirement history (SR4.4). Note that the change history is arranged in reverse chronological order and records changes to both the text (change 1.0001 versus 1.0000) and the values of selected attributes.

Project Name: HOLIS 2000   **SR4.4**

Revision: 1.0003, Version Label: Printed By: Don

SR4.4

Text:	Message Acknowledgement. In reply to the message from the Control Switch, the CCU shall respond with the following message:
Requirement type:	Rqmt
Location:	HOLIS CCU SRS
Traced from:	
Traced to:	
Attributes:	

Priority	Status	Cost	Difficult.	Stability	Assign..
Medium	Approve.		Medium	Medium	

Revisions:

1.0001	04/18/99 9:06 AM by: Don
Change description:	Major revision to requirement to facilitate testing. Requirement Text Changed.
Text:	Message Acknowledgement. In reply to the message from the Control Switch, the CCU shall respond with the following message:

1.0000	04/15/99 5:32 PM by: Don
Change description:	Requirement created. DIFFICULTY: <no entry> - Medium. PRIORITY: <no entry> - Medium. STABILITY: <no entry> - Medium. STATUS: <no entry> - Approved.
Text:	Checksum. The checksum for the message is calculated and checked per the CRC2.3 standard.

Figure 34–7   SR4.4 change history

Text changes can be very tiny, such as a change in punctuation, or, as in the case of SR4.4, a major revision. Nevertheless, any change is a change and should be logged appropriately by the change management tool.

Configuration Management and Change Management

A change history should exist at three levels within your project.

1. At the finest level of detail, the change history records all changes to each individual requirement within the project. This is the level of detail exhibited in Figure 34–7.
2. At a middle level of detail, you should automatically maintain a similar change history for each project document. Document-level history is typically maintained by your source code control system or document control system.
3. At the most general level of detail, you should automatically maintain a similar change history for the entire project. Both the project and the archives can be fully integrated into a configuration management system.

In other words, you need a set of tools providing a fully automatic, comprehensive, and seamless integration to common applications that will assist you in the configuration management tasks involved in running a large software development project.

Summary

Although requirements will change during project development, change itself need not destabilize the development process. With a comprehensive change control process in place and with requirements artifacts placed under the control of the development team's configuration management system, the team will be well prepared for the key requirements challenge of managing change.

It is important to realize that managing change in a large project is usually too big to handle by manual methods. Yes, you need a *process* to control the manner in which change enters the project. However, we have found it to be a formidable task to attempt to *understand the ramifications* of the change without tools that help you find all of the affected elements of the project.

Team Skill 6 Summary

Team Skill 6, Building the Right System, completes the transition from understanding the problem to implementing the solution system.

Designing and implementing the correct system is tough. One useful technique is to use the requirements and the use cases to drive the implementation architecture and design. We also learned about *verification*, an analytic approach that constantly monitors the evolution of the project's features, requirements, design, and implementation. Verification is supported by the use of *traceability* techniques to relate parts of your project to one another.

Traceability techniques allow you to make certain that everything required for the project is present and accounted for. Also, the same techniques allow you to ferret out unnecessary or superfluous items that will only bog down your development efforts in useless side roads. Although verification is an analytical technique, it is important to remember that *thinking* is important. You can't simply apply the verification techniques mechanically.

Validation is the other half of the V&V approach to ensuring that the system is built correctly. Validation uses testing activities and traceability techniques to ensure that the system conforms to its requirements. Acceptance testing is then applied to ensure that the system works as intended in the customer's environment and that it really does solve the customer's problem.

You may also need to apply hazard analysis and risk analysis to help you decide which portions of your system need verification and validation and in what amounts. Your investments in these activities should be controlled by your return on investment (ROI) analysis.

Finally, a critical feature of building the right system is the matter of managing change. Change is a way of life; we can *plan* for change and *manage* it. Managing change helps us make sure that the system we built is the *right* system and, moreover, that it continues to *be* the right system over time.

With the completion of Team Skill 6, we are ready to move to the last chapter. Chapter 35 is intended to help you apply the skills you have learned and to help you get off to a good start on your next project.

Chapter 35
GETTING STARTED

Dedication

Over the course of many years, we and others who have contributed to this book have taught, and have been taught by, thousands of students interested in requirements management. As you are aware, there is no one right way to perform requirements management; no one single elicitation technique applies in every circumstance; no one single process fits all teams. Projects have varying degrees of scope and complexity. Application types vary tremendously and come from many different industries.

Yes, requirements management is a very broad topic and also very deep. A recurring theme from the classroom is that students feel the need to have a more prescriptive process—a recipe, if you will—for applying what they learned in class. "You've told us too much," our students might say. "Just give us a single generic process that we can start with," they continue. "We know it's not that simple, but we'll be happy to modify it as necessary for *our* project, but we need a more prescriptive starting point, a step-by-step process so that we can better apply what we learned. *Just tell me how to get started*!"

OK, you've got it. *This chapter is dedicated to these students, and to those of you who share their point of view and this common "user need."*

What We've Learned So Far

Before we can kickstart your project requirements process, however, we need to summarize what we've learned in the book.

Introduction

In the introductory chapters, we learned that our industry often does a poor job of delivering quality applications on time and on budget. Some of the root causes of this problem are also clear. *Lack of user input, incomplete requirements and specifications, and changing requirements and specifications* are commonly cited problems in projects that failed to meet their objectives.

Perhaps developers and customers alike have a common attitude that "even if we're not really sure of the details of what we want, it's better to get started with implementation now, because we're behind schedule and in a hurry. We can pin down the requirements later." But all too often, this well-intentioned approach degenerates into a chaotic development effort, with no one quite sure what the user really wanted or what the current system really does.

How do we know what the system is supposed to do? How do we keep track of the current status of requirements? How do we determine the impact of a change? To address these issues, we recommend an encompassing philosophy of requirements management, which we defined as

> *a systematic approach to eliciting, organizing, and documenting the requirements of the system, as well as a process that establishes and maintains agreement between the customer and the project team on the changing requirements of the system.*

Since the history of software development—and the future for at least as far as we can envision it—is one of ever increasing complexity, we also understand that the software development problem must be addressed by well-structured and well-trained software *teams*. Every team member will eventually be involved in helping manage the requirements for the project. These teams must develop the requisite skills to understand the user needs, to manage the scope of the application, and to build systems that meet these user needs. The team must work *as a team* to address the requirements management challenge.

Team Skill 1: Analyzing the Problem

In Team Skill 1, we introduced a set of skills that your team can apply to *understand the problem to be solved before application development begins*. We introduced a simple, five-step problem analysis technique that can help your team gain a better understanding of the problem to be solved.

1. Gain agreement on the problem definition.
2. Understand the root causes of the problem.
3. Identify the stakeholders and the users whose collective judgement will ultimately determine the success or failure of your system.

4. Determine where the boundaries of the solution are likely to be found.

5. Understand the constraints that will be imposed on the team and on the solution.

All in all, following this process will improve your team's ability to address the challenge ahead, *providing a solution to the problem to be solved.*

We also noted that a variety of techniques can be used in problem analysis. Specifically, we looked at business modeling, a specific problem analysis technique that works quite well in complex information systems that support key business infrastructures. The team can use business modeling to both understand the way in which the business evolves and to define where within the system we can deploy applications most productively. We also recognized that the business model we defined will have parallel constructs in the software application, and we use this commonality to seed the software design phases. We will also use the business use cases we discovered again later to help define requirements for the application itself.

For the embedded-system software applications, we used systems engineering as a problem analysis technique to help us decompose a complex system into subsystems. This process helps us to understand where software applications should lie and what overall purpose they serve. In so doing, we also learned that we complicate the requirements matter somewhat by defining new subsystems, for which we must, in turn, come to understand the requirements to be imposed.

Team Skill 2: Understanding User Needs

We started Team Skill 2 by introducing three "syndromes" that increase the challenge of understanding the real needs of users and other stakeholders. The "Yes, But," the "Undiscovered Ruins'" and the "User and the Developer" syndromes were used as metaphors to help us better understand the challenge ahead and to provide a context for the elicitation techniques that we developed in this Team Skill.

We also recognized that since we rarely have been given effective requirements specifications for the systems we are going to build, in order to do a better job of building these systems, we are going to have to go out and *get* the information we need to be successful. Requirements elicitation is the term we used to describe this process, and we concluded that the team must play a more active role in this process.

To help the team on this mission, we then presented a variety of techniques for addressing these problems and better understanding the real needs of users and other stakeholders. These techniques were

- Interviewing and questionnaires
- The requirements workshop
- Brainstorming and idea reduction
- Storyboarding
- Use cases
- Role playing
- Prototyping

Although no one technique is perfect in every circumstance, each represents a proactive means of pushing knowledge of user needs forward and thereby converting "fuzzy" requirements to requirements that are "better known." Although all of these techniques work in certain circumstances, we did admit to a favorite: the requirements workshop/brainstorming technique.

Team Skill 3: Defining the System

In Team Skill 3, we moved from understanding the needs of the user to starting to define the solution. In so doing, we took our first baby steps out of the problem domain, the land of the user, and into the solution domain, wherein our job is to define a system to solve the problem at hand.

We also learned that complex systems require comprehensive strategies for managing requirements information, and we looked at a number of ways to organize requirements information. We recognized that we really have a hierarchy of information, starting with user needs, transitioning through features, then into the more detailed software requirements as expressed in use cases or traditional forms of expression. Also, we note that the hierarchy reflects the level of abstraction with which we view the problem space and the solution space.

We then "zoomed in" to look at the application definition process for a stand-alone software application and invested some time in defining a Vision document for such an application. We maintain that the Vision document, with modifications to the particular context of a company's software applications, is a crucial document and that *every* project should have one.

We also recognized that without someone to champion the requirements for our application and to support the needs of the customer and the development team, we would have no way to be certain that the hard decisions are made. Requirements drift, delays, and suboptimum decisions forced by project deadlines are likely to result. So, we decided to appoint someone or to anoint someone to own the Vision document and the features it contains. In turn, the champion and the team will empower a change control board to help with the really tough decisions and to ensure that requirements changes are reasoned about before being accepted.

Team Skill 4: Managing Scope

In Team Skill 4, we learned that the problem of project scope is endemic. It is not unusual that projects are initiated with twice the amount of functionality that the team can reasonably implement in a quality manner. We shouldn't be surprised by this, as it is the nature of the beast: Customers want more, marketing wants more, and the team wants more. We just need to make sure that we can deliver *something* on time.

In order to manage scope, we looked at various techniques for setting priorities, and we defined the notion of the baseline, an agreed-to understanding of what the system will do, as a key project work product. We learned that if scope and the concomitant expectations exceed reality, in all probability, some bad news is about to be delivered. We decided on a philosophy of approach that engages our customer in the hard decisions. After all, we are just the resources, not the decision makers; it's our customer's project. So, the question is, What, exactly, *must* be accomplished in the next release, given the resources that are available to the project?

Even then, we expect to do some negotiating. We briefly mentioned a few negotiation skills and hinted that the team may need to use them on occasion.

We cannot expect that the process described so far will make the scope challenge go away, any more than any other single process will solve the problems of the application development world. However, the steps outlined can be expected to have a material effect on the scope of the problem, allowing application developers to focus on critical subsets and to incrementally deliver high-quality systems that meet or exceed the expectations of the user. Further, engaging the customer in helping solve the scope management problem increases commitment on the part of both parties and fosters improved communication and trust between the customer and application development teams.

With a comprehensive project definition, or Vision document, in hand and scope managed to a reasonable level, we at least have the *opportunity* to succeed in the next phases of the project.

Team Skill 5: Refining the System Definition

In Team Skill 5, we learned that requirements are *the* key communication technique to capture the user's needs in such a way that the developer can develop a system to meet those needs. In addition, requirements need to have sufficient specificity so that we can tell when they have been met. We needn't be alarmed by this, as it is often our team members—after all, we are closest to the project—who can provide this specificity. This is one of our opportunities to make sure that the right system gets defined.

These requirements can be organized and documented in a variety of ways. We focused on what we called a Modern SRS Package, a logical construct that allows us to document requirements in use cases, documents, database forms, or other techniques. Although we made some suggestions on how to organize this package, we don't really care what form it takes, so long as it contains the right things.

All development should flow from the requirements specified in the Modern SRS Package. Nothing should be developed outside this package, and all specifications in the package should be reflected in the development activities. Since these are the governing elements, it follows that all activities, such as regulatory constraints, should reflect the package and vice versa. The Modern SRS Package is a living package that should be reviewed and updated throughout the lifetime of the project. The package should specify *what* functions are to be accomplished, not *how* they are to be accomplished. The Modern SRS Package should be used to specify functional requirements, nonfunctional requirements, and design constraints.

We also provided a set of quality measures for assessing the quality of your package and the various elements contained therein. Where necessary, the requirements documentation may be supplemented by one or more formal, or more structured, methods of specification. The Modern SRS Package provides the detail you need to proceed to *implement*, or *build*, the right system.

Team Skill 6: Building the Right System

Designing and implementing the correct system is the biggest job of all. One useful technique is to use the requirements and use cases to drive the implementation architecture and design.

Verification is an analytic approach that allows you to constantly monitor the evolution of the project's features, requirements, design, and implementation. Verification is supported by the use of *traceability* techniques to relate parts of your project to one another. By using traceability, you can verify that

- All project elements are accounted for, and
- All project elements have a purpose

Although verification is an analytical technique, it is important to remember that *thinking* is important. You can't simply apply the verification techniques mechanically.

Validation, the other half of the V&V approach to ensuring that the system is built correctly, focuses on testing and uses traceability techniques to select system components that will require testing. As in verification, we use the validation techniques to ensure that

- All project elements are properly tested
- All tests have a useful purpose

You may also need to apply hazard analysis and risk analysis to help you decide which portions of your system need verification and validation, and in what amounts.

We also described how periodic acceptance testing could help keep our projects on track.

Finally, building the right system also depends on managing change. We learned that change is just part of life, that we must *plan* for change and develop a process whereby we can *manage it*. Managing change helps us make sure that the system we built *is* the *right* system and, moreover, that it continues to *be* the right system over time.

Your Prescription for Requirements Management

With this little refresher course behind us, we can now proceed to provide a prescription. However, if we are going to oversimplify the prescription, as is necessary to manage our level of abstraction—and to help us *manage the scope* of the prescription—we must first make some simplifying assumptions.

These will help us communicate more clearly what type of system the prescription can be applied to and also helps *manage your expectations* for what the prescription can deliver as well.

Simplifying Assumptions

- The followers of the prescription have read and understood the book and/or received some training reasonably consistent with the methodology in this book.
- The application being described is a single, stand-alone application, not a system of subsystems or a much larger-scope project. Also, there are no contractual requirements for documents in a specific format.
- The team size is small to moderate, perhaps 10–30 members.
- The software is being designed for use by others: an external customer who is fairly readily available to the team.
- It's a new application, so the team can "start from scratch" in building the project.
- The team will use modern software methods and they are familiar with the basic concepts of use cases and iterative development.
- The team has reasonable tool support, including requirements management tools, modeling tools, and a change request system and change management tools.

The Recipe

Step 1: Understand the Problem Being Solved

a. *Execute* the five-step problem analysis process.

   1. Gain agreement on the problem being solved.
   2. Understand the root cause, if applicable to your situation.
   3. Identify the stakeholders and users, or actors, in your system.
   4. Define the system boundary.
   5. Identify constraints imposed on the solution.

   (Use Team Skill 1 as a guideline for your work.)

b. *Circulate* the problem statement to external stakeholders and insist that you gain agreement on the problem statement before moving forward.

Step 2: Understand User Needs

a. Create a *structured interview*, using the generic template from Team Skill 2, pertinent to your application.
b. *Interview* 5–15 users/stakeholders identified in Step 1.

c. Summarize the interviews by aggregating the top 10–15 user needs, or use the "pithy quote approach"; that is, document 10 or 15 particularly memorable stakeholders quotes that reflect their needs in their own words.

d. Use the quotes or the restated needs to start your requirements pyramid. Start requirements traceability now.

e. Facilitate a requirements workshop for your project. Use "out-of-box" and "in-box" warm-up papers (use "in-box" data from item c).

1. Run a brainstorming session to identify/refine features.
2. Perform idea reduction and feature prioritization.
3. Use the critical, important, and useful classification.

f. Rerun the workshop once or twice a year to provide a format for ongoing structured customer input.

g. Create storyboards for all innovative concepts. Present them and show an appropriate set of use cases to your users to make sure you get it right.

h. Try to make sure that your process yields at least one user prototype system to evaluate, which the users can test in their environment.

Step 3: Define the System

a. Adopt the Vision document concept and create a template to suit your project's needs.

b. Create a product position statement. Circulate it *widely* and make sure that you have agreement. If you don't have it, stop and get it. Make sure that your customer is in agreement.

c. Enter all features identified in step 2 and through other inputs, such as development, help desk, and marketing, in the Vision document. Trace them back to user needs. Use attributes of priority (critical, important, useful), risk (H, M, L), effort (team-months), stability (H, M, L), and Release (v1.0 and so on). Also define the general requirements (licensing, documentation, legal and regulatory, and so on) in the Vision document.

d. Develop illustrative use cases in the Vision document's Appendix so the features in the Vision document can be understood by all.

e. Make the Vision document be *the* living document for your project. Publish it for easy access and review. Make the owner of the document, by default, the *official channel* for changing features. Use a Delta Vision document going forward. Addict your company to having a current Vision document at all times.

Step 4: Continuously Manage Scope and Manage Change

a. Based on effort estimates from the team, determine the *baseline for each release* in the Vision document, using an attribute of "version number."

b. Get *customer agreement on scope.* Help the team make the hard scope decisions *and get the decisions behind you.*

c. Preach and teach *iterative development.* Communicate and manage expectations everywhere.

d. *Manage change* by using the baseline. Use the Delta Vision document to capture all new features that arise through the normal course of events. Make sure that all suggested features are recorded so that none are lost. Empower a change control board to make the hard decisions.

e. Install a *change request management system* to capture all requests for change, and ensure that all requests go through that system to the change control board.

Step 5: Refine the System Definition

a. Mandate that there shall be, at all times, a software requirements specification—using the Modern SRS Package organizational structure—that defines the complete set of functional and nonfunctional behaviors of the product. Develop detailed use cases for core functionality of the system.

b. Have the development team or test team adopt and manage this workload. Assist them with training and find them help if they need it. Use formal analysis methods only where you cannot afford to be misunderstood.

c. Trace requirements to and from use cases and features.

d. Also, make sure that you define all of the nonfunctional requirements for your system. The template you use should prompt you to make sure that you have asked the right questions.

Step 6: Build the Right System

a. Perform a hazard analysis (risk assessment) to determine what things you can't afford to have go wrong in the implementation. Develop a verification and validation plan, based on these results.

b. Engage the test department in the requirements management challenge now. Have testers involved in test planning from the beginning. Have the test team build test procedures and test cases that trace back to the use cases, as well as functional and nonfunctional requirements.

c. If you have an independent QA department, have it assume a role in the monitoring and assessment of the requirements *process* and the V&V plan.

d. Rely on the use cases and use-case realizations in the design model to integrate design elements with the requirements. Use inferred traceability through the use-case realizations for impact assessment as change occurs.

e. Provide periodic acceptance testing milestones to validate your work and ensure your customer's continuous involvement.

Step 7: Manage the Requirements Process

a. The champion should personally maintain responsibility for the Vision document, have weekly reviews with the team to assess status, and set up default reports and queries to assist this effort.

b. Monitor the software requirements specification process to make sure that the vision is properly fulfilled in the detailed requirements.

c. Engage QA to help monitor the requirements maintenance, change management, and test processes.

d. Lead the change control review process (CCB) and make certain that impact assessment is done before significant changes are allowed into the system.

Step 8: Congratulations! You've Shipped a Product!

Now, On to the Next Release!

Congratulations! You and your team have shipped a quality, albeit scope-managed, first release of your new system. You did it with quality and even a little style, and you got to spend the year-end holidays at home with your family. And your customers are *happy*. OK, they are not ecstatic; many of them were hoping for more. But they are *still your customers*, and they eagerly await the next release.

a. Go back to (about) step 2(e)! and build the next iteration of your system.

By the way, don't forget to have some fun! Building great products and systems is a blast! We love this business!

Appendixes

- **Appendix A**   HOLIS Artifacts
- **Appendix B**   Vision Document Template
- **Appendix C**   Modern SRS Package Template
- **Appendix D**   Requirements Management in the SEI-CMM and within ISO 9000
- **Appendix E**   Requirements Management in the Rational Unified Process

Appendix A
HOLIS Artifacts

Note: This case study, including the names of the company, the participants, and the invented product, is entirely fictional.

Background of the Case Study

Lumenations, Ltd.

Lumenations, Ltd., has been a worldwide supplier of commercial lighting systems for use in professional theater and amateur stage productions for more than 40 years. In 1999, its annual revenues peaked at approximately $120 million, and sales are flattening. Lumenations is a public company, and the lack of growth in sales—no, worse, the lack of any reasonable prospect for improving growth in sales—is taking its toll on the company and its shareholders. The last annual meeting was quite uncomfortable, as there was little new to report regarding the company's prospects for growth. The stock climbed briefly to $25 last spring on a spate of new orders but has since crept back down to around $15 a share.

The theater equipment industry as a whole is flat, and there is little new development. The industry is mature and already well consolidated, and since Lumenations' stock is in the tank and its capitalization is only modest, acquisition is not an option for the company.

What's needed is a *new* marketplace, not too remote from what the company does best, but one in which there is substantial opportunity for growth in revenue and profits. After conducting a thorough market research project and spending many dollars on marketing consultants, the company has decided to enter a new market, that of *lighting automation for high-end residential systems*. This market is apparently growing at 25%–35% a year. Even better, the market is immature, and none of the established players has a dominant market position. Lumenations' strong worldwide distribution channel will be a real asset in the marketplace, and the distributors are hungry for new products. Looks like a great opportunity.

The HOLIS Software Development Team

The project for the case study is the development of HOLIS, our code name for an innovative new HOme LIghting automation System to be marketed by Lumenations. The HOLIS team is typical in terms of its size and scope. For the purposes of our case study, we've made it a fairly small team, only 15 team members, but it's large enough that all of the necessary skills can be fairly represented by individuals with some degree of specialization in their roles. Also, it's the structure of the team that's most important, and by adding more developers and testers, the structure of the HOLIS team scales well to a size of 30–50 people and commensurately larger software applications than HOLIS will require.

To address the new marketplace, Lumenations has set up a new division, the Home Lighting Automation Division. Since the division and the technology are mostly new to Lumenations, the HOLIS team has been assembled mostly from new hires, although a few team members have been transferred from the Commercial Automation Division. Figure A–1 is an organization chart showing the development team and the relationships among the team members.

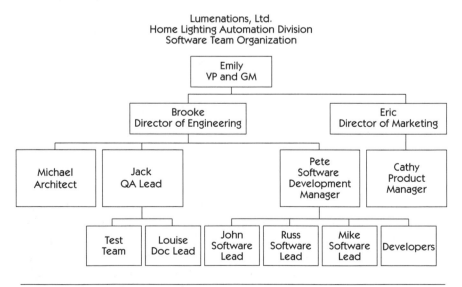

Figure A–1   Lumenations software team organization

Team Skill 1: Analyzing the Problem

Lumenations Problem Statement

The team decided to develop three problem statements, one of which seemed to state the obvious problem from the company's perspective.

For Lumenations	
The problem of	slowing growth in the company's core professional theater marketplaces
Affects	the company, its employees, and shareholders.
The result of which	is unacceptable business performance and lack of substantive opportunities for growth in revenue and profitability.
Benefits of	new products and a potential new marketplace for the company's products and services would include
	▪ Revitalizing the company and its employees
	▪ Increased loyalty and retention of the company's distributors
	▪ Higher revenue growth and profitability
	▪ Upturn in the company' stock price

The team also decided to see whether it could understand the "problem" that the existing solutions offered to the marketplace from the perspectives of both a future customer (end user) and potential distributors/builders (Lumenations' customers). Here's what the team came up with.

For the Homeowner	
The problem of	the lack of product choices, limited functionality, and high cost of existing home lighting automation systems
Affects	the homeowners of high-end residential systems.

Continued on next page.

For the Homeowner	
The result of which	is unacceptable performance of the purchased systems or, more often than not, a decision "not to automate."
Benefits of	the "right" lighting automation solution could include
	▪ Higher homeowner satisfaction and pride of ownership
	▪ Increased flexibility and usability of the residence
	▪ Improved safety, comfort, and convenience

For the Distributor	
The problem of	the lack of product choices, limited functionality, and high cost of existing home lighting automation systems
Affects	the distributors and builders of high-end residential systems.
The result of which	is few opportunities for marketplace differentiation and no new opportunities for higher-margin products.
Benefits of	the "right" lighting automation solution could include
	▪ Differentiation
	▪ Higher revenues and higher profitability
	▪ Increased market share

System Block Diagram with Actors Identified

Figure A–2 identifies the actors in this case study. Figures A–3, A–4, and A–5 show the subsystem block diagrams.

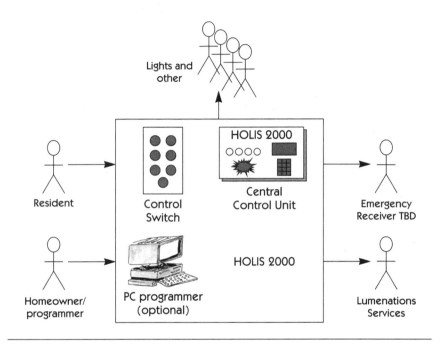

Figure A–2 Actors in the HOLIS case study

Actor Survey

Item Name	Comments
Lights and other	Output devices, lights and dimmer controls, others TBD
Homeowner/ programmer	Homeowner programs direct to CCU or through programmer PC
Emergency Receiver	Unknown; under investigation
Resident	Homeowner using Control Switch to change lighting
Lumenations Services	Lumenations employees supporting remote programming and maintenance activities

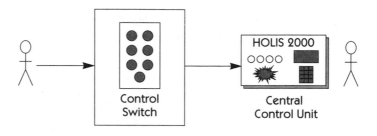

Figure A–3 Control Switch block diagram, with actors

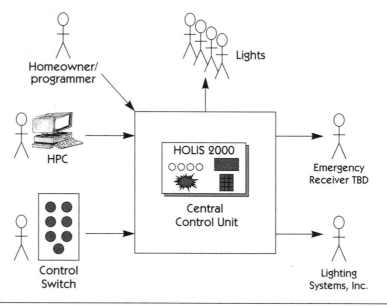

Figure A–4 Central Control Unit subsystem, with actors

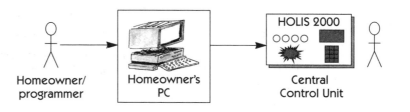

Figure A–5 PC programmer subsystem, with actors

Stakeholder Survey

HOLIS has a number of nonactor stakeholders, both external and internal.

Item Name	Comments
External	
Distributors	Lumenations' direct customer
Builders	Lumenations' customer's customer: the general contractor, responsible to the homeowner for the end result
Electrical contractors	Responsible for installation and support
Internal	
Development team	Lumenations' team
Marketing/product management	Will be presented by Cathy, product manager
Lumenations general management	Funding and outcome accountability

Constraints to Be Imposed on the Solution

Over a period of 45 days at the beginning of the product development effort, the HOLIS development team and Lumenations management identified, discussed, and agreed on the following constraints.

ID	Description	Rationale
1	A version 1.0 initial product release would be released to manufacturing by January 5, 2000.	The only product launch opportunity this year.
2	The team would adopt UML modeling, OO-based methodologies, and the Unified Software Development Process.	We believe these technologies will provide increased productivity and more robust systems.
3	The software for the Central Control Unit and PC programmer would be written in C++. Assembly language would be used for the Control Switch.	For consistency and maintainability; also, the team knows these languages.
4	A prototype system *must* be displayed at the December Home Automation trade show.	To take distributors' orders for Q1 FY 2000.
5	The microprocessor subsystem for the Central Control Unit would be copied from the Professional Division's advanced lighting system project (ALSP).	An existing design and an inventoried part.

ID	Description	Rationale
6	The only homeowner PC programmer configuration supported would be Windows 98 compatible.	Scope management for release 1.0.
7	The team would be allowed to hire two new full-time employees after a successful inception phase, with whatever skill set was determined to be necessary.	Maximum allowable budget expansion.
8	The KCH5444 single-chip microprocessor would be used in the Control Switch.	Already in use in the company.
9	Purchased software components were permissible, so long as there was no continuing royalty obligation to the company.	No long-term cost-of-goods-sold impact for software.

Team Skill 2: Understanding User Needs

Summary of User Needs as Collected from Interviews

Three homeowners, two distributors, and one electrical contractor were interviewed.

From the homeowner's perspective:

- Flexible and modifiable lighting control for entire house
- "Futureproof" ("As technology changes, I'd like compatibility with new technologies that might emerge.")
- Attractive, unobtrusive, ergonomic
- Fully independent and programmable or (reconfigurable) switches for each room in the house
- Additional security and peace of mind
- Intuitive operation ("I'd like to be able to explain it to my 'technophobic' mother.")
- A reasonable system cost, with low switch costs
- Easy and inexpensive to fix
- Flexible switch configurations (from one to seven "buttons" per switch)
- Out of sight, out of mind
- 100% reliability
- Vacation security settings

- Ability to create scenes, such as special housewide lighting settings for a party
- No increase in electrical or fire hazard in the home
- Ability, after a power failure, to restore the lights the way they were
- Program it myself, using my own PC
- Dimmers wherever I want them
- Can program it myself, without using a PC
- Somebody else will program it for me
- If system fails, I still want to be able to turn some lights on
- Interfaces to my home security system
- Interfaces to other home automation (HVAC, audio/video, and so on)

From the Distributor's Perspective:

- A competitive product offering
- Some strong product differentiation
- Easy to train my salespeople
- Can be demonstrated in my shop
- High gross margins

The Case Study: The HOLIS 2000 Requirements Workshop

While the interviewing process was under way, the development team met with marketing and decided to hold a requirements workshop for the HOLIS 2000 project. The following attendees were identified.

Name	Role	Title	Comments
Eric	Facilitator	Director of Marketing	
Cathy	Participant	HOLIS 2000 Product Manager	Project champion
Pete	Participant	Software Development Manager	Development responsibility for HOLIS 2000
Jennifer	Participant		Prospective homeowner
Elmer	Participant		Prospective homeowner
Gene	Participant		Prospective homeowner
John	Participant	CEO Automation Equip	Lumenations' largest distributor
Raquel	Participant	GM, EuroControls	Lumenations' European distributor

Name	Role	Title	Comments
Betty	Participant	President, Krystel Electric	Local electrical contractor
David	Participant	President, Rosewind Construction	Custom home builder
Various members	Observer	Development team	All team members who were available

The Workshop Prior to the workshop, the team put together a warm-up package consisting of

- A few recent magazines articles highlighting the trends in home automation
- Selective copies of the interviews that had been conducted
- A summarized list of the needs that had been identified to date

Eric brushed up on his facilitation skills, and Cathy handled the logistics for the workshop.

The Session The session was held at a hotel near the airport, and began promptly at 8 A.M. Figure A–6 provides a perspective on the workshop.

Eric introduced the agenda for the day and the workshop rules, including the workshop tickets. In general, the workshop went very well, and all participants

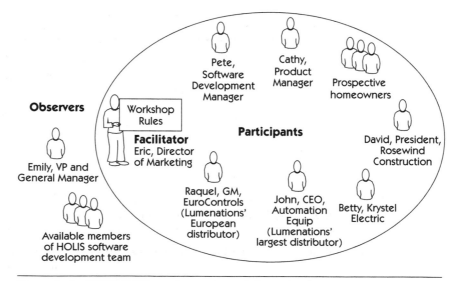

Figure A–6 HOLIS 2000 requirements workshop structure

were able to have their input heard. Eric did a fine job of facilitating, but one awkward period occurred when Eric got into an argument with Cathy about priorities for a couple of features. (The team decided that, if it had to do the workshop over again, it would bring in an outside facilitator.) Eric led a brainstorming session on potential features for HOLIS, and the team used cumulative voting to decide on relative priorities. The results follow, sorted by priority.

ID	Features from Workshop, Sorted by priority	Votes
23	Custom lighting scenes	121
16	Automatic timing settings for lights, etc.	107
4	Built-in security features—lights, alarms, and bells	105
6	100% reliability	90
8	Easy to program, non-PC control unit	88
1	Easy-to-program control stations	77
5	Vacation settings	77
13	Any light can be dimmed	74
9	Uses my own PC for programming	73
14	Entertain feature	66
20	Close garage doors	66
19	Automatically turn on closet lights when door opened	55
3	Interface to home security system	52
2	Easy to install	50
18	Turn on lights automatically when someone approaches a door	50
7	Instant lighting on/off	44
11	Can drive drapes, shades, pumps, and motors	44
15	Control lighting, etc., via phone	44
10	Interfaces to home automation system	43
22	Gradual mode: slowly increase/decrease illumination	34
26	Master control stations	31
12	Easily expanded when remodeling	25
25	Internationalized user interface	24
21	Interface to audio/video system	23
24	Restore after power fail	23
17	Controls HVAC	22
28	Voice activation	7
27	Web site–like user presentation	4

Analysis of Results The results of the process turned out as expected, except for two significant items.

1. The feature "built-in security" appeared very high on the priority list. This feature had been mentioned in passing in interviews but had not made it to the top of anyone's priority list. After a quick offline review, Cathy noted that built-in security—the ability to flash lights, optional horn, and optional emergency call-out system—was apparently not offered by any competitive system. The distributors commented that although they were surprised by this input, they felt that it *would* be a competitive differentiation and agreed that this should be a high-priority feature. Krys and David agreed. Based on this conclusion, marketing decided to include this functionality and to position it as a unique, competitive differentiator in the marketplace. This became one of the *defining features* for HOLIS.

2. In addition, you should note feature 25, the need to have the software's user interface fully "internationalized." Although the feature did not get a lot of votes—this seemed to make sense to the team, because the U.S.-based homeowners present could not have cared less about how well the product sold in Europe!—Raquel stated flatly that if the product was not internationalized at version 1.0, it would *not* be introduced in Europe. The team noted this position and agreed to explore the level of effort necessary to achieve internationalization in the 1.0 release.[1]

HOLIS System-Level Use-Case Model Survey

Use Case Name	Description	Actor(s)
Create Custom Lighting Scene	Resident creates a custom lighting scene	Resident, Lights
Initiate Emergency Receiver	Resident initiates emergency action	Resident
Control Light	Resident turns light(s) on or off or sets desired dim effect	Resident, Lights
Program Switch	Change or set the actions for a particular button/switch	Homeowner/ programmer
Remote Programming	Lumenations service provider does remote programming based on request from resident	Lumenations Services
On Vacation	Homeowner sets vacation setting for extended away period	Homeowner/ programmer
Set Timing Sequence	Homeowner programs time-based automated lighting sequence	Homeowner/ programmer

---

1. This demonstrates one of the issues with cumulative voting. Not all stakeholders are created equal. Failure to achieve internationalization, which had not been on the "radar screens" of the team prior to the workshop, would have been a strategic requirements misstep.

Note: The remainder of the use cases are deleted for brevity; a total of 20 system-level use cases are defined for v1.0 release.

Team Skill 3: Defining the System

HOLIS Requirements Organization

Figure A–7 shows the HOLIS requirements organization.

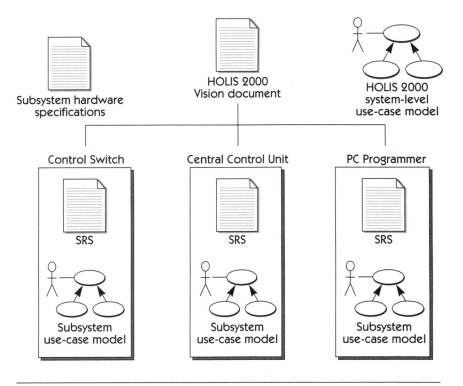

Figure A–7 HOLIS requirements organization

HOLIS Vision Document

For brevity, we present an abbreviated form of the HOLIS Vision document here, with some sections omitted. The full Vision document template, which you might wish to adopt, is provided in Appendix B.

Lumenations, Ltd.

HOLIS 2000
Vision Document

© 1999 Lumenations, Ltd.
102872 Cambridge Ave.
Marcy, NJ 12345

REVISION HISTORY

Date	Revision	Description	Author
1/21/99	1.0	Initial version	Cathy Mole
2/11/99	1.1	Updated after requirements workshop	Cathy Mole

TABLE OF CONTENTS

1 Introduction

1.1 Purpose of the Vision Document

This document provides the current vision for the HOLIS 2000-series home lighting automation system.

1.2 Product Overview

1.3   References

- HOLIS 2000 Control Unit Software Requirements Specification
- HOLIS 2000 Switch Software Requirements Specification
- HOLIS 2000 PC Programmer Software Requirements Specification
- Safety and Reliability Standards for Home Security Systems, Overwriters Laboratory 345.22, 1999

2   User Description

2.1   User/Market Demographics

2.2   User Profiles

2.3   User Environment

2.4   Key User Needs

The following user needs were gathered by the marketing department in a series of interviews conducted with prospective homeowners and distributors in fall 1998. These interviews are on file on the corporate intranet at www.HOLIShomepage.com/marketing/HOLIS/interviews.

2.4.1   From the Homeowner's Perspective

- Flexible and modifiable lighting control for entire house
- "Future-proof" ("As technology changes, I'd like compatibility with new technologies that might emerge.")
- Attractive, unobtrusive, ergonomic
- Additional security and peace of mind
- Intuitive operation ("I'd like to be able to explain it to my 'technophobic' mother.")
- A reasonable system cost, with low switch costs
- Easy and inexpensive to fix
- Out of sight, out of mind
- 100% reliability
- No increase of electrical or fire hazard in my home
- After power failure, able to restore the lights the way they were
- Ability to easily modify switch functionality
- Program it myself, using my own PC
- Can program it myself without using a PC

- Somebody else to program it for me
- If system fails, I still want to be able to turn some lights on
- Interfaces to my home security system
- Interfaces to other home automation (HVAC, audio/video, etc)

2.4.2   From the Distributor's Perspective

- A competitive product offering
- Some strong product differentiation
- Easy to train my salespeople
- Can be demoed in my shop
- High gross margins

2.5   Alternatives and Competition

3   Product Overview

3.1   Product Perspective

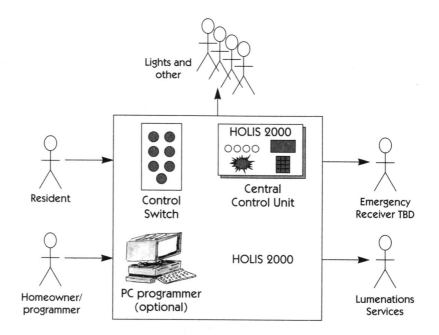

Text deleted for brevity.

3.2   HOLIS 2000 Product Position Statement

For	homeowners building new, high-end homes
Who	would like to enhance their residence and their convenience, comfort, and safety
The HOLIS 2000	is a home lighting automation system
That	brings unprecedented, state-of-the-art lighting automation functionality, with ease of use and a reasonable price.
Unlike	the Lightomation Systems series from Herb's Industrial Controls
Our product	combines the very latest in home automation functionality with built-in security features, and costs less to install and to maintain.

3.3   Summary of Capabilities

3.4   Assumptions and Dependencies

3.5   Cost and Pricing

3.6   Licensing and Installation

4   Feature Attributes

4.1   Priority

Used a mandatory versus optional prioritization.

4.2   Status

4.3   Votes

The votes attribute carries the priorities that were established in the HOLIS 2000 requirements workshop.

4.4   Effort

Low, medium, and high as set by the development team.

4.5   Risk

Set by development team.

4.6   Stability

4.7   Target Release

4.8   Assigned to

4.9   Reason

5   Product Features

5.1   Mandatory Features for v1.0

- **Fea23 Custom lighting scenes:** The system gives the homeowner the ability to create up to TBD custom lighting scenes. Each scene provides a preset level of illumination for each lighting bank throughout the residence. Scenes may be activated from either the Control Switch or the Central Control Unit.

- **Fea16 Automatic lighting settings:** The homeowner can create preset, time-based schedules for certain lighting events to happen.

- **Fea4 Security sequence:** The system has a built-in security feature that provides a one-button, panic alarm emergency sequence activation from any control switch in the house. The security sequence sets the lights to a predetermined scene setting and will also (optionally for each) flash the lights, activate an alarm claxon, and make a dial-up call to a predetermined number and deliver a voice-based preprogrammed message. The system also closes a relay contact, which the homeowner can use to attach devices of his or her choice.

- **Fea6 Reliability:** Our homeowners have repeatedly stressed that the system be as close to 100 percent reliable as possible. This is a particular concern with the security sequence.

(Remainder of features deleted for brevity.)

5.2   Optional Features

- **Fea20 Garage door control:** The system supports the "garage door" as one of the controlled output devices. The software must manage the control of the output accordingly and will need to provide a garage door metaphor/icon and support for programming the feature.

- **Fea2 Smart Install:** Ease of installation has been a key concern of our distributor/customers and will be a key differentiator for us with our channels organization. The software should support this need by whatever means are determined to be reasonable and viable. This could include online help for an installer's guide and instruction manual, a troubleshooting guide, in-process status assessment indication, automated fault detection, and so on.

(Note to Brooke: The engineering team should investigate this need and get back to marketing with a list of ideas and rough cost parameters so we can determine how far we can go on v1.0.)

(Remainder of optional features deleted for brevity.)

5.3   Future Features

Appendix A in the Vision document lists features that have been identified for possible future versions of the system. Although we agree that no significant investment is to be made in these in v1.0, we do ask that the marketing and engineering teams review this list and, wherever possible, keep these needs in mind as the design and development of the v1.0 system proceeds.

6   Exemplary cases

Text deleted for brevity.

7   Other Product Requirements

7.1   Applicable Standards

7.2   System Requirements

7.3   Licensing and Installation

7.4   Performance Requirements

8   Documentation Requirements

8.1   User Manual

8.2   Online Help

8.3   Installation Guides, Configuration, Read Me File

8.4   Labeling and Packaging

Team Skill 4: Managing Scope

After the requirements workshop, the team was chartered with the responsibility to assess the level of effort for each feature and to come up with a first draft of the v1.0 baseline. It was necessary to apply rigorous scope management because of the constraints on the team, including the "drop dead" date of having a prototype available at the trade show in December and the (even tougher) date of a release to manufacturing in January.[2] The team used the high-medium-low heuristic to estimate the level of effort for each feature and then added the risk assessment for each feature. The team went on to perform the suggested scope management activities, with the results shown in Tables A–1 and A–2.

Table A–1   HOLIS 2000 features, sorted by effort and risk attributes added

ID	Feature	Votes	Effort	Risk
23	Create custom lighting scenes	121	Med	Low
16	Automatic timing settings for lights, etc.	107	Low	Low
4	Built-in security features—lights, alarms, and bells	105	Low	High
6	100% reliability	90	High	High
8	Easy-to-program, non-PC control unit	88	High	Med
1	Easy-to-program control stations	77	Med	Med
5	Vacation settings	77	Low	Med
13	Any light can be dimmed	74	Low	Low
9	Uses my own PC for programming	73	High	Med
14	Entertain feature	66	Low	Low
20	Close garage doors	66	Low	Low
19	Automatically turn on closet lights when door opened	55	Low	High
3	Interface to home security system	52	High	High

---

2. Although given manufacturing lead times, the team decided that it actually had until the end of February for the final v1.0 software release. This was a crucial additional 6 weeks that the team was convinced it would need for final modifications, based on feedback from the trade show.

ID	Feature	Votes	Effort	Risk
2	Easy to install	50	Med	Med
18	Turn on lights automatically when someone approaches a door	50	Med	Med
7	Instant lighting on/off	44	High	High
11	Can drive drapes, shades, pumps, and motors	44	Low	Low
15	Control lighting, etc., via phone	44	High	High
10	Interfaces to home automation system	43	High	High
22	Gradual mode: slowly increase/decrease illumination	34	Med	Low
26	Master control stations	31	High	High
12	Easily expanded when remodeling	25	Med	Med
25	Internationalized user interface	24	Med	High
21	Interface to audio/video system	23	High	High
24	Restore after power fail	23	N/A	N/A
17	Controls HVAC	22	High	High
28	Voice activation	7	High	High
27	Web site–like user presentation	4	Med	Low

Table A–2   V1.0 baseline for HOLIS

ID	Feature	Votes	Effort	Risk	Marketing Comments
23	Create custom lighting scenes	121	Med	Low	As flexible as possible
16	Automatic timing settings for lights, etc.	107	Low	Low	As flexible as possible
4	Built-in security features—lights, alarms, and bells	105	Low	High	Marketing to do more research
6	100% reliability	90	High	High	Get as close to 100% as possible
8	Easy-to-program, non-PC control unit	88	High	Med	Provide dedicated controller
1	Easy-to-program control stations	77	Med	Med	As easy as feasible with measure effort
5	Vacation settings	77	Low	Med	
13	Any light can be dimmed	74	Low	Low	
9	Uses my own PC for programming	73	High	Med	Only one configuration supported in 1.0
25	**Internationalized CCU user interface**	24	Med	Med	Per agreement with European distributor
~~14~~	~~Entertain feature~~	66	Low	Low	(Not applicable, included in 23)
7	Instant lighting on/off	44	High	High	Make intelligent investments

V1.0 mandatory baseline: Everything above the line must be included, or we will delay release.

| 20 | Close garage doors | 66 | Low | Low | May be little impact on software |
| 2 | Easy to install | 50 | Med | Med | Level of effort basis |

Table continued on next page.

Table A–2   V1.0 baseline for HOLIS   (*continued*)

ID	Feature	Votes	Effort	Risk	Marketing Comments
11	Can drive drapes, shades, pumps, and motors	44	Low	Low	May be little impact on software
22	Gradual mode: slowly increase/decrease illumination	34	Med	Low	Nice if we can get it

V1.0 optional: Do as many of these as you can (Cathy)

Future features (Below this line, no current development)

29	**Internationalize PC Programmer interface**	N/A	High	Med	Will become mandatory for version 2.0
3	Interface to home security system	52	High	High	Can we at least provide a hardware interface? (Eric)
19	Automatically turn on closet lights when door opened	55	Low	High	
18	Turn on lights automatically when someone approaches a door	50	Med	Med	
15	Control lighting, etc., via phone	44	High	High	
10	Interfaces to home automation system	43	High	High	
26	Master control stations	31	High	High	
12	Easily expanded when remodeling	25	Med	Med	
25	Hand-held remote controls	24	Med	High	
21	Interface to audio/video system	23	High	High	
24	Restore after power fail	23	N/A	N/A	
17	Controls HVAC	22	High	High	
28	Voice activation	7	High	High	
27	Website-like user presentation	4	Med	Low	

Team Skill 5: Refining the System Definition

HOLIS Sample Use Case: Control Light

REVISION HISTORY

Date	Issue	Description	Author
14 April 1999	1.0	Initial creation of Control Light use case	Don Widrig
15 April 1999	1.1	Added second precondition to clarify operation	Jack Bigrig, QA Lead

Brief Description This use case prescribes the way in which lights are turned on or off or are dimmed by how the user presses a light switch.

Basic Flow Basic flow begins when the Resident presses any button on a Control Switch. If the Resident removes pressure on the Control Switch within the timer period, the system "toggles" the state of the light.

- If the light was On, the light is turned Off, and there is no illumination.
- If the light was Off, the light is turned On to the last remembered brightness level.

End of Basic Flow

Alternative Flow of Events If the Resident keeps pressure on the Control Switch for more than 1 second, the system initiates a dimming activity for the indicated Control Switch button. While the Resident continues to press the Control Switch button:

1. The brightness of the controlled light is smoothly increased to a systemwide maximum value at a rate of 10 percent a second.
2. When the maximum value is reached, the brightness of the controlled light is smoothly decreased to a systemwide minimum value at a rate of 10 percent a second.
3. When the minimum value is reached, processing continues at alternate flow step 1.

When the Resident ceases to press the Control Switch button:

4. The system ceases to change the brightness of the light.

Preconditions for Control Light Use Case The selected CS button must be "Dim Enabled." The selected CS button must be preprogrammed to control a light bank.

Postconditions for Control Light Use Case On leaving this use case, the current brightness level for the selected Control Switch button is remembered.

Extension Points None.

HOLIS 2000

Central Control Unit

Software Requirements Specification

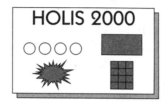

© 1999 Lumenations, Ltd.

Figure A–8   Title page of the HOLIS Modern SRS Package

HOLIS Central Control Unit Software Requirements Specification

For brevity, we present an abbreviated form of the HOLIS Modern SRS Package here. Figure A–8 shows the title page. The full SRS template, which that you might wish to adopt, is in Appendix C.

REVISION HISTORY

Date	Revision	Description	Author
4/11/99	1.0	Initial version	John Altinboy
4/15/99	1.1	Converted to ReqPro	Don Widrig
4/18/99	1.2	Revised to support Test Plans	Don Widrig and Dean Leffingwell

Table of Contents

1 Introduction

1.1 Purpose

This is the software requirements specification for the v1.0 release of the HOLIS 2000 Central Control Unit subsystem.

1.2 Scope

1.3 References

- HOLIS 2000 Vision Document
- HOLIS 2000 System-Level Use-Case Model: http://www.Lumenations.com/Engineering/HOLIS/Rose.mdl
- HOLIS 2000 Control Switch Software Requirements Specification
- HOLIS 2000 PC Programmer Software Requirements Specification

1.4 Assumptions and Dependencies

2 Use-Case Model Survey

The Central Control Unit for the home automation system participates in all system-level use cases. In addition, as the central subsystem, CCU also participates in a number of additional use cases that focus mostly on installation and setup, monitoring, and communication with the Control Switch, PC programmer. These subsystem use cases are as follows:

Name	Description	Actor(s)
System Diagnostic	This use case is run on command or whenever activated manually.	Control Switch Homeowner/programmer Lumenations Services Emergency Receiver Lights
Calibration	Calibrates dimming illumination levels	Homeowner/ programmer Lights
Assign Lighting Banks	Assigns physical-to-logical lighting bank mapping.	Homeowner/programmer
Program Switch	Change or set the actions for a particular button/switch	Homeowner/programmer

Note: The remainder of the use cases are deleted for brevity. A total of 11 use cases are defined for v1.0 release.

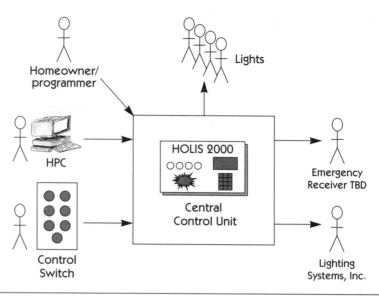

Figure A–9   CCU in system context

3   Product Context

The block diagram shown in Figure A–9 places the CCU into the overall system context.

4   Actor Survey

The actors that interact with the CCU are as follows:

Actor Name	Description
Homeowner/programmer	Homeowner/programmer (also maintenance technician) who interacts with the control panel
Lumenations Services	Actor at the end of the phone line; supports remote programming and diagnostics
Emergency Receiver	Actor receiving the emergency message
Lights	Lights and other control outputs, garage doors, etc.
Control Switch	Lighting switch control devices
PC programmer	Attached and optional homeowner's PC

Note: The actor Resident does not interact with the CCU. Resident can interact only with Control Switch, which in turn interacts with the CCU.

5 Requirements

5.1 Functional Requirements

- **SR1 System clock**. The system shall use and maintain a system clock. Precision of this clock shall be as specified in the ALSP requirements.

- **SR1.1 Synchronizing the clock time**. The homeowner shall have the ability to set the clock, using the numeric keys and the special function keys provided on the CCU operator panel. The GUI for doing so should appear as in the screen shot.
- **SR1.2 Synchronizing the month**. The homeowner shall also have the ability to set the month, using the numeric keys and the special function keys provided on the CCU operator panel.
- **SR2 OnLevel illumination parameter**. Each controlled lighting bank that is Dim Enabled shall have a data field. The lighting output is controlled by the parameter OnLevel, which controls the percent of illumination to the light. The nine possible OnLevel settings are 10%, 20%, 30%, 40%, 50%, 60%, 70%, 80%, and 90%.
- **SR3 Support for up to 255 event-time-schedules**. SR3.1 The allowable programming precision of an event-time-schedule shall be 1 minute. SR3.2 HOLIS shall execute event-time-schedules with an accuracy of 1 minute, ± 5 seconds as measured by the system clock. SR3.3 Event-time-schedules can be programmed on either a 12-hour or 24-hour clock. The user shall enter the data in the following format:

```
SR3.3.1 Event number (1-256), Time of day
(in 24-hour HH:MM format)
```

SR3.3.2 Then, for each lighting bank to be affected by the event, the user must fill out the following data to complete the schedule:

Lighting Bank ID	Action (on, off, or OnLevel) (entered as % of full on in 10% increments). Examples follow.
73	On
34	Off
73	60%

SR3.3.3 When finished entering data, the user must press the End key to signify that the schedule is complete.

- **SR4 Message protocol from Control Switch**. Each button press on the control initiates a single 4-byte message to the CCU. The message protocol is as follows

Address of sending device	Message number	Data	Checksum

The data fields in the message are mapped as follows:

SR4.1 Address 0–254, the logical address of the specific control switch sending the message

SR4.2 Message Number 0–255. Message numbers supported are

1. Normal key press

2. Emergency

3. Held down for the last 0.5 second

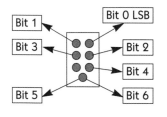

SR4.3 Data field, with each bit corresponding to a specific button on the key switch.

SR4.4 Message Acknowledgment. In reply to the message from the Control Switch, the CCU shall respond with the following message:

[55]	[FF]	Received data	Checksum

where 55 (hex) is the dedicated address of the CCU, FF (hex) is the Acknowledge Message code, Received data returns the data byte received from the CCU, and Checksum is the calculated checksum for the returned message.

All remaining requirements are deleted for brevity.

5.2   Nonfunctional Requirements

5.2.1   Usability

5.2.2   Reliability

- Customers have requested that the HOLIS system operate as close to 100 percent reliable as possible.
- SR5 The CCU must have no defects that can interfere with normal operation of the homeowner's residence.

5.2.3 Performance

5.2.4 Supportability

6 Online User Documentation and Help System Requirements

7 Design Constraints

DC1 Control subsystem design is based on the controller module from the ALSP product line. BIOS should not be modified unless absolutely necessary.

DC2 The use case and supporting infrastructure for the emergency sequence must be validated to the highest reasonable commercial reliability standards.

8 Purchased Components

9 Interfaces

9.1 User Interfaces

9.2 Hardware Interfaces

9.3 Software Interfaces

9.4 Communications Interfaces

10 Licensing Requirements

There are no licensing requirements for the CCU.

11 Legal, Copyright, and Other Notices

- SR6 Include standard corporate copyright notice, corporate logo, and HOLIS 2000 product logo for a minimum of 5 seconds during start-up mode.
- SR7 In steady-state mode, when no programming is active, the display shall show the HOLIS 2000 logo at all times.

12 Applicable Standards

SRS Index

SRS Glossary

SRS Appendix: CCU Subsystem Use-Case Specifications

Team Skill 6: Building the Right System

HOLIS 2000 Sample Test
Case 01: Test Control Light

REVISION HISTORY

Date	Revision	Description	Author
14 April 1999	1.0	First draft	Jack Bigrig
15 April 1999	1.1	Correction to increase/ decrease rate	Jean McBill

Description This test case, used to test instances of the use case Control Light, is used only to test Dim-enabled Control Switch buttons that have been preassigned to a light bank.

Test Case ID	Event Description	Input 1	Input 2	Expected Result
		Basic flow		
2001	Resident presses Control Switch (CS).	Any enabled button	Light was on before button was pressed (tester must record level).	Light is turned off.
2002			Light was off before button was pressed.	Light is turned on to OnLevel.
2003	Resident releases button in less than 1 second.	Light on		Stays off.
2005	Resident releases button in less than 1 second. (This ends path 1 through use case.)	Light off		Stays on at OnLevel.

Test Case ID	Event Description	Input 1	Input 2	Expected Result
2006	Resident presses button again and releases it in less than 1 second.	Same enabled button as in 2003	Light off before	Light is turned on to same illumination level as in 2002.
	Resident presses button again and releases it in less than 1 second.		Light on before	Light is turned off.

Alternative flow

Test Case ID	Event Description	Input 1	Input 2	Expected Result
2007	Button held longer than 1 second.	Enabled button	Light off before	Light turned on. Brightness increases 10% to maximum level for each second held, then decreases 10% for each second held until minimum reached, then increases again. Cycles continuously while held.
2008	Resident releases button.			Brightness held at last reached level.

Note: Run test case multiple times and with different lengths of hold-button time to verify that system is restoring OnLevel properly.

HOLIS 2000 Sample Test Case 02: Test Round-Trip Message Protocol

REVISION HISTORY

Date	Revision	Description	Author
14 April 1999	1.0	First draft	Jean McBill

Description This test case tests the round-trip message protocol between the CCU and CS, the control switch. In so doing, this test case tests the following requirements from the CCU and Control Switch SRS:

CCU SRS	Control Switch SRS
SR4, SR4.1, SR4.2, SR4.3, SR4.4	CSSR88, CSSR91–97, CSSR100–107

(Note to file: The table above can be deleted after the traceability matrix is established. To minimize maintenance, the trace matrix is the only place we will maintain these links.)

Events

Test Case ID	Event Description	Input 1	Input 2	Expected result
5300	Press switch button 0 on Control Switch 1 and initiate message from CS to CCU.	Button only		CCU message-received indicator is lit, and CS message-received indicator is lit.
5301	Examine received message in diagnostic line of CCU display.			[01][01][01][5A]
5302	Examine sent message in CCU display.			[55][FF][01][F7]
5303	Press Control Switch button 0–5 simultaneously and hold for 3 seconds.	All buttons depressed 3+ seconds		CCU message-received indicator is lit. Three messages should be in the message display buffer.
	Examine message 1. (Remainder of test case deleted for brevity.)			[01][01][3F][3C]

VISION DOCUMENT TEMPLATE

Fundamental to the success of a project is a Vision document that identifies and organizes the high-level user needs and features of an application. This document is updated as needed and is shared among team members and other involved personnel. The document template below is intended to be used as a starting point and may be customized according to your organization's needs.

Company Name

Project Name
Vision Document

© 1999 Company Name

REVISION HISTORY

Date	Revision	Description	Author
06/23/99	1.0	Initial version	Author name
mm/dd/yy			

Table of Contents

This section should not be used to state specific requirements. Instead, provide the background and the justification for why the requirements specified in Section 5 are needed.

2.1   User/Market Demographics

Summarize the key market demographics that motivate your product decisions. Describe and position target-market segments. Estimate the market's size and growth by using the number of potential users or the amount of money your customers spend trying to meet needs that your product/enhancement would fulfill. Review major industry trends and technologies. Answer these strategic questions: What is your organization's reputation in these markets? What would you like it to be? How does this product or service support your goals?

2.2   User Profiles

Describe each unique user of the system here. User types can be as divergent as gurus and novices. For example, a guru might need a sophisticated, flexible tool with cross-platform support, whereas a novice might need an easy-to-use and user-friendly tool. A thorough profile should cover the following topics for each type of user:

- Technical background and degree of sophistication
- Key responsibilities
- Deliverables the user produces and for whom
- Trends that make the user's job easier or more difficult
- Problems that interfere with success
- The target user's definition of success and how the user is rewarded

2.3   User Environment

Detail the working environment of the target user. Here are some suggestions.

- How many people are involved in completing the task? Is this changing?
- How long is a task cycle? How much time is spent in each activity? Is this changing?
- Are there any unique environmental constraints: mobile, outdoors, in-flight, and so on?

- Which systems platforms are in use today? Future platforms?
- What other applications are in use? Does your application need to integrate with them?

2.4   Key User Needs

List the key problems or needs as perceived by the user. Clarify the following issues for each problem.

- What are the reasons for this problem?
- How is it solved now?
- What solutions does the user envision?

It is important to understand the relative importance the user places on solving each problem. Ranking and cumulative-voting techniques indicate problems that *must* be solved versus issues they would like addressed.

2.5   Alternatives and Competition

Identify alternatives the user perceives as available. These can include buying a competitor's product, building a homegrown solution, or simply maintaining the status quo. List any known competitive choices that exist or that may become available. Include the major strengths and weaknesses of each competitor as perceived by the end user.

2.5.1   Competitor 1

3   Product Overview

This section provides a high-level view of the product capabilities, interfaces to other applications, and systems configurations. This section usually consists of three subsections, as follows:

3.1   Product Perspective

This subsection should put the product in perspective to other related products and the user's environment. If the product is independent and totally self-contained, state it here. If the product is a component of a larger system, this subsection should relate how these systems interact and should identify the relevant interfaces among the systems. One easy way to display the major components of the larger system, interconnections, and external interfaces is via a block diagram.

3.2   Product Position Statement

Provide an overall statement summarizing, at the highest level, the unique position the product intends to fill in the marketplace. Moore (1991) calls this the product position statement and recommends the following format:

For	(target customer)
Who	(statement of the need or opportunity)
The (product name)	is a (product category)
That	(statement of key benefit, that is, compelling reason to buy)
Unlike	(primary competitive alternative)
Our product	(statement of primary differentiation)

A product position statement communicates the intent of the application and the importance of the project to all concerned personnel.

3.3   Summary of Capabilities

Summarize the major benefits and features the product will provide. For example, a Vision document for a customer support system may use this subsection to address problem documentation, routing, and status reporting—without mentioning the amount of detail each of these functions requires.

Organize the features so that the list is understandable to the customer or to anyone else reading the document for the first time. A simple table listing the key benefits and their supporting features might suffice.

Customer Support System

Customer Benefit	Supporting Features
Benefit 1	Feature 1

3.4   Assumptions and Dependencies

List assumptions that, if changed, will alter the vision for the product. For example, an assumption may state that a specific operating system will be available for the hardware designated for the software product. If the operating system is not available, the vision will need to change.

3.5   Cost and Pricing

For products sold to external customers and for many in-house applications, cost and pricing issues can directly impact the application's definition and implementation. In this section, record any cost and pricing constraints that are relevant. For example, distribution costs (number of diskettes and CD-ROMs, CD mastering) or other cost-of-goods-sold constraints (manuals, packaging) may be material to the project's success or irrelevant, depending on the nature of the application.

4   Feature Attributes

As with requirements, features have attributes that provide additional project information that can be used to evaluate, track, prioritize, and manage the product items proposed for implementation. This section provides suggested attributes for use in your Vision document. This section need describe only the attributes you've chosen and their meaning, so all parties can better understand the context of each feature.

4.1   Status

Set after negotiation and review by the project management team. Status information tracks progress during definition of the project baseline.

- **Proposed:**   Used to describe features that are under discussion but have not yet been reviewed and accepted by the "official channel," such as a working group consisting of representatives from the project team, product management, and user or customer community
- **Approved:**   Capabilities that are deemed useful and feasible and have been approved by the official channel for implementation
- **Incorporated:**   Features incorporated into the product baseline at a specific time

4.2   Priority

Product priorities (benefits) are set by marketing, the product manager, or the business analyst. Ranking features by their relative priority to the end user opens a dialogue with customers, analysts, and members of the development team. Priorities are used in managing scope and determining development priority. One possible prioritization scheme follows.

- **Critical:**   Essential features. Failure to implement means that the system will not meet customer needs. All critical features must be implemented in the release, or the schedule will slip.
- **Important:**   Features important to the effectiveness and efficiency of the system for most applications. The functionality cannot be easily provided in another way. Lack of inclusion of an important feature may affect customer or user satisfaction or even revenue, but release will not be delayed due to lack of any important feature.
- **Useful:**   Features that are useful in less typical applications, will be used less frequently, or for which reasonably efficient workarounds can be achieved. No significant revenue or customer satisfaction impact can be expected if such an item is not included in a release.

4.3   Effort

Set by the development team and used in managing scope and determining development priority. Because some features require more time and resources than others, estimating the number of team or person-weeks, lines of code required, or function points, for example, is the best way to gauge complexity and to set expectations of what can and cannot be accomplished in a given time frame.

4.4   Risk

Set by development team, based on the probability that the project will experience undesirable events, such as cost overruns, schedule delays, or even cancellation. Most project managers find categorizing risks as high, medium, and low sufficient, although finer gradations are possible. Risk can often be assessed indirectly by measuring the uncertainty (range) of the project team's schedule estimate.

4.5   Stability

Set by the analyst and development team, based on the probability that the feature will change or the team's understanding of the feature will change. This information is used to help establish development priorities and to determine those items for which additional elicitation is the appropriate next action.

4.6   Target Release

Records the intended product version in which the feature will first appear. This field can be used to allocate features into a particular baseline release. When the target release is combined with the status field, your team can propose, record, and discuss various features of the release without committing them to development. Only features whose status is set to Incorporated and whose target release is defined will be implemented. When scope management occurs, the target release version number can be increased so the item will remain in the Vision document but will be scheduled for a later release.

4.7   Assigned To

In many projects, features will be assigned to "feature teams" responsible for further elicitation, writing the software requirements, and implementation. This simple list will help everyone on the project team better understand responsibilities.

4.8   Reason

This text field is used to track the source of the requested feature. Features exist for specific reasons. This field records an explanation or a reference to an explanation. For example, the reference might be to a page and line number of a product requirement specification, or to a minute marker on a video of an important customer interview.

5   Product Features

This section documents the product features. Features provide the system capabilities that are necessary to deliver benefits to the users. Each feature provides a service that fulfills a user need. For example, a feature of a problem-tracking system might be the ability to "provide trending reports." Trending reports might in turn support a user need of "better understand the status of my project."

Because the Vision document is reviewed by a wide variety of involved personnel and serves as the basis of agreement, features should be expressed in the user's natural language. Features descriptions should be short and pithy, typically one or two sentences.

To effectively manage application complexity, we recommend that for any new system or increment to an existing system, capabilities be abstracted to a high enough level to result in 25–99 features. These features provide the fundamental basis for product definition, scope management, and project management. Each feature will be expanded in greater detail in the follow-on specifications.

Throughout this section, each feature should be perceivable by users, operators, or other external systems.

5.1   Feature #1

5.2   Feature #2

6   Exemplary Use Cases

Describe a few exemplary use cases, perhaps those that are architecturally significant or those that will most readily help the reader understand how the system is intended to be used.

7   Other Product Requirements

7.1   Applicable Standards

List all standards the product must comply with, such as legal and regulatory (FDA, FCC), communications standards (TCP/IP, ISDN), platform compliance standards (Windows, UNIX), and quality and safety standards (UL, ISO, CMM).

7.2   System Requirements

Define any system requirements necessary to support the application. These may include the supported host operating systems and network platforms, configurations, memory, peripherals, and companion software.

7.3   Licensing and Installation

Licensing and installation issues can also directly impact the development effort. For example, the need to support serializing, password security, or network licensing will create additional system requirements that must be considered in the development effort. Installation requirements may also affect coding or create the need for separate installation software.

7.4   Performance Requirements

Performance issues can include such items as user load factors, bandwidth or communication capacity, throughput, accuracy, reliability, or response times under a variety of loading conditions.

8   Documentation Requirements

This section describes the documentation that must be developed to support successful application deployment.

8.1   User Manual

Describe the purpose and contents of the user manual. Discuss its desired length, level of detail, need for index and glossary, tutorial versus reference manual strategy, and so on. Formatting and printing constraints should also be identified.

8.2   Online Help

Many applications provide an online help system to assist the user. The nature of these systems is unique to application development, as they combine aspects of programming, such as hyperlinks, with aspects of technical writing, such as organization and presentation. Many people have found that the development of an online help system is a project within a project that benefits from up-front scope management and planning activity.

8.3   Installation Guides, Configuration, Read Me File

A document that includes installation instructions and configuration guidelines is important to a full solution offering. Also, a Read Me file is typically included as a standard component. The Read Me file may include a "What's New with This Release" section and a discussion of compatibility issues with earlier releases. Most users also appreciate documentation defining any known bugs and workarounds in the Read Me file.

8.4   Labeling and Packaging

Today's state-of-the-art applications provide a consistent look and feel that begins with product packaging and manifests itself through installation menus, splash screens, help systems, GUI dialogs, and so on. This section defines the needs and types of labeling to be incorporated into the code. Examples include copyright and patent notices, corporate logos, standardized icons and other graphic elements, and so on.

9   Glossary

The glossary defines all terms that are unique to the project. Include any acronyms or abbreviations that may not be understood by users or other readers of this document.

MODERN SRS PACKAGE TEMPLATE

This template provides an outline for a Modern Software Requirements Specification (SRS) Package applying both traditional document-based techniques and use-case modeling. For large systems, optional packaging is recommended at the feature (or other appropriate subsystem grouping) level. For example, if feature-level packaging is used, this specification will include or reference *all* software requirements related to the implementation of that feature. In some cases, a Modern SRS Package may be specified as one or more documents, for which this outline serves as an annotated template starting point. In other cases, the package is a logical construct that may consist of only one physical document, with references to other model- or tool-based physical representations (UML models, use cases, requirements tool repositories, or other) of the data described herein.

Company Name
Division Name, if appropriate

Project Name
Software Requirements Specification
Document Number, if appropriate

© 1999 Company Name

REVISION HISTORY

Date	Revision	Description	Author
mm/dd/yyyy	1.0	Initial version	Author name

TABLE OF CONTENTS

1 Introduction

1.1 Purpose

Specify the purpose of this SRS. The SRS should fully describe the external behavior of the application or subsystem identified, as well as nonfunctional requirements, design constraints, and other factors necessary to provide a complete, comprehensive description of the software requirements.

1.2. Scope

This section provides a brief description of the software application that the SRS applies to, the features or other subsystem grouping, what use-case model(s) it is associated with, and anything else that is affected or influenced by this document.

1.3 References

Provide a list of project-related references or applicable documents that bear on this project.

1.4 Assumptions and Dependencies

This section describes any key technical feasibility, subsystem, or component availability or other project-related assumptions on which the viability of the software described by this SRS may be based.

2 Use-Case Model Survey

This section provides an overview of the use-case model. The survey is used by people interested in the behavior of the system, such as the customer, users, architects, use case authors, designers, use case designers, testers, managers, reviewers, and writers. This section lists for each use case

- The use case name.
- A brief description explaining the use case's function and role in the system.
- A list of actors for the use case. The aggregation of these actors is further defined in the accompanying actor survey.
- Diagram of the use-case model. A diagram of the entire use-case model is included here.

3 Actor Survey

All of the actors mentioned in the use-case model survey are reported here. For each actor, you should list

- The actor's name
- A brief description of the actor

4 Requirements

4.1 Functional Requirements

This section describes the functional requirements of the system for those requirements that are expressed in the natural-language style. For many applications, this may constitute the bulk of the package, and thought should be given to the organization of this section. This section is typically organized by feature, but alternative organization methods, by user or by subsystem, may also be appropriate.

Where application development tools (requirements tools, modeling tools, and so on) are used to capture the functionality, this section of the document will refer to the availability of that data and will indicate the location and name of the tool used to capture the data.

4.2 Nonfunctional Requirements

Most nonfunctional requirements are typically recorded in natural language in this section of the specification. However, nonfunctional requirements may also be included with a specific use case specification.

4.2.1 Usability

This section should include all of those requirements that affect usability. These often include:

- Specify the required training time for normal users and power users to become productive at particular operations.
- Specify measurable task times for typical tasks; alternatively, base usability requirements of the new system on other systems that the users know and like.
- Specify requirements to conform to common usability standards, such as IBM's CUA standards or the GUI standards published by Microsoft for Windows 98.

Refer to the User's Bill of Rights in Chapter 23 for additional guidelines.

4.2.2 Reliability

Requirements for system reliability should be specified here.

- Availability: Specify percent of time available (xx.xx%), hours of use, maintenance access, degraded-mode operations, and so on.
- Mean time between failures (MTBF): This is usually specified in hours but could also be specified in terms of days, months, or years.
- Mean time to repair (MTTR): How long is the system allowed to be out of operation after it has failed?
- Accuracy: Specify precision (resolution) and accuracy (by some known standard) that is required in the system's output.
- Maximum bugs or defect rate: Usually expressed in terms of bugs/KLOC (thousands of lines of code) or bugs per function-point.
- Bugs or defect rate: Categorized in terms of minor, significant, and critical bugs. The requirement(s) must define what is meant by a "critical" bug (such as complete loss of data or complete inability to use certain parts of the functionality of the system).

4.2.3 Performance

The performance characteristics of the system should be outlined in this section. Include specific response times. Where applicable, reference related use cases by name.

- Response time for a transaction (average, maximum)
- Throughput (transactions per second)
- Capacity (the number of customers or transactions the system can accommodate)
- Degradation modes (the acceptable mode of operation when the system has been degraded)
- Resource utilization (memory, disk, communications)

4.2.4 Supportability

This section indicates any requirements that will enhance the supportability or maintainability of the system being built, including coding standards, naming conventions, class libraries, maintenance access, and maintenance utilities.

5   Online User Documentation and Help System Requirements

Describes the requirements, if any, for online user documentation, help systems, help notices, and so on.

6   Design Constraints

This section should indicate any design constraints on the system being built. Design constraints represent design decisions that have been mandated and must be adhered to. Examples include software languages, software process requirements, prescribed use of developmental tools, architectural and design constraints, purchased components, and class libraries.

7   Purchased Components

This section describes any purchased components to be used with the system, any applicable licensing or usage restrictions, and any associated compatibility/interoperability or interface standards.

8   Interfaces

This section defines the interfaces that must be supported by the application. This section should contain adequate specificity, protocols, ports, and logical addresses, and so on, so that the software can be developed and verified against the interface requirements.

8.1   User Interfaces

Describe the user interfaces that are to be implemented by the software.

8.2   Hardware Interfaces

Define any hardware interfaces that are to be supported by the software, including logical structure, physical addresses, and expected behavior.

8.3   Software Interfaces

Describe software interfaces to other components of the software system. These may be purchased components, components reused from another application, or components being developed for subsystems outside of the scope of this SRS but with which this software application must interact.

8.4   Communications Interfaces

Describe any communications interfaces to other systems or devices, such as local area networks or remote serial devices.

9   Licensing Requirements

Define any licensing enforcement requirements or other usage restriction requirements that are to be exhibited by the software.

10   Legal, Copyright, and Other Notices

Describe any necessary legal disclaimers, warranties, copyright notices, patent notice, wordmark, trademark, or logo compliance issues for the software.

11   Applicable Standards

Describe by reference any standards (and the specific sections of any such standards) that apply to the system being described. For example, this could include legal, quality, and regulatory standards, as well as industry standards for usability, interoperability, internationalization, operating system compliance, and so on.

Index

The index is provided to assist the reader in locating key concepts and topics that occur throughout the document.

Glossary

Describe any terms that are unique to this application context and any definitions, acronyms, abbreviations, or other project or company-specific shorthand that is necessary for an understanding of this document and the application.

Appendixes

You should insert appendixes here as appropriate. Note that the following template appendix is provided specifically to allow you to record use cases. Feel free to insert as many appendixes as you need.

APPENDIX: USE CASE SPECIFICATIONS

This appendix contains references the elaborated use cases for the system. The following template is provided as a starting point.

REVISION HISTORY

Date	Issue	Description	Author
dd/mmm/yy	x.x	Details	Author name

Note that the revision history is provided for each use case included in the appendixes. The current revision history block should be on the first page of each use case appendix.

TABLE OF CONTENTS

Normally, a use case specification will not be long enough to warrant a table of contents for the use case. But this element may be required if the use case presents unusual problems in finding portions of the specification.

USE CASE NAME

BRIEF DESCRIPTION

The role and purpose of the use case. A single paragraph should suffice for this description.

FLOW OF EVENTS

Basic Flow

This use case starts when the actor does something. An actor always initiates use cases. The use case should describe what the actor does and what the system does in response. The use case should be phrased in the form of a dialogue between the actor and the system.

The use case should describe what happens inside the system but not how or why. If information is exchanged, be specific about what is passed back and forth. For example, it is not very illuminating to say that the actor enters customer information; it is better to say that the actor enters the customer's name and address. A glossary is often useful to keep the complexity of the use case manageable; you may want to define customer information there, to keep the use case from drowning in details.

Simple alternatives may be presented within the text of the use case. If it takes only a few sentences to describe what happens when there is an alternative, do it directly within the flow-of-events section. If the alternative flows are more complex, use a separate section. For example, an alternative flow describes how to describe more complex alternatives.

A picture is sometimes worth a thousand words, although there is no substitute for clean, clear prose. If doing so improves clarity, feel free to include graphical depictions of user interfaces, process flows, or other figures into the use case. If a technical method, such as an activity diagram is useful to present a complex decision process, by all means use it! Similarly for state-dependent behavior, a state-transition diagram often clarifies the behavior of a system better than do pages upon pages of text. Use the right presentation medium for your problem, but be wary of using terminology, notation, or figures that your audience may not understand. Remember that your purpose is to clarify, not to obscure.

Alternative Flows

1. **First alternative flow:** More complex alternatives should be described in a separate section, which is referred to in the basic flow-of-events section. Think of the alternative flow sections as *alternative behavior*; each alternative flow represents alternative behavior (many times, because of exceptions that occur in the main flow). They may be as long as necessary to describe the events associated with the alternative behavior. When an alternative flow ends, the events of the main flow of events are resumed unless otherwise stated.

Alternative flows may, in turn, be broken down into subsections.

2. **Second alternative flow:** There may be, and most likely will be, a number of alternative flows in a use case. Keep each alternative separate, to improve clarity. Using alternative flows improves the readability of the use case, as well as prevents use cases from being *decomposed* into hierarchies of use cases. Keep in mind that use cases are just textual descriptions and that their main purpose is to document the behavior of a system in a clear, concise, and understandable way.

Special Requirements

These are typically nonfunctional requirements that are specific to a use case but are not easily or naturally specified in the text of the use case's event flow. Examples of special requirements include legal and regulatory requirements, application standards, and quality attributes of the system to be built, including *usability, reliability, performance, or supportability requirements.* Other requirements, such as operating systems and environments, compatibility requirements, and design constraints, should also be captured in this section.

   1. First special requirement

Preconditions

Precondition of a use case is the state of the system that must be present prior to a use case being performed.

   1. Precondition 1

Postconditions

Postcondition of a use case is a list of possible states the system can be in immediately after a use case has finished.

   1. Postcondition 1

Extension Points

Extension points of the use case.

   1. Name of extension point

Definition of the location of the extension point in the flow of events.

REQUIREMENTS MANAGEMENT IN THE SEI-CMM AND WITHIN ISO 9000

Requirements Management in SEI-CMM

In November 1986, the Software Engineering Institute (SEI), at Carnegie-Mellon University, began developing a process maturity framework to help developers improve their software process. In September 1987, the SEI released a brief description of the process maturity framework, later amplified in Watts Humphrey's *Managing the Software Process* (1989). By 1991, this framework had evolved into what has become known as version 1.0 of the Capability Maturity Model, or CMM. In 1993, version 1.1 of the CMM was released (SEI 1993). Version 1.1 defines five levels of software maturity for an organization and provides a framework for moving from one level to the next, as illustrated in Figure D–1. The CMM guides developers through activities designed to help an organization improve its software process, with the goal of achieving repeatability, controllability, and measurability.

Despite the ongoing debate and controversy about the advantages and disadvantages of the CMM, an accumulating body of data shows that adherence to the CMM and corresponding improvements in software quality have significantly lowered the cost of application development within many companies. By now, the CMM has been in use by many organizations long enough so that meaningful and positive return-on-investment statistics are appearing. These payoffs should, ideally, provide results in productivity and significant reduction in time to market. In an era of increasingly competitive environments, any improvements to software productivity cannot be ignored.

The CMM provides a framework for process improvement that consists of "key process areas," or organizational activities that have been found, through experience, to be influential in various aspects of the development process and resultant software quality. Table D–1 identifies the key process areas of each of the five levels of the CMM. (The reason we're discussing all

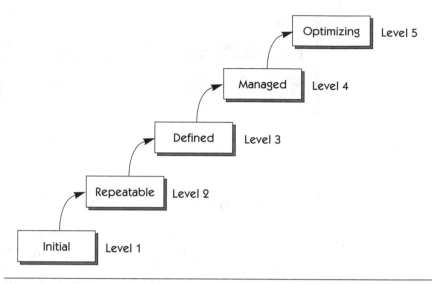

Figure D–1   CMM maturity levels

of this at length in this book is that Table D–1 shows that the *first* key process area that must be addressed to move from level 1 to level 2 is requirements management.)

The CMM summarizes the process area of requirements management as follows: *The purpose of requirements management is to establish a common understanding between the customer and the software team of the customer's requirements.*

This common understanding serves as the basis of agreement between the customer and the development team and, as such, is the central document that defines and controls the activity to follow. Requirements are controlled to establish a *baseline* for software engineering management use. Throughout the CMM, guidelines specify that all activities, plans, schedules, and software work products are to be developed and modified as necessary to be consistent with the requirements allocated to software. In this manner, the CMM moves the organization toward an integrated view wherein technical requirements must be kept consistent with project plans and activities. To support this process, software requirements must be documented and reviewed by software managers and affected groups, including representatives of the customer and user community.

The software requirements specification serves as a central project document, a defining element with relationships to other elements of the project

Table D–1 Levels of the CMM with key process areas

Level	Key Process Areas
1. Initial: Ad hoc, even chaotic; success depends solely on individual heroics and efforts.	Not applicable
2. Repeatable: Basic project management to track application functionality and cost and schedule.	Requirements management Software project planning Software project tracking and oversight Software subcontract management Software quality assurance Software configuration management
3. Defined: The process for management and engineering is documented, standardized, and integrated. All projects use an approved, tailored version of the process.	Organization process focus Organization process definition Training program Integrated software management Software product engineering Intergroup coordination Peer reviews
4. Managed: Detailed measures of the software process and software quality metrics are collected. Both process and software products are understood and controlled.	Quantitative process management Software quality management
5. Optimizing: Continuous process improvement is enabled by use of metrics and from piloting innovative ideas and technologies.	Defect prevention Technology change management Process change management

plan. The requirements include both technical (the behavior of the application) and nontechnical (other project requirements, including schedule, budget, and other) requirements. In addition, acceptance criteria, which are the tests and measures that will be used to validate that the software meets its requirements, must be established and documented.

In order to accomplish these objectives and to demonstrate compliance with the CMM process area of requirements management, adequate resources and funding must be provided for managing requirements. Members of the software engineering group and other affected groups should be trained to perform their requirements-management activities. Training should cover methods and standards, as well as training activities designed to create an understanding on the part of the engineering team as to the unique nature and problems of the application domain.

The CMM further specifies that requirements should be managed and controlled and should serve as the basis for software plans, work products, and activities. Changes to the requirements should be reviewed and incorporated into the project plans, and the impact of change must be assessed and negotiated with the affected groups. In order to provide feedback on the results of these activities and in order to verify compliance, the CMM provides guidelines for measurements and analysis, as well as activities for verifying implementation. Suggested measures include

- Status of each of the allocated requirements
- Change activity of the requirements, cumulative number of changes
- Total number of changes that are open, proposed, approved, and incorporated into the baseline

One of the most enlightened aspects of the CMM is its understanding that requirements management is not simply a "document-it-up-front-and-go" process of the sort often prescribed in the waterfall methodologies of the 1970s. With the CMM, requirements are living entities at the very center of the application development process. Not surprisingly, the process of effective requirements management appears at virtually all levels of the process model and within many key process areas. As an organization moves to level 3 on the CMM scale, the focus is on managing software activities based on defined and documented standard practices. Key process areas for level 3 include organization process focus, organization process definition, training program, integrated software management, software product engineering, intergroup coordination, and peer reviews. The software product engineering key practice is designed to cause an organization to integrate all software engineering activities to produce high-quality software products effectively and efficiently. The software engineering key practice states that the "*software requirements are developed, maintained, documented, and verified by systematically analyzing the requirements according to the project's defined software process*" (SEI 1993).

The analysis process is necessary to ensure that the requirements make sense and are clearly stated, complete and unambiguous, consistent with one another, and testable. Various analysis techniques are suggested, including simulations, modeling, scenario generation, and functional and object-oriented decomposition. The results of this process will be a better understanding of the requirements of the application, which are then reflected in revised requirements documentation. In addition, the group responsible for system and acceptance testing also analyzes the requirements to ensure testability.

The resulting software requirements document is reviewed and approved by the affected parties to make sure that the points of view represented by these parties are included in the requirements. Reviewers include customers and end users, project management, and software test personnel. In order to manage change in a controlled way, the CMM also calls for placing the software requirements document under configuration management control.

Another important concept in the CMM is *traceability*. Under the CMM, all worthwhile software work products are documented, and the documentation must be maintained and readily available. The software requirements, design, code, and test cases are traced to the source from which they were derived and to the products of the subsequent engineering activity. Requirements traceability provides a means of analyzing impact before a change is made, as well as a way to determine what components are affected when processing a change. Traceability also provides the mechanism for determining the adequacy of test coverage.

All approved changes are tracked to completion. The documentation that traces the allocated requirements is also managed and controlled. Measurements are made to determine the functionality and the quality of the software products and to determine the status of the software activity. Example measurements include

- Status of each allocated requirement throughout the lifecycle
- Change activity of the allocated requirements
- Allocated requirements summarized by category

Finally, the CMM recognizes that change is an integral part of software activity in any development project. In place of frozen specifications, we instead strive for a stable baseline of requirements that are well elicited, documented, and placed into systems that provide support for managing change. Specifically, the CMM requires that

- As understanding of the software improves, changes to the software work products and activities are proposed, analyzed, and incorporated as appropriate. Where changes to the requirements are needed, they are approved and incorporated before any work products or activities are changed.

- The project determines the impact of change before the change is made.
- Changes are negotiated and communicated to the affected groups.
- All changes are tracked to completion.

In summary, the CMM provides a comprehensive view of the activities that must be applied to improve software quality and to increase productivity. Requirements management is an integral part of this process, wherein requirements serve as living entities that are at the center of development activity. Once elicited, requirements are documented and managed with the same degree of care that we provide to our code work products. This process puts the team in control of its project and helps team members manage both the project and its scope. Lastly, actively managing changing requirements keeps the project under control and helps ensure the reliable, repeatable production of high-quality software products.

Although all of this provides an important "validation" of the concept of requirements management, along with some high-level advice for inserting requirements-oriented processes into the development lifecycle, it doesn't tell us how to *do* requirements management. The detailed activities of eliciting, organizing, documenting, and managing requirements are the subject of this book, and these activities have been influenced by the CMM framework.

Requirements Management in ISO 9000

For the past decade or so, a number of organizations around the world have been using a series of quality management standards known as ISO 9000 to improve operating efficiency and productivity and to reduce costs. ISO 9000 has been adopted by the European Community as EN29000 and has become an important fact for international trade; organizations wishing to do business in Europe, for example, often have to demonstrate ISO 9000 certification. The certification requires an on-site assessment by an ISO-approved assessor; the companies that pass realize that they will be reassessed periodically to maintain their certification.

ISO 9000 consists of five quality standards:

1. ISO 9000: Guidelines for selection and use
2. ISO 9001: Quality assurance guidelines for design, development, production, installation, and servicing

3. ISO 9002: Quality assurance guidelines for those companies involved primarily in manufacturing
4. ISO 9003: Quality assurance guidelines for those companies involved primarily in distribution
5. ISO 9004: A guide for the application of various elements of a quality management system

Within these documents, ISO 9000-3 provides guidelines for the application of the ISO 9001 "design and development" standard for the development, supply, and maintenance of software. Part 5.3 of that document stipulates *"In order to proceed with development, the supplier should have a complete, unambiguous set of functional requirements."* The same document also stipulates that the information thus provided to the supplier (which we've described as the "developer" throughout this appendix) should include all performance, safety, reliability, security, and privacy requirements that collectively determine whether the delivered system is acceptable.

Like the CMM, ISO 9000 standards have been the subject of considerable debate, particularly in U.S. organizations that worry about the possibility of the standards degenerating into a bureaucratic demand for excessive documentation. Our purpose here is not to endorse or attack ISO 9000; like all such "common sense" concepts, it can be used or misused. But to the extent that many organizations are adopting ISO 9000 because they think it's a good idea or because it's a necessary prerequisite for doing business in Europe and other parts of the world, it's interesting to note the emphasis that the standard puts on requirements management. For example, ISO 9000 emphasizes the need for *mutual cooperation* between the customer and the developer for software systems; specifically, it calls for

- Assignment of people from both groups to be responsible for establishing requirements
- Establishment of methods and procedures for agreement and approval of changes to the requirements
- Efforts to prevent misunderstandings of the requirements
- Establishment of procedures for recording and reviewing the results of discussions about the requirements

Although it's easy to dismiss all of this as "obvious" and "common sense," remember what happens during the assessment required to achieve certification. An assessor will visit the organization and ask, "Where are your methods and procedures for approving changes to the requirements? Show them to me in writing. Let me visit some project teams and make some spot-checks to ensure that the procedures are actually being followed."

ISO 9000 also stipulates that the input to the development phase of a project—the lifecycle activity in which technical design and programming usually take place—should be defined and documented. These "inputs" are, of course, *requirements*, and ISO 9000 states that the requirements should be defined so that their achievement can be verified. ISO 9000 also calls for processes to ensure that incomplete, ambiguous, or conflicting requirements will be resolved in an orderly fashion. One of the important consequences of this kind of emphasis on requirements at the beginning of a development effort is that it helps ensure that, if the technical design and development efforts are carried out in a disciplined fashion, it will be possible to produce a system that meets specifications, or requirements, rather than relying on frantic testing and validation activities at the end of the lifecycle for assurance of quality.

Like the SEI-CMM, ISO 9000 doesn't tell us *how* to do requirements management. The fact that we have an official process that forces us to choose an "official" user representative and an "official" developer to discuss the requirements of a system obviously doesn't guarantee that these two individuals will be capable of identifying and documenting the correct requirements. But armed with the procedures and techniques described in other chapters of this book, we should be able to create a comprehensive requirements management approach that will satisfy the most demanding of ISO 9000 assessors, as well as CMM assessors.

REQUIREMENTS MANAGEMENT IN THE RATIONAL UNIFIED PROCESS

With Philippe Kruchten and Leslee Probasco

T his book provides an overview of a requirements management software best practice. The Team Skills described in the book, along with the requirements prescription provided in Chapter 35, will help your team start down the right path on your next project. However, to better ensure success, some way is needed to reinforce and to support the application of these best practices throughout the course of development. This must be accomplished in a way that integrates requirements management smoothly with other software development activities, including design, implementation, test, and deployment. Ideally, this information would be provided online, in the team's desktop environment. Further, it would be prescriptive in describing which team members performed which activities and when they needed to produce the outputs of these activities for other team members to use. This is the role of a *software development process*. In this appendix, we will look at an example of an industrial software development process, the Rational Unified Process, and see how the skills we have presented map into it.

The Rational Unified Process, a software engineering process developed and commercialized by the Rational Software Corporation (1999), captures some of the best practices of the industry for software development. It is use case driven and takes an iterative approach to the software development life cycle. It embraces object-oriented techniques, and many of its activities focus on the development of *models*, all described using the UML. The Unified Process is a descendant of Objectory (Jacobson, Christerson, and Jonsson 1992) and of the Rational Approach. It has benefited over the years from the contributions of many industry experts, including the authors of this book and the teams from Requisite, Inc.; SQA, Inc.; and many others.

As a product, the Rational Unified Process is a Web-enabled guidebook that brings process guidance directly onto the desktop of the software developers. It is composed of approximately 2,800 files presenting an HTML-based interactive desktop coach, which can be tailored to suit the needs of a wide range of software development organizations.

Although it uses slightly different terminology from that presented in this book, the Rational Unified Process provides an effective implementation of the requirements management best practices offered in this book, in a form that can be readily applied by the software development team.

Structure of the Rational Unified Process[1]

A process describes *who* is doing *what*, *how*, and *when*. The Rational Unified Process is described using four key modeling elements:

- Workers, the "who"
- Activities, the "how"
- Artifacts, the "what"
- Workflows, the "when"

(See Figure E–1.) A *worker* defines the behavior and responsibilities of an individual or a group of individuals working together as a team. The behav-

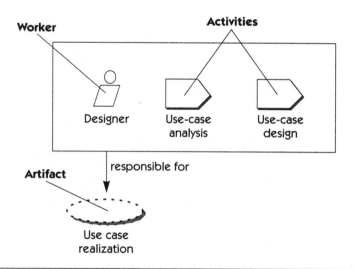

Figure E–1   Worker, activities, and artifact

---

1. This section is extracted from Philippe Kruchten, *The Rational Unified Process—An Introduction* (Reading, MA: Addison Wesley Longman, 1999), pp. 35–48, and reproduced with permission from the publisher.

ior is expressed in terms of *activities* the worker performs, and each worker is associated with a set of cohesive activities. The responsibilities of each worker are expressed in relation to certain *artifacts*, or work products, that the worker creates, modifies, or controls.

Workflows allow the grouping of activities into meaningful sets that provide some result for the development organization and show how various workers interact. Beyond these four main concepts, the Rational Unified Process introduces specific techniques in the form of *guidelines* mapped to activities, *templates* for major artifacts, and *tool mentors*, that is, guidance on how to proceed using software development tools.

Requirements Management in the Rational Unified Process

The best practice of requirements management is captured in the Rational Unified Process in the requirements *workflow*, one of nine core workflows described in the process. This requirements workflow produces and updates the following *artifacts* (see Figure E–2):

- *Stakeholder requests*, the collection of any type of requests, including formal change requests, needs, or other input from any stakeholders, during the life cycle of the project, that might affect the product requirements
- The *Vision document*, which summarizes the overall vision of the system under consideration: main characteristics, major features, key stakeholder needs, and key services provided
- The *use-case model*, the organized set of use cases that constitute the bulk of the requirements
- The *supplementary specification*, which captures any requirements that cannot be tied directly to any specific use case, in particular, many of the nonfunctional requirements and design constraints

The last two artifacts constitute collectively one form of what in this book we have called the Modern Software Requirements Specification Package.

Other artifacts are also developed as a result of this workflow, including

- *Requirements attributes*, a repository of information containing requirements-related information that is used to track requirements status and to maintain traceability to other project elements

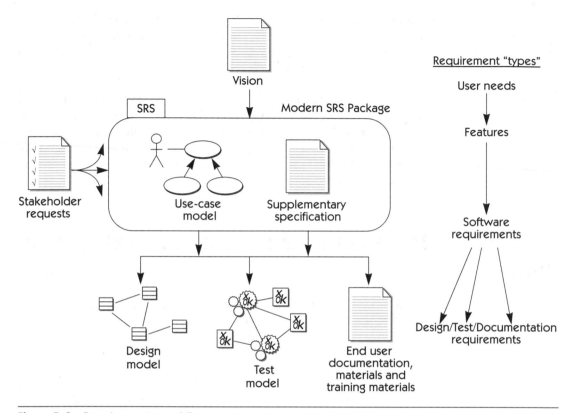

Figure E–2   Requirements workflow

- *Use case storyboards*, systematically derived from the essential use cases involving human actors to model the user interface and to elaborate some of the usability requirements
- *User interface prototypes*, developed to get feedback from the various stakeholders
- A project's *glossary*, which captures and defines the terms used in the project domain

Workers involved in this workflow include

- *Stakeholder, customer, end user,* or whoever within the development organization represents the role of anyone providing input to the requirements process (it is often the marketing manager who plays this role in some companies)
- *System analyst,* who leads and coordinates requirements elicitation and use-case modeling by outlining the system's functionality and

delimiting the system: for example, establishing what actors and use cases exist and how they interact, along with nonfunctional requirements and design constraints

- *Use case specifier,* who details the specification of a part of the system's functionality by describing the requirements aspect of one or several use cases
- *User interface (UI) designer,* who develops use case storyboards and UI prototypes and involves other stakeholders in their evaluation
- *Requirements reviewer* (a role usually played by several team members), who plans and conducts the formal review of the use-case model and other requirements specified in the supplementary specifications

The description of the requirements workflow activities and steps is organized in the Rational Unified Process into six smaller workflows (called workflow details) which directly parallel the six team skills described in this book.

Analyze the Problem

As shown in Figure E–3, the purpose of this workflow detail is to

- Produce a *Vision* document for the project
- Agree on system features and goals

This workflow detail may be revisited several times during *inception* and *early elaboration*. As *requests from stakeholders* are more clearly understood, both business process solutions and technical solutions will evolve.

The primary activity in this workflow is to develop the *Vision* document, which identifies the high-level user or customer view of the system to be built. In the Vision document, initial requirements are expressed as key features the system must possess in order to solve the most critical problems. The features should be assigned *attributes,* such as rationale, relative value or priority, source of request, and so on, so that dependencies can begin to be managed. As the *vision* develops, the *system analyst* identifies users and system interfaces—the *actors* of the system.

Understand Stakeholders' Needs

The purpose of this workflow detail is to elicit and to collect information from *stakeholders* of the project (Figure E–4). The collected *stakeholder requests* can be regarded as a "wish list" that will be used as primary input to

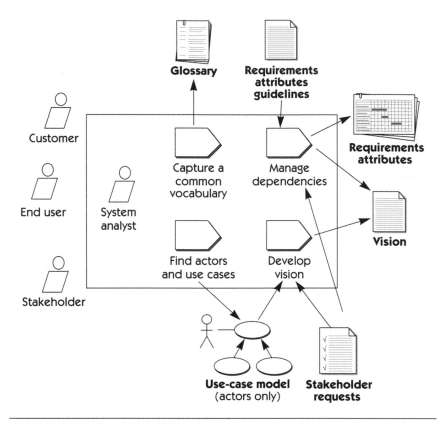

Figure E–3   Analyze the problem

defining the *use-case model, use cases, and supplementary specifications.* Typically, this is performed only during iterations in the *inception* and *elaboration* phases.

The key activity is to *elicit stakeholder requests.* The primary outputs are collection(s) of prioritized *stakeholder requests,* which enable refinement of the *Vision* document, as well as a better understanding of the *requirements attributes.* Also, during this workflow, you may start discussing the system in terms of its *use cases* and *actors.* Another important output is an updated *glossary* of terms to facilitate a common vocabulary among team members.

Define the System

The purpose of this workflow detail (see Figure E–5) is to

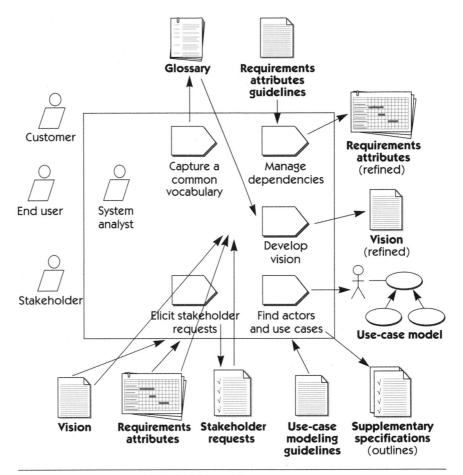

Figure E–4   Understand stakeholder needs

- Align the project team in its understanding of the system
- Perform a high-level analysis on the results of collecting *stakeholder requests*
- More formally document the results in models and documents

Typically, this is performed only in iterations during the inception and elaboration phases.

Problem analysis and *understanding stakeholder needs* create early iterations of key system definitions, including the *Vision* document, a first outline to the *use-case model*, and the *requirements attributes*. In defining the system, you will

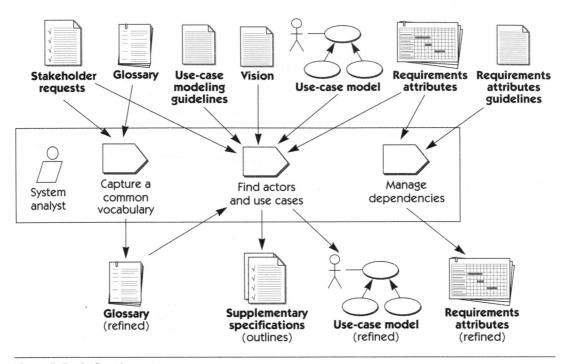

Figure E–5   Define the system

focus on identifying *actors* and *use cases* more completely and adding *supplementary specifications*.

Manage the Scope of the System

The purpose of this workflow detail (Figure E–6) is to

- Define input to the selection of *requirements* to be included in the current iteration
- Define the set of *features* and *use cases* (or scenarios) that represent some significant, central functionality
- Define which *requirement attributes* and *traceabilities* to maintain

Although project scope should be managed continuously, the better understanding of system functionality obtained from identifying most *actors, use cases,* and *supplementary specifications* will allow the *system analyst* to apply priority, effort, cost, risk values, and so on, to *requirements attributes* more accurately and will enable the *architect* to identify the *architecturally significant use*

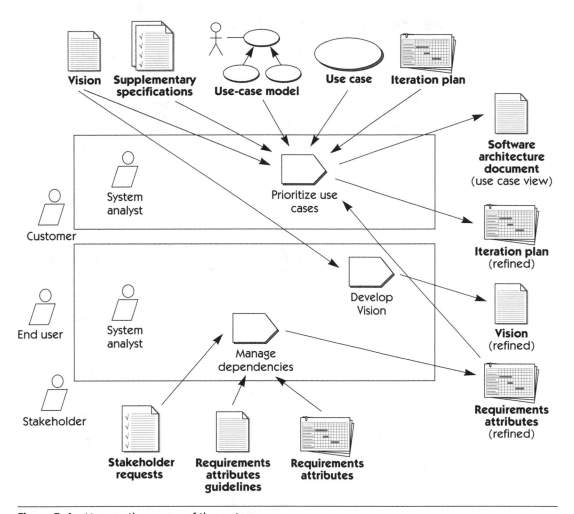

Figure E–6   Manage the scope of the system

cases. An input to managing scope not seen in other workflow details of the requirements workflow is the *iteration plan*, developed in parallel by *project and development management*. The iteration plan defines the number and frequency of iterations planned for the release. The scope of the project defined in managing scope will have a significant impact on the *iteration plan*, as the highest-risk elements within scope will be planned for early iterations. Other important outputs from managing scope include the initial iteration of the *software architecture document* and a revised *Vision document* that reflects *system analyst's* and *key stakeholders'* better understanding of system functionality and project resources.

Refine the System Definition

The purpose of this workflow detail (Figure E–7) is to further refine the *requirements* in order to

- Describe the *use case's* flow of events in detail.
- Detail *supplementary specifications*
- Model and prototype the user interfaces

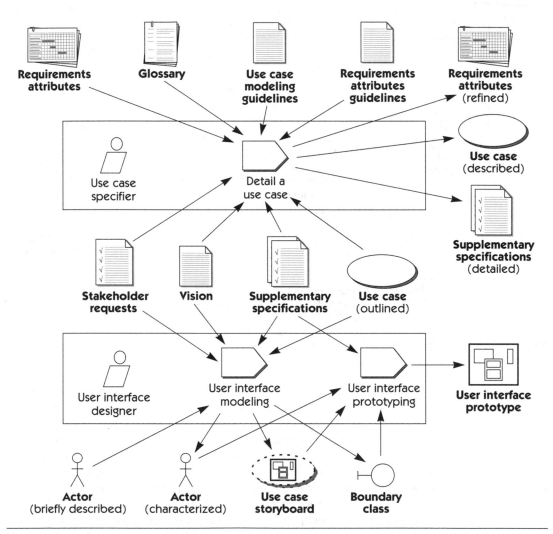

Figure E–7   Refine the system definition

Refining the system begins with *use cases* outlined, *actors* described at least briefly, and a revised understanding of project scope reflected in reprioritized *features* in the *vision* and believed to be achievable by fairly firm budgets and dates. The output of this workflow is more in-depth understanding of system functionality expressed in detailed *use cases*, revised and *detailed supplementary specifications*, and user interface elements.

Manage Changing Requirements

The purpose of this workflow (Figure E–8) detail is to

- Structure the *use-case model*
- Set up appropriate *requirements attributes and traceabilities*
- Formally verify that the results of the requirements workflow conform to the customer's view of the system

Changes to *requirements* naturally impact the *models* produced in the *analysis and design workflow*, as well as the *test model* created as part of the *test workflow*. *Traceability* relationships between requirements identified in the *manage dependency* activity of this workflow and others are the key to understanding these impacts.

Another important concept is the tracking of requirement history. By capturing the nature and rationale of requirements changes, *reviewers* (in this case, the role is played by anyone on the software project team whose work is affected by the change) receive the information needed to respond to the change properly.

Process Integration

The Rational Unified Process defines flows of information, transformations, guidelines, heuristics, and formal traceability links that tie these artifacts to other software development activities and artifacts. For example, the requirements artifact may be tied upstream in the process to a business model, constructed also using object-oriented technology and business use cases, and downstream to such artifacts as an analysis model or a design model, as well as to test cases and user documentation (see Figure E–2).

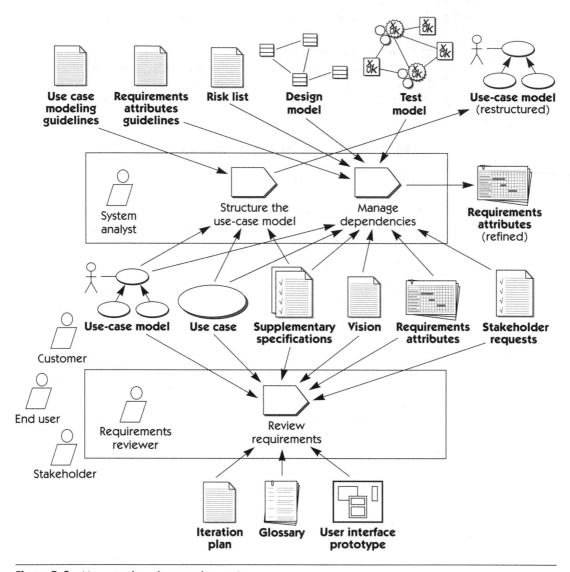

Figure E–8 Manage changing requirements

Software engineering tools support many of the best practices presented in the Rational Unified Process—from requirements management and visual modeling to report generation, configuration management, and automated testing. Tool mentors are also included, which provide detailed descriptions on how Rational's software tools can be used to support particular steps and activities within the process.

BIBLIOGRAPHY

Boehm, Barry W. *Software Engineering Economics*. Englewood Cliffs, NJ: Prentice-Hall, 1981.

———. "A Spiral Model of Software Development and Enhancement." *IEEE Computer* 21, 15 (May 1988), pp. 61–72.

Boehm, Barry W., and Philip N. Papaccio. "Understanding and Controlling Software Costs." *IEEE Transactions on Software Engineering* 14, 10 (October 1988), pp. 1462–1473.

Booch, Grady, James Rumbaugh, and Ivar Jacobson. *The Unified Modeling Language User Guide*. Reading, MA: Addison Wesley Longman, 1999.

Brooks, Frederick P. Jr. *The Mythical Man Month: Essays on Software Engineering*. Reading, MA: Addison-Wesley, 1975.

Davis, Alan M. *Software Requirements: Objects, Functions, and States*. Englewood Cliffs, NJ: Prentice-Hall, 1993.

———. "Software Prototyping." In *Advances in Computers*, Vol. 40, pp. 39–62. Chestnut Hill, MA: Academic Press, 1995.

———. *201 Principles of Software Development*. New York: McGraw-Hill, 1995.

———. "Achieving Quality in Software Requirements." *Software Quality Professional* 1, 3 (June 1999), pp. 37–44.

Dorfmann, Merlin, and Richard H. Thayer. *Standards, Guidelines, and Examples of System and Software Requirements Engineering*. Los Alamitos, CA: IEEE Computer Society Press, 1990.

European Software Process Improvement Training Initiative. *User Survey Report*. 1995.

FDA. "Medical Devices; Current Good Manufacturing Practice (CGMP) Final Rule; Quality System Regulation." *Federal Register* 61, 195 (7 October 1996), Subpart C, pp. 52657–52658.

FDA/ODE. "ODE Guidance for the Content of Premarket Submission for Medical Devices Containing Software." (Draft 1.3, 12 August 1996).

Fisher, Roger, William Ury, and Bruce Patton. *Getting to Yes: Negotiating Agreement without Giving In.*, 2nd ed. New York: Penguin Books, 1983.

Gause, D., and G. Weinberg. *Exploring Requirements: Quality Before Design*. New York: Dorset House Publishing, 1989.

Grady, R. *Practical Software Metrics for Project Management and Process Improvement*. Englewood Cliffs, NJ: Prentice-Hall, 1992.

Humphrey, Watts S. *Managing the Software Process*. Reading, MA: Addison-Wesley, 1989.

IEEE. *IEEE Standards Collection, Software Engineering*. IEEE Standards Collection, Software Engineering. New York, NY: IEEE, 1994.

International Council on Systems Engineering (INCOSE). "An Identification of Pragmatic Principles—Final Report." INCOSE WMA Chapter, 1993. Available at www.incose.org/workgrps/practice.html.

———. 1999. Available at www.incose.org.

Jacobson, Ivar, Grady Booch, and James Rumbaugh. *The Unified Software Development Process*. Reading, MA: Addison Wesley Longman, 1999.

Jacobson, Ivar, Magnus Christerson, Patrik Jonsson, and Gunnar Övergaard. *Object-Oriented Software Engineering: A Use Case Driven Approach*. Harlow, Essex, England: Addison Wesley Longman, 1992.

Jacobson, Ivar, Maria Ericsson, and Agneta Jacobson. *The Object Advantage: Business Process Reengineering with Object Technology*. Wokingham, England: Addison-Wesley, 1995.

Jones, Capers. "Revitalizing Software Project Management." *American Programmer* 6, 7 (June 1994), pp. 3–12.

Karat, Claire-Marie. "Guaranteeing Rights for the User." *Communications of the ACM* 41, 12 (December 1998), p. 29.

Kruchten, Philippe. "The 4+1 View of Architecture." *IEEE Software* 12, 6 (November 1995), pp. 45–50.

———. *The Rational Unified Process: An Introduction.* Reading, MA: Addison Wesley Longman, 1999.

Moore, Geoffrey A. *Crossing the Chasm: Marketing and Selling Technology Products to Mainstream Customers.* New York, NY: HarperCollins, 1991.

Rational Software Corporation. "Rational Unified Process V5.1." Cupertino, CA: Rational Software Corporation, 1999.

Rechtin, Eberhardt, and Mark W. Maier. *The Art of Systems Architecting.* Boca Raton, FL: CRC Press, 1997.

Royce, Walker. *Software Project Management: A Unified Approach.* Reading MA: Addison Wesley Longman, 1998.

Royce, Winston W. "Managing the Development of Large Software Systems: Concepts and Techniques." *Proceedings of WESCON*, August 1970. Also available in *ICSE9 Proceedings, IEEE-CS*, 1987.

Rumbaugh, James, Ivar Jacobson, and Grady Booch. *The Unified Modeling Language Reference Manual.* Reading, MA: Addison Wesley Longman, 1998.

Scharer, Laura. "Pinpointing Requirements." In *Software Requirements Engineering.* Los Alamitos, CA: IEEE Computer Society Press, 1990. (Article reprinted from *Datamation*, 1981.)

Schneider, Geri, and Jason P. Winters. *Applying Use Cases: A Practical Guide.* Reading, MA: Addison Wesley Longman, 1998.

SEI. *Capability Maturity Model for Software.* Version 1.1, Document No. CMU/SEI-93-TR-25, ESC-TR-93-178. Pittsburgh, PA: Carnegie-Mellon University Software Engineering Institute, 1993.

Shaw, Mary, and David Garlan. *Software Architecture: Perspective on an Emerging Discipline*. Upper Saddle River, NJ: Prentice-Hall, 1996.

Snyder, Terry, and Ken Shumate. "Kaizen Project Management." *American Programmer* 5, 10 (December 1992), pp. 12–22.

The Standish Group. "Charting the Seas of Information Technology— Chaos." The Standish Group International, 1994.

Weinberg, Gerald. *The Psychology of Computer Programming*. New York: Van Nostrand Reinhold, 1971.

———. "Just Say No! Improving the Requirements Process." *American Programmer* 8, 10 (October 1995), pp. 19–23.

Wood, Bill J. and Julia W. Ermes. "Applying Hazard Analysis to Medical Devices" (Part I) *Medical Device & Diagnostic Industry Magazine* 15, 1 (January 1993), pp. 79–83.

———. "Applying Hazard Analysis to Medical Devices" (Part II). *Medical Device & Diagnostic Industry Magazine* 15, 3 (March 1993), pp. 58–64.

Index

Object Solutions
Managing the Object-Oriented Project
Grady Booch
Addison-Wesley Object Technology Series

Object Solutions is a direct outgrowth of Grady Booch's experience with object-oriented projects in development around the world. This book focuses on the development process and is the perfect resource for developers and managers who want to implement object technologies for the first time or refine their existing object-oriented development practice. Drawing upon his knowledge of strategies used in both successful and unsuccessful projects, the author offers pragmatic advice for applying object technologies and controlling projects effectively.

0-8053-0594-7 • Paperback • 336 pages • ©1996

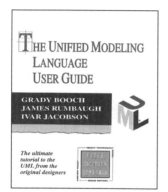

The Unified Modeling Language User Guide
Grady Booch, James Rumbaugh, and Ivar Jacobson
Addison-Wesley Object Technology Series

The Unified Modeling Language User Guide is a two-color introduction to the core eighty percent of the Unified Modeling Language, approaching it in a layered fashion and showing the application of the UML to modeling problems across a wide variety of application domains. This landmark book is suitable for developers unfamiliar with the UML or modeling in general, and will also be useful to experienced developers who wish to learn how to apply the UML to advanced problems.

0-201-57168-4 • Hardcover • 512 pages • ©1999

Surviving Object-Oriented Projects
A Manager's Guide
Alistair Cockburn
Addison-Wesley Object Technology Series

This book allows you to survive and ultimately succeed with an object-oriented project. Alistair Cockburn draws on his personal experience and extensive knowledge to provide the information that managers need to combat the unforeseen challenges that await them during project implementation. Independent of language or programming environment, the book supports its key points through short case studies taken from real object-oriented projects, and an appendix collects these guidelines and solutions into brief "crib sheets"—ideal for handy reference.

0-201-49834-0 • Paperback • 272 pages • ©1998

Objects, Components, and Frameworks with UML

The Catalysis^SM Approach
Desmond Francis D'Souza and Alan Cameron Wills
Addison-Wesley Object Technology Series

Catalysis is a rapidly emerging UML-based method for component and framework-based development with objects. The authors describe a unique UML-based approach to precise specification of component interfaces using a type model, enabling precise external description of behavior without constraining implementations. This approach provides application developers and system architects with well-defined and reusable techniques that help them build open distributed object systems from components and frameworks.

0-201-31012-0 • Paperback • 816 pages • ©1999

Doing Hard Time

Developing Real-Time Systems with UML, Objects, Frameworks, and Patterns
Bruce Powel Douglass
Addison-Wesley Object Technology Series

Doing Hard Time is written to facilitate the daunting process of developing real-time systems. The author presents an embedded systems programming methodology that has been proven successful in practice. The process outlined in this book allows application developers to apply practical techniques—garnered from the mainstream areas of object-oriented software development—to meet the demanding qualifications of real-time programming.

0-201-49837-5 • Hardcover with CD-ROM • 800 pages • ©1999

Real-Time UML, Second Edition

Developing Efficient Objects for Embedded Systems
Bruce Powel Douglass
Addison-Wesley Object Technology Series

The Unified Modeling Language is particularly suited to modeling real-time and embedded systems. *Real-Time UML, Second Edition,* is the completely updated and UML 1.3–compliant introduction that developers of real-time systems need to make the transition to object-oriented analysis and design with UML. The book covers the important features of the UML, and shows how to effectively use these features to model real-time systems. Special in-depth discussions of finite state machines, object identification strategies, and real-time design patterns to help beginning and experienced developers alike are also included.

0-201-65784-8 • Paperback • 384 pages • ©2000

UML Distilled, Second Edition

A Brief Guide to the Standard Object Modeling Language
Martin Fowler, with Kendall Scott
Addison-Wesley Object Technology Series

Thoroughly revised and updated, this best-selling book is a concise overview that introduces you to the Unified Modeling Language, highlighting the key elements of the standard modeling language's notation, semantics, and processes. Included is a brief explanation of UML's history, development, and rationale, as well as discussions on how UML can be integrated into the object-oriented development process. The book also profiles various modeling techniques associated with UML—use cases, CRC cards, design by contract, dynamic classification, interfaces, and abstract classes. The first edition of this classic work received *Software Development* magazine's 1997 Productivity Award.

0-201-65783-X • Paperback • 224 pages • ©2000

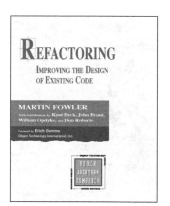

Refactoring

Improving the Design of Existing Code
Martin Fowler, with contributions by Kent Beck, John Brant, William Opdyke, and Don Roberts
Addison-Wesley Object Technology Series

Refactoring is the process of changing a software system in such a way that it does not alter the external behavior of the code, yet improves its external structure. In this book, Martin Fowler, Kent Beck, John Brant, William Opdyke, and Don Roberts show you where opportunities for refactoring can typically be found, and how to go about reworking a bad design into a good one. In addition to discussing the various techniques of refactoring, the authors provide a detailed catalog of more than seventy proven refactorings.

0-201-48567-2 • Hardcover • 464 pages • ©1999

Applied Software Architecture

Christine Hofmeister, Robert Nord, and Dilip Soni
Addison-Wesley Object Technology Series

Applied Software Architecture provides practical guidelines and techniques for producing quality software designs. The authors give an extensive overview of software architecture basics and a detailed guide to architecture design tasks, focusing on four fundamental views of architecture—conceptual, module, execution, and code. This book reveals the insights and best practices of the most skilled software architects in designing software architecture, and presents these through four real-life case studies.

0-201-32571-3 • Hardcover • 432 pages • ©2000

The Unified Software Development Process

Ivar Jacobson, Grady Booch, and James Rumbaugh
Addison-Wesley Object Technology Series

The Unified Software Development Process goes beyond other object-oriented analysis and design methods by detailing a family of processes that incorporate the complete lifecycle of software development. This new book, representing the collaboration of Ivar Jacobson, Grady Booch, and James Rumbaugh, clearly describes the different higher-level constructs—notation as well as semantics—used in the models. Thus, stereotypes such as use cases and actors, packages, classes, interfaces, active classes, processes and threads, nodes, and most relations are described intuitively in the context of a model.

0-201-57169-2 • Hardcover • 512 pages • ©1999

The Rational Unified Process

An Introduction
Philippe Kruchten
Addison-Wesley Object Technology Series

This concise book offers a quick introduction to the concepts, structure, content, and motivation of the Rational Unified Process. This revolutionary software development process provides a disciplined approach to assigning, managing, and completing tasks within a software development organization, and is the first development process to exploit the full capabilities of the industry-standard Unified Modeling Language. *The Rational Unified Process* is unique in that it captures many of the proven best practices in modern software development and presents them in a form that can be tailored to a wide range of projects and organizations.

0-201-60459-0 • Paperback • 272 pages • ©1999

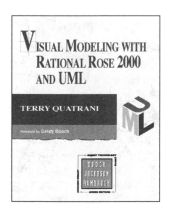

Visual Modeling with Rational Rose 2000 and UML

Terry Quatrani
Addison-Wesley Object Technology Series

Terry Quatrani, the Rose Evangelist from Rational Software Corporation, uses a simplified case study to teach readers how to analyze and design an application using UML and how to implement the application using Rational Rose 2000. With the practical direction offered in this updated book, you will be able to specify, visualize, document, and create software solutions. Highlights include an examination of system behavior from a use case approach, a discussion of the concepts and notations used for finding objects and classes, an introduction to the notation needed to create and document a system's architecture, and a review of the iteration planning process.

0-201-69961-3 • Paperback • 240 pages • ©2000

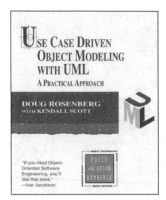

Use Case Driven Object Modeling with UML
A Practical Approach
Doug Rosenberg, with Kendall Scott
Addison-Wesley Object Technology Series

This book presents a streamlined approach to UML modeling that includes a minimal but sufficient set of diagrams and techniques you can use to get from use cases to code quickly and efficiently. *Use Case Driven Object Modeling with UML* provides practical guidance that shows developers how to produce UML models with minimal startup time, while maintaining traceability from user requirements through detailed design and coding. The authors draw upon their extensive industry experience to present proven methods for driving the object modeling process forward from use cases in a simple and straightforward manner.

0-201-43289-7 • Paperback • 192 pages • ©1999

Software Project Management
A Unified Framework
Walker Royce
Addison-Wesley Object Technology Series

This book presents a new management framework uniquely suited to the complexities of modern software development. Walker Royce's pragmatic perspective exposes the shortcomings of many well-accepted management priorities and equips software professionals with state-of-the-art knowledge derived from his twenty years of successful from-the-trenches management experience. In short, the book provides the software industry with field-proven benchmarks for making tactical decisions and strategic choices that will enhance an organization's probability of success.

0-201-30958-0 • Hardcover • 448 pages • ©1998

The Unified Modeling Language Reference Manual
James Rumbaugh, Ivar Jacobson, and Grady Booch
Addison-Wesley Object Technology Series

James Rumbaugh, Ivar Jacobson, and Grady Booch have created the definitive reference to the UML. This two-color book covers every aspect and detail of the UML and presents the modeling language in a useful reference format that serious software architects or programmers should have on their bookshelf. The book is organized by topic and designed for quick access. The authors also provide the necessary information to enable existing OMT, Booch, and OOSE notation users to make the transition to UML. The book provides an overview of the semantic foundation of the UML through a concise appendix.

0-201-30998-X • Hardcover with CD-ROM • 576 pages • ©1999

Applying Use Cases
A Practical Guide
Geri Schneider and Jason P. Winters
Addison-Wesley Object Technology Series

Applying Use Cases provides a practical and clear introduction to developing use cases, demonstrating their use via a continuing case study. Using the Unified Software Development Process as a framework and the Unified Modeling Language as a notation, the authors step the reader through applying use cases in the different phases of the process, focusing on where and how use cases are best applied. The book also offers insight into the common mistakes and pitfalls that can plague an object-oriented project.

0-201-30981-5 • Paperback • 208 pages • ©1998

Enterprise Computing with Objects
From Client/Server Environments to the Internet
Yen-Ping Shan and Ralph H. Earle
Addison-Wesley Object Technology Series

This book helps you place rapidly evolving technologies—such as the Internet, the World Wide Web, distributed computing, object technology, and client/server systems—in their appropriate contexts when preparing for the development, deployment, and maintenance of information systems. The authors distinguish what is essential from what is incidental, while imparting a clear understanding of how the underlying technologies fit together. The book examines essential topics, including data persistence, security, performance, scalability, and development tools.

0-201-32566-7 • Paperback • 448 pages • ©1998

Addison-Wesley Computer and Engineering Publishing Group

How to *Interact* with Us

1. Visit our Web site

http://www.awl.com/cseng

When you think you've read enough, there's always more content for you at Addison-Wesley's web site. Our web site contains a directory of complete product information including:

- Chapters
- Exclusive author interviews
- Links to authors' pages
- Tables of contents
- Source code

You can also discover what tradeshows and conferences Addison-Wesley will be attending, read what others are saying about our titles, and find out where and when you can meet our authors and have them sign your book.

2. Subscribe to Our Email Mailing Lists

Subscribe to our electronic mailing lists and be the first to know when new books are publishing. Here's how it works: Sign up for our electronic mailing at **http://www.awl.com/cseng/mailinglists.html**. Just select the subject areas that interest you and you will receive notification via email when we publish a book in that area.

3. Contact Us via Email

cepubprof@awl.com
Ask general questions about our books.
Sign up for our electronic mailing lists.
Submit corrections for our web site.

bexpress@awl.com
Request an Addison-Wesley catalog.
Get answers to questions regarding your order or our products.

innovations@awl.com
Request a current Innovations Newsletter.

webmaster@awl.com
Send comments about our web site.

jcs@awl.com
Submit a book proposal.
Send errata for an Addison-Wesley book.

cepubpublicity@awl.com
Request a review copy for a member of the media interested in reviewing new Addison-Wesley titles.

We encourage you to patronize the many fine retailers who stock Addison-Wesley titles. Visit our online directory to find stores near you or visit our online store: **http://store.awl.com/** or call **800-824-7799**.

Addison Wesley Longman
Computer and Engineering Publishing Group
One Jacob Way, Reading, Massachusetts 01867 USA
TEL 781-944-3700 • FAX 781-942-3076